ANCIENT EGYPT

UNDER

THE PHARAOHS.

By JOHN KENRICK, M.A.

By Volume 1 of 2

ISBN: 978-1-63923-647-3

All Rights reserved. No part of this book maybe reproduced without written permission from the publishers, except by a reviewer who may quote brief passages in a review to be printed in a newspaper or magazine.

Printed: January 2023

Published and Distributed By:
Lushena Books
607 Country Club Drive, Unit E
Bensenville, IL 60106
www.lushenabks.com

ISBN: 978-1-63923-647-3

RICHARD AND JOHN EDWARD TAYLOR,

PREFACE.

EGYPTIAN archæology and history have undergone a complete revolution since the commencement of the present century, and especially since the discovery of the hieroglyphical character. Hitherto, however, no work has appeared in our language from which the historical student can obtain a comprehensive view of the results of the combined labours of travellers and artists, interpreters and critics, during the whole of this period. The object of my work is to supply this deficiency. It describes, according to the present state of our knowledge, the land and the people of Egypt, their arts and sciences, their civil institutions, and their religious faith and usages; and relates their history from the earliest records of the monarchy to its final absorption in the empire of Alexander. Strictly speaking, the dominion of the Pharaohs ceased with the conquest of Egypt by Cambyses. But it was not without reason that Manetho carried on his Dynasties to the flight of Nectanebus the Second. The struggle of two centuries, renewed at intervals, for the recovery of the national independence, belongs essentially to the history of the native sovereigns.

The references which the work contains will indicate the sources, ancient and modern, from which it has been derived. No accessible materials have been intentionally neglected. It may seem presumptuous in one who possesses but a limited acquaintance with hieroglyphics, to undertake a work, of which the historical part, before the commencement of the Greek accounts, must be derived from hieroglyphical legends. I may plead, however, that the province of the decipherer and the antiquary has always been held to be distinct from that of the historian, who is only required to follow the best authority that he can obtain. In the uncertainty which still prevails in regard to the interpretation of hieroglyphics, the reader is perhaps most safe in the hands of one who has no system of his own to defend. Whereever a doubt appeared to exist, I have acknowledged it; where no materials for history are found, I have left the blank to be filled up by subsequent discovery.

The history of Egypt, down to the seventh century B.C., is almost entirely derived from inscriptions on monuments. Their number has been greatly increased by the researches of individual travellers, and still more by those of the French, Tuscan and Prussian expeditions, so that on the surface at least of Egypt and Nubia very few remain that have not been accurately copied, nor many of which the general purport and evidence is not understood. I should gladly have waited for the results of the last-mentioned of these undertakings, had the time of their complete publication been more definite. It is not probable, however, that the promised work of Lepsius will effect any change in the great divisions of Egyptian history, as laid down by his friend and fellow-labourer, the Chevalier Bunsen. Whatever period were chosen for a publication like the present, the same difficulty would still exist; the evidence would not be exhausted; there would still be doubtful questions of criticism, interpretation and chronology.

What is now published, although complete in itself, is only a portion of a contemplated work comprehending the history of those countries of the East, whose civilization preceded and influenced that of Greece. Syria and Phœnicia will form the next volume. The rapidity with which the discovery and interpretation of the Assyrian and Persian monuments have lately advanced, justifies the hope that it may be possible before long to relate the history of these monarchies with something of the copiousness and certainty which Egyptian history has attained.

CONTENTS.

VOL. I.

ANCIENT EGYPT.

CHAPTER I.

The Valley of the Nile and its Monuments.

Antiquity of Egyptian civilization.—The White River.—The Blue River.—Meroe.—The Tacazzè.—Gebel-el-Birkel.—The Third Cataract.—Island of Argo.—Semneh.—The Second Cataract.—Aboosimbel.—Ibrim.—Derr.—Amada.—Pselcis.—Kalabsche.—Beitoualli.—Taphis.—Philæ.—Syene.—Ombi.—Apollinopolis Magna (Edfoo).—Eilithya (El-kab).—Latopolis (Esneh).—Gebelein.—Hermonthis.—THEBES.—Apollinopolis Parva.—Coptos.—Tentyra.—Diospolis Parva.—Abydos.—Panopolis.—Hermopolis Magna.—Speos Artemidos (Benihassan).—Alabastron.—Oxyrrynchus.—Heracleopolis.—The Fyoum.—The Pyramids.—MEMPHIS.—Branches of the Nile.—The *Pelusiac*.—Heliopolis.—Bubastus.—Pelusium.—Lake Menzaleh.—Tanis.—The *Sebennytic*.—Busiris (Bahbeit).—The *Canopic*.—Terenuthis.—Sais.—Naucratis.—Lake Mareotis.—Coast of Egypt.. 1–60

CHAPTER II.

The Country between Egypt and the Red Sea.

Wadi Magara.—Surabit-el-Kadim.—Geological structure.—Routes from the Nile to the Red Sea.—Emerald mines.—Wadi Jasoos.—Gold mines.—Population of the coast and the interior 61–66

CONTENTS.

CHAPTER III.

The Western Desert.

False conceptions of the Desert.—Its extent.—The Oases.—Ammonium (Siwah).—Bahr-be-la-Ma.—Natron lakes.—Fountain of the Sun.—El-Bacharieh.—Artesian wells.—El-Khargeh.—El-Dakkel.—El-Farafreh 67–76

CHAPTER IV.

The Inundation of the Nile, Soil, Productions and Climate of Egypt.

Geology of the Delta.—Petrified forest.—Alluvium of the Nile.—Theories of the ancients.—Commencement, amount and end of the inundation.—Quality of the Nile water.—Botany of Egypt.—Zoology.—Climate.—Differences of Upper and Lower Egypt 77–95

CHAPTER V.

Population and Language.

Complexion and hair of the ancient Egyptians.—The Coptic language.—Relation to the Syro-Arabian languages.—Identity with the old Egyptian.—Origin of Egyptian population.—Supposed connexion with India 96–110

CHAPTER VI.

Memphis and the Pyramids.

Foundation of the city.—Site.—Pyramids of Gizeh.—The Sphinx.—Tombs near the Pyramids.—Causey.—Quarries of Mokattam.—Pyramids of Abouseir—of Saccara—of Dashour—of Lisht—of Meydoom—of Illahoun.—The Pyramid of El-Koofa.—Pyramids of Meroe 111–148

CHAPTER VII.

Thebes.

Deposition of the soil.—*Western bank.*—Qoorneh.—The Menephtheion.—The Ramescion.—Sepulchre of Osymandyas.—The Amenophion.—The Vocal Memnon.—Medinet Aboo.—The Thothmeseion.—Pavilion of Rameses.—The Hippodrome.—Sepulchres.—The Bab-el-Melook or Valley of the Kings.—Sepulchres of the Queens.—*Eastern bank.* — Luxor. — Obelisks. — The Amenophion. — Dromos of Sphinxes.—Karnak.—Obelisks of Thothmes I.—Hypostyle hall.—Victories of Sheshonk.—The hundred gates of Thebes 149–178

CHAPTER VIII.

Amount of Population.

Estimates of Diodorus, Josephus, De Pauw, Goguet, Jomard. —Calculation from the data of Tacitus.—Causes of its being over-estimated.—Present amount 179–182

CHAPTER IX.

Agriculture and Horticulture.

Agricultural instruments.—Species of grain.—Flax.—Cotton. —Esculent vegetables.—Lotus and papyrus.—Wine.—Pasturage of cattle.—The ass.—The horse.—The persea.— The palm.—Ornamental gardening.................... 183–200

CHAPTER X.

The Chase. Fisheries.

Wild animals.—The hippopotamus.—The crocodile.—Fishery of the Lake Mœris.—Aquatic birds.—Hatching by artificial heat... 201–207

CHAPTER XI.

Navigation and Commerce.

Egyptian dislike to the sea.—Navigation of the Nile.—Form and structure of boats.—The Baris.—Route to Cosseir.— Egyptians not active in foreign commerce 208–213

CONTENTS.

CHAPTER XII.

Mechanical and Industrial Arts.

Stone engraving.—Chemistry.—Spinning and Weaving.—Metallurgy.—Use of iron.—Quarrying.—Carpentry.—Different kinds of wood; whence imported................ 214–220

CHAPTER XIII.

Military Equipment, Armour, and Warfare.

Calasirians and Hermotybians.—Enrollment and drill.—Defensive armour.—Weapons.—War-chariots.—Use of cavalry.—Military ensigns.—Encampment.—Fortification.—Naval warfare...................................... 221–231

CHAPTER XIV.

Domestic Life and Manners. Amusements.

Size and arrangement of houses.—Decorations.—Furniture.—Chairs.—Headstools.—Posture at meals.—Diet.—Introduction of a mummy at feasts.—Song of Maneros.—Exhibitions of agility and strength.—Amusements on the river.—Dice.—Game resembling draughts.—*Mora.*—Tricks of jugglers 232–244

CHAPTER XV.

Dress.

The calasiris.—Dress of the lower orders—of the king.—Double crown or *Pschent.*—Head-dress of the queen.—Distinction of princes of the blood.—Use of artificial hair.—Sandals.—Collars and bracelets.—Rings.—Mirrors.—Use of stibium and henneh.......................... 245–251

CHAPTER XVI.

Architecture.

Earliest style.—Resemblance to the Doric.—Two kinds of capital.—Proportions of the shaft.—The abacus.—Cornice.—Portico.—Width of intercolumniation.—Osiride columns.—Convergence of architectural lines.—The arch.—Arrangement of temples.—The dromos.—The pylones.—The naos.—The sekos.—Typhonia.—Colour applied to architecture . 252–262

CHAPTER XVII.

Sculpture and Painting.

Characteristics of early art.—Unchangeableness of Egyptian forms.—Influence of religion on art.—Type of the human face.—Colossal sculpture.—Carving in wood.—Superiority of historical sculpture and painting to religious.—Defects in drawing and perspective.—Caricature.—Number of colours and mode of applying them.—Fresco painting.—Knowledge of anatomy.—Peculiarity of Egyptian relief.—Correspóndence of the progress and decline of art with that of national power and prosperity.—Art under the Ptolemies and the Romans.................................... 263-278

CHAPTER XVIII.

Music.

Control exercised by religion.—Variety of instruments.—Knowledge of harmony.—The harp, lyre and guitar.—The sistrum.—The flute.—The drum.—The dance 279-282

CHAPTER XIX.

Art of Writing.

Frequency of its use in Egypt.—Account of Egyptian writing by Herodotus, Plato, Diodorus, Tacitus, Pliny, Ammianus, Clemens.—Opinions of the moderns, Warburton, Zoega.—The Rosetta Stone.—Discoveries of Young and Champollion.—*Pictorial, symbolical* and *phonetic* hieroglyphics.—Evidence of the reading and interpretation of hieroglyphics.—Enchorial or demotic character.—Hieratic.—Anaglyphs.
Note.—Interpretation of a line from the Rosetta Stone.—Hieroglyphics of grammatical inflexions.............. 283-324

CHAPTER XX.

Science.

Geometry.—Whether learnt by the Greeks in Egypt.—Pythagoras, Thales, Anaxagoras, Plato.—Astronomy.—Knowledge of the meridian line.—Months originally lunar.—Length of solar year.—Sothiac period.—The Phœnix.—Cycle of twenty-five years.—Division into weeks.—Precession of the equinoxes.—Solar eclipses.—Astrology.—Divisions of the zodiac.—Mechanical science.—Arithmetical notation.—Weights and measures.—Medicine.—Iatromathematic.. 325–348

CHAPTER XXI.

Religion.

Sect. 1.—*Theology*.

Accounts of the Egyptian religion given by Herodotus, Manetho, Diodorus, Plutarch.—The later Pythagoreans and Platonists.—Modern writers—Jablonsky, Zoega.—Discoveries by means of hieroglyphics.—Dynasties of gods.—Threefold division of Herodotus.—Egyptian theology not originally a system.—Eight gods—Amun, Noum or Kneph, Amun Khem, Ptah, Maut, Sate, Thriphis, Pasht.—Children of the great gods—Khons, Anouke, Harka.—Other gods—Athor, Neith, Ra, Horhat, Sebek, Athom, Mandoo.—Physical gods—Sun, Moon, Heaven (Tpe), the Nile.—Æsculapius.—Osiris and Isis.—Osiris Pethempamenthes.—The judgement scene.—The Typhonian mythe.—Seth.—Obliteration of his figure on monuments.—Horus, Harpocrates, Nephthys, Anubis, Thoth.—Gods of the second and third order not to be distinguished.—Religious honours paid to deceased persons.—Serapis, Mars, Hercules, Hecate.—Whether the unity of God, as an intellectual principle, was a doctrine of Egyptian theology 349–438

Sect. 2.—*Sacrificial Rites. The Sacerdotal order.*

Different kinds of sacrifices.—Human sacrifices in Egypt.—Offering of victims.—Unbloody sacrifices and offerings.—Habits of the priests.—Circumcision.—Gradation of ranks.—Whether women were admitted to the priesthood.—Divination.—Oracles.—Stellar influences.—Religious processions.—Festivals appropriate to different parts of the year.—Panegyries.—Feast of Mars—of Isis-Neith at Sais—of Dionusos.—Mysteries.—The Triaconterides 438–472

Sect. 3.—*Doctrine of a Future Life.*

State of the dead according to the Jewish belief.—The Homeric conception of the shades.—Motive for embalmment

CONTENTS. xiii

Page

among the Egyptians.— Doctrine of Metempsychosis—
whether connected with retribution.—Adoption of this doctrine by the Greeks.—Pindar.—Plato.—The Book of the
Dead.—Representations in the tombs.—No uniformity of
opinion on this subject among the Egyptians themselves.. 472–489

CHAPTER XXII.

Embalmment, Sepulture, and Funeral Rites.

Office of the *Taricheutæ*.—Three different kinds of embalmment.—Judgement preliminary to interment.—Mode of
conveyance to the sepulchre.—Objects deposited in tombs.
—Offerings made to deceased persons by the *Choachutæ*.—
Whether the Greek scenery of the unseen world was borrowed from Egypt................................. 490–509

PLATES.

I. Sections of the Pyramids.   Hieroglyphics of the Months.

II. Shields and Banner of Egyptian Kings.
General Phonetic Alphabet.

III. Hieroglyphic Characters.

IV. Grammatical Inflexions.
Hieroglyphic and Hieratic Numerals.
Facsimile of a portion of the Rosetta Inscription.

ANCIENT EGYPT.

ANCIENT EGYPT.

CHAPTER I.

ANTIQUITY OF EGYPTIAN CIVILIZATION.—THE VALLEY OF THE NILE AND ITS MONUMENTS.

THE seats of the earliest civilization in the ancient world extend across the southern part of Asia, in a chain, of which China forms the extremity towards the east and Egypt towards the west. Syria, Mesopotamia, Assyria, the Medo-Bactrian countries and India are its intermediate links. The civilization of Medo-Bactria appears to have been the lowest, as its history is the most obscure; but in all these countries, when they become known to us, we find the people cultivating the soil and dwelling in cities, living under regular forms of government, practising the mechanical arts, possessed of at least a tincture of science and a written character more or less perfect. All that lies beyond and around them is involved in barbarism and ignorance. The origin of this earliest civilization, however, and its transmission from one country to another, cannot be fixed by direct historical evidence. In all, the belief of the nation attributes to itself the immemorial possession of its own soil; and to its progenitors or to the gods the invention of the arts and sciences. Whether these have really had a single origin, and what has been their primitive seat, is a question which the present state of historical knowledge does not enable us to answer. But there is no difficulty in fixing on the country from which Ancient History must begin. The monuments of EGYPT, its records and its literature, surpass those of India and China in antiquity by many centuries[1]. Babylon and Assyria have no literary records, and their monuments of brick or a perishable marble, though their absolute age is unknown, bear on their face the evidence of a much more recent date than the pyramids and obelisks of Egypt. Abraham, a wanderer from Mesopotamia, where as yet no great monarchy had arisen[2], found Egypt already ruled by a Pharaoh, and in all probability as far advanced in social improvement as we know it to have been in the days of his great-grandson Joseph. Herodotus had seen the stupendous remains of Babylon, but neither the sight of these, nor the claims of the Chaldæan priests, induced him to assign more than a very moderate antiquity to the Assyrian monarchy, of which he reckoned it the second capital[3]. In Egypt, on the

---

[1] See Lepsius, Chronologie der Ægypter, Einleitung, p. 28–54.
[2] Genesis xiv. 1.
[3] Ἀσσυρίων ἀρχόντων τῆς ἄνω Ἀσίης ἐπ' ἔτεα εἴκοσι καὶ πεν- τακόσια, πρῶτοι ἀπ' αὐτῶν Μῆδοι ἤρξαντο ἀπίστασθαι. 1, 95. Τῆς Ἀσσυρίης ἐστὶ τὰ μέν κου καὶ ἄλλα πολίσματα μεγάλα πολλά· τὸ δὲ ὀνομαστότατον καὶ ἰσχυρότατον καὶ

contrary, he received without questioning even the most extravagant statements respecting the antiquity of the nation[1]. Neither his belief nor that of Plato, expressed in more unmeasured terms[2], affords indeed any proof of the soundness of Egyptian chronology: but they are an evidence of the impression which the monuments and records, the institutions and general aspect of the country, had made on two men, who had travelled widely and observed acutely —an impression of immemorial, unchangeable antiquity.

Even if it were doubtful whether Egypt preceded the other nations which have been mentioned, in the establishment of law and the cultivation of science, letters and art, it must still be the starting-point of *our* Ancient History. India exercised no perceptible influence on the West till the time of Alexander; China remained in its insulation till the Roman Empire. The religion of the Medo-Bactrian nations, and the science of the Babylonians may, through intermediate channels, have been conveyed even to our times; but the genealogy which connects European with Egyptian civilization is direct and certain. From Egypt it came to Greece, from Greece to Rome, from Rome to the remoter nations of the West, by whom it has been carried throughout the globe. The indigenous culture of Asia has either become extinct, or is in rapid decay; that which had its first germ in the valley of the Nile, still lives and grows in other

ἔνθα σφι Νίνου ἀναστάτου γενομένης τὰ βασιλήϊα κατεστήκεε, ἦν Βαβυλών. 1, 178.

[1] Her. 2, 142. 145. Αἰγυπτίους δοκέω αἰεὶ εἶναι, ἐξ οὗ ἀνθρώπων γένος ἐγένετο.

[2] Εὑρήσεις αὐτόθι τὰ μυριοστὸν ἔτος γεγραμμένα ἢ τετυπωμένα, οὐχ ὡς ἔπος εἰπεῖν μυριοστὸν, ἀλλ' ὄντως. Plat. de Leg. 2, s. 3, p. 657 E.

climates, and in its diffusion seems destined to overshadow and exterminate the ancient civilization of the East.

The geography and history of every country are closely connected with the origin and course of its rivers. In cold and humid climates like our own, their neighbourhood may have been avoided by the early inhabitants, who found more healthy abodes on the open sides of the hills. But in the East, where many months succeed each other without any supply of rain, the vicinity of a perennial stream is the first condition of a settled and civilized life. The history of the world begins on the banks of the great rivers of China, India, Assyria and Egypt. The Nile, however, holds a far more important relation to the country through which it flows than any other river of the world. The courses of the Rhine, the Danube or the Rhone, are only lines on the surface of Germany or France; the valleys of the Euphrates and the Tigris were a very small part of the dominions of the Assyrian and Babylonian kings; but the banks of the Nile *are* Egypt and Nubia. To live below the Cataracts and to drink of its waters, was according to the oracle of Ammon to be an Egyptian[1]. Upwards or downwards, it is through the valley of the Nile that civilization and conquest have taken their course. We should therefore naturally begin by tracing it from its origin to the sea. But this is still impracticable. The Mesopotamian rivers have been followed to their sources amidst the mountains of Armenia and Kurdistan; the traveller has even penetrated to the

[1] Herod. 2, 18.

place where the Ganges bursts forth from the everlasting snows of the Himalaya; but the sacred river of Egypt still conceals its true fountains. The question which Herodotus asked of the priests of Egypt, and Alexander of the oracle of Ammon[1], which learned curiosity has so often addressed to geographical science, has been only partially answered. We must therefore begin our survey from the confluence of the two tributaries, whose united stream has been known in all ages as THE NILE.

In the latitude of 15° 37' N. and longitude 33° E. from Greenwich, two rivers meet near the modern village of Khartoum. The broader but less rapid stream comes from the S.W., and from the colour of its waters, mixed with argillaceous matter during the inundation[2], it is called the Bahr-el-Abiad, or White River. This is considered as the true Nile, both because its course is the same which the united streams afterwards pursue, and because the volume of water which it furnishes is larger and more constant. Even in the dry season it has a depth of from eighteen to twenty-five feet, and a breadth of a mile: in the inundation it attains a depth of from thirty-six to fifty feet, and a breadth of four miles[3]. From the remotest times the origin of this branch of the Nile has been the subject of speculation, and as its course, immediately above the junction, is considerably from the west, it was

---

[1] Herod. 2, 28. Max. Tyr. 41, 1.
[2] Hoskins's Travels in Ethiopia, p. 119. It is singular that even this circumstance should be doubtful. Dr. Beke (Journal of Royal Geographical Society, 7, p. 34, N. S.) suggests that the river derives its name *white* from the absence of mud; while Russegger (Reisen, 2, 82) denies that it is white at all.
[3] Russegger, Reisen, 2, 46.

conjectured to be one of the great rivers known to exist in the western regions of Africa, whose termination was unknown. Juba[1], on the authority of Carthaginian writers, described the Nile as rising in Mauritania, losing itself twice in the sands, and at length emerging as the Niger, which after dividing the continent across, entered Ethiopia as the Nile; and this opinion was long current at Rome[2]. Herodotus believed that the great river flowing eastward, which his Nasamonians reached, when they had passed the Great Desert, was the Nile[3]. When Park discovered the Joliba at Timbuctoo to have an easterly course, this ancient hypothesis was revived. The travels of Lander showed its fallacy by tracing the Niger to the Bight of Benin. As the Bahr-el-Abiad is followed further to the south, it recovers its ordinary direction towards the north. For our knowledge of its course above Khartoum, we are indebted to the expeditions undertaken by the Pasha of Egypt, in the hope of discovering gold mines, and the more disinterested researches of MM. d'Abbadie and Dr. Beke. It receives several tributaries from the east, between N.L. 11° and 9°, and in 9° 20' a large stream from the west, called the Keilak, whose origin is unknown. The expedition of 1841, led by M. d'Arnaud, ascended to N.L. 4° 42', where its further progress was stopped by a ridge of gneiss which crossed the river. At this point its longitude was nearly that of Cairo. After the junction of the Keilak it receives only

---

[1] Plin. N. H. 5, 10. Juba lived in the reign of Augustus.
[2] Dion. Hist. Rom., lib. 75, p. 1266, ed. Reimar. Ὁ Νεῖλος ἐκ τοῦ Ἄτλαντος σαφῶς ἀναδίδοται.
[3] 2, 33.

trifling accessions from the west; but it is probable, that above the point where the Egyptian expedition halted, a large tributary from the east brings with it the waters of the country between Abessinia and the equator. If the Mountains of the Moon, and the lakes which from their melted snows supply, according to Ptolemy[1], the sources of the Nile, have any existence, it must be south of the equator.

The remotest origin of the Nile, therefore, remains a problem still to be solved; nor indeed can it be said to have any single source[2]. Its course above Khartoum, however, is more interesting to the geographer and ethnologist than to the historian. Its banks are inhabited by tribes, partly Arab, partly negro, deep sunk in barbarism, and contain no traces of a more ancient civilization. Neither the Pharaohs, the Ptolemies, nor the Romans ever carried their arms so high; and the researches of a peaceful traveller are embarrassed by the hostility which the black nations feel towards neighbours who from time immemorial have reduced them to slavery.

The Bahr-el-Azrek, Blue or Dark River, the Astapus of ancient geography, unites with the Bahr-el-Abiad at Khartoum. It rises, according to Bruce[3], in N.L. 10° 59′, E.L. 36° 55′ in the kingdom of Abessinia, at a height of nearly 6000 feet above the sea[4]. He visited its sources, which had not been seen by any European for seventy years, and pro-

---

[1] Ptolemy, Geogr. 4, 8. Τοῦτον τὸν κόλπον (the coast opposite to Madagascar) περιοικοῦσιν Αἰθίοπες ἀνθρωποφάγοι, ὧν ἀπὸ δυσμῶν διήκει τὸ τῆς Σελήνης ὄρος, ἀφ᾽ οὗ ὑποδέχονται τὰς χιόνας αἱ τοῦ Νείλου λίμναι.

[2] So the Troglodytes maintained. Πολλῶν πηγῶν εἰς ἕνα τόπον ἀθροιζομένων συνίσταται τὸ ῥεῦμα τοῦ Νείλου. Diodor. 1, 37.

[3] Travels, vol. 5, p. 308.

[4] 955 toises (about 5730 feet), Humboldt, Central Asien, p. 33.

fessed to have discovered the true sources of the Nile. They are three springs, regarded by the natives with superstitious veneration; not large, but deep. The stream in which they unite flows N.W. for about eighty miles, when it falls into the Lake of Tzana or Dembea, the Koloe of Ptolemy, entering on its western and issuing again on its south-eastern side. Its current is so rapid, that it scarcely mingles its waters with those of the lake. Descending from this high region by many cataracts, and bearing the name of Abai, it flows southward to about 10° N.L., and washes the eastern side of the province of Amhara, receiving all the streams from the mountainous region of Gojam. Its course is so circuitous, that it almost surrounds this district, returning by a bend to the north, till it is within seventy miles of its source. Its banks are little known before it reaches the country of Fazuglo, recently explored, in search of gold mines, by the Pasha of Egypt. Indeed, until the Bahr-el-Azrek is traced upward, or the Abai of Bruce downward, continuously, which no traveller yet has done, their identity must be regarded as problematical. From the elevated and hilly district of Fazuglo, the river, enlarged by the influx of the Tumet from the south-west, reaches the plains of Sennaar, by another series of cataracts and rapids. After passing Sennaar, it rapidly verges towards the White River: near the junction, it is even in the dry season a quarter of a mile broad, and in the rainy seasons swells to double this breadth. To its sweetness and purity the Nile is said to owe the reputation which its waters have in all ages maintained.

Northward of the junction at Khartoum, between that point and the influx of the Tacazzè or Astaboras, in N.L. 17° 40′, E.L. 34°, lay the ancient kingdom of Meroe. It is called an island by the Greek and Roman writers, who were accustomed to give this name to the irregular spaces included between confluent rivers[1]; and as the Nile itself was composed of two branches, the island of Meroe is variously described as formed by two rivers or by three. The country of Sennaar appears sometimes to have been included in its limits, but nothing has been discovered in this region to prove that it partook in the civilization for which Meroe was celebrated[2]. According to Diodorus, the island of Meroe was 375 miles long and 125 broad, measures which appear to be derived rather from some political division, than from the natural boundaries of the island. The " Libyan sands," by which he says that it was bordered on one side, are the Desert of Babiouda on the left bank of the Nile: the "steep precipices on the side of Arabia" are the high mountains of the north of Abessinia[3]. Through the channel of the Tacazzè the Nile receives the rains which fall on these mountains. The country rises rapidly from the Red Sea to the height of 8000 or 9000 feet, and consequently the course of the rivers on the eastern side is short and their streams scanty.

[1] So the space included between the Rhone, the Isère and the Alps, was called the Island of the Allobroges (Polyb. Bell. Pun. 2, 49).

[2] Cailliaud, Voyage à Meroe (1, 206), describes some small remains of Egyptian or Ethiopic architecture and a fragment of a sphinx, at Soba, a little to the south of the junction of the Bahr-el-Azrek with the Nile.

[3] Diod. 1, 33. Παρήκειν δὲ τῆς νήσου τὸν περικλυζόμενον πάντα τόπον ἀπὸ μὲν τῆς Λιβύης θῖνας, ἔχοντας ἄμμου μέγεθος ἀέριον, ἀπὸ δὲ τῆς Ἀραβίας κρημνοὺς κατερρωγότας.

The Tacazzè is the last tributary that the Nile receives in its course of 1500 miles to the Mediterranean.

The remains which have identified the site of Meroe, the ancient capital of the island, all lie between 16° and 17° N.L., and not far from the Nile. The most southerly are found at Naga, distinguished as Naga-gebel-ardan, from another place of the same name, a little further to the north[1]. There are remains of four temples, all of Egyptian architecture, with slight variations, and evidently dedicated to gods of the Egyptian pantheon. In one a king appears holding a number of captives by the hair, who stretch their hands towards him in an attitude of supplication, while he threatens to strike them with a hatchet. The largest temple has been consecrated to the worship of the principal god of Thebes, commonly called Ammon, and represented with the head of a ram. An alley of sphinxes with the heads of rams, seven feet high, led up to the principal portico, which is insulated from the temple in a manner not seen in Egyptian architecture; and the bas-reliefs of the principal entrance exhibit the god, receiving the homage of a queen. Woad-Naga stands only about a mile from the river: here are the remains of a sandstone temple 89 feet in length, bearing on the capitals of the columns the figures of Athor and Typhon, or Pthah-Sokari[2]. The mounds and heaps of brick with which the ground is strewed indicate that these are only the remains of more extensive buildings. The ruins of El-Mesaourat are sixteen or seventeen miles from

[1] Cailliaud, Voyage à Meroe.   [2] Hoskins's Travels, p. 112.

the river, the most remote which have yet been discovered; they stand in a valley among the sandstone hills, surrounded by the Desert. A wall, 2800 feet in circumference, encloses the remains of eight temples or sanctuaries, and a great number of courts, galleries and chambers, constituting an assemblage of buildings, the destination of which it is difficult to assign. That no great city has existed here is evident from the entire absence of pyramids and excavated sepulchres; and if it had been a college of priests, it is singular that no hieroglyphics should be found on the walls. The style is Egyptian, but of a late age, and the sculpture resembles that of the temples erected under the Ptolemies.

The site of the city of Meroe was placed by Eratosthenes 700 stadia south of the junction of the Nile with the Astaboras[2]. This does not exactly correspond with the position of Assour, a little north of the present town of Shendy; but the difference is not so great as to invalidate the evidence of the antiquities still existing there. Its position in N.L. 16° 44' answers also to the statement of Philo, that the sun was vertical there forty-five days before the summer solstice[3]. A space of more than three-quarters of a mile in circumference near the river is covered with the traces of buildings, and marks the site of the city. Its dwelling-houses, consisting of sun-baked bricks and branches of palm, would easily perish in a latitude to which the tropical rains partially extend[4]. Groups of pyramids are scattered

---

[1] Hoskins, p. 99.
[2] Strabo, B. 17, p. 786.
[3] B. 2, p. 77.

[4] Strabo, 15, p. 690, says, the region of no rain extends from the Thebaid to near Meroe. The rain

on the sandstone hills which rise a little to the east; the most distant of them are about two leagues from the river, and they mark the necropolis of ancient Meroe. They are eighty in number and of various sizes: the most lofty is about 160 feet in height; the largest has a base of 63 feet square; the smallest, of not more than 12 feet[1]. The material is the sandstone of the hills; the entrance is usually on the eastern side, but not facing exactly to the east; nor do their angles correspond to the cardinal points. In front is a portico with sides pointing inwards, like the gateways of the Egyptian temples, often covered with sculpture: the interior of the portico next to the pyramid also contains sculpture. The angles of some of the pyramids form a series of steps, others are a sloping line, and others again are covered with a square beading. At about two-thirds of their height most of them have a small opening like a window. In one, which was examined by demolition from the top, sepulchral chambers were found at different elevations, and at the bottom pits excavated in the rock, in which mummies were deposited. Some of the pyramids have evidently been royal tombs; Lepsius has found the distinct names of thirty sovereigns in various parts of Meroe, and queens appear receiving the honours and performing the functions which commouly belong to kings—a confirmation of the account of the ancients that female sovereignty prevailed in Ethiopia[2]. This mode of interment con-

of Shendy is violent, but not continuous in the wet season (Ritter, Africa, p. 542).

[1] Hoskins, ch. 6. Cailhaud, Voyage.
[2] Wetstein on Acts, 8, 27.

tinued to a late age: in one of the pyramids opened by Ferlini[1], engraved stones, evidently of Greek workmanship, were found, and an arch remains in another.

What other monuments the island of Meroe may contain is uncertain. Besides the dangers to which the traveller is exposed from the barbarous inhabitants of the country, the wild beasts which everywhere infest it make researches difficult. Cailliaud heard a rumour of the existence of ruins, which he supposes, in connection with those of Soba on the Blue River, may have formed a line of stations, by which trade was carried on between Meroe, and Axum and Adulis on the Red Sea. If they exist, they must belong, like everything else in Meroe, to the Ptolemaic and Roman times. The land near the rivers appears in ancient times to have been used in agriculture, the interior in pasturage; the forests and swamps abounded with elephants, which the natives caught for sale or used for food. Rain falls scantily in the north; and therefore the parts remote from the rivers must always have been nearly desert; but in the south, where the hills rise towards Abessinia, the rain, though not so violent as among the mountains, is sufficient to maintain a considerable degree of fertility. The banks of the Nile are so high that Meroe derives no benefit from the inundation. The Tacazzè[2], like the Bahr-el-Azrek, descends from its source among the mountains of Abessinia, in lat. 11° 40′, by a precipitous course, in which lakes and rapids alternate. It

[1] Ferlini, Fouilles de la Nubie. Rome, 1838.
[2] Tacazzè is Ethiopic for river, "Tacazzè Gihon," the river Nile. See Beke, Trans. of Royal Geogr. Soc. 7, 1, 7.

receives on its way, in lat. 14°, the Mareb, which rises in the chain of mountains parallel to the Red Sea; and where it joins the Nile, it has a breadth of 1000 feet[1]. The valley of the Tacazzè is lower and warmer than the rest of Abessinia.

The course of the river from this point to Syene, being about 700 miles, exhibits a series of rapids and cataracts, in consequence of which the fall per mile is double the average of Egypt. The cataracts are seven in number, all composed of granite or kindred rocks, which being harder than the sandstone through which they rise, resist the action of the water, divide the stream, and preserve the inequality of the descent. The Nile, much enlarged after its union with the Tacazzè[2], continues to flow nearly north for 120 miles, through the country of the Berbers. A strip of arable land, about two miles in breadth, borders the river; beyond it all is desert, the inundation not extending further. Nowhere in this part of the Nile's course have any antiquities been discovered, to mark whether in ancient times it was subject to Egypt or Meroe. At the point where it makes its great bend to the south-west, its stream is divided by the rocky island of Mogreb. Here the caravans leave the banks of the river and proceed by the shorter route of the Eastern Desert to rejoin it either at Syene, or at Derr, between the First and Second Cataracts. In all this part of the Nile's course, as the land susceptible of cultivation is so small, the inhabitants avail themselves of the patches of loamy soil which the river deposits in the rocky hollows. The navigation too, for more than 100

[1] Rüppell, Reisen. Hoskins, p. 63.   [2] Cailliaud, 1, 349.

miles, is impeded by rapids. The deflection to the S.W. continues, till the Nile reaches, not, as Eratosthenes asserted, the latitude of the city of Meroe[1], but very nearly that of the most northern point of the peninsula. The space on the left bank included in this great bend, now called the Desert of Babiouda, was occupied in ancient times by the Nubæ, whose name has extended itself to the whole valley as far as Syene, and into the eastern desert, where, in the time of Eratosthenes, the Megabari and the Blemmyes dwelt[2].

Where the Nile skirts the Desert of Bahiouda on the north, its banks are little known, since travellers seldom follow its windings; but it is ascertained that they contain no antiquities. The traces of ancient civilization re-appear below the Fourth Cataract, at Nouri, Gebel-el-Birkel and Merawe. Nouri, on the left bank, exhibits the remains of thirty-five pyramids, of which about half are in good preservation; but they have no sculptures or hieroglyphics; no temples stand near them, nor are there any ruins which indicate the former existence of a city. It can only be conjectured that they may be the necropolis of such a city, of which the traces have been buried in the sands. Gebel-el-Birkel[3], about eight miles lower down, on the right bank, is a hill of crumbling sandstone, between 300 and 400 feet in height, and a mile distant from the river. On its western side, standing in the Desert, are two groups of pyramids, from 35 to 60 feet in height, amounting together to thirteen. Like those of

---

[1] Strabo, B. 17, p. 786.
[2] Strabo, *ubi supra*.
[3] Cailliaud, 3, 197. Hoskins, ch. 11.

Meroe, some of them have a sanctuary and sloping walls in front, with arched roofs and sculpture. The Egyptian deities Osiris and Athor, with their usual emblems, and the ornaments common in Egyptian architecture, are found here. In one of the sanctuaries, a personage apparently royal, holding a bow of great length and thickness, is receiving oblations similar to those which are represented in the Egyptian tombs. Gebel-el-Birkel contains also the remains of several temples, two of them so far preserved, that their original plan and dimensions can be discovered. The largest has been nearly 500 feet in length, and consisted of two courts, the first 150 feet long and 135 wide, the second 125 feet long and 102 wide. The sanctuary contains a granite altar, on which the name of Tirhakah is inscribed, and another of basalt, with the shield of an Egyptian king[1]. The sculptures with which the walls appear to have been adorned have almost entirely perished, and such is the havoc which time and barbarism have made, that of more than eighty columns which the temple must have contained, one only remains erect.

Another of much smaller dimensions, being only 115 feet in length, and partly excavated in the rock, was constructed by Tirhakah, whose name, with that of his queen, is read upon the walls of the excavated part[2]. It was dedicated to the god Typhon or Pthah-Sokari. The sculptures exhibit offerings made to various gods of the Egyptian pantheon, and the whole style of the building is decidedly of an

---

[1] Hoskins (p. 146) says the name is Papi, but he has not given a copy.

[2] Hoskins, p. 136.

Egyptian character. Two other temples, one 85 feet in length, remain surrounded by ruins which indicate the ancient importance of the city in which they stood. In one of them a king appears lifting a battle-axe on some captives tied together by their hair[1]. Two lions of red granite, one bearing the name of Amunoph III., the other of Amuntuonch, perhaps his son or brother, were found among the ruins and brought to England by Lord Prudhoe[2]. They are now appropriately placed at the entrance of the Gallery of Egyptian antiquities in the British Museum. Notwithstanding the mutilation they have suffered, their grand and simple outlines and attitude of majestic repose reveal to a discriminating observer the high perfection of taste and skill which characterized Egyptian art under the eighteenth dynasty. The characters for Amun, in the first part of the name, have been obliterated, as in many other instances; and a king Amunasso, of a much later age, perhaps of the Ptolemaic or Roman times[3], has engraved his own name on one of them, in characters which show the decline of art. Whether these lions mark the southern limits of the dominions of Egypt, or are trophies of conquest, brought from Thebes or Soleb by Ethiopian kings, is a doubtful question. A fragment has also been found here, which appears to have borne the name of Rameses II., and another with that of *Aspelt* or *Osport*.

No monument has yet been discovered, by which

---

[1] Hoskins, p. 141.
[2] Birch's Gallery of Antiquities, p. 50.
[3] Hoskins, 161, 288. Rosellini, Dyn. 25. Sir G. Wilkinson in Trans. Royal Soc. Lit. 2nd Ser. 1, 54.

the name of this city could be fixed; but it is probably Napata, the capital of Candace, the queen of the Ethiopians, which was taken by Petronius in the reign of Augustus[1], and also of those kings of Ethiopia, who are mentioned in the history of the Ptolemies and the Pharaohs. The name *Merawe*, given to a village a short distance below Gebel-el-Birkel, on the right bank of the Nile, has been identified by some writers with *Meroe*. But the site of that kingdom has been fixed by decisive evidence; and if the modern name have any connexion with the ancient, it can only be that Merawe marks the northern limit of the kingdom of Meroe. It stands very near the commencement of the route which conducts across the Desert of Bahiouda to the banks of the Nile, opposite Shendy. Another route through the Desert from the north, commencing at the isle of Argo, appears also to have terminated at Napata, by which the bend of the river to Dongola was cut off[2]. The importance which it thus acquired, as an entrepôt between Nubia and Meroe, would account for its size and population.

The south-western deflection of the Nile continues, after it has passed Merawe, till it reaches the 18th degree of N. latitude, when it turns again to the north. In this part of its course it is about half a mile wide. Scarcely any land is now under cultivation, except in the islands, and the desert spreads in interminable extent everywhere beyond the banks. The kingdom of Dongola begins just

[1] Strabo, 17, p. 820. Plin. 6, 35.
[2] See Russegger's Karte von Nubien.

where the river resumes its northern direction, and continues to near the Second Cataract. The whole of this district much surpasses in fertility that which has been just described. The banks are no longer rocky; the inundation consequently diffuses itself further over the surrounding country; fine pastures abound, and maintain a breed of valuable horses. No remains of antiquity are found till we reach the island of Argo, in lat. 19° 12′ N., a little above the Third Cataract[1]. It is twelve miles in length and tolerably fruitful, and is probably the *Gagaudes insula* of Pliny[2]. Two overthrown colossal statues of grey granite, in Ethiopian costume, with Egyptian features, are without a name; but near them lies a fragment of a statue of Sabaco. They all appear to have belonged to a temple which once stood upon this spot, and the two statues may have been erected before its entrance[3]. They were cut from a quarry at Toumbos, near the Third Cataract, where a similar, but smaller statue still exists, and a hieroglyphic tablet, bearing the names of Thothmes I. and Amunoph III.

Below the Third Cataract, a little to the north of the island of Argo, the Nile makes a considerable deflection to the east, and travellers usually take a straight line through the desert to Soleb or Dherbe on the left bank. In this deflection, the only ruins that occur are those of Seghi or Sesce, on the right bank; they consist of a few columns, on the base of which captives are represented; but no name has been found to determine whose triumph they

[1] Hoskins's Ethiopia, ch. xv. [3] Hoskins, p. 212.
[2] N. H. 6, 35.

record[1]. Soleb presents the ruins of a temple, equally remarkable for the elegance of its architecture, and its imposing and picturesque position, on the very line of separation between the verdure and fertility of the Nile, and the desolation of the Desert, spreading to the horizon in a monotonous plain of sand[2]. A *dromos* or avenue 136 feet long, of granite sphinxes, with bodies of lions and heads of rams, led up to a portico or *propylon*, opening into a court 90 feet in length and 113 in width, ornamented with twenty-eight columns. It is succeeded by another 78 feet long, where the remains of thirty-two columns, each 17 feet in circumference, can be traced. A chamber beyond this second court contained twelve columns, on the bases of which prisoners of different nations are represented, as on Egyptian monuments, by embattled ovals. Thirty-eight of these have been counted, but they have neither been drawn nor described with such accuracy as to enable us to identify them. Amunoph III. is the king whose victories are recorded, and the temple was dedicated to Amuura, the chief god of Thebes. The foundations were of crude brick, which in Egypt also has been used for the same purpose, though apparently a slight support for the enormous masses of stone which were placed upon them. Sukkot, also on the left bank, a little lower down, contains some ruins of the age of Amunoph III., and traces of a town of considerable size[3]. The river is divided, a few miles below Sukkot, by

---

[1] Ritter, Africa, 611. They were not seen by Hoskins, who took the Desert-road.

[2] Cailliaud, 1, 375. Hoskins, p. 245.

[3] Hoskins, 255.

the island of Sais, the next in magnitude to that of Argo, and soon after enters the district called Batu-el-Hajar, abounding with granitic rocks which approach each other so nearly, that the Nile is contracted in one place into two passages, scarcely a stone's throw wide. The rocks impend over the shore and fill the bed with shoals, among which the river runs with so many eddies, rapids and shallows, that navigation, even in the time of the highest waters, is dangerous, and at other times impracticable[1]. A short distance below the island of Sais, on the right bank, stand the remains of the small temple of Amara. The two columns of the portico, which alone remain, have square bases, an appendage not found in the oldest specimens of Egyptian architecture; and this, joined to the indifferent execution of the sculpture, leads to the conclusion that they are not of the Pharaonic times[2]. The shields, which might have given us precise information of the builder's name, have never been filled up[3].

Semneh, on the left bank, in lat. 21° 29', about half-way between the island of Sais and the Second Cataract, exhibits the remains of a temple, on an elevated rock near the river, surrounded by a covered gallery supported by columns and square pillars. The walls are ornamented with sculpture, in which the Egyptian king Thothmes III. appears, making offerings to a predecessor of the name of Sesortasen or Osortasen[4], who is joined in a triad with the gods Noum or Cnuphis, and Totoun. The names of Amenemhe III., the founder of the La-

[1] Ritter, Africa, p. 617.
[2] Cailliaud, 3, 253. Hoskins, p. 261.
[3] Cailliaud, 1, 348.
[4] Hoskins, p. 269.

byrinth and of Sebekatep, or Sebekopth, have also been found here[1]. Directly opposite, on the right bank, stands another temple of larger dimensions, but so decayed and buried in the sand, that its plan has not been traced. It is, however, of equal antiquity, the name of Thothmes III., joined with that of Amunoph III., being found on the sculptures. No spot on the upper course of the Nile exhibits a more impressive or picturesque view. The temples on their opposite eminences appear like the ruins of fortresses, guarding the narrow pass through which the river forces its way. Though now surrounded only by the sands of the Desert, they no doubt mark the site of a populous city, whose buildings have vanished, as its name has disappeared from history[2]. In the flourishing times of the monarchy of the Pharaohs, it was strongly fortified as being the frontier town of their dominions towards Ethiopia. It was also the highest point on the course of the Nile on which its rise was recorded[3], as in later times at Elephantine.

The district of Batn-el-Hajar continues to the Second Cataract, or Wadi Halfa, in lat. 22°, anciently called Behni[4]; but as the river approaches this place, the porphyritic and granitic rocks on its banks give place to sandstone, forming hills of a less rugged character. The Cataract of Wadi Halfa, called by the ancients the Great Cataract[5], is itself composed, like all the others, of primitive rocks, rising

---

[1] Birch, Trans. of Royal Soc. of Lit. 2, 322, N. S.
[2] Hoskins, p. 276.
[3] The inference of Lepsius, that *the place* of the inscriptions which he has copied, marks the *height* of the inundation, appears to me very doubtful.
[4] Rosellini, Monumenti del Culto, p. 15.
[5] Strabo, B. 17, p. 786.

through the sandstone. In depth it exceeds that of Syene, and its roar may be heard at the distance of half a league; yet it appeared to Burckhardt[1] rather a collection of rapids than a fall, and Belzoni ascended it during the inundation. It is not a single shoot of water, extending across the channel of the river; but a succession of islands dividing the stream, which foams and rushes between them. This has been the site of an ancient town: large remains of pottery are spread over what is now the Desert, and three temples have been traced with the names of Sesortasen, Thothmes III. and Amenophis II., all on the left bank. The largest and most southern of these was probably dedicated to Thoth, who was an object of special reverence in Nubia. Its walls and propylon were constructed of crude bricks, the columns and pilasters of the pronaos, of stone. Like those of Benihassan, which will be hereafter mentioned, they were fluted in eighteen facets. A flight of steps led from the Nile to the front of the temple, which stands on rising ground. In the sanctuary of a smaller temple was excavated a *stele* or tablet of the age of Sesortasen, now placed in the Museum of Florence, and recording his victories over the neighbouring African tribes[2]. In the pronaos of the same edifice was found a similar monument of the age of Menephtha I., indicating that the temple had been built by his father Rameses I., and dedicated to Amun-Khem[3].

The whole interval of 220 miles from Wadi Halfa

---

[1] Travels in Nubia, p. 85.
[2] Rosellini, Monumenti del Culto, p. 15; Monumenti Stor. 3, 38.
[3] Rosellini, Mon. del Culto. p. 14.

to Syene is remarkable for the number of the temples which are found, some on the right, some on the left bank, detached, or excavated in the sandstone rock, according to the width of the interval between it and the river[1]. At the distance of a day's navigation from Wadi Halfa, at Meschiahit, on the right bank, is a small grotto temple, in which is sculptured the homage of an Ethiopian prince, named Poeri, to an Egyptian sovereign. He kneels in the presence of three deities, the goddess Anuke or Vesta, the crocodile-headed Sebak, Anubis and a king, probably deceased, whose shield appears to identify him with the Sesortasens. A little lower down, on the right bank, is the grotto temple of Gebel Addah, now a christian church, but originally dedicated by King Horus of the 18th dynasty to the god Thoth. It appears also to have been a place of sepulture, and perhaps served as a necropolis to some of the neighbouring towns, which would otherwise appear to have been wholly destitute of cemeteries.

The most remarkable of all the temples between the Second Cataract and Syene is that of Aboosimbel or Ipsambul, anciently Ibsciak, two days' journey below Wadi Halfa, and on the left bank. It was nearly covered by the sands of the Desert, which have poured down in a stream through an opening in the hill, when Belzoni[2] undertook to clear them away, and discovered that the rock had been hewn

---

[1] The monuments of Lower Nubia are faithfully delineated in the work of Gau, Antiquités de la Nubie, 1822; but his speculations on the respective antiquity of buildings and excavations, as they preceded the discovery of the hieroglyphic character, are often erroneous.

[2] Belzoni, Researches, 1,316. fol.

into two grotto temples, one dedicated to Athor by Nofreari, the queen of Rameses the Great, the other to Amun and Phre, by Rameses himself. The front of the larger temple has a cornice of apes, sacred to Thoth, and is adorned with colossal figures 51 feet in height, yet so deeply buried in the sand that only a portion of the head of one was visible. The pronaos is 57 feet long and 52 wide; many apartments lie beyond it, covered with hieroglyphics and historical paintings and sculptures, which have been preserved with scarcely any injury even to the brilliancy of the colours, through so long a series of ages. Champollion and Rosellini, following the footsteps of Belzoni with ampler means, have explored every part of the temple, ascertained the age of its construction, and discovered that it records the victories of Rameses III. over various nations of Africa and Asia. Its importance as an historical document will appear when we come to treat of this sovereign's reign. Smaller excavations of the same kind are found at Ibrim, the Premis of the Greek and Roman geographers, after another day's navigation; one is a chapel of the age of Thothmes I., another of Thothmes III., another of Amunoph II., his successor, and a fourth of Rameses III.[1]

After passing Ibrim the channel of the river is compressed between a range of sandstone hills, which for two miles rise almost perpendicularly, and scarcely allow room to pass between them and its bed. Derri or Derr (anciently *Teiri*), the present capital of Lower Nubia, situated on the left bank,

[1] Rosellini, Monumenti del Culto, p. 37. That in honour of Amenophis II. appears to have been sculptured by a prince of the blood royal, who was governor of Nubia.

contains an excavated temple dedicated by Rameses the Great (III.) to the gods Pthah and Phre, whose sacred bark appears carried in procession by twelve priests. Amada, about two hours' sail below Derri, has a temple founded by Thothmes III., continued by Amenophis II., and completed by Thothmes IV. Its sculptures are of a high order of merit, and the columns of the pronaos bear a striking resemblance to the early Doric. It is at this point of the Nile's course, that the long *Akaba*, or valley of Korosko, leads from the right bank into the heart of the eastern Desert. The caravans, avoiding the circuitous course by which we have followed the Nile through Upper Nubia and Dongola, rejoin it after a desert journey of twelve to fourteen days (250 miles), at the point between Napata and Meroe, where it makes its great deflexion to the south-west[1]. Wadi Esseboua, the Valley of Lions, on the right bank, has derived its name from the sphinxes, the remains of a line of sixteen, which once led up from the Nile to the temple. It is partly an excavation in the rock, and partly a detached building of the age of Rameses III., dedicated to Amun. Its architecture is of an ordinary kind[2]. The temple of Affeedonee or Meharraka appears from its architecture to be of low antiquity; its remains are considerable, but it contains no hieroglyphical inscriptions or sculptures by which its precise age can be determined. Dakkeh, twenty miles lower down, the ancient Pselcis[3], was the site of a temple of Thoth, erected by Thothmes III.; but

---

[1] See before p. 14. Hoskins, p. 17.
[2] Rosellini, Mon. Stor. 3. pt. 2, 194; Mon. del Culto, p. 60.
[3] Selk, with the article Pselk, was a form of Isis, to whom the city was dedicated.

its principal temple was begun by the Ethiopic king Erkamen, the Ergamenes of Diodorus[1], one of a dynasty who appear to have made themselves independent after the fall of the ancient throne of the Pharaohs. The temple was continued by Ptolemy Euergetes, who reunited Nubia to Egypt. The Libyan chain, bending to the Desert, leaves here a considerable space on the left bank, on which the ruins stand. They are only the central part of a vast square which once occupied the plain. An inscription of the Roman times designates the Great Hermes (Thoth) as sharing in the border land of Egypt and Ethiopia. The central part of Nubia was specially under his protection; the southern under that of Anuke and Sate; the northern, near Philæ, of Kneph and Osiris. Pselcis is the furthest point to the south at which any traces of Greek or Roman dominion have been found on monuments; northward they are abundant. Ghirscheh, or Gerf Hussein, on the right bank, a few miles below Dakkeh, has been partly constructed, partly excavated in the rock: the construction has been destroyed; the excavation appears to have been a sanctuary dedicated by Rameses III. to the honour of the god Pthah, from whom the place was called, like Memphis, *Phthah-hei*. The temple of Dandour is of a very different age, that of the emperor Augustus. Kalabsche, the ancient Talmis, which, like Dandour, stands on the left bank, contains a temple dedicated to the god Mandulis or Malulis, as appears both by a hieroglyphical and a Greek inscription; and its

---

[1] Diod. 3, 6. He was contemporary with the second Ptolemy.

[2] Rosellini, Mon. del Culto, p. 65.

bas-reliefs exhibit his mythological history. It had been founded by Amunoph II., rebuilt by one of the Ptolemies, and repaired by Augustus, Caligula and Trajan. The Libyan chain, which rises directly behind the temple, offered in its sandstone hills inexhaustible materials for building, and ancient quarries may be traced in various parts of it. Kalabsche stands in lat. 23° 30′, consequently immediately under the Tropic of Cancer. The temple of Beitoualli, at a short distance from Kalabsche, is filled with memorials of the victories of Rameses II., forming one of the most important documents of the history of his reign. The first portion represents his triumphs over the Ethiopian nations; the others, the tribute brought by them, and his Asiatic victories[2]. The temple of Beitoualli probably escaped the devastation which fell on the rest of the buildings of Lower Nubia, in the invasion of Cambyses, by the circumstance of its being excavated in the rock. The space between Kalabsche and Beitoualli is covered with heaps of earth and fragments of pottery, mixed with human bones and bandages impregnated with bitumen, the evident traces of a large necropolis. Tafa, the ancient Taphis, contains some temples of the Roman times, and Kardassi, a temple of Isis without any sculptures. That of Deboud (Parembole), a short distance above the First Cata-

---

[1] Wilkinson, Mod. Eg. and Thebes, 2, 312. It contains a monument in the Greek language, supposed to be of the age of Diocletian, in which Silco, a king of Ethiopia and Nubia, records his victories over the Blemmyes. Mandulis is represented as the son of Horus and Isis, though commonly Isis appears as the mother of Horus.

[2] Gallery of Antiquities of the British Museum, p. 94. One of the rooms of the Museum exhibits a coloured *facsimile* of the sculptures of this temple, from the drawings of Mr. Hay.

ract, was chiefly built by Atharaman, an Ethiopian king of the same dynasty as Ergamenes, and dedicated to the ram-headed god of Thebes and Meroe.

Such a line of sacred edifices as we have described from the Second Cataract to the First, implies a population very different from the scattered and impoverished tribes that now inhabit the valley of Lower Nubia. Their habitations may easily have disappeared, but the traveller is surprised to find so few traces of their sepulchres. Not many, however, have explored this region; they have gone, till lately, in haste and fear, without time or means to make excavations, and not venturing beyond the immediate neighbourhood of the river. An ample field of inquiry remains for any scientific expedition which should be able to explore what lies buried, as well as measure and delineate what stands on the surface. The climate of Nubia is superior to that of Egypt, and its mean temperature ten degrees higher, but its general fertility is less; and Lower Nubia especially, from the near approach of the hills to the river, which prevents the deposit of alluvium, contains less land capable of culture, and is more exposed to the encroachment of the sand[1]. The rise of the Nile is in some places as much as thirty feet, but the height of the banks denies the adjacent land the benefit of the inundation, unless powerful wheels be used to raise its waters to a higher level.

Just above the Cataract of Syene, where the Nile is 3000 feet wide, lies the island of Philæ[2], which

---

[1] Wilkinson, Manners and Customs, 1, 117, 223.

[2] Φίλαι is plural in Greek and Latin, the smaller island being included. The access to the larger is from the southern side. The

might be considered as the boundary between Egypt and Ethiopia. It is not above a quarter of a mile long, but is covered with picturesque ruins of temples almost entirely of the times of Ptolemy Philadelphus, Epiphanes and Philometor, with additions by the Roman emperors. The small remains of the temple of Athor are of the age of the last of the Pharaohs, Nectanebus. The principal monuments lie at the southern end of the island; a wall, erected on the rocks which rise abruptly from the river, ran round the whole, and made it an *Abaton* or inaccessible sanctuary[1]. From the landing-place two parallel colonnades conducted to the chief temple, before which lay two colossal lions of granite in front of a pair of obelisks, forty-four feet in height. The angles of the sanctuary were occupied by two monolithal shrines, in which a sacred hawk used to be kept. One of these is now in the Louvre, the other in the Museum of Florence. Right and left of the entrance are two small buildings, one of which, dedicated to Athor, represents the birth of Ptolemy Philometor, under the form of Horus. Philæ was dedicated to the worship of Osiris, said to be buried here[2], whose mythic history is displayed in the sculptures which everywhere cover the walls, and especially two secret chambers. A still smaller island, anciently called *Snem* or *Senmut*, now *Beghé*, lies near Philæ. The inscriptions show that it was a place of sanctity in the Pharaonic times. The hieroglyphic name, *Philak*, (or *Manlak*) is said to mean boundary land. Rosellini, Mon. del Culto, p. 179.

[1] Plut. Is. et Osir. p. 359. The Egyptians fabled that neither birds flew over it, nor fish approached the shore. Senec. N. Q. 4, 2, 7.

[2] Diod. 1, 22.

names of Amunoph III., Rameses the Great, Psammitichus, Apries and Amasis, all appear on its granite rocks[1], along with memorials of the Ptolemies and Roman emperors.

The falls begin immediately below Philæ, and extend to Syene and the island of Elephantine. The granite rocks by which they are caused, cross the river and extend into the Desert on either side. They are much higher and more rugged than those of the Second Cataract; rising to the height of forty feet, their fracture exhibits a beautiful rose colour, but their bare sides and peaks are brown. There are three principal falls; at the steepest, which is about thirty feet wide, the descent is from ten to twelve feet in 100; yet during the high water it may be shot, though not altogether without danger[2]. The entire descent in a space of five miles, is only eighty feet[3]. The description given by the ancients of the deep fall and deafening sound of the waters is an exaggeration, for no change of level can have taken place since the days of Cicero and Seneca[4], which could reconcile their accounts with the fact. From them the whole neighbourhood obtained the name of *Manebmou*, "the place of pure waters."

---

[1] Rosellini, Mon. del Culto, p. 186. The resort of visitors to Philæ was so great in the time of the Ptolemies, that the priests petitioned Physcon not to allow public functionaries to come and live at their expense. The obelisk on which this petition was inscribed was brought to England by Mr. Bankes, and the comparison of its hieroglyphics with those of the Rosetta stone, assisted in the discovery of the phonetic alphabet.

[2] Seneca, N. Q. 4, 2, gives a lively picture of this operation. "Bini parvula navigia conscendunt, quorum alter navem regit, alter exhaurit; cum toto flumine effusi navigium ruens minus temperant, magnoque spectantium metu in caput nixi, quum jam adploraveris, mersosque atque obrutos tanta mole credideris, longe ab eo in quem ceciderant loco navigant, tormenti modo missi."

[3] Russegger, Reisen, 1, 213.

[4] Somn. Scip. 5. Nat. Quæst. 4, 2.

The Egyptians considered this as in a certain sense the source of the Nile, and in a sculpture of the temple, the river is represented in a human form, crowned with lotus, at the bottom of a grotto, pouring a perennial stream from two urns, which he holds upright in his hands[1]. When the course of the Nile above Egypt was little known, as it would be to the natives of the Delta, the violent agitation of the waters at this place was not unnaturally accounted for by the bursting forth of a subterraneous stream. It was even believed in Lower Egypt, or at least so Herodotus was told by a learned functionary of Sais[2], that the Nile rose here, and flowed half towards Ethiopia and half towards Egypt.

The quarries on either bank have furnished the colossal statues, obelisks and monolithal shrines[3] which are found throughout Egypt, or as trophies of conquest adorn Rome and Constantinople. The marks of the wedges and tools are still visible; an obelisk, fifty-four feet long, lies wholly detached and ready for transport; others are marked out by a line of holes in which the wedges were to be inserted[4]. Notwithstanding the many centuries which have elapsed since these quarries were wrought, their fracture still appears fresh and of a much brighter colour than the natural rock; so short is the time since the tool of an Egyptian quarryman laid open their surface, compared with that during which their brown sides and peaks have been exposed to the action of the atmosphere. The road which leads from Philæ to Syene on the right bank

---

[1] Rosellini, Mon. del Culto, pl. xxvii. 3.
[2] Her. 2, 28.
[3] Her. 2, 175.
[4] Description de l'Egypte, Ant. vol. 1, p. 140.

is about four miles in length, and is bordered on both sides by round masses of the granite rock, piled upon one another. The remains of a large square enclosure of crude brick are supposed to indicate the prisons or barracks, in which the slaves were lodged by whom these quarries were wrought[1]. Inscriptions and tablets in various parts commemorate acts of homage by the Pharaohs and other illustrious persons to the divinities of the Cataract, Kneph or Chnuphis, Sate and Anuke. The island of Elephantine[2], just opposite to Syene, diversifies by its fertility and verdure the dreary aspect which sand and granite give to the neighbourhood of the Cataracts. Two temples which stood upon it, one dedicated by Amunoph II. to Kneph, the other to Amun, have been recently destroyed by the Pacha of Egypt to build warehouses and a barrack. The remains of the Nilometer described by Strabo[3] are still visible. The waters of the Nile were admitted into a receptacle of squared stone, into which a long flight of steps descended; and the walls were graduated so as to mark the progressive rise of the inundation. The measures inscribed upon it are of the Greek and Roman age[4].

The latitude of Assuan, the ancient Syene, is 24° 5′ 23″, and it consequently lies 35′ 23″ north of the true tropic[5]. The ancients believed that it

---

[1] Rosellini, Mon. del Culto, p. 189.

[2] The ancient name of Elephantine was Ebo. *Eb* is the name of the elephant and of ivory in hieroglyphics. Rosellini, Mon. Stor. 4, 204.

[3] Strabo, B. 17, 817. Heliod. Æth. 9, 22.

[4] Hieroglyphics published by the Egyptian Soc., pl. 57–62. Wilkinson, Manners and Customs, 2, 47.

[5] Ritter's Africa, p. 694, from the observations of the French.

was immediately under the tropic; that the sun's disc was reflected in a well at noon on the day of the solstice, and that an upright staff cast no shadow[1]. It has been thought that these observations, though untrue for historical times, had been handed down from very remote ages, when the position of the tropic was different. The northern limb of the sun's disc would however be nearly vertical over Syene, though not the centre, and the length of a shadow, being only $\frac{1}{400}$th of the staff, would be scarcely appreciable. Considering the entire want of accurate astronomical instruments among the Egyptians, an inaccuracy of observation or exaggeration of statement is far more probable than such a change in the inclination of the earth's axis[2].

At Syene we enter upon Upper Egypt, which continues as far as Hermopolis Magna, in lat. 28°, where Middle Egypt, called in later times the

---

[1] Ἐν Συήνῃ κατὰ θερινὰς τροπὰς ὁ ἥλιος κατὰ κορυφῆς γίγνεται (Strabo, 2, 133). Ἐν Συήνῃ καὶ τὸ φρέαρ ἐστὶ τὸ διασημαῖνον τὰς θερινὰς τροπὰς, διότι τῷ τροπικῷ κύκλῳ ὑπόκεινται οἱ τόποι οὗτοι καὶ ποιοῦσιν ἀσκίους τοὺς γνώμονας κατὰ μεσημβρίαν. (17, p. 817).

[2] Syene is supposed to have been so called from a goddess Suan (opener), answering to the Ilithya of the Greeks. Rosellini, *u. s.*

It may be convenient to exhibit here a table of the distances in English miles of the principal places in Egypt. They are taken from Sir Gardner Wilkinson's Manners and Customs, 3, 404, and Russegger's Map:—

Syene to Latopolis	100
Latopolis to Thebes	38
Thebes to Keneh, opposite to Tentyra	49
Keneh to Panopolis	83
Panopolis to Lycopolis	85
Lycopolis to Speos Artemidos	80
Speos Artemidos to Minieh	26
Minieh to Benisooef, opposite the Fyoum	85
Benisooef to Cairo	83
Cairo to Rosetta	110
	739

Heptanomis, begins. From Syene to the apex of the Delta the Nile runs with a declivity without falls or rapids, the whole descent to the Mediterranean being only between 500 and 600 feet. The valley through which it flows varies in breadth, as the hills which are parallel to it approach or recede, its average width being seven, its greatest not exceeding eleven miles. A short distance below Syene begins a district of sandstone-rock which continues nearly to Latopolis in lat. 25°. This part of the valley is narrow, and as the Nile can deposit little fertilizing matter, the general aspect of the shores is dreary and barren. The first place at which any remains of antiquity occur is Koum-Ombos, the ancient Ombi, on the right bank. The two temples, of which considerable ruins are standing, of an imposing architecture, and still showing the brilliant colours with which they were adorned, are of the Ptolemaic age; but a fragment of a much earlier foundation has been discovered, a doorway of sandstone, built into a wall of brick. It was part of a temple built by Thothmes III., in honour of the crocodile-headed god Sebak[1]. The king is represented, on the jambs, holding the measuring reed and chisel, the emblems of a construction, and in the act of dedicating the temple. The crocodile was held in special honour by the people of Ombi, whose feud with the people of Tentyra has been celebrated by Juvenal[2]. Crocodile mummies have been found in the adjacent catacombs, confirming the ancient accounts of the veneration in which it was held here; the Roman coins of the Ombite nome also exhibit the

---

[1] Rosellini, Mon. del Culto, 196.   [2] Sat. 15.

crocodile[1]. The river here inclines strongly to the Arabian side, and threatens to undermine and bury in its waters the hill on which the temples stand. Sixteen miles below Ombi[2], at Gebel Selsileh, or the Hill of the Chain, the Arabian and Libyan range draw so near to each other, that the river, contracted to about half its previous width, seems to flow between two perpendicular walls of sandstone. This spot was appropriately chosen for the special worship of the Nile, who seems here to occupy the whole breadth of Egypt. Under the name of Hapimoou, and the emblem of the crocodile, Rameses II. consecrated a sanctuary to him. On both sides of the river, but especially on the eastern bank, are vast quarries of the beautiful and durable stone of which the temples of Upper Egypt are constructed. The opening of a quarry for such a purpose appears to have been regarded by the Egyptians as a religious act; inscriptions record the event and the edifices for which the stone was wrought, the officers who superintended the works, and the sovereigns who visited this part of Egypt for religious or festive purposes. One excavation in the western rock, of superior dimensions to the rest, with five entrances from the bank of the river, was begun in the reign of Horus of the eighteenth dynasty, and records his expedition into Ethiopia and triumph over its inhabitants. On the internal walls of this gallery, which runs parallel to the Nile, successive sovereigns and princes of this and the following dynasty have inscribed their names,

---

[1] Tochon d'Annecy, Recherches sur les Médailles des Nomes, p. 54.

[2] Wilkinson, Modern Egypt and Thebes, 2, 283.

with acts of adoration. The position of these quarries, so close to the banks of the river, made it easy to transport columns and architraves of any size to the most distant parts of Egypt. The block of a colossal sphinx is still lying on the shore; others are traced for excavation on the rock : and it was hence, no doubt, that the criosphinxes were brought, which form the long *dromos* uniting the temple of Luxor at Thebes with the palace of Karnak. Two monolithal shrines are lying fractured on the ground, one of which bears the date of the twenty-seventh year of Amenophis-Memnon[1].

Edfu, or Apollinopolis Magna, stands on the right bank in lat. 25°, and here the valley begins to expand sufficiently to allow some effect to the inundation. The remains of the principal temple, distant about a third of a mile from the river, give a very perfect idea of the usual construction of an Egyptian temple. Of all the edifices of this class in Egypt it is the best preserved, but its beauty is impaired by the sands which have accumulated against its sides and the heaps of rubbish which hide the columns to two-thirds of their height—the ruins of the huts of mud with which the Arabs have covered the platform of the temple. The whole of the sacred precincts is surrounded by a strong wall 20 feet high, and is entered by a gateway (or *pylon*) which is 50 feet in height, and is flanked by two converging wings, rising to 107 feet[2]. A large square

---

[1] Rosellini, Mon. del Culto, p. 234.

[2] Writers on Egyptian antiquities frequently give the name of *pylon* to the converging piles which rise on each side the gateway; but πυλών is properly a lofty gate, bearing the same analogy to πύλη, as *portone* in Italian to *porta*. The converging piles are called πτερά,

court, surrounded by a colonade, is in front of the pronaos or portico, which is 53 feet in height, and has a triple row of columns, whose capitals exhibit a rich variety of graceful foliage. The temple is 145 feet wide; and from the entrance to the opposite end 424 feet long, and every part is covered with hieroglyphics. It was dedicated to Hor-hat, the Horus-Apollo of the Greeks; but it is wholly of the Ptolemaic times, its earliest portion having been erected by Ptolemy Philometor. The smaller temple, which had been called a Typhonium, is properly an appendage, in the hieroglyphics *Manmisi*, representing the birth and education of the youthful god, whose parents were adored in the larger edifice[1].

Eilithya (El Kab), a few miles lower down the Nile and on the eastern bank, is remarkable for its hypogæa, which pierce the sandstone rock in every direction and mark the ancient importance of the town. Two of them deserve more especial notice. They are tombs of the family of the sacred scribes and high priest of the temple of Eilithya, whose names have been read *Pipe*, *Sotepau*, and *Ranseni*, and are as old as the reign of Rameses Meiamun. Almost the whole domestic life of the Egyptians is here portrayed, in sculptures and stucco, with colours as vivid as when the artist had just ceased to work upon them. The operations of husbandry, the gathering of the vintage and the making of wine, the capture and preservation of fish, the navigation

---

wings; and the whole front, including gateway and wings, πρόπυλον. Diodorus, 1, 47, gives the name of πυλών, *a parte potiori*, to the whole front. Russegger (1, 180) gives 90 feet as the height of the converging wings. They contain ten stories, and probably served as lodgings for the priests or servitors of the temple.

[1] Rosellini, Mon. del Culto, p. 269; Mon. Stor. 3, 1, 215.

of the Nile, trades and manufactures, the song and the dance, the preparation of a mummy, are all delineated on these walls. Another tomb belonged to the commander of the fleet in which Amasis, the first of the eighteenth dynasty, ascended the Nile for the subjugation of Ethiopia; and a third records the names of several sovereigns of the same dynasty, whose succession would not otherwise have been known. From this point a valley opens which conducts in a south-eastern direction through the Desert to Berenice on the Red Sea. Eilithya has probably been a seat of the commerce of ancient Egypt; a wall of unburnt bricks, 27 feet in height, 34 in thickness, and 2000 each way in length, enclosed the ruins of the town, and one of larger extent the temples. The latter, of which the remains were drawn by the French Commission[1], have wholly disappeared under the hands of the present ruler of Egypt, but the fragments are sufficient to show that they belonged to the same epoch as the tombs, and that the tutelary goddess was Suan. The sandstone rock which has hitherto bordered the valley on both sides, is found only on the eastern from a short distance below Edfu; four miles below Eilithya, the limestone makes its appearance. The pyramid of El Koofa, which is about two miles from the river, is built of it[2].

At Esneh (Latopolis) on the western bank, in lat. 25° 30′, the valley of the Nile receives a great expansion and attains the width of between four and five miles. The remains of its temple are magnifi-

[1] Description de l'Egypte, Antiq. vol. 1, 343. 6. 7.
[2] Vyse on the Pyramids, 3, 85, 1, pl. 66–71.

cent and resemble in style that of Edfu, but are wholly of the Roman times, extending from Claudius to Geta, whose hieroglyphics have been erased by his brother and murderer Caracalla. What now exists is only the pronaos. When the Roman emperors began their work, they appear to have destroyed even the foundations of the temple. A fragment still remains, the jamb of a gateway, converted into a doorsill, of the age of Thothmes II., and a doorway in the pronaos, bearing a dedication by Ptolemy Epiphanes; and it is true generally, that the Ptolemies erected their splendid works only on sites already consecrated to the ancient divinities of the country. Kneph or Chnuphis, Neith or Sate and Hak, their joint offspring, appear to have been the tutelary deities of Edfu. The architectural effect of the temple is imposing, but the sculptures and hieroglyphics are very badly executed, showing the deep decline of art in the imperial times[1]. Two zodiacs found here, gave rise at their first discovery to inferences respecting the antiquity of Egyptian astronomy, which have been set aside by further investigation. The pronaos of the greater temple, on the ceiling of which one of them is found, was begun by the Emperor Claudius. The smaller temple, sometimes called of Esneh, but which stood at E'Dayr, two miles and three-quarters north of Esneh, lately destroyed[2], contained another zodiac, but was not older than Ptolemy Euergetes. Strabo says that Latopolis derived its name from the wor-

---

[1] Rosellini, Mon. del Culto, p. 283.

[2] It was destroyed to construct a canal. The larger temple has been cleared and preserved for a cotton warehouse (Lepsius, Einleitung, p. 63).

ship of Minerva and the fish Latus[1], which accordingly appears among the sculptures of the temple, surrounded by that oval ring or shield which usually marks royalty or divinity[2].

The course of the river is again contracted by the rocks of Gebelein or *the two mountains,* which on opposite sides approach so near to it and rise so steeply, that to avoid them the road quits the vicinity of the Nile. With these hills the sandstone wholly disappears[3], and limestone hills border the valley till it opens into the Delta below Memphis. Its character is consequently changed, the banks slope more gently from the stream, especially on the western side, and afford a wider interval of cultivated land. In a plain of this enlarged valley stands Hermonthis on the western bank. Its temple was built under the reign of the last Cleopatra, the contemporary of Julius Cæsar and Antony; and the sculptures appear to allude to the birth of Cæsarion, her son by the former, symbolized as that of the god Harphre, the son of Mandou and Ritho. Its astronomical ceiling can therefore afford no evidence of the state of science under the Pharaohs; it is probably *genethliacal, i.e.* refers to the aspect of the heavens at the time of the birth.

A much wider expansion of the valley takes place at the plain on which stood THEBES, the city of a hundred gates. Both the chains of hills make a sweep away from the river, approaching and again contracting the valley at Gournah to the north, where the plain of Thebes and the remains of its

---

[1] Strabo, 17, p. 812, 817.
[2] Wilkinson, Manners and Customs, 5, 253.
[3] On Russegger's Geognostical Chart of Egypt the sandstone is represented as terminating a few miles south of Gebelein.

edifices end. The river is enlarged to the width of a mile and a quarter, and is divided by islands. On the Libyan or western side, the hills, which are 1200 feet high[1], form precipitous rocks, and are penetrated by hypogæa, in which all classes of the Theban population found sepulchres. The Arabian or eastern chain is a succession of hills rising more gradually to the summit; it contains no sepulchral monuments. The ancient city was divided by the river. On the right bank the plain is occupied by two modern villages, Luxor to the south and close to the river; Karnak nearer to the hills and about a mile and a quarter to the north. On the other side of the Nile, Medinet Abou and Gournah stand on the ground which the western half of Thebes anciently occupied. But the monuments of this capital of the Pharaohs, in the times of their most extensive dominion, are so vast and important as to require a more detailed account than can be given of them now, when our object is rather to trace the course of the Nile, and we shall return to Thebes hereafter.

In descending the river from Thebes, the traveller passes, at a little distance from the eastern bank, Medamoot[2], the site of a town whose ancient name is not ascertained. It contains, along with remains of the Roman and Ptolemaic times, some fragments of the age of Amunoph II. and Rameses II. At Apollinopolis Parva (Koos) on the same bank, the propylon of a temple was till lately seen, nearly buried in the sand, dedicated by Cleopatra (Cocce) and her son Ptolemy to the god Aroeris; but among the ruins a tablet has been found bearing date the sixteenth

---

[1] Wilkinson, M. and C. 4, 119. Russegger, Reisen, 2, 1, 114.
[2] Wilkinson, Mod. Eg. and Thebes, 2, 133.

year of Rameses Meiamun[1]. Coptos (now Keft, in hieroglyphics Kobto), also on the right bank, contains monuments of the Roman times, but none of ancient Egypt. Among the stones which the Christians have employed in the construction of their church, the royal legends of Thothmes III. and Nectanebus have however been discovered[2]. From this place a second valley opens to the south-east, leading to the quarries of porphyry in the Arabian Desert and to Cosseir on the Red Sea. Coptos was enriched by the commerce with India carried on by this route, and was a flourishing city till its destruction by Diocletian[3]. The traffic with Cosseir still continues, but it is chiefly carried on from Keneh, a little further to the north. The river, after passing the opening of this lateral valley, bends to the northwest, and follows for some distance the line of its prolongation, but soon recovers its normal direction to the north.

About thirty-eight miles below Thebes, on the left bank, stands Dendera, the ancient Tentyra, whose inhabitants, celebrated for their skill in hunting the crocodile[4], were involved in hostility with the people of Ombi, whose devotion to the god Sebak, worshiped under this emblem, has been already noticed[5]. No remains of Egyptian archi-

---

[1] Champollion, Lettres d'Egypte, p. 92.
[2] Wilkinson, *u. s.*, 2, 129.
[3] Gibbon, vol. 2, ch. 13.
[4] Pliny, N. H. 8, 25. Ælian, Hist. Anim. 10, 21.
[5]   Inter finitimos vetus atque antiqua simultas
   Ardet adhuc Ombos et Tentyra; summus utrinque
   Inde furor vulgo, quod numina vicinorum
   Odit uterque locus.—Juv. Sat. 15, 33.

Ombi and Tentyra are not so near as the words of the poet would lead us to suppose; but the Tentyrites had probably exercised their skill in catching crocodiles within the limits of the Ombite nome.

tecture have excited the admiration of travellers more than the temple of Athor at Tentyra[1]. It is the first in tolerable preservation which they meet as they ascend the Nile; it stands remote from the river and the abodes of men, amidst the sands of the Desert, at the foot of the Libyan hills. The majestic architecture of its portico, composed of six columns, from which the features of the goddess Athor look down with a mysterious tranquillity, and the supposed primæval antiquity of its zodiac, combined with its situation to produce admiration and awe. Under the influence of such feelings, it was natural that, as it is certainly one of the most impressive of Egyptian monuments, it should be regarded as one of the oldest. This, however, is not the case. The sculpture with which every part is crowded, betrays itself to be of a late age; the Greek inscriptions on the pronaos refer to Tiberius and Hadrian[2], and the hieroglyphic legends on the oldest portions of the walls to the last Cleopatra. Tentyra contains, behind the great temple, a smaller one, dedicated to Isis, and a Typhonium; but they are also of the Roman times. The zodiac is delineated on the ceiling of the pronaos; the conclusion which Visconti drew from the position of the signs, that it must have been constructed between A.D. 12 and A.D. 132, was confirmed by Mr. Hamilton's reading of the name of Tiberius in the Greek inscription[3], and the hieroglyphical discoveries of Champollion. In an upper apartment a circular planisphere is de-

[1] Tentyra has been explained as *Tei-n-athor*, the abode of Athor (Wilkinson, Mod. Eg. 2, 119).
[2] Letronne's Inscriptions, 1, p. 89.
[3] Wilkinson, Mod. Eg. and Thebes, 2, 121. Lepsius, Einleitung, p. 103.

lineated on the ceiling[1], the object of which has not yet been ascertained. Chenoboscion (Quesr-Syad) on the right bank is remarkable for some very ancient grottos, in which are inscribed the names of several kings of Egypt, earlier than any which remain on obelisks or temples.

Near Diospolis Parva (How) on the left bank, opposite to Chenoboscion, begins the canal or ancient branch of the Nile, called the Bahr-Jusuf, or River of Joseph, which flows between the river and the Libyan hills to the entrance of the Fyoum. One of the first places which it passes is Abydos or This. If modern discoveries have disproved the high antiquity of Dendera, they have fully confirmed the claims of Abydos. In the times of the native kings of Egypt, it had been the second city of the Thebaid[2], the birth-place of Menes the founder of the monarchy; the origin of its temple was attributed to Memnon, and it was supposed to be the place of sepulture of Osiris. As he was the god of the unseen world, pious votaries desired to rest here under his auspices. It became therefore a celebrated necropolis, and the adjacent Libyan hills are full of sepulchres, some of which date as far back as the time of Sesortasen. Its remains are found at Arabat el Matfoon, buried in sand, which reaches to the capitals and architraves of the columns. Here in 1818 Mr. Bankes discovered a tablet inscribed with the shields of a series of Egyptian kings, which has contributed more than any other monument, except the Rosetta stone, to advance our knowledge of

[1] Denon's Voyage en Egypte, 1, p. 34, plate 48.
[2] Strabo, B. 17, p. 813.

Egyptian history. Abydos contains two edifices; one, called by the ancients the Palace of Memnon[1], built by the father of Rameses the Great; the other, a temple built or finished by Rameses himself. The royal tablet just mentioned was placed on the wall of one of the side apartments of this temple, and as it terminates with his name, and records his offerings to his predecessors, it is presumed that it was erected in his reign. It unfortunately suffered great mutilation in the interval between its discovery and its final removal by the French Consul Mimaut, on whose death it came into the British Museum[2]. A road passed by Abydos to the Greater Oasis.

Ekhmin, Chemmis or Panopolis on the eastern bank, which was anciently inhabited by linen weavers and masons, contains some ruins of the age of Ptolemy Philopater, dedicated to Amun Khem[3]. The Greeks confounded him with their Pan, whose name appears in the inscription on the temple. It is doubtful whether anything remains of a temple described by Herodotus[4], dedicated to Perseus, the son of Danae, and said to have been founded by him. E' Syout, the ancient Lycopolis, in lat. 27° 10' 14", on the western bank, has no conspicuous ruins, but in the excavated chambers of the adjacent rocks mummies of wolves are found, confirming the etymology of the name[5]. The shield of a king preserved here has been read *Rekamai*; he lived probably during the dominion of the Shep-

---

[1] Plin. N. Hist. 5, 11.
[2] Gallery of Egyptian Antiquities in the British Museum, p. 66.
[3] Strabo, B. 17, p. 813. Steph. Byz. s. v. Πανόπολις.
[4] Her. 2, 91.
[5] See the account of these hypogæa in the Description de l'É_gypte, Antiquités, tom. 2, ch. 13. Rosellini, Mon. Civ. 1, 81.

herds. Near Manfalout, a little lower down, the eastern and western banks contain grottos which have served as repositories to embalmed dogs, cats and crocodiles. The latter animal was especially worshiped at Athribis on the western side of the river, nearly opposite to Ekhmin. The magnificent portico of Hermopolis Magna, on the western side, was of the Pharaonic times. The remains of Antinoe, built by Hadrian in honour of his favourite, exhibited Roman architecture in singular contrast with the native style of Egypt. This district was more exposed than the Thebaid to the ravages of invading armies, and the material of buildings offered a temptation to burn them into lime. Hermopolis and Antinoe had escaped those perils, but have perished in our own age from the ignorance and cupidity of a semi-barbarous people. A little to the south of Antinoe is a grotto, the tomb of Thoth-otp of the age of Sesortasen, containing a representation of a colossal statue dragged by the force of men's arms to the place of its erection[1].

To the north of Antinoe, on the eastern bank, are the grottos of Benihassan, the Speos Artemidos of the Greeks. The name has been explained by the united French and Tuscan expedition, who found in a desert valley of the Arabian chain, a temple constructed by the kings of the eighteenth dynasty, and dedicated to Pasht, the Bubastis of the Greek writers on Egypt, identified by them with their Artemis[2]. The hypogæa near this temple are filled with the mummies of cats and some dogs,

---

[1] Minutoli, Reisen, Atlas, plate 13.

[2] Herod. 2, 58. Rosellini, Mon. Civ. 1, p. 78.

and others are buried under the sands of the Desert. The grottos of Benihassan itself, which are above thirty in number, appear to have been the general cemetery of the nome of Hermopolis, to whose inhabitants it was more convenient to transport their dead for interment to the eastern hills, which here approach very near to the river, than to carry them to those on their own side, which recede to a considerable distance from it. This is a singular instance of a religious usage controlled by convenience; for in general the western hills were exclusively appropriated to interments. Two of these hypogæa are especially deserving of notice; one is the tomb of Nevopth, a military chief of the reign of the early king Sesortasen, and of his wife, Rotei. It has in front an architrave excavated from the rock, and supported by two columns of 23 feet in height and slightly fluted with sixteen faces, which are just worked to a sufficient depth in the rock to allow them to be insulated from it. They have no base or capital, but a square abacus is interposed between the architrave and the head of the column, and over the architrave a denteled cornice has been cut, giving to the whole an air of grace and lightness. The chamber within is 30 feet square, and the roof is divided into three vaults. of elegant curvature by two architraves, each of which was once supported by a column no longer existing. The vaults are painted in checkers of the most vivid colouring. The walls represent Nevopth himself, engaged in fishing and the chase; or husbandmen in various operations of agriculture, and artisans plying their respective handicrafts. In one compartment we see a procession of three Egyptians and thirty-seven strangers, apparently prisoners, with the date of the sixth year of the reign of Sesortasen II.[1] Adjacent to the tomb of Nevopth, and very similar in construction, is that of Amenheme, of nearly the same age; one of the walls is covered with representations of men in various postures of wrestling. The other grottos exhibit scenes from the domestic and civil life of the Egyptians. The hope expressed by an intelligent English traveller[2], who visited Egypt early in this century, that by their means we might obtain as accurate a knowledge of the domestic antiquities of Egypt, as Herculaneum and Pompeii had given us of Roman life and manners, has been amply fulfilled by the publications of the French Commission, of Rosellini, and of our countryman, Sir Gardner Wilkinson. The grottos of Koum-el-Ahmar, nine miles lower down, supposed to stand on the site of Alabastron, are inferior in size and splendour to those of Benihassan, but they contain the names of some of the earliest Egyptian kings[3]. The quarries of the beautiful white or veined alabaster, which the Egyptians employed for their sarcophagi and other works of art, are in the Arabian Desert, near this place[4]. The ruins of Oxyrrynchos (Behneseh) and Heracleopolis (Anasieh), both on the western bank, and near the Libyan hills, are inconsiderable; nor does the course of the Nile present any remark-

[1] Some writers have thought that this was a representation of the arrival of Jacob and his family in Egypt; but they were not thirty-seven in number, nor were they captives, and they came in wheel-carriages (Gen. xlvi. 27, xlv. 21).
[2] Hamilton, Ægyptiaca, p. 290.
[3] Wilkinson, Mod. Egypt. 2, 43.
[4] Russegger, Reisen, 21, 298.

able feature till it arrives at Benisooef, opposite to the latter town, in lat. 29°. The Libyan chain of hills here begins to retire from the vicinity of the river, and bends towards the north-west, and again returning towards the east and approaching the river, incloses the ancient province of Arsinoe, the modern Fyoum[1], in which were the Lake of Mœris, the Labyrinth, and the city of Crocodilopolis.

The entrance to this insulated region is by a valley about four miles wide, through which the canal or branch of the Nile called the Bahr Jusuf, passes. Its present surface is about 340 square miles; its extent anciently about forty miles in one direction and thirty in another. It is one of the most fertile districts of Egypt[2], though the inferiority of the modern to the ancient system of irrigation has much lessened the extent of productive soil. Besides grain and vegetables, it abounds with groves of dates and fig-trees, and the vine, which is a stranger to the valley of the Nile, thrives in the Fyoum. The basin in which it lies consists of the same limestone rock as the rest of this district, but it is covered by the deposit of the Nile. As it lies higher than Egypt, it must have become fertile at a later period, a rise in the bed of the river by deposition being necessary, before the water could reach it, from the Nile at Heracleopolis. But many circumstances render it probable that the Bahr Jusuf is an ancient branch of the river; no mounds of earth are seen beside it, such as accompany the course of ancient canals,

---

[1] The name is ancient, *Phioum*, signifying in Coptic "the waters," i. e. the Lake of Mœris.

[2] Strabo, B. 17, p. 809. It produces good olive oil, which the rest of Egypt does not (Jomard, Descr. de l'Égypte, 4, 440).

and the windings of its bed indicate a natural rather than an artificial channel[1]. The point at which it originates is about 130 feet higher than the present level of the Nile opposite to the entrance of the Fyoum, and in this way it may have been fertilized in very remote times, though subsequent, as history informs us, to the establishment of the monarchy.

On the side of the Desert the Fyoum was bounded by the natural lake called the Birket-el-Kerun, seven miles broad and about thirty-five miles from S.W. to N.E., which seems to have been the Lake of Mœris[2], as described by Herodotus, Strabo and Pliny. Its waters are brackish, being strongly impregnated with the alkaline salts with which the Desert abounds, and with muriate of lime washed by the rains from the hills which border it. But it is not absolutely salt, and in the season of the inundation the fishermen of the Nile come here to pursue their business. Of its north-western shore very little is known, but it does not appear to contain any antiquities of the Pharaonic times. The present level of its surface is about that of the sea, and from the quality of its waters and the sandy nature of the soil around, Strabo conjectured that it had once been connected with the Mediterranean. Herodotus too represents it as the tradition of the country, that the Lake of Mœris, at its northern extremity, turned westward and had a subterranean outlet into the Syrtes. No such outlet is known; the tradition of

[1] Linant, Mémoire sur le Lac Mœris. Translated in Borrer's Travels, p. 553. The author has been long employed as a surveyor by the Pacha of Egypt, and has examined as an engineer the levels of the Fyoum.

[2] Herod. 2, 149. Strabo, u. s. Pliny, N. H. 36 12, 75.

Herodotus is probably of the same origin as the hypothesis of Strabo, and if either of them had a foundation in fact, it must have been in geological, not historical times. The present average depth of water is not more than twelve feet, in the deepest part twenty-eight, and the bottom is the limestone rock; but it is probable that in ancient times, when it received larger supplies from the Nile, the water may have stood rather higher than at present[1]. Herodotus, indeed, speaks of two pyramids which stood in the lake, and were fifty fathoms above the water and fifty below it[2]. This is not only irreconcilable with the actual depth of the Birket-el-Kerun, or any that it can have had in ancient times, but equally with Linant's supposition that the Lake of Mœris was an artificial excavation in the centre of the Fyoum. The only remains that in any way answer to the description of Herodotus are the truncated pyramids of Biahmu, about five miles from Medinet-el-Fyoum. They may have stood formerly in the waters of the inundation; indeed their sides bear traces of immersion[3], and thus Herodotus may have been led to describe them as in the lake. They appear also anciently to have served as the pedestals to statues; but at present they are only about thirty feet in height, and from the size of the base, they can never have been fifty fathoms high. Perhaps their truncated form may have led the guides to exaggerate their original height. The Fyoum contains an obelisk, probably the oldest in existence, near

---

[1] Linant, *ubi supra*. Wilkinson, Mod. Egypt, 2, 345.
[2] Her. 2, 149.
[3] Perring in Vyse on the Pyramids, 3, 84.

Bijij, bearing the shield of Sesortasen[1]; and the site of the Labyrinth, which had been long a subject of doubt, has been fixed by the researches of the Prussian Expedition where the French Commission had placed it, in the neighbourhood of the ancient Crocodilopolis. The pyramid and sepulchre of the founder, Amenemhe III. adjoins the Labyrinth. For a fuller account of these remains we must await the publication of the great work which Lepsius is preparing.

Returning to the Nile, opposite to the opening which leads to the Fyoum, we find nothing remarkable on its banks, till approaching Cairo the Pyramids are seen. The first that are passed, in descending the stream, are those of Dashour, on the eastern edge of the Libyan chain, which has again approached and overlooks the valley. From these, the pyramids of Saccara are separated by a short interval. Those of Gizeh and Abousir close the long line of monuments which mark the necropolis of the ancient Memphis, the former by their size and towering height proclaiming their superior dignity as royal sepulchres. Memphis, however, like Thebes, is too important to be treated of incidentally, and its monuments will be reserved to a separate chapter. The hills of Gebel-el-Mokattam correspond on the eastern side to those on which the Pyramids stand. From the quarries of Tourah and Massarah the limestone was obtained for the casing and finer work of the Pyramids, and the causey by which the stones were conveyed, may still be traced across the intervening plain.

[1] Wilkinson, Mod. Eg. and Thebes, 2, 342.

The double chain of hills, between which the Nile has so long flowed, here terminates. Those on the eastern side turn off towards the head of the Red Sea, the Libyan chain retiring at the same time towards the north-west. The Nile has thus room to expand, its current is weakened, and the divided stream finds its way to the sea in sluggish branches. The point of the first separation, the apex of the Delta, was, according to the earliest records at Cercasoros[1], about ten miles below Memphis, but by a process common to all rivers[2], this point has gradually advanced, and the Delta now commences at Batu-el-Bakarah, six or seven miles lower. It spreads out to the north, east and west, a boundless plain of alluvial land, without a natural rock, a hill, or any variation of the surface, except where some high mound marks the site of an ancient city. Though *seven* mouths of Nile were reckoned by the ancients, only three branches appear ever to have carried down any great amount of water—the PELUSIAC or eastern arm, the CANOPIC or western, and the SEBENNYTIC, which continuing in the direction of the undivided stream, may with most propriety be considered as the Nile. The Pelusiac arm is now become dry; on the eastern side of it, and almost close to the apex of the Delta, stood Heliopolis, the On of Scripture, the Ain Shems, or fountain of the sun, of the modern Arabs. The only remains of this ancient city, where the father-in-law of Joseph filled the office of priest, where Moses perhaps was initiated into the wisdom of the Egyptians[3], where

---

[1] Herod. 2, 15, 16.
[2] Rennell's Geography of Herodotus, 2, 133.
[3] Gen. xli. 45. Acts vii. 22. Joseph. c. Ap. 1, c. 26.

in the days of Strabo were still shown the halls in which Plato had studied[1], is an obelisk of granite, bearing the name of Sesortasen. The place in which it stands is now distant between four and five miles from the river, but it was probably nearer in ancient times. Heliopolis stood at the verge of the Desert, and may have had a considerable mixture of Arabian population[2]. Twenty miles lower down, on the same branch, was Bubastus, now Tel Basta, conspicuous for its lofty mounds of brick, raised to protect it from the inundation, and inclosing a space now covered with ruins[3]. These are sufficient to attest its ancient magnificence; the names of Rameses the Great, Osorkon and Amyrtæus have been found here. Pelusium, even in the time of Strabo[4], was twenty stadia from the sea; its remains are now more than four times that distance; yet originally it was probably a harbour, and from its position was the key of Egypt on the side of Arabia and Palestine. The soil in which the ruins stand corresponds with the name which the city has borne in Hebrew, Coptic, Greek, and Arabic[5], all signifying a marsh; and such is the pestilent malaria which it exhales, that no traveller has ventured thoroughly to explore the ruins[6].

The wide expanse of the Lake of Menzaleh, which extends along the coast from Pelusium to Damietta, has absorbed the ancient Tanitic and Bucolic mouths of the Nile; but the ruins of San, in lat. 31°, identify

[1] Strabo, B. 17, p. 806.
[2] Juba, ap. Plin. N. H. 6, 34. Juba tradit Solis quoque oppidum, quod non procul Memphi in Egypto situm diximus, Arabas conditores habere.
[3] Herod. 2, 137. Wilkinson, 1, 428.
[4] Strabo, 17, p. 803.
[5] Champollion, Egypte sous les Pharaons, 2, 86.
[6] Wilkinson, 1, 406.

the site of Tanis, the Zoan of Scripture, one of the oldest cities of the Delta. Monuments found here show that it existed in the days of Rameses the Great; others bear the names of Menephthah, Sesortasen III., and Tirhakah[2]; the fragments of obelisks and columns, of pottery and glass, show its ancient size and importance. The present canal of Moueys probably coincides nearly with the Tanitic branch, and the ruins of Attrib, at the point where this canal leaves the Nile, represent the ancient Athribis[3]. The Mendesian branch, a derivation from the Sebennytic, has equally been lost in Lake Menzaleh, but the former channel may be traced by soundings through the present shallow waters.

The modern branch of Damietta corresponded in the upper part of its course with the ancient Sebennytic branch, as far as Semenhoud (Sebennytus), a little to the north of Mansoora; but in its lower part with the Phatnitic or Phatmetic, which though artificial has drawn to itself the greater portion of the water. Where the Sebennytic had its mouth, nearly due north of Memphis, the Lake of Bourlos has collected and obliterated the channel. Busiris stood near the middle of the Delta, on the left bank of the Damietta branch. Its name is preserved in Abousir, a little to the north of Semenhoud. There are some extensive ruins of a temple of Isis at Bahbeit, a little below 'Semenhoud[4], which from their size and destination appear to correspond with that which Herodotus describes as existing at Busiris[5].

[1] Ps. lxxviii. 12, 43.
[2] Wilkinson, 1, 448.
[3] Wilkinson, 1, 423.
[4] Minutoli, Reisen, 301. Wilkinson, 1, 432, 434.
[5] The modern Abousir is several miles distant from Bah-beit, but we often find ancient names transferred to places in their neighbourhood.

The temple stood in the midst of an extensive inclosure of crude brick, 1500 feet long and 1000- broad. It has been of extraordinary magnificence, being entirely built of granite. The remains of the sculpture, which is all of the age of Ptolemy Philadelphus, show that it was dedicated to the worship of Isis. Being in true relief, contrary to the usual Egyptian style of art, it seems to betray the hand of a Greek artist.

The Canopic branch, the most westerly, is represented by the first part of the present Rosetta branch as far as the lat. of 31°, where it turned off to the west and discharged itself into the sea, very near the promontory and bay of Aboukir. A shallow lagoon has formed here, as at the other mouths of the Nile, called the Lake of Madieh. The Canopic branch, in the first part of its descent from the apex of the Delta, closely skirted the western Desert. At Teranieh, the ancient Terenuthis, a pass through the hills communicated with the Valley of the Natron Lakes, about thirty miles from the Nile. Continuing to descend the river, we find the site of the ancient Sais on the right bank,—ascertained not only by the modern name of Sa-el-Hadjar, but by ruins corresponding in extent to the important place which this city occupied under the later Pharaohs. They have been raised high above the level of the plain, to avoid the inundation; and though they now present only a confused mass of ruins of brick, the fragments of granite and marble found among them, and the evident traces of a large inclosure, give reason to conclude that valuable remains lie buried here, and that excavation might bring to light the plan of the celebrated temple of Neith and the sepulchres of the Saitic kings[1]. Naucratis, long the Canton of the Greek merchants, the only port which they were permitted to frequent[2], was a few miles lower down than Sais and on the left bank, but its exact site has not been ascertained. That part of the present Rosetta branch which lies between the ancient course of the Canopic and the sea, represents the Bolbitine mouth, originally an artificial canal, and it appears from Herodotus[3] that in his time a branch from the Sebennytic must have joined the Canopic, passing near Sais. Westward of the Canopic mouth, there was no town of any importance in the Pharaonic times. The lake Mareotis extended parallel to the sea, as far as the Tower of Perseus on the Plinthinetian Bay, about twenty-six miles S.W. of Alexandria, the western limit of Egypt; and it is closely bordered by the sands of the Libyan Desert.

From the western limit of Egypt to Pelusium, the coast, as far as so irregular an outline can be measured, extends about 180 geographical miles; but the space now included between the Rosetta and Damietta branches is probably not equal to more than half the ancient Delta. The coast has that fan-shaped form which the deposits of a great river naturally assume where it meets the sea, being carried out the furthest opposite to the direct line of its course, the lateral and therefore weaker currents depositing their burden nearer the shore. Cape

---

[1] Champollion, Lettres d'Egypte, p. 50. Wilkinson, Mod. Egypt and Thebes, 1, 183, 185.
[2] Her. 2, 179.
[3] Her. 2, 17.

Bourlos, the most projecting point of the low sandy shore, is nearly in the same line with the bisection of the stream at the apex of the Delta. To the operations of the Nile it has been chiefly owing that Egypt presents a coast not only inhospitable, but dangerous to the navigator. He finds himself in shallow water before he has discovered the low alluvial shore, which scarcely lifts itself above the level of the horizon. From Parætonium in Libya to Joppa in Syria, there was not a single good harbour except that of Pharos[1]. The influence of the river extends far out into the sea, which is discoloured by the great volume of turbid water during the inundation; and the sounding-line, at the distance of seventeen leagues from shore, brings up alluvial mud[2]. The action of the waves upon the sandy shore has formed, and continues to form along the whole coast a rock of grey sandstone, in which the fragments of land and sea shells are blended together[3]. Where the shore is lowest, the sea, impelled by the north winds, sometimes breaks in, as on the coast of Holland, converts freshwater lakes into salt lagoons, or covers what had been dry land, leaving only a few insulated spots above the water. In the early ages of the Church, these islands, like the Desert of the Thebais, afforded a refuge to the holy men, who wished to seclude themselves from the world[4].

We have thus described the course of the Nile from the junction of its principal branches to the

[1] Diodor. Sic. 1, 31.
[2] Herod. 2, 5. Bruce, Travels, 1, 6.
[3] Russegger, Reisen, 11, p. 363.
[4] Cassianus, quoted by Jablonsky, Pantheon Ægyptiacum, lib. 5, 2, p. 89.

sea, and the antiquities which are found along its banks. Those which belong to the history of Ancient Egypt extend for more than 1000 miles from Upper Nubia to the Mediterranean. They have been so minutely specified because they are in fact our documents; and as the historian of other countries enumerates the archives in which his authorities are deposited, the necessary preliminary to Egyptian history is the description of the temples, palaces and sepulchres, on whose walls the names and actions of her sovereigns are inscribed.

CHAPTER II.

THE COUNTRY BETWEEN EGYPT AND THE RED SEA.

ALTHOUGH the nucleus of the population of Egypt and the origin of its national peculiarities are to be sought within its double chain of hills and the extended arms of the Delta, it was not entirely cut off from all that lay beyond these limits. The Red Sea is nowhere more than 150 miles from the valley of the Nile; the Gulf of Suez is only sixty from the most eastern branch of the ancient Nile, and we shall find the sovereigns of Egypt in very early times endeavouring to unite their country with it by means of a canal, and thus place themselves in communication with the Indian Ocean. They early established colonies within the peninsula of Mount Sinai. Wadi Magara, in this district, exhibits names contemporaneous with the erection of the Great Pyramid; Surabit-el-Kadim, on the road from Suez to Sinai, contains hieroglyphical inscriptions and fragments of pottery, showing the existence of a colony or settlement under the 18th dynasty[1]. Copper mixed with iron ore is found in the sandstone which borders the primitive rocks of Sinai; the scoriæ produced by their smelting yet remain in large heaps[2], and to obtain these metals was no doubt the purpose for which this desert region was occupied.

[1] Laborde, Petra, p. 80, Eng. Translation. Sinai, p. 14. Wilkinson, Mod. Eg. and Thebes, 1, 405.
[2] Lepsius's Journey to Mount

When we ascend beyond the head of the Delta, the space between the Red Sea and the valley of the Nile is occupied by tertiary limestone hills, the Gebel-el-Mokattam and Gebel-Attaka of modern geography, resting on a cretaceous formation which is found at Suez and on the opposite shore[1]. For the space of thirty miles from the river they rise gradually towards the east, and after continuing for some distance at nearly the same level sink again, in a space of fifty miles to the Red Sea. A general line of elevation appears to run north and south through this region, westward of which the country slopes to the Nile and eastward to the sea. It has been caused probably by the intrusion of the plutonic rocks, which everywhere abound[2]. In the latitude of 28° 26′ a primitive region begins, which rises into a mountain of 6000 feet in height[3]. The same cause appears to have produced the gorges by which the limestone and sandstone hills are penetrated; most of them soon terminate, but there are two which being more prolonged served as routes of communication with the Red Sea. The most northerly is at Coptos and Keneh, the other opposite to Apollinopolis Magna or Edfu. The routes from both these places to Berenice unite about three days' journey in the Desert[4], and from their point of junction a branch goes north-westward to Kosseir, the ancient Philoteras, in lat. 26° 9′, and to Myos Hormos, 27° 32′. Berenice is in the lat. of 23° 50′,

---

[1] Russegger's Reisen, 1, P. 1, 264.
[2] Russegger's Geognostische Karte. An insulated mass of the granite of the Cataracts is found as far north as 27° 10′.
[3] Wilkinson, Manners and Customs, pl. 18; Modern Egypt, 2, 383.
[4] Belzoni, pl. 38.

a little to the south of the promontory of Cape Nose. There is also a route which goes nearly due west from Coptos to Kosseir. This road is almost throughout desert, but not difficult, as the French passed their artillery through it without impediment except at one point. It is bordered by hills of limestone, sandstone, and further on, at the distance of two days' and a half journey, green breccia. From the latter the Egyptians derived the beautiful material which under the name of *Verde d'Egitto* is so much admired among their remains of art[1]. These quarries were opened at a very early period in the history of the monarchy, and continued to be wrought even in the Roman times. The inscriptions go back as far as to the sixth dynasty of Manetho, and record the names of those who directed the workings and the kings under whom they held office. The god in whose honour the more recent *proscynemata* are made is Amun-Khem, answering to the Pan of the Greeks and Romans, to whom deserts especially belonged. The road from Apollinopolis to Berenice presents more remains of antiquity than that from Coptos to Kosseir. At intervals of from seven to twelve miles, inclosures with walls or cisterns occur, which appear to mark the site of ancient stations of caravans on their way from the Nile to the Red Sea[2]. About thirty miles from the river is a temple in which the figure of an Egyptian king appears, holding captives by the hair as if about to immolate them. Pyramidal masses of masonry are seen on the hills, apparently designed as landmarks

[1] It is composed of rounded fragments of greenstone, gneiss and porphyry, cemented by a slightly calcareous paste. Newbold, Geology of Egypt, Proc. of Geol. Soc. 1842, 3, 2, 91 foll.
[2] Belzoni, 2, 34.

through these deserts, in which the wind speedily obliterates all traces of a route. The porphyry and granite which are found towards the western side were quarried for purposes of art[1]; the mines of emeralds also attracted the ancient Egyptians into these barren regions, and have caused them to be again explored in modern times. They lay out far from the Red Sea, between 24° and 25° N.L. Mount Zabareh was the principal mine, but at Bender-el-Sogheir to the north and Sekket to the south, there are traces of ancient mining operations. The temple at the latter place is indeed of the Ptolemaic times, but it is certain that the mines were known and wrought in those of the Pharaohs, at least as early as Amunoph III. At Wadi Jasoos, to the north of Kosseir, the shields of Sesortasen II. and his predecessor Amenemhe II. occur with a record of victories[2]. In the road from Coptos to Kosseir, Mr. Burton and Sir Gardner Wilkinson have copied inscriptions of various sovereigns from the early reign of Papi or Apappus down to Darius, Artaxerxes and Nectanebus, and Lepsius has recently added to their number[3]. There were gold-mines also on the eastern side of the Nile, in the primitive district which lies between the Cataracts and the Red Sea[4]. The workings belong to the Ptolemaic times, yet they can hardly have been unknown to the Pharaohs[5].

---

[1] There were quarries of granite at Mons Claudianus (now Gebel Fatireh), and of porphyry at Mons Porphyrites (now Gebel Dochan).
[2] Wilkinson, Manners and Customs, 1, 45, 231; Mod. Eg. 2, 385, 388.
[3] Journey to M. Sinai, p. 5.
[4] Wilkinson, M. and C. 3, 229. Mr. Birch thinks that what Lepsius supposed to be a plan of the tomb of Sethos, is a plan of an ancient gold-mine.
[5] Wilkinson, Mod. Egypt and Thebes, 2, 389.

The general character of this region and its geological structure resembles that of the peninsula of Sinai, and is wholly unlike that of the Libyan Desert on the western side of the Nile. Its surface is varied, and a scanty vegetation in the valleys affords the means of pasturage to a wandering population. As it is Arabian, not African in its features, so its inhabitants have probably in all ages been of the Arabian family. The Desert between Kosseir and Berenice is now occupied by the Ababdeh, who represent the population of the Ptolemaic and Pharaonic times. The tribes who live to the north of these are Arabs of more recent immigration, but probably the successors of others of the same origin. According to the Greek geographers[1], the coast from the Gulf of Suez to Berenice was inhabited by the Troglodytes, a nomadic people, who, as their name indicates, made their dwellings in the excavated rock. Hence we may infer, that they did not extend further than the limestone and sandstone districts of the coast, and they may have belonged to various races, agreeing in this mode of habitation. The practice of circumcision appears to connect them with the Arabic or Ethiopian tribes[2]; they were in the lowest state of civilization, characteristic of a people who have not industry or skill to procure themselves habitations, but take up with such as nature or the labour of others has provided. Dwelling promiscuously in caves, they had no distinctions of family, but their wives and children were in

---

[1] Artemidorus apud Strab. B. 16, p. 768, 775.
[2] Her. 2, 104. Strabo, B. 16, p. 775, 786. Herodotus, 4, 183, speaks of Ethiopian Troglodytes.

common, except those of the chief. Southward of the Troglodytes dwelt on the sea-coast tribes who lived on fish, and others more inland, of whose figure and mode of life strange tales were related by the Greek and Roman writers[1].

The country between Egypt and the Red Sea was no doubt virtually subject to the Egyptian kings; but, except where its mines and quarries invited a settlement, or traffic rendered a line of communication necessary, it could not repay the expense of a permanent occupation, or reward any attempt to cultivate the soil and civilize the inhabitants.

[1] Pliny, N. H. 6, 30.

CHAPTER III.

THE WESTERN DESERT.

THE country which borders Egypt on the west, presents even a more striking contrast to the luxuriant fertility and overflowing population of the Valley of the Nile, than the rough and barren region on the east. Since the Libyan Desert has been examined by scientific travellers, it has been divested of many of its fabulous terrors; its hosts of serpents, which by their number and venom could even impede the march of armies[1]; its tribes who shrieked like bats, instead of speaking with a human voice[2]; its pestilential blasts. extinguishing life instantaneously wherever they reached; and its whirlwinds of sand, burying armies as they fell. Enough, however, remains to characterize it as one of the most inhospitable regions of the earth, and perhaps the most formidable barrier anywhere interposed to the intercourse of nations. It is not in Africa alone that it produces this effect. Egypt intersects it with a narrow stripe of fertile land, but it immediately reappears in the Desert which separates Egypt from Palestine, and Palestine from the country on the Euphrates; it occupies the coast beyond the Persian Gulf, and only ends on the Indus. Probably among the changes which our globe has undergone, in ages before the existence, or at least the history

---

[1] Lucan, Pharsalia, 9, 765.   [2] Herod. 4, 183.

of man, the Sahara may have formed the bed of the sea, the level of which even now it does not greatly exceed[1]. As it yields no exhalation, so it receives no rain, and hence appears condemned to perpetual barrenness.

The vague descriptions of the ancients had led to the opinion that in the midst of this ocean of sand, verdant spots called Oases appeared, like islands in the sea[2], having escaped by their greater elevation the sand with which the wind had covered all the rest of the cultivated soil. The oases, however, are not elevations, but depressions in the surface. They are composed of sandstone and clay, on which the limestone which forms the basis of the western Desert everywhere rests; the limestone rises in mural escarpments around them, and the clay retaining the water, supports a vegetation which made them appear like a paradise to the Desert traveller, and procured them the name of Islands of the Blessed[3]. They serve to keep up communication between Egypt and the countries of western and southern Africa: without such resting-places and supplies of water, even the adventurous caravans could not traverse the Desert. Though it is in general destitute of life and vegetation, it is not a mere plain of sand; it has considerable inequalities and even hills of gravel. The effects of the hot wind[4] of the Desert have been much exaggerated. In the summer months, blowing from the south and

[1] Russegger, Reisen, vol. 2, part 1, p. 279.
[2] Wilkinson, Manners and Customs, 4, 119.
[3] Herod. 3, 26.
[4] Called in Egypt *Khamsin* (fifty), from the number of days that it is supposed to blow; in the Desert, Simoum, by a corruption of the Arabic *Semen*, poison.

south-east, over a soil scorched by an almost vertical sun, it acquires an intensity of heat which dries up all moisture, relaxes the muscular power and renders respiration difficult, but does not smite with sudden death as Oriental exaggeration represents. The same wind, sweeping over a surface where nothing breaks its force, raises eddies of sand high in the air[1], which falls in a heavy shower, inconvenient but not dangerous to the traveller, except as it effaces his track[2]. The failure of his supply of water, or the illness of himself or his beast of burden, is the danger which he has most to dread on a journey, where every one is too fully occupied with his own wants to have aid or even sympathy to spare for others.

Herodotus describes a chain of these oases extending from east to west through the Desert of Libya[3]. Some of these, as Augila and Fezzan, assume the size of kingdoms, while others are mere halting-places for caravans[4]; we have here only to speak of those which border on Egypt and are connected with its history. They are five in number. The most northerly, the largest and the most remote from the Nile, is the oasis of Siwah, the ancient Ammonium. It lies nearly in the latitude of Fyoum, and in longitude 26° 20′ E. From Lower Egypt it is approached from Terenieh on the Rosetta branch of the Nile, by a route to the W.S.W., which passes the Natron Lakes[5]. They are six in

---

[1] Bruce, Travels, 6, 458. Compare Burckhardt's Nubia, 1, 207.
[2] Arrian, Exp. Alex. 3, 3.
[3] Herod. 4, 181.
[4] The Coptic *Ouah*, whence Oasis is derived, means *Mansio*. See Peyron, Lex. Ling. Copt. *s. v.*
[5] Minutoli, Reise zum Tempel des Jupiter Ammon.

number, lying in a valley which runs N.W. about twelve miles in length. They swell with the rains, which fall in the months of December, January and February, and are therefore highest when the Nile is lowest. They thus imbibe saline matter from the sand of the Desert, impregnated with it by the ancient ocean which has covered this part of Africa, since the deposition of the tertiary strata. The heat of summer produces strong evaporation; a crust forms upon the surface and edges of the lakes[1] containing muriate, carbonate and sulphate of soda, which is collected and carried off to be used in the operations of glass-making and bleaching. The Bahr-be-la-Ma or River with no Water, a name given by the Arabs to many valleys which they think have the appearance of ancient streambeds, runs parallel to the valley of the Natron Lakes, and is only separated from it by a narrow ridge. The water-worn pebbles which are found on the sides of the hills have suggested the hypothesis, that the Nile may once have found its way to the Mediterranean from above Memphis by this channel; and the agatized wood which is strewed about has been considered an evidence of ancient navigation. Such appearances, however, are very common in other parts of Libya, and there is nothing in the configuration of the country which warrants the supposition of a connexion either with the Nile or the Birket-el-Kerun. The Bahr-be-la-Ma is entirely destitute of that sedimentary deposit which a river flowing through it would have left; the peb-

---

[1] Quo iter est ad Hammonem lacus sunt palustres, qui ita sunt salsi, ut habeant insuper se salem congelatum (Vitruv. 8, 3).

bles are found abundantly in the limestone of Lower Egypt and the adjacent Desert, and are derived from its decomposition; the agatized wood has no doubt the same origin as the petrified forest near Cairo, which we shall hereafter describe[1]. The road towards Ammonium inclines from the Natron Lakes towards the south; the soil is in some places so salt that it is covered with an incrustation through which the foot of the camel breaks as through a thin coat of ice. Yet it is not all desert; springs occur at intervals which nourish a scanty vegetation and a few groves of palms. The oasis of El-Gerah[2], distant two days' march from Siwah, consists of a little district four or five miles in circumference, formerly no doubt dependent on the neighbouring oasis.

Siwah itself is about six miles in length, and two or three in breadth. The ground is strongly impregnated with salt, which in ancient times Ammonium furnished in the greatest purity for sacrifice and the royal table[3]; yet the abundance of water maintains a high degree of fertility, especially in the production of fruit, and dates form an article of extensive commerce. The present population has been estimated at 8000. The ruins of the temple of Ammon are found at Ummebeda, about two miles from the principal village and fortress. Its style and arrangement bespeak its Egyptian origin and its consecration to the worship of the

---

[1] Russegger, Reisen, vol. 1, p. 267. Wilkinson, Mod. Eg. and Thebes, 1, 300.

[2] The Ummesogeir of Hornemann and others.

[3] Arrian, Exp. Alex. B. 3, c. 4.

ram-headed god of Thebes[1], but it is probably not older than the Persian times. The oracle, however, was no doubt of much higher antiquity than the temple; the name was derived from Amun, and the population in the time of Herodotus partly from Egypt and partly from Ethiopia, in both which countries this god was worshiped[2]. Etearchus, the name of the king whom Herodotus mentions, in his account of the expedition of the Nasamonians in search of the sources of the Nile[3], appears to be Greek. Danaus founded it according to one tradition[4]; another made its establishment contemporaneous with that of the most ancient oracle of Greece, the Dodonæan[5]. It could not long remain unknown to the Greeks after the colonization of Cyrene in the seventh century B.C. The fountain of the Sun, of which the ancients from Herodotus downwards have related so many wonders[6], is near the ruins of the temple, and appears to be a tepid spring, such as are found elsewhere in the oases, which during the day feels colder, and during the night warmer, than the surrounding air. Alexander the Great, in visiting the oracle of Ammon, followed the coast of the Mediterranean as far as Parætonium and then turned inland, but probably

> .... Stat certior illic
> Jupiter, ut memorant; sed non aut fulmina vibrans
> Aut similis nostro, sed tortis cornibus Ammon.
>
> Lucan, Phars. 10, 38.

---

[2] Herod. 2, 42.
[3] Herod. 2, 32.
[4] Diod. 17, 50.
[5] Herod. 2, 54.
[6] Herod. 4, 181. Comp. Wilkinson's Mod. Eg. and Thebes, 2, 358.

returned to the neighbourhood of Memphis by the route which has been just described[1].

Of the oases which lie near to Egypt the most northerly is that of El-Bacharieh, of which the principal village, Zabou, is in lat. 28° 21', and E. long 29° 10'. It is about 100 miles distant from Oxyrrhynchus or Bahneseh on the Nile, and has sometimes been called the oasis of Bahneseh. It is also reached by a route from the Fyoum. The soil is good and produces many fruit-trees, but there are no inscriptions or remains of buildings which decisively prove that it was permanently occupied by the Egyptians, even in the Persian times. A triumphal arch, the ruins of an aqueduct and hypogæa containing sarcophagi, mark its occupation by a Roman force. It was necessary for the maintenance of order in Egypt under the Empire, as well as the security of commerce, to take possession of these solitary spots, which would otherwise have become banding-places for the malefactors of the province.

It is in the oasis of El-Bacharieh that the remarkable discovery has been made of the use of Artesian wells by the ancients. Olympiodorus, a native of Egyptian Thebes, who lived about the beginning of the fifth century after Christ, has described them in a manner which cannot be mistaken, in a passage of his history preserved by Photius[2]. Their depth,

---

[1] Arrian, B. 3, c. 4 *ad fin.* It is singular that such a point should have been doubtful. Q. Curtius (4, 33) makes him return by the coast.

[2] Ὅτι περὶ τῆς Ὀάσεως πολλὰ παραδοξολογεῖ καὶ τῶν ὀρυσσομένων φρεάτων ὡς εἰς διακοσίους καὶ τριακοσίους, ἔσθ' ὅτε δὲ καὶ ἐς πεντακοσίους πήχεις ὀρυσσόμενα ἀναβλύζουσι τὸ ῥεῖθρον αὐτοῦ τοῦ στομίου προχεόμενον. (Phot. Bibl. 80, p. 191, ed. Hoesch.)

200 to 500 cubits, far exceeds that of wells of the ordinary construction, and the spontaneous rise of the water in a rushing stream shows that no machinery was employed to pump or lift it. A Frenchman who has established himself in this oasis, to manufacture alum, with the elements of which it abounds, has discovered and re-opened several of them, having a depth of 360 to 480 feet[1]. How long they had been in use before Olympiodorus wrote we do not know. There is no trace of Artesian wells being known to the ancient Egyptians, nor to the Greeks and Romans; but the art of boring them has been long known in China[2], and it may have been brought thence, like the culture of the silk-worm, in the imperial times, and introduced into the oases. The water which supplies them is supposed to be derived by infiltration from the Nile[3].

The largest of all the oases is El-Khargeh, which extends from the latitude of Dendera to that of Edfu, its central part being nearly opposite to Thebes, whence it has been called the oasis of Thebes. In the 'Notitia Imperii' its chief town is called Hibe, and from the hieroglyphics its Egyptian name appears to have been Heb. Its nearest point is about ninety miles from the river; it is eighty miles in length, and eight to ten in breadth; the cultivated land in ancient times extended further than at present to the north. The limestone hills, which are higher here than in the oases already described, rise in precipices above it, and the doum

---

[1] Russegger, Reisen, vol. 2, P. 1, p. 284, 339.

[2] Ritter, Asien, part 4, vol. 3, p. 416.

[3] Russegger, Reisen, *ubi supra*.

palm and the acacia of the Nile grow luxuriantly at the base. A multitude of ruins attest its ancient importance and population, but none of them are of the Pharaonic times. Herodotus calls it the city of Oasis, and says that it was occupied by Samians of the Æschrionian tribe[1], who had probably settled here in consequence of their friendship with the Cyrenians[2]. It was garrisoned under the Persians, the names of Darius and Amyrtæus having been found here[3]; but the principal buildings which remain are of the Greek, if not the Roman times. The great temple dedicated to Amun is 468 feet in length; its architecture resembles that of Hermonthis and Apollinopolis Magna. Besides its convenience as a station, the alum found in its neighbourhood attracted the Egyptians, to whom it was a source of wealth[4], as well as of essential importance in the processes of art. The oasis of El-Dakkel, sometimes called The Little Oasis, lies to the N.W. of the oasis of Thebes, from which it is separated by a high calcareous ridge. A temple at Ain Amour, on the route between them, shows that it was used by the Egyptians; the oasis itself has tombs and a temple of the Ptolemaic times. Its productions are now chiefly dates, fruits and olives; under the Romans it was celebrated for its wheat. It contains a number of springs, some of them thermal, which are used for irrigation. The oasis of El-Farafreh, which lies nearly north of El-Dakkel, at the distance of about eighty miles, served as an intermediate station both to Ammonium and El-Khargeh.

[1] Herod. 3, 26.
[2] Herod. 4, 152.
[3] Sir G. Wilkinson, Mod. Egypt and Thebes, 2, 367.
[4] Herod. 2, 180. Amasis gave 1000 talents of alum towards rebuilding the temple of Delphi.

The absence of all positive traces of establishments in these oases by the Egyptians, under their native rulers, is contrasted with the records which we have found of their earliest kings in the deserts near the head of the Red Sea and on the road to Kosseir. But on the west, Egypt was itself the frontier of civilization; till the settlements of the Phœnicians and Greeks, only barbarous tribes dwelt beyond it in Africa, from whose hostility it had nothing to fear, and who had nothing to communicate which it could not more easily obtain from the interior by the channel of the Nile. The Isthmus of Suez and the ports of the Red Sea, on the contrary, placed it in connexion with the wealth and fertility of Asia. The difficulty of traversing the Sahara must have been almost insurmountable[1] for numerous companies before the introduction of the camel, which never appears in the monuments of the Pharaonic times[2]. Its use had been long known to the Persians, and by them the oases were first permanently occupied. Cambyses failed to reach Ammonium, and has been unjustly charged with madness for an attempt, which appears to have been dictated by sound policy. Darius however succeeded in establishing his power in the oases: in the time of Herodotus they were the resting-places of a traffic which penetrated Africa nearly from east to west, and under the Ptolemies and the Romans they became military outposts of their empire.

---

[1] Psammitichus, when he wished to explore the Deserts of Africa, trained youths to endure unusual degrees of thirst; very few of them however escaped with life (Athen. 8, p. 345).

[2] The camels mentioned among Pharaoh's cattle (Exod. ix. 3) had probably been obtained from the Israelites. We have such ample representations of Egyptian life, that if the camel had been naturalized here as a beast of burden, it must have occurred in the paintings.

CHAPTER IV.

THE INUNDATION OF THE NILE, SOIL, PRODUCTIONS AND CLIMATE OF EGYPT.

IF we carry back our thoughts to the commencement of those changes which have given to Egypt its actual form, we see a long rocky valley of sandstone and limestone, terminating in a deep bay, where the Arabian and Libyan chains now give place to the plain of the Delta. Its aspect from this point suggested the earliest geological speculation on record, if we except those which may have taken the form of mythical traditions. "The greater part of Egypt," says Herodotus[1], "appears to me also, as the priests represented, to be acquired land. For the space which lies between the mountains above Memphis seemed to me, like the country about Ilium and Teuthrania and Ephesus and the plain of the Mæander, to have been once a gulf of the sea, if we may compare small things with great. For the rivers which have filled up these places with their deposit are not to be compared in magnitude with any one of the five mouths of the Nile, which is so large and so energetic in its operations, that in the time which has elapsed before I was born it may well have filled up even a much larger gulf than this. That this has been the case with Egypt I believe, not only on the authority of those who have

[1] Herod. 2, 12.

told me so, but because I have myself observed that it projects beyond the adjacent country, and that shells are found upon the hills, and that salt effloresces so as even to injure the pyramids; and that this hill above Memphis is the only one which has sand upon it; and that the soil of Egypt does not resemble that of either of the conterminous countries, Libya or Syria. It is dark and friable, as being the mud and alluvial deposit brought down by the river from Ethiopia[1]; whereas the soil of Libya is reddish, with a substratum of sand; that of Arabia and Syria clayey, with a substratum of rock."

Modern science has added little to this simple hypothesis. Borings made in the Delta to the depth of forty-five feet have shown that the soil consists of vegetable matter and an earthy deposit such as the Nile now brings down; but as no marine remains are found in the mud which covers the upper and middle portion of the Delta, it appears that the present alluvium must have been deposited upon a surface previously elevated above the Mediterranean. That Egypt has undergone changes not recorded in history, nor surmised by its ancient inhabitants or visitors, is evident from the phænomena of the petrified forest in the neighbourhood of Cairo. The platform on which it lies is considerably above the present level of the Nile, on the side of the Mokattam range. The trees, some of which are from fifty to sixty feet in length, are scattered over a space of three and a half miles wide and four miles long;

---

[1] Ἰλύντε καὶ πρόχυσιν ἐξ Αἰθιοπίης κατενηνειγμένην ὑπὸ τοῦ ποταμοῦ (Her. u. s.).

their substance is in many cases converted into silex, agate and jasper, and they are partially covered with rolled pebbles and sand. It is difficult to account for these appearances without supposing that they have been submerged subsequently to their growth and again elevated to their present position[1]. If the agatized wood in the Bahr-be-la-Ma is of the same origin and was deposited there before the valley of the Nile intervened, we are carried far back into that indefinite antiquity which Herodotus prudently assumes[2].

In supposing the alluvial deposit by which the Delta had been formed to have been brought down from Ethiopia, Herodotus was perhaps influenced by an opinion which prevailed among the ancients[3], that as the people of Ethiopia were black, so must the soil be. The deposit of the Nile is composed of clay[4], lime and silicious sand, but the proportion of these ingredients varies with the nature of the formation over which the river has flowed. In the granitic and sandstone regions of Upper Egypt and Lower Nubia, less calcareous and argillaceous matter and a larger proportion of silex is found than in the neighbourhood of Cairo and in the Delta. The annual deposit varies in the same situation from an inch to a few lines, and therefore all calculations must be very uncertain which attempt to deduce the

---

[1] Newbold, Geology of Egypt. Proc. Geol. Soc. 3, 2, 91 (1842).
[2] Εἰ ἐθελήσει ἐκτρέψαι τὸ ῥέεθρον ὁ Νεῖλος ἐς τὸν Ἀράβιον κόλπον, τί μιν κωλύει ἐκχωσθῆναι ἐντός γε δισμυρίων ἐτέων; 2, 11.
[3] Et viridem Ægyptum *nigra* fœcundat arena
Usque *coloratis* devexus amnis ab Indis.
Virg. Georg. 4, 291.
[4] According to the analysis of Regnault (Wilkinson, 4, 50. Mémoires sur l'Egypte, H. N. 20, 77), the proportion of clay (alumen) is 48 in 100.

antiquity of the country from the rate of increase. The whole amount of the alluvial deposit, however, bears a general proportion to the distance from the sea and the slope of the soil. In Nubia and Upper Egypt cliffs of alluvium are found of the height of forty feet; the average height in Middle Egypt is thirty feet, at the apex of the Delta eighteen. The earthy matters which the water contains are also deposited in different quantities and proportions in the vicinity of the river and at a distance from it[1]. The largest quantity settles close to the stream, the smallest at the edge of the inundation; and hence a transverse section of the valley exhibits a convex line, gradually rising to the level of the highest Nile, and again declining in the opposite direction. In consequence of this fall from the bank towards the Desert, the limit to which the inundation reaches is gradually extending; the sites of ancient cities disappear beneath an increasing accumulation of deposited soil, and even the colossal statues of the plain of Thebes must be ultimately buried. If less land be now under cultivation than in the time of the Pharaohs and the Ptolemies, it has not been because the Nile is fulfilling the prediction of Herodotus[2] and raising the land by its alluvion above the reach of its own waters, but because there is less security and less encouragement for the labours of the husbandman. Despotism is the Typhon that resists and defeats the benevolent labours of Osiris-Nilus to extend the fertility of Egypt.

---

[1] Wilkinson, Manners and Customs, 4, 50, 108.

[2] Her. 2, 13. He had overlooked the circumstance that the Nile raises its own bed, as well as its banks, so that the relative proportion is preserved.

Similar effects to those now described are produced by every great river on the country through which it flows; but they are very much increased and modified in Egypt by the periodical inundation of the Nile. This phænomenon was variously explained by the ancients. It was natural that an inhabitant of Greece, accustomed to see the rivers of his own country swollen in summer by the melting of snow upon the mountains, should attribute the rise of the Nile to the same cause. Such was the opinion of Anaxagoras, adopted by Æschylus, Sophocles[1] and Euripides[2], but rejected by Herodotus on the ground that no snow could fall in the climate of Ethiopia[3]. Thales supposed that there was no real increase of the waters of the Nile, but that the Etesian winds, blowing from the north in summer full upon its mouth, prevented their discharge into the sea and threw them back upon the low grounds of Egypt[4]. This is a real cause, but not adequate to explain the whole effect. Democritus and probably Hecatæus attributed its rise to its connexion with the ocean, which was conceived to flow round the south of Libya, and thought its waters had been sweetened by long exposure to the sun[5]. Probably some vague notion of the tides of the ocean was combined in their minds with that of the origin of the Nile, to explain its periodical swelling. Another explanation attributed the increase of the waters to an exudation from the earth, saturated with condensed moisture

---

[1] Schol. Apoll. Rhod. 4, 269.
[2] Helen. init.
[3] 2, 22.
[4] Diodor. 1, 38–40.
[5] Diodor. 1, 40.

during the winter, which the summer heat expanded and set free[1]: Herodotus himself supposed that he had explained the phænomenon by the remark, that the rivers in Southern Libya were necessarily lowest in winter, when the sun was vertical over those regions, though this offered no solution of the overflow in summer. The true cause, the rainy season in Ethiopia, was first assigned by Agatharchides of Cnidus, in the second century B.C.[2] It is the progress of the sun from the Equator to the Tropic of Cancer. As he becomes successively vertical over different points northward of the Equator, the air is heated and rarefied, and colder currents set in from the Mediterranean to restore the equilibrium. They deposit none of their moisture in their passage over the heated and level soil of Egypt, but when they reach the lofty mountains of Abessinia, some of which rise to the height of 13,000 feet[3], the cold condenses their vapours into torrents of rain, such as are hardly known in any other country. So close, according to Bruce, is the connexion between the sun's position in the ecliptic and the rains of Abessinia, that they usually begin on the very day on which he is vertical over any particular place. While they last, the forenoon of each day is usually clear, but a violent storm comes on between two o'clock and six[4]. The high grounds of Abessinia, in which the Bahr-el-Azrek, the Tacazzè and their tributaries rise, receive a large proportion of this rain, which from the form of the country nearly all drains towards the western side, and is ultimately

[1] Ephorus, ed. Marx, p. 213.
[2] Diodor. 1, 41.
[3] Ruppell, Reisen.
[4] Bruce, Travels, vol. 5, p. 332.

poured into the channel of the Nile. The Bahr-el-Abiad is also affected by the periodical rains, and begins to rise about twenty days earlier; but as its course is less precipitous, the variation in the volume of its waters is not so great. It is not till the last days of June or the beginning of July that the rise begins to be visible in Egypt. The change is at first scarcely perceptible; in a few days, however, it becomes more rapid; it reaches half its extra height about the middle of August, when the dykes are usually cut[1], and its maximum from the 20th to the 30th of September. It then remains stationary for fourteen days, sinks about the 10th of November to the same height as in the middle of August, and continues to decrease slowly till the 20th of May in the following year, when it reaches its minimum. At this time its depth at Cairo is not more than six feet, and its waters are nearly stagnant throughout the level plains of Lower Egypt. The mean increase in the quantity of water discharged into the sea, when the inundation is at its height, is ninefold; the velocity is increased at the same time, according to observations made at Lycopolis (E' Siout), near the middle of Egypt, to nearly six feet in a second[2]. The rise in the height of the river varies of course in different parts of its channel; at Cairo, where it is most regularly observed, because the amount of tribute paid depends upon it, its highest rise was to twenty-four feet, its lowest to eighteen, according to the register kept by the French for four years while they were in possession of the country[3].

[1] Wilkinson, Manners and Customs, 4, 9, note.
[2] Ritter, Africa, p. 849, from Girard.
[3] Ritter, ibid. p. 838.

This quantity appears to have been constant as far back as observations have been recorded. Fifteen or sixteen cubits was the height of a *good Nile* in the time of Herodotus[1]. The statue of the Nile placed by Vespasian in the Temple of Peace, of which a copy is still to be seen in the Vatican, was surrounded by sixteen diminutive figures, emblematic of the number of cubits to which the river should rise[2]. Sixteen cubits is assigned by Abdollatiph as the medium between defect and excess. The sixteenth cubit on the Meqyas or Nilometer is called "the water of the Sultan," because no tribute is paid if it do not reach this height. Its rise was carefully noted in ancient times on the Niloscopeum at Memphis, and the news of its beginning to rise or decline was communicated by letters to different parts of Egypt, that the peasants might be relieved from apprehension and be able to regulate their agricultural operations[3]. Sometimes the Nile exceeds its normal height and reaches thirty feet, spreading devastation over the country. Houses are undermined, cattle are drowned, and the stored-up produce of former years swept away. The waters retire more slowly than usual; the labours of the husbandman are delayed, and the following harvest endangered; pestilential diseases arise from the stagnant waters and the unburied remains of animals. If the rise falls short of twenty-four feet, a proportional diminution of the produce of Egypt ensues; but if it be below eighteen feet, dreadful famines

---

[1] Herod. 2, 13.
[2] Pliny, Nat. Hist. 36, 9. Visconti, Mus. Pio-Clement. 1, p. 291.
[3] Diod. 1, 36. Description de l'Egypte, vol. 18, p. 595, fol.

ensue, such as the failure of the rice-crop has produced in India, and the population, who in both countries live ordinarily on the smallest quantity of food that can support life, perish by thousands. Diodorus relates that in a famine the people of Egypt consumed human flesh, and the same thing has happened in more recent times[1].

The mean quantity of water brought down by the Nile, in normal years, as it depends on cosmical causes, probably continues the same from age to age, and the extent of land which it is capable of fertilizing by its overflow tends to increase, till its diffusion is stopped by the Arabian and Libyan hills. Long before the inundation reaches its maximum, the dykes which close the communication between the canals and the Nile are opened, and the water diffuses itself first of all over the lands which lie towards the Desert; gradually as it rises it irrigates the nearer country, but the immediate banks of the river are seldom covered, and serve as a highway for the people while the inundation continues. In the Delta, where the slope is small, the whole country is laid under water during an extraordinary rise, and boats take the place of the ordinary modes of communication. European travellers commonly choose the winter and spring for a journey through Egypt, and therefore do not see the Nile at its height; but those who have resided there through

---

[1] Diod. 1, 84. See an account of a famine caused by a *low Nile* (less than 13 cubits) in the year 1200 A.D., in Abdollatiph's History of Egypt (White's Ed. p. 197). Very little rain had fallen in Ethiopia. Volney (l,c.11) gives an account of a famine in the years 1784–5, the consequence of two low Niles, which reduced the inhabitants to the lowest depth of misery, and drove them in crowds into Palestine and Syria.

all seasons assure us that the description of Herodotus is still realized, the villages on their elevated sites rising out of a lake, like the Cyclades from the Egean Sea[1]. The effects of such a mighty volume of water upon the surface of the country through which it is discharged are great; the bank of sand deposited by one flood is mined and scattered by another; and thus its materials gradually travel onward towards their final resting-place in the sea, or in places which the river subsequently abandons.

Having created the soil of Egypt, the Nile thus renews it from year to year, and maintains it in that state of perpetual fertility which in other countries is the result of the toil and skill of the cultivator[2]. Besides clay, which as already mentioned amounts to 48 parts in 100 of Nile water, it contains 9 parts of carbon, 18 of carbonate of lime and 4 of carbonate of magnesia, besides portions of silica and oxide of iron. These ingredients form a compost of such richness that no artificial manure is needed, to enable the same land to produce in succession heavy crops of corn[3]. As the inundation spreads, the peasants receive its waters into their fields and confine it there by mounds, till it has at once saturated them with the moisture which must be their sole supply for three quarters of the year, and fully deposited

---

[1] Belzoni, Researches, 2, 26. Herod. 2, 97.

[2] Pliny (N. H. 18, 21) reckons that the soil of Egypt returns 150-fold to the cultivator; but he says the same thing of the soil of Leontini, which, according to Cicero, in the most favourable years produced only tenfold (Verr. 3, 47).

[3] Ποία βασιλεία οὕτως γέγονε πολύχρυσος; Οὐ γὰρ τὰ ἐκ Περσῶν καὶ Βαβυλῶνος λαβοῦσα χρήματα, ἢ μέταλλα ἐργασαμένη, ἢ Πακτωλὸν ἔχουσα χρυσοῦν ψῆγμα καταφέροντα (sc. γέγονε πολύχρυσος). Νεῖλος μετὰ τροφῶν ἀφθόνων καὶ χρυσὸν ἀκίβδηλον καταφέρει, ἀκινδύνως γεωργούμενον ὡς πᾶσιν ἐξαρκεῖν ἀνθρώποις (Athenæus, 5, 36).

all its earthy particles. The sun and N.W. wind soon evaporate the superfluous moisture from the surface, and the seed scattered upon it or in a shallow furrow was trodden in by the feet of cattle. In the absence of natural springs, the Nile is the great resource of the inhabitants of Egypt for water. In its medium state it is clear, but becomes feculent in its lowest; the first rise of the waters covers it with a greenish vegetable matter, and it then is said to produce an eruptive disease[1]. In the Amenophion at Luxor are two figures of the Nile; one, which represents its ordinary state, is coloured blue, the other red[2]. The red is the symbol of the inundation, the water assuming this colour soon after it has begun, owing to a mixture of the red oxide of iron. These changes have been conjecturally attributed to the overflowing of lakes, or the passage of the rivers through strata which they do not ordinarily reach[3]; but their real cause is unknown, and must remain so till the upper course of the Blue and White Rivers is explored. The long continuance of the green fecula indicates that the river is sluggish and stagnant, and is ominous of a low Nile. Even when the water is most turbid it is not unwholesome, and may be easily cleared by filtration; when pure, it is said to be delicious to the taste. The Persian kings used it for their own drinking after the conquest of Egypt[4]; and Pescennius Niger[5] reproached his soldiers with wanting wine when they had the water of the Nile. A natural filtration

[1] Volney, 1, 146.
[2] Pliny (N. H. 31, 5), after Ctesias, speaks of a red fountain in Ethiopia.
[3] Rosellini, Mon. Stor. 3, 1, 29.
[4] Athen. 2, 67.
[5] "Nilum habetis et vinum quæritis." Hist. Aug. 1, 663, with Casaubon's notes. Clarke's Travels, 5, 283.

appears to be carried on through its sandy banks in the lower part of its course, so that water may be obtained by sinking, but it is brackish[1]. The inundation not only prepared the fields for harvest, but filled the streams and canals with fish, and revived the various kinds of aquatic plants which require comparatively still waters for their growth.

Both the general aspect of Egypt and the nature of its productions have been determined by its relation to the Nile. There can be no variety of surface in a country which has risen out of the water, and is annually overspread by it. The Delta, whether it be in the condition of a sandy plain, a lake of fresh water, or a carpet of verdure and flowers[2], has a monotonous character which soon becomes wearisome to the traveller. In Middle and Upper Egypt the view is bounded by the double line of hills; the eastern side has something of grandeur from its height and abruptness; the west is lower and covered with sand, and both are alike destitute of foliage and verdure. The trees which grew in Egypt were not numerous; two species of palm, besides their fruit, furnished materials from different parts of the tree for every kind of work for which solid timber or tough fibre can be employed[3]. The sycamore and various species of acacia also abounded, but no other trees of a large size were indigenous to the country. The products of the fields of Egypt were almost all the results of cultivation. Grain,

---

[1] Herod. 2, 108.
[2] Volney, Voyage en Egypte et Syrie, vol. 1, p. 7.
[3] "The inhabitants of Egypt and Arabia feed camels on the datestone, and from the leaves make couches, baskets, bags, mats and brushes; from the branches, cages for poultry and fences for their gardens; from the fibres of the boughs, thread, ropes and rigging." (Clarke's Travels, 5, 409.)

herbs, and leguminous vegetables were produced in an abundance which no other country could rival; but its native botany was scanty, the yearly renewal of the soil preventing the seeds which had fallen on the surface from vegetating, and culture exterminating all plants which cannot be made serviceable to man. The fragrance of flowers was wanting in its landscapes, for those of Egypt had very little odour[1]. The sandy desert which lies beyond the reach of the inundation has a scanty vegetation of its own—stunted shrubs and herbs, which have generally an aromatic smell.

The most characteristic part of the botany of Egypt are the aquatic plants. These are not generally found near the borders of the river itself[2], which in its upper course is too impetuous to allow of their tranquil growth, and perpetually undermines and carries away its own banks; but in the numerous canals which distribute the water to distant parts, in the ancient channels of the river, now nearly dry, or on the edges of the lakes and marshes. Of these the papyrus and the lotus are identified with the history of Egyptian literature, art and religion. The papyrus was found chiefly in the shallow waters of Lower Egypt, and hence became in hieroglyphics the emblem of that district and of the northern nations who bordered upon it. The lotus, abounding more in Upper Egypt, was employed to denote that kingdom as well as Nubia and the South generally. The papyrus had various economic uses; the root and lower part of the stem were eaten raw

---

[1] Pliny, Nat. Hist. 21, 7.   [2] Irby and Mangles, Travels, p. 161. Plin. N. H. 13, 22.

or roasted by the inhabitants of the marshes to supply the deficiency of grain[1]. Its coarser species furnished mats, wrappers and baskets, and the stems bound together made a rude float on which the river might be crossed. But that which has preserved the name of the papyrus in the history of civilization is its use as a writing material in Egypt and throughout the ancient world when Egypt became known to them. The pith being taken out and divided by a pointed instrument into the thin pellicles of which it is composed, was flattened by pressure and the strips glued together[2], other strips being placed at right angles to them, so that a roll of any length might be manufactured. The bulb of the lotus afforded a sweet and wholesome food; the seeds taken from the capsule or *ciborium*[3] were pounded and baked; its blue and white flowers[4] enlivened all the lesser streams and pools, and furnished a graceful ornament to architectural sculpture.

The same causes which made the vegetable productions of Egypt few, limited also the number of the birds and beasts which inhabited it. Its birds are chiefly those which, like the ibis and various species of *anas*, haunt the water or lodge in sandy banks; those which live in trees and thickets found no shelter in its naked plains and hills. All large land animals but those which man had subdued

[1] Herod. 2, 92.
[2] Plin. Nat. Hist. 13, 23; whose account of the manufacture, however, is erroneous, especially in attributing to the Nile water the quality of paste.
[3] Diod. 1, 34.
[4] The *Nymphæa Lotus* and *N. cærulea* still grow in Egypt; the *N. Nelumbo*, the sacred lotus, has not been found there. See the Botanical plates to the Description de l'Egypte, pl. 61. Wilkinson (M. and C. 4, 411) says the *N. Lotus* is the sacred emblem.

to his own use, must early have disappeared from a region so populous and so level. The crocodile and the hippopotamus were protected by their amphibious habits[1]; the wolf, the hyæna and the jackal found a refuge in the Desert or the mountains, but the larger carnivorous animals, though abounding in Libya, were rarely seen upon the soil of Egypt[2]. The Nile, on the contrary, teemed with fish of various sorts adapted for the sustenance of man, and the inundation diffused an annual supply of them through every part of the country[3]. The children of Israel longed in the Desert for the fish of Egypt, not less than its cucumbers and melons, its onions and garlic[4]. The occupation of catching and curing fish employed a large number of the people, and forms a prominent subject in those curious pictures of Egyptian life and manners which adorn the walls of the sepulchres.

The species of reptiles and insects of Egypt are not many, but their numbers were immense. Gnats and flies swarmed in the neighbourhood of the river[5] and the canals. Frogs appeared in such multitudes, when the dry pools were visited by the inundation, that they were ignorantly believed to be generated from the mud[6]; and vermin could only be prevented by the most scrupulous cleanliness from infesting the person. Egypt is not exempt from the devastations of the locust, but they are much less frequent here.

---

[1] At present the crocodile is not seen in Lower Egypt; the hippopotamus only in Southern Nubia. (Russegger, Reisen, 2, 287.)

[2] Herod. 2, 65. Αἴγυπτος, ἐοῦσα ὅμουρος τῇ Λιβύῃ, οὐ μάλα θηριώδης ἐστί.

[3] Herod. 2, 93.

[4] Numbers, xi. 5. Wilkinson, M. and C. 3, p. 63.

[5] Herod. 2, 95.

[6] Diod. 1, 10. Horapollo, 1, 25.

than in Arabia, Ethiopia or Western Africa[1]. Scarabæi abound; one species (*Ateuchus sacer*) was commonly employed as a symbol of the sun or the world.

The climate of Egypt is very little subject to the variations of more northern regions, or even of those adjacent to it in position, but less uniform in surface, as Syria. The mean annual temperature is rather higher than in neighbouring countries under the same latitude, being at Cairo 72°·32 Fahrenheit[2] (22° above that of London); mean temperature of winter 58°·46, of summer 85°·10. Egypt can scarcely be said to have a winter; it is covered with verdure when countries of our latitude are buried in snow; the trees begin to be clothed with new leaves in February, almost as soon as they are stripped of the old. The sensation of cold, however, is often severe from the great difference of the diurnal and nocturnal temperature. The inundation of the Nile divides the year into three natural portions of four months each, discriminated in their hieroglyphical characters as the season of Vegetation, the season of Ingathering, and the season of the Waters. Wheat is now sown in November and reaped in April; barley, sown about the same time, is ripe a month earlier. Herodotus remarks the great healthiness of Egypt, and attributes it to the absence of those changes of the seasons[3] which are elsewhere so injurious to health. He referred probably to the diseases which in our climates prevail during the transition from winter to summer and from sum-

---

[1] Hasselq. Travels in Levant, 446.
[2] Humboldt in Murray's Encyclopædia of Geography, 1, 164; Russegger, Reisen, 1, p. 209.
[3] Her. 2, 77. Compare Isocrates, Busiris, 2. p. 164, edit. Battie.

mer to winter. Spring and autumn are not marked in Egypt by such contrasts to the other seasons as in northern latitudes. The inundation leaves no *malaria* behind it; the north winds, which prevail during three-fourths of the year, at once cool and dry the air, and the east and west winds, blowing from Arabia or Libya, arrive in Egypt deprived of moisture and contribute to its desiccation. The Khamsin in the spring brings whirlwinds of sand which are injurious to the eyes, and, like the Scirocco of the shores of the Mediterranean, produces languor and a difficulty of respiration; but its effects are transient. When the inhabitants were described as so healthy, it is impossible that Egypt should have been subject to those visitations of the plague, which now are almost regular. The plague of Athens had not originated in Egypt, but in Ethiopia[1]; nor does it appear that in the age of the Ptolemies it was more subject to it than other countries of the East. Indeed at the present day it is not indigenous in Egypt, but is brought thither from Syria, Barbary, and above all Constantinople, where filth and fatalism perpetuate the seeds of the disease[2]. Diseases of the eye, in all stages from inflammation to blindness, are now very common in Egypt; and the glare of its dusty plains and its driving sands must at all times have had a tendency to produce them. Eruptive diseases, and especially that dreadful kind of leprosy, *elephantiasis*, were very prevalent in the Roman times[3].

---

[1] Thuc. 2, 48. The Emperor Severus visited Egypt, but was prevented entering Ethiopia by the plague (Dion. Cass. 75, 21).

[2] Volney, Voyage, 1, 150.

[3] Ægypti peculiare hoc malum, Plin. N. H. 26, 5, who has an idle tale, that if kings were attacked with it they washed themselves in human blood as a cure. Lucr. 6, 1112.

Although we have spoken of Egypt as one country, in reference to its climate and productions, yet in the seven degrees of latitude which intervene between Syene and the sea, great variety must manifest itself, giving to the southern and northern parts the aspect of two different countries. Lower Egypt is a boundless plain, Upper Egypt a narrow valley. Lower Egypt, though it has its peculiar character, in the main resembles the other countries which border the Mediterranean on the south. Upper Egypt seems to belong to Nubia: its temperature ranges seven degrees higher than that of Lower Egypt[1]. Rain is an exceptional phænomenon in the Thebaid, though the arrangements for carrying off water from the temple-roofs, and the deep ravines into which the hills are worn, indicate that even within historical times it must have been different in this respect[2]. The traveller who ascends the Nile, perceives that he is entering a different world when he passes E' Siout and the 27th degree of N. latitude. The Theban or Doum palm, with its divided branches, begins to prevail along with the date-palm, and the sycamore becomes rare. The crocodile is seen in the waters, though of small size compared with the inhabitant of the Nubian rivers, and scarcely formidable to man. The sphere of vegetation is more limited, but its power more vigorous and intense. The flora of the Thebaid approaches that of Nubia and the Desert. The jackal and the hyæna abound, being

---

[1] Russegger, Reisen, 2, 1, 265. Comp. p. 92.

[2] Οὐ ὕεται τὰ ἄνω τῆς Αἰγύπτου τὸ παράπαν (Her. 3, 10). "Showers fall annually, perhaps on an average four or five in the year, and every eight or ten years heavy rain, which fills the torrent-beds of the mountains. The lions on the cornices have tubes in their mouths to let the rain run off." (Wilkinson, Thebes, p. 75.)

protected from the pursuit of man by the recesses of the hills, which rise close on either side of the stream. Even the mollusks which are found in the Nile and its canals, correspond with those of Nubia and the Blue and White Rivers[1]. Had not the barrier of the Cataracts intervened, Ethiopia would have been reckoned to extend to Thebes; and now the Arabic language, with its hoarse gutturals, gives place to the smoother Barabra, above the pass of Gebel-Silsileh.

[1] Russegger, Reisen, 2, 1, 374.

CHAPTER V.

POPULATION AND LANGUAGE.

We possess means for ascertaining the form, physiognomy and colour of the ancient Egyptians, such as no other people has bequeathed to us. We find in Greek, Roman or British sepulchres only the ashes, or at most the skeleton of the occupant; but the Egyptian reappears from his grotto after the lapse of 3000 years with every circumstance of life except life itself. Even had no mummies been preserved, the remains of art, especially the paintings with which the walls are so profusely covered, would have enabled us to represent to ourselves very exactly the ancient inhabitants of the valley of the Nile. They are also described to us by the Greek and Latin writers, but these seldom go beyond the colour of the face and hair in their ethnographical sketches. The name of Ham, given by the Hebrews to the progenitor of the Egyptian people, as it signifies *adust*, shows that their complexion struck their Asiatic neighbours as darker than their own. Herodotus, speaking of the Colchians[1], indirectly informs us that the Egyptians had curling hair and black complexions.

---

[1] Αὐτὸς εἴκασα τῇδε (that the Colchians were an Egyptian colony) καὶ ὅτι μελάγχροές εἰσι καὶ οὐλότριχες (2, 104). Ammianus Marcellinus says, "Homines Ægyptii plerumque *subfusculi* sunt et *atrati*." (22, 16, 23.)

The inference which has been drawn from this, that they were negroes, has been founded on a mistranslation of the word which I have rendered *curling*, as if it meant *woolly*, and a strained sense of *black*. The ancient Egyptians had none of the osteological characters of the true negro of the west coast and the interior of Africa, who often appears in the same paintings with the Egyptians themselves, with traits wholly dissimilar. The only approach to the negro physiognomy is in a fullness of the lips[1], which may be remarked in the Sphinx of the Pyramids, the heads of some of the Egyptian sovereigns, and many representations of individuals[2]. The elongation of the eye is said to be a Nubian peculiarity[3]. No doubt, intermarriages took place between the Egyptians and the Ethiopians, that is, the Nubians. Of the two wives of Amenophis I., one who is always represented black[4] was probably an Ethiopian princess; and if the royal family did not keep their blood pure, the common people would be less likely to do so, especially during the occupation of Egypt by the Ethiopians[5]. The figure of the Egyptians was generally slight, and their average stature, judging from the mummies, did not exceed five feet and a half[6]. The hair of the mummies is sometimes crisp and sometimes flowing; the former seems to have been considered more beautiful and to have

---

[1] Lucian, 8, 15, ed. Bipont., speaking of an Egyptian youth, says, πρὸς τῷ μελάγχρους εἶναι καὶ προχειλός ἐστι καὶ λεπτὸς ἄγαν τοῖν σκελοῖν. This is the nearest approach to the negro peculiarities that we find in any description.

[2] See the heads of Rameses the Great and some others in the British Museum (Gallery of Antiquities, P. 2, pl. 39, 42).

[3] Madden, in Pettigrew on Mummies, p. 159.

[4] Gallery of Antiquities, P. 2, pl. 30.

[5] Herod. 2, 100.

[6] Pettigrew on Mummies, *u. s.*

been imitated by art, as it is now among the Barabras. The original colour of the skin of the mummies is not easily distinguishable, owing to the effect of embalmment; but on the exterior cases, as in the paintings, men are represented of a red-brown, and women of a green-yellow complexion. Both these colours must have been in some degree conventional. Had the ancient Egyptian complexion exactly corresponded to the colours of the paintings, there must have been a difference between the two sexes such as we nowhere else meet with; and the men must have resembled the copper-coloured Indians, and could never have been described as black or dusky. Their real colour was probably that of the Copt and the Barabra at the present day —brown with a tinge of red—a hue sufficiently dark to be called black by the natives of the northern shores of the Mediterranean; darker also than that of the people of Arabia and Palestine[1]. The Egyptians may therefore be said to be intermediate between the Syro-Arabian and the Ethiopic type, but a long gradation separates them from the negro. The evidence derived from the examination of the skulls of the mummies approximates the Egyptians rather to the Asiatic than the African type[2]. It has been thought that traces could be discovered of two stocks, one fairer and more nearly allied to the Caucasian, to which the ruling castes belonged, the other darker and more Ethiopic. But whatever elements may have mingled in Egyptian blood in

---

[1] Prichard, Researches, 2, chap. 11. At this day an Egyptian is at once recognized in Syria "à son peau noirâtre" (Volney, Voyage, 1, c. 11, p. 114).

[2] Morton, Crania Ægyptiaca.

antehistoric times, had been blended in a homogeneous population before the age of the monuments, in which we discover no marks of a distinction of race, except in the case of foreigners, or of the children of Egyptians by Ethiopian women[1].

The distinction between the Egyptians and their Syro-Arabian neighbours is more strongly marked in language than in complexion and form. Since the researches of M. Quatremère de Quinçy[2], it has been universally admitted that the Coptic, the language of the native Christian population of Egypt, is in the main the same as the old Egyptian spoken under the Romans, the Ptolemies, the Persians and the Pharaohs. As a medium of ordinary communication, this language ceased to be used in the twelfth century; and the last person who could speak it is said to have died A.D. 1633[3]; but considerable remains of it still exist in translations of the Scriptures, liturgies, hymns, lives of saints and other religious works. The versions are no doubt considerably older than the Mahometan conquest of Egypt in the seventh century. The alphabet is borrowed from the Greek, with the exception of five letters expressing sounds unknown to the Greeks, and which were furnished by the hieratic character; the oldest known specimen of it is an inscription of the age of Severus[4]. It has two dialects, corresponding to the two great natural and political divisions of Egypt, the Memphitic and the Sahidic or

---

[1] Dr. Morton (Transactions of American Ethnological Society, vol. 2) mentions skulls of a *negroid* type in the catacombs, belonging to the offspring of mixed marriages.

[2] Recherches Critiques et Historiques sur la Langue et la Litérature de l'Egypte. Paris, 1808.

[3] Adelung, Mithridates, 3, 78.

[4] Niebuhr, Appendix to Gau Monuments of Nubia.

Theban, from the Arabic name for Upper Egypt. The Bashmuric is a variation of the Sahidic. Many Greek, and not a few Arabic and Persian words are intermixed with the language; the Greek are especially abundant in those works which were written in the Memphitic dialect[1]: but when these are thrown aside (and their foreign aspect readily betrays them), there remains a language having all the marks of originality. Very few of the principal objects of nature and art are the same as in the Syro-Arabian languages, and the structure is characteristically different. Its roots appear to have been generally monosyllabic, and the derivatives have been formed by a very simple system of prefixing, inserting and affixing certain letters, which have usually undergone but little change, not having been incorporated with the root, nor melted down by crasis, nor softened by any euphonic rules. The language has the appearance of having undergone very little cultivation; the derivative and figurative meanings are few, as if it had been fashioned by the use of a people whose genius was precise and formal, and never luxuriated in poetic and imaginative literature. The conclusion of an author who has elaborately compared the system of inflexions in the Egyptian and the Syro-Arabian languages, is that both must have separated themselves from some parent tongue, long before this system was established[2]. A connexion so remote belongs not to history.

That this is in the main the original language of

---

[1] Peyron, Lex. Copt. Præf. p. xxx. Prichard, 2, 205.

[2] Benfey Ueber das Verhältniss der ægyptischen Sprache zum semi-

the native population of Egypt cannot be doubted. There is a vitality in national language which preserves it from extinction, except by the absorption of the race that speak it. Neither the Romans nor the Ptolemies nor the Persians attempted the destruction of Egyptian nationality; the religious persecutions under the Byzantine dominion diminished the numbers of those by whom the ancient language was spoken and confined them to the limits of the Thebaid, but had no tendency to produce any intermixture by which the language could have been changed. The Persians were at first intolerant, and the impatience of the Egyptians under their yoke led them into revolts, in which many perished; but no incorporation of the conquered and conquerors took place. The presumption which hence arises, that the remains of the Coptic literature contain a language essentially the same as that spoken in Egypt since it became known to the Greeks, is confirmed by direct evidence. Herodotus relates, that when Hecatæus was in Egypt he deduced his own descent from a god in the sixteenth degree, and that the priests of Thebes, to whom he made this boast, took him into the inner house of the temple and showed him the wooden statues of 340 high priests in succession, among whom none had been either god or hero, but every one a *piromi* the son of a *piromi*[1]. Their argument evidently required that *piromi* should signify *man*, and *rome*, with the ar-

tischen Sprachstamm. Bunsen, who has examined the subject of the Egyptian language with great care (Ægypten's Stelle, &c. V. 1, B. 1, sect. 4), thinks (see Preface) that it affords proof of a connexion between the oldest population of Egypt and the Caucasian stock.

[1] Her. 2, 143. He was not himself aware of the truth which he has preserved, and renders Πίρωμι by καλὸς κἀγαθός.

ticle *perome*, is Coptic for *man*. Herodotus (2, 69) says the crocodile was called χάμψα; in hierogly-phics it is *hamso*, in Coptic *amsah*. On the cubit measure *half* is marked by the hieroglyphic M, the initial of *Met*, Coptic for *half*; fractions by R, the initial of *Re*, Coptic for *part*. Instruction was called by the Egyptians *Sbo*[1]; which is the Coptic word for *learning*. The water-plants of the Nile were called by the Egyptians, according to St. Jerome[2], *achi*; a name preserved in the Alexandrian version of Gen. xli. 2, 18, and Isaiah xix. 7; and this word is Coptic. *Erpis* was an Egyptian word for wine[3]; removing the Greek termination, it is the Coptic *erp*[4]. An Egyptian priest informed Aristides, that the name Canopus was not derived, as the Greeks supposed, from the pilot of Menelaus, but signified in the Egyptian language " golden soil[5]." *Kahi* in Coptic is earth, and *nub* gold. *Chemia*, the native name of Egypt, signified, according to Plutarch[6], "black," and Amenthes the Egyptian Hades[7]; both these words are found in Coptic in this sense. That many false explanations should have been assigned by Greek and Roman writers to Egyptian words will not surprise any one who has observed how careless they were in regard to foreign languages. The recent discoveries in hieroglyphics have extended this proof of the

---

[1] Horapollo, 1, 38.
[2] St. Jerome ad Esaiam (19, 7). Quum ab eruditis quærerem quid hic sermo (ἄχει τὸ χλωρόν) significaret, audivi ab Egyptiis hoc nomine lingua eorum omne quod in palude virens nascitur appellari.
[3] Eustath. ad Od. *i*. p. 1633, 5.
[4] Peyron, Lex. Copt. *s. voc.*

[5] Op. ed. Jebb. 2, 360.
[6] Plut. Is. et Osir. c. 33. Peyron, p. 270.
[7] Plut. Is. et Osir. c. 29. But he is wrong in his etymology when he explains it by τὸν λαμβάνοντα καὶ διδόντα. It means the West, the land of darkness (Peyron, p. 35).

identity of the Coptic with the ancient Egyptian to the Pharaonic times. A great multitude of groups of characters, including the grammatical flexions of the language, have been read by the phonetic alphabet into Coptic words, and in many cases all doubt is precluded by the addition of the object itself. It is true that no single hieroglyphical inscription has yet been read completely into Coptic; but this is not wonderful, since the remains of Coptic literature are imperfect and limited. Even in Egypt, too, unchangeable as it was, language could not remain unaltered for more than 2000 years. In the time of the Ptolemies some words had become obsolete, and a distinction existed between the common and the sacred dialect[1].

As we know nothing of the language spoken along the banks of the Nile in Nubia in primitive times, we cannot from this source obtain any materials for deciding on the origin of the Egyptian people or their affinities with their Ethiopian neighbours. The Pharaohs made so many settlements in Nubia, that a considerable Egyptian population must have been introduced among the native Ethiopian tribes as far south as Argo or even Gebel-el-Birkel. It is not certain whether any tribe now existing can be considered as descendants of these Ethiopians, the population having undergone many changes. Diocletian, finding the country above Syene nearly depopulated, transferred hither the Nobatæ from the "city of Oasis" or El-Khargeh. The Barabras, who under various names inhabit the Nubian valley, and to the southern limit of Dongola cultivate such parts

[1] Joseph. c. Ap. 1, 14, quoting Manetho.

of it as are susceptible of cultivation, would appear to be the descendants of the ancient Ethiopians, if we could rely on the judgement of travellers respecting their physiognomy. Their language, however, has no affinity either to Coptic or Arabic, and the resemblances which have been pointed out to the language of the hill-district of Kordofan[1], are too slight to found an argument of identity of race, especially as the people of Kordofan are negroes, which the Barabras are not. The marked distinction which the ancients always make, between the Egyptians who lived below and the Ethiopians who lived above the Cataracts of Syene, leads to the conclusion that in all historical times Egypt has been inhabited by a distinct race, and that what is said of its being peopled from Meroe is only an hypothesis, grounded on the probability that population would follow the course of the descending river and the extension of the land. Herodotus adopted this view as regards Upper and Lower Egypt[2], but does not carry it above the First Cataract. Diodorus, who is the principal authority for the opinion that Egypt derived everything from Meroe, had seen in Egypt the ambassadors of Ethiopia, and appears readily to have adopted the statements by which they endeavoured to establish the higher antiquity of the population, religion and arts of their own country[3]. The monuments of Meroe have been sufficiently examined by Lepsius and his associates to prove that they are all of younger date than those of

---

[1] Prichard, Researches, 2, 178.
[2] Her. 2, 15. Δοκέω προιούσης τῆς χώρης, πολλοὺς μὲν τοὺς ὑπολειπομένους αὐτῶν γενέσθαι, πολλοὺς δὲ τοὺς ὑποκαταβαίνοντας.
[3] Diod. 3, 11.

Egypt, not ascending beyond the times of the Ptolemies and the Romans. This indeed is not decisive of the question of priority in population or religion; but no historical fact confirms the opinion that Egypt was indebted to Ethiopia for its settlement or civilization; whereas we know that the Pharaohs possessed the valley of the Nile, 600 miles above Syene, at least fifteen centuries before Christ.

The high antiquity of civilization in India, and some remarkable coincidences in doctrine and usages between this country and Egypt, have led to the supposition of an early connexion, by which one of them has communicated, if not its population, at least its institutions and opinions to the other. Of such a connexion there is no historic trace. The ancient Egyptians never surmised an Indian origin of their nation; they believed themselves to be in the strictest sense *autochthones*, not only figuratively but literally, natives of the soil[1]; nor have the Indians any tradition of having received or sent forth an Egyptian colony. The passages in their sacred books, in which Ethiopia and Egypt were supposed to have been mentioned, are now known to be forgeries by which the Bramins imposed on a too eager and credulous European[2]. After the conquests of Alexander, India became well known to the West; and the resemblance of the Indians of the South to the Ethiopians and those of the North to the Egyptians was noticed[3]. During the reigns of the Ptolemies an active commerce was carried on between Egypt and India;

---

[1] Diodorus Sic., 1, 10.
[2] Asiatic Researches, vol. 3, p. 46.
[3] Arrian, Indica, 6, 9.

yet in no author of these times do we find even a tradition of the colonization of one of these countries from the other. The Sophist Philostratus in the beginning of the third century[1] speaks of the Ethiopians as having once dwelt in India[2]. The Christian chronologers described the Ethiopians as quitting the Indus and establishing themselves on the frontiers of Egypt, and assigned the supposed migration to the reign of Amenophis[3]. The application of the name Ethiopian from early times to the dark nations of the East, as well as those of the valley of the Nile, would naturally give rise to such an hypothesis, especially as the Nile was supposed by some to have its source in India[4], and the name India was used for Ethiopia[5].

The physiognomy of the two nations, if we compare their monuments, appears to be very different; the Indian is even less Ethiopic than the Egyptian, and in stature and features approaches much nearer to the Caucasian standard. Blumenbach, it is true, pronounced that in all his collection of skulls no two more resembled each other than those of a native of Bengal and a mummy. Independently, however, of their vagueness, osteological resemblances, even if more clearly established than by an insulated

---

[1] Vit. Apoll. 3, 20. Ἦν τοίνυν χρόνος ὅτε Αἰθίοπες μὲν ᾤκουν ἐνταῦθα γένος Ἰνδικόν. 6, 8. ἄποικοι Ἰνδῶν Αἰθίοπες. Αἰθιοπία δ' οὔπω ἦν, ἀλλ' ὑπὲρ Μερόην τε καὶ Καταδούπους ὥριστο Αἴγυπτος.

[2] Van Bohlen's Indien, v. 1, p. 119. The author is known to have abandoned his opinion of the original connexion between Egypt and India.

[3] Chron. Gr. ed. Scal. p. 26. Amenophis was supposed to be Memnon, and Memnon son of Aurora a prince coming from the East, and thus the date of the migration was arbitrarily fixed.

[4] See Joseph. Antiq. 1, 1, referring to Gen. ii. 13—"the river that boundeth the whole land of Cush"—Γηὼν (Gihon) ὃν Νεῖλον Ἕλληνες προσαγορεύουσι.

[5] Virg. Georg. 4, 293, quoted p. 79 note.

fact of this kind, do not deserve that authority in historical inquiries which is often attributed to them. The unity of race, which is all that they can prove, when most perfect, is no proof of historical unity; *that* is determined by causes which leave no trace upon the bony structure. Unity of speech, on the contrary, is essential to historical unity in the first coalescence of a nation, and the strongest presumption of identity or affinity between different nations. Judged by this criterion, no two nations of the ancient world appear to have less relation to each other than the Indians and the Egyptians. The Sanscrit, now the sacred idiom, but once no doubt the vernacular tongue of India, is the most polished and copious language ever spoken by man; the Coptic the most rude of all which were used by the civilized nations of antiquity. The resemblances between their roots are few and slight; their whole genius and almost their whole stock of words are entirely different.

In the institutions and religious systems of Egypt and India there is, on the contrary, a close and most remarkable resemblance. The principle of hereditary caste prevailed with great original strictness in both, and the divisions of society arising from it were nearly the same. Their systems of theology appear to have originated in the same source—the personification of the powers of nature under male and female forms, whose images were multiplied and varied by sculpture and painting. The assignment of animals to each of the gods and their consequent worship, the minuteness of the temple ritual, the doctrine of the transmigration of souls, the phallic orgies of Osiris and Sceva—are all circumstances which seem strongly to identify the religions of Egypt and India. Yet before we infer that one country was colonized from the other, we must not overlook their differences. The Egyptian and Hindu Pantheons have each a perfectly native character. The ram-headed Kneph or Amun, the hawk-headed Osiris, the ibis-headed Thoth, the jackal-headed Anubis, the scarabæus, the ostrich-feather, the hippopotamus, belong as exclusively to Egypt, as the elephant, the peacock and the eagle to the gods of India. The bull, the cow, the lion, the serpent, the lotus, belong alike to the two countries and the two mythologies. The hieroglyphic system of Egypt is clearly indigenous in the valley of the Nile, and no such mode of writing ever prevailed in India. The Egyptians had practised circumcision from time immemorial in common with the Ethiopic tribes, but this rite was unknown in India before the Mahometan conquest. On the other hand, we have reason to conclude that the system of castes is a form naturally assumed by society in an early state[1], and therefore affording no proof of the identity of the nations by whom it was admitted: the doctrine of metempsychosis prevails in a ruder shape among the negroes, who have certainly not learnt it either from the Bramins or the Egyptians. In the fine arts India remained far below Egypt, and it is only in the most barbarous

---

[1] Meiners de Causis Castarum. Reg. Soc. Götting. 10, p. 184. Kenrick's Essay on Primæval History, p. 130.

specimens of Egyptian sculpture that any resemblance to the Indian can be traced[1]. The same practice of excavating temples in the native rock prevailed in both countries; but Aboosimbel and other grotto temples of Nubia existed fourteen centuries before the Christian æra. Those of India, Ellora, Kennery, Ceylon, are not mentioned before the reign of Heliogabalus[2]. They were indeed then old, because they were described as a work of nature; but were they even of equal antiquity with those of Nubia, there would be no ground for concluding that one was copied from the other, since their style and decoration are entirely different. Taking coincidences as well as differences into the account, it appears that there has been some connexion between the civilization of Egypt and India, while the nations themselves have as much claim to be considered distinct as any others of antiquity. We should be quitting altogether the domain of history were we to endeavour to devise an explanation of this connexion. Both of them are in a remarkable degree insulated by their geographical position; both were averse from intercourse with foreigners and from navigation; both were chained to their native soil by religious prejudices and political institutions. Even the traditions of Egyptian conquest, which is now known to have spread far into Asia, do not extend to India; and the intervening countries were inhabited by nations differing from both in their language and institutions.

---

[1] Rosellini, Monumenti del Culto, 77.
[2] See the account of the Embassy of Bardesanes in Ritter's Indien, 4, 489, Part 1.

We must be content to leave their similarity unexplained, among many other historical phænomena, the origin of which belongs to ages of which no record has been preserved[1].

[1] Dr. Prichard (Researches, 2, p. 214) has pointed out some curious analogies between the Coptic language and those of South Africa, especially the Kafir. Kolben (Zoega de Orig. et Us. Obeliscorum, p. 450) found the worship of the Scarabæus among the barbarous nations in South Africa.

It may deserve remark, that in Gen. x. 8, Nimrod, the sovereign of Babylon and founder of Nineveh, is said to be a son of Cush, the son of Ham, and consequently a brother of Mizraim. The nation which occupied the plain of Shinar, and built there the city of Babylon and Tower of Babel, is said (xi. 2) to come from the East; and these conquerors and colonists are clearly distinguished from the children of Shem,—Elam, Assar and Aram. So the original occupation of Southern Arabia is attributed to the sons of Cush (x. 7), though Seba and Havilah, which were in this region, are said to have been occupied by the descendants of Shem (x. 26). Thus Africa, Egypt and Southern Asia, according to the conceptions of this age, were occupied by Cushite nations, and to them the first movements of conquest and migration are attributed. India was not known to the Jews till the Captivity (Esther, i. 1), but no doubt its dark inhabitants would have been classed by them with Cushites, as by the Greeks with Ethiopians. In this early and wide diffusion of a people allied at least in colour to the Egyptians (which is all that the name proves), we have a glimpse of the means by which Egypt may have been brought into relations with India.

CHAPTER VI.

MEMPHIS.—THE PYRAMIDS.

MEMPHIS appears to have been the earliest capital of the united Egyptian monarchy, although the first king of the whole country was a native of Upper Egypt. Driven into the Thebaid by the Shepherd invaders, the Pharaohs, after their expulsion, retained Thebes as their capital, and made more extensive conquests in Ethiopia. As the Ethiopians grew formidable, after the decline of the power of the Rameses, and became invaders in their turn, the Pharaohs fixed themselves again in Lower Egypt. It is the natural site for the capital of a kingdom connected with Syria and Palestine, Asia Minor and Greece, and here accordingly it has remained with little change of place, under the Macedonians, the Romans, the Saracens and the Turks.

Memphis was situated, according to Strabo[1], three schoenes, between eleven and twelve miles, from the apex of the Delta. At the distance of about ten miles to the south of the modern capital of Cairo, but on the opposite or western bank, stands the village of Mitrahenny or Mitranieh, in a plain covered with palm-trees, where are found the only remains which identify the site of the ancient Memphis. The name of Memf, which the district bears traditionally among the Copts, confirms the

[1] Lib. 17, p. 807.

evidence of the ruins and the correspondence of the measures. A circuit of 150 stadia, at least fifteen miles, is attributed to the former capital[1], but its outline cannot now be traced. Its position accords very well with the account of Herodotus[2], that Memphis was in the narrow part of Egypt; for it is just below the great expansion of the valley of the Nile to Fyoum, and above the still wider opening of the Delta. Thus commanding the connexion between the Upper and Lower countries, it was pointed out as a suitable site for the metropolis of the kingdom of Menes[3].

The founder of this kingdom obtained the ground on which he built his capital, according to Herodotus, by diverting the course of the Nile, which had previously flowed past the foot of the Libyan hills, and compelling it to take a channel which divided the valley more equally[4]. But as it is not likely that he would turn the whole body of water in a river of such depth and width to found a city on its former bed, we must suppose that in ancient times the first bifurcation of the Nile took place higher up than Cercasorus, where the apex of the Delta stood when the Greeks became acquainted with

---

[1] Diod. 1, 50. The mounds which mark the ancient site extend, according to the French Commission, three leagues in circumference. It probably occupied the whole space between the river and the hills, here about three miles.

[2] Herod. 2, 8, 99.

[3] Diod. 1, 50. Συνέβη τὴν πόλιν, εὐκαίρως κειμένην ἐπὶ τῶν κλείθρων, εἶναι κυριεύουσαν τῶν εἰς τὴν ἄνω χώραν ἀναπλεόντων.

[4] Τὸν Μῆνα, τὸν πρῶτον βασιλεύσαντα Αἰγύπτου, οἱ ἱρέες ἔλεγον ἀπογεφυρῶσαι τὴν Μέμφιν· τὸν γὰρ ποταμὸν πάντα ῥέειν παρὰ τὸ ὄρος τὸ ψάμμινον πρὸς Λιβύης· τὸν δὲ Μῆνα ἄνωθεν, ὅσον τε ἑκατὸν σταδίους ἀπὸ Μέμφιος τὸν πρὸς μεσαμβρίης ἀγκῶνα προσχώσαντα τὸ μὲν ἀρχαῖον ῥέεθρον ἀποξηρᾶναι, τὸν δὲ ποταμὸν ὀχετεῦσαι, τὸ μέσον τῶν οὐρέων ῥέειν (Her. 2, 99). This passage has been misunderstood, as if it described the Nile as originally flowing through the Libyan Desert and by the channel of the Bahr-be-la-Ma. See p. 70.

Egypt, and to the south of Memphis. Appearances now give some colour to this supposition. At Kasr-el-Syat, about fourteen miles above Mitrahenny, the Nile makes a bend to the N.W., and in the low ground between this and the Libyan hills an ancient bed may be traced. The canal, a continuation of the Bahr Jusuf, flows here through a natural depression, while to the south it is an excavation[1]. This bend is the *elbow*, of which Herodotus speaks, where Menes built the dam by which he diverted the river from its western course. If this arm were already nearly dried up in the age of Menes, and the great body of the water were carried down by the Eastern arm, the project of excluding the river altogether, and employing the ground thus gained for the site of a city, will not appear extravagant. It was necessary however to guard this point with great care; the bed of the river would rise, but the land from which it was excluded would not rise, and hence Memphis would be exposed to the same danger, if the embankment gave way, by which New Orleans is threatened from the Mississippi. Even during the Persian occupation of Egypt this dam was annually repaired[2]. At present the rise of the soil has obliterated its traces. The ancient arm of the Nile, thus excluded, served to feed a lake which protected Memphis on the north and west, as the main stream did on the east[3]. Some traces of it are said to be still visible.

[1] Perring in Howard Vyse on the Pyramids, vol. 3, p. 2.
[2] Herod. 2, 99.
[3] Herod. ibid. Strabo, p. 807. Browne's Travels, p. 173.

The motive which led the founder of Memphis to place his capital on the western bank of the Nile may easily be divined. Egypt has never been exposed to invasion from the west. The scattered tribes of the Desert could not be formidable to it in any stage of its power. But on the east it had very dangerous neighbours in the Arabs, the Syrian, Mesopotamian and Persian nations; it was not even beyond the wide-sweeping excursions of the Scythians[1]. It was therefore of the utmost importance to oppose a strong barrier to an invader on that side, and such a barrier the Nile supplied. When the Saracens established themselves in Egypt, the eastern bank was pointed out to them as the proper site of their capital, by the necessity of maintaining their connexion with the country which had been the cradle of the Mahometan religion; and here Old and New Cairo successively arose, commanding more completely than Memphis the connexion between the Delta and the Upper Country.

The actual remains of Memphis at Mitrahenny are not great, though sufficient to identify it; but as late as the beginning of the fourteenth century, when Abulfeda wrote, they were very considerable[2]. In the description of Abdollatiph, a century earlier, we can distinguish a monolithal shrine, nine cubits in height, seven in depth and eight in breadth, with the remains of a temple in which it stood; a gateway whose lofty jambs were of a single piece; a

---

[1] Herod. 1, 105. Psammitichus prevailed on them to retire by gifts and entreaties.

[2] Rennell's Geography of Herodotus, 2, 119.

statue thirty cubits high of red granite and of perfect symmetry, and two colossal lions couched over against each other[1]. The actual remains begin about a mile from the river, on the bank of which the village of Bedreshein now stands. Between it and Mitrahenny are two long parallel hills, the remains of the immense enclosure of crude brick, which according to the analogy of Thebes and Sais appears to have surrounded the principal edifices of Memphis. Within this enclosure lies a colossal statue of Rameses II. of crystalline limestone, mutilated at the upper and lower extremities, but which when perfect must have been nearly forty-three feet in height[2]. Its features exactly resemble those of known statues of this king, and all doubt has been removed by the discovery of his name and title, on his girdle and on a scroll which he holds in his hand. We know from Herodotus, that Sesostris, who corresponds most nearly with the Rameses II. and III. of the monuments, erected in front of the temple of Pthah, the chief divinity of Memphis, two colossal statues thirty cubits (forty-five feet) high; and as we find from the remains of Thebes, that such statues did not stand isolated, the temple may be concluded to have been placed near the spot where the colossus now lies. Some other fragments are scattered in the neighbourhood, two of red granite, probably of the same king, whose banner and name are still visible on one of them; and a fragment of a block of limestone, on which the god Nilus is sculptured. The excavations of Caviglia and Champollion have also

---

[1] Abdollatiph, by White, p. 121, Appendix.
[2] Bonomi, in Trans. of Royal Soc. of Literature, 2, 293, 800.

ascertained the existence, to the north of the colossus, of a temple dedicated to Pthah and Athor, *i. e.* Vulcan and Venus, the two chief divinities of Memphis. Of the temple of Apis, and the enclosure in which he was exhibited, which stood near the temple of Pthah, no traces have been discovered. Little indeed has been done towards elucidating the vestiges of this ancient capital, and it is to be feared that the accumulation of the soil will diminish the likelihood of the necessary researches being undertaken.

Were these vestiges, however, even less distinct than they are, the vicinity of a great capital would be sufficiently marked, by the pyramids[1] which at intervals cover the crests of the Libyan hills, and by the mummy plain of Saccara which lies at their feet, nearly in the line of the ruins of Mitrahenny. The pyramids are best seen in their whole extent and succession from the Hill of Tourah, above Cairo. Looking across the Nile, but a little to the south, are first seen the pyramids of Gizeh, to which from their superior size the name has been often exclusively given; then about seven miles to the south those of Abouseir, followed at shorter intervals by those of Saccara and Dashour. These last are the most remote that we can with any probability suppose to have served as cemeteries to Memphis; but the line is continued into the Fyoum by the pyramids of Lisht, Meidoun and Illahoun. The pyramid of Abouroash, about five miles below Gizeh, is the furthest remaining to the north.

---

[1] Memphis is designated in hieroglyphics "the land of the pyramid." Wilkinson, M. and C. 3, 278, Lepsius, Einleitung, p. 173.

THE PYRAMIDS OF GIZEH.

The pyramids of Gizeh are about five miles distant from the bank of the Nile. As the traveller approaches them first across the plain and then the sandy valley to which the inundation does not extend, he is usually disappointed by their appearance, which falls short of the conception which their fame had raised. Their height and breadth are lessened by the hills of sand and heaps of rubbish which have accumulated around them. The simplicity and geometrical regularity of their outline is unfavourable to their apparent magnitude; there is nothing near them by which they can be measured; and it is not till, standing at their base, he looks up to their summit, and compares their proportions with his own or those of the human figures around them, that this first error of the judgement is corrected. And when he begins to inquire into their history, and finds that 2300 years ago, their first describer was even more ignorant than ourselves of the time and purpose of their erection, he feels how remote must be their origin, which even then was an insoluble problem. They stand upon a rocky platform of unequal height, but where highest, elevated about 100 feet above the plain, and forming a kind of promontory in the Libyan chain, whose greatest projection is towards the north-east. Such a range of low rock, the first step in the ascent of the Libyan hills, borders the valley of the Nile to the entrance of the Fyoum, and on it all the pyramids which occur in this district are placed. This range of hills rises northward also from the entrance to the Fyoum, so that the pyramid of Meidoun, which is the furthest to the south, is the least elevated above the plain. The First or Great Pyramid is the nearest to the river, and furthest to the north, the Second being placed about as much more to the west, as the breadth of the First, and the Third in like manner retiring to the west, by somewhat more than the breadth of the Second. The pyramids have been recently explored, more completely than before, by Colonel Howard Vyse, and we are indebted to his liberality and the intelligence of his engineer, Mr. Perring, for establishing some most important points in Egyptian history.

The GREAT PYRAMID, or that of Cheops, had originally a square base of 764 feet[1] (now reduced to 746), and consequently an area of thirteen acres, and a perpendicular height of 480 feet, now reduced by the dilapidation of the summit to 450 feet. The rock around was carefully leveled to furnish a horizontal base for the structure, yet not throughout the whole area, for a nucleus of the native rock has been discovered in the interior, rising, according to the latest account, to the height of 22 feet. The sides now present the appearance of a series of steps, each course projecting beyond that above it; and by these projections it is easy to reach the top, where is a platform of about 30 feet square. But in its original state the pyramid probably presented a perfectly smooth surface, the spaces between the courses being filled up by the insertion of casing-

---

[1] Perring says 767·424. He observes that "the proportion that seems to have regulated the exact form of the Great Pyramid and several others was a ratio of height to size of base of 5 to 8; and this gives on a direct section—as half the base : perpendicular height : the apotheme or slant height : the whole base." See Bunsen's Ægypten's Stelle, &c. B. 2, p. 365, Germ.

stones, wrought with the most perfect finish, after they were fixed in their places[1], so that from top to bottom there was no projection. It appears that not a very long time elapsed before a forcible entrance was made or attempted. A very inconsiderable depth of the Desert sand lies beneath the stones at the base of the northern front; and as these must have been stripped off in the first attempt to find an entrance, it is evident that it was made at so short an interval, that there had not been time for any great accumulation. Though Herodotus does not expressly say that the pyramid was open in his time, it is evident that it was or had recently been, since he speaks, not very accurately it is true, of the interior. Strabo[2] describes the entrance as at a moderate elevation, and as made by means of a *moveable* stone. It should seem therefore not to have been permanently open; and when the Caliphs established themselves in Egypt, they entered it by a forced passage[3].

The original opening (see Pl. I.) is, like that of all the other pyramids, in the northern face, but a little on one side of the centre, about 45 feet from the ground, and in the fifteenth course of stones. A block of unusual size is immediately over it, on which rest four others, meeting so as to form a kind of pointed arch or pediment—an arrangement by which the pressure from above was lessened and the opening preserved from being crushed in. This peculiarity must always have pointed out the entrance when

---

[1] This was begun at the top. Ἐξεποιήθη δ' ὧν τὰ ἀνώτατα αὐτῆς πρῶτα (Her. 2, 125).
[2] Lib. 17, p. 808.
[3] Howard Vyse, 2, 341 note.

the casing was removed. From this entrance the passage descends at an angle of 26° 41', as in the other pyramids; it is of the height and width of 3 feet 5 inches, and is roofed with stones finely wrought and fitted together. After a descent of 63 feet it divides, one passage continuing in the same straight line and with the same dimensions, the other ascending towards the centre of the pyramid. The entrance to this upper passage was closed by a block of granite, the position of which was hidden by the roof of the lower passage. To pass round it an entrance has been forced through the masonry of the pyramid. The upper passage thus entered is continued by an ascent, at an angle of 26° 18', for 125.feet, when it again divides; one branch runs horizontally, with only the descent of a single step, for 110 feet, and terminates in the Queen's Chamber, as it is called, an apartment about 17 feet long, 16 feet wide, and 20 feet high. It is roofed with blocks meeting in a point, which to give them strength have been carried a long way into the masonry and cut so as to have a perpendicular bearing. This chamber stands immediately under the apex of the pyramid, and from the careful finish of the slabs with which it is lined, appears to have been intended for the reception of an embalmed body. Nothing however has been found in it; if a sarcophagus should be concealed anywhere, it must be in the floor. Returning to the junction of the passages, a well is to be noticed, just at the point of divergence, which descends partly through the masonry of the pyramid and partly through the natural rock, till it meets the prolongation of the descending passage by which the pyramid was entered. It is 191 feet in depth, perpendicular in the first 26 feet, afterwards more or less inclined; its dimensions are 2 feet 4 inches square, and it can be ascended or descended by means of projections which have been left in it. Though called a well, its purpose appears to have been to afford a means of communication and ventilation, after the passage into the upper part of the pyramid had been closed by the mass of granite before described; and as it has been cut through the masonry, it is evident that it was an afterthought.

The great gallery, leading to the King's Chamber, begins where the horizontal passage to the Queen's Chamber goes off. It continues to ascend at the same angle as before; it is 150 feet long, 28 feet high, and $6\frac{1}{2}$ feet wide; but this width is lessened by a projecting stone seat or ramp, which runs along each side, 19 inches wide and 2 feet high. Holes are cut in it at intervals, which are supposed to have served for the insertion of the machinery by which the sarcophagus was raised. The side walls are formed of eight assizes of stone, which projecting inward over each other, give the passage the appearance of being arched. A landing-place at the upper end leads into a vestibule, designed to be closed by four portcullises of granite[1]. Three had been lowered, the fourth remained in its original position, the lower part of the groove never having been cut away to allow of its descent. Beyond

---

[1] In the sepulchral mounds of the North of Europe, it was customary to place a shutter, of wood or stone, let down in a groove, between the central chamber and the passage which led to it (Guide to Northern Archæology, p. 101).

these lies the principal apartment of the pyramid, the King's Chamber. It is 34 feet long and 17 feet wide; its height is 19 feet; its position is not exactly in the centre of the pyramid, but a little southward and eastward of the vertical line. The roof is flat, formed of single slabs of granite, and the side walls on which they rest are of the same material. The sarcophagus, also of red granite, but without hieroglyphics or even ornamental carving, stands north and south; its exterior length is 7 feet 6 inches, and its breadth 3 feet 3 inches. No body or any indication of its former presence remains, and the sarcophagus is without a lid.

It was known, from the researches of Mr. Davidson, who was Consul at Algiers in 1764, that ten feet above the King's Chamber, there was a vacant space, thirty-eight feet long and seventeen wide, varying in height from two feet and a half to three feet and a half. Col. Howard Vyse has discovered that there are four more spaces, in the same perpendicular line, of similar dimensions. The four lowest have flat roofs; the highest has its roof formed of blocks, meeting at an angle, and is eight feet and a half in height in the centre. These spaces have been left vacant, evidently with the design of lessening the pressure upon the king's chamber, and preventing its flat roof from being crushed in. For its ventilation, two small passages were left open, one on the north, the other on the south side, which terminate in the exterior faces of the pyramid. It was on the stones of these chambers that the hieroglyphics were discovered drawn in red ochre, presenting, besides the quarry-marks of the workmen, the shield of the king, and thus establishing the fact of their being used at the time of the erection of the pyramid, notwithstanding their absence from every other part of the structure.

If, returning to the point where the upper passage branches off, we continue in the line of the passage of entrance, we find it prolonged for 320 feet from the opening in the side of the pyramid, and with such exactness that the sky is visible from the further end[1]. It then runs for 27 feet further in a horizontal direction, and terminates in a subterranean chamber, immediately under the Queen's Chamber, and 90 feet below the base of the pyramid. It is 46 feet in length and 27 in breadth; no sepulchral remains of any kind have been found in it. There is a passage, 2 feet 7 inches high, issuing from it on the southern side, which continues for a little more than 50 feet, but ends in nothing. Col. Vyse sunk through the floor of this chamber to the depth of 36 feet, without any result. As Herodotus[2] speaks of a communication with the Nile, by means of which its water was introduced, so as to insulate the sepulchral chambers which Cheops constructed for himself, and the excavation of which preceded the erection of the pyramid, it was natural that it should be sought for, in connection with this, the lowest apartment hitherto discovered. It is, however, considerably above the level, even of the High Nile of the present day, and must have been still more beyond the reach of water drawn directly from the river in ancient times, when its own bed was so much lower. From the account

[1] Richardson's Travels, 1, 130. [2] 2, 124.

of the same author[1], it was concluded that the exterior of the Great Pyramid was once covered with a smooth coating from the bottom to the top, such as still remains on some part of the Second. But until recently no trace of this coating could be discovered. Col. Vyse, however, found under the rubbish accumulated at the base, two of the casing-stones in their original position. They are of the limestone of the Mokattam quarries, which being almost free from fossils, is much fitter for fine work than the stone of the Libyan hills. In perpendicular height they are 4 feet 11 inches, and 8 feet 3 inches long, the outer face sloping with an angle of $51° 50'$. Being inserted in the spaces left between the successive courses of the pyramid, they were shaped to the required angle, and then polished down to an uniform surface. The operation began at the top, as Herodotus asserts, and was carried downwards[2]. The joints are scarcely perceptible, and not wider than the thickness of silver paper, and the cement so tenacious, that fragments of the casing-stones still remain in their original position, notwithstanding the lapse of so many centuries, and the violence by which they were detached. All the fine work of the interior passages, where granite is not expressly mentioned, is of the same stone, and finished with the same beautiful exactness. The great mass of the pyramid, however, is not constructed with equal care; the mortar is formed of crushed red brick, gravel and earth of the Nile mixed with lime, and sometimes a liquid *grout* of lime mortar, Desert sand and gravel has been used.

[1] 2, 125.   [2] See p. 119 note.

A pavement, with two steps, worked with the greatest exactness, so as to obtain a perfect level for the foundation, extended under, and 33 feet in its widest part around the base.

The loss of the casing-stones, which appear to have been stript off by the Caliphs, discloses the exterior arrangement. The first assize is laid into the rock; above this are 202 others, varying from 2 feet 2 inches to 4 feet 10 inches in depth, and projecting about a foot, furnishing the means of an easy ascent to the top. Herodotus asserts that none of the stones was less than 30 feet long, but this is by no means true either of the casing or the interior; from 5 feet to 12 is the common range; the longest are the slabs of granite in the King's Chamber, which approach to 20 feet. Two assizes at least have been torn away from the top, which now presents a platform of about 25 feet square.

The manner in which the pyramids were built is not clearly ascertained either from the descriptions of the ancients or by researches into their structure. The stones bear marks of having been raised by machinery, fixed into holes in them which are yet visible, but the width of the projection of each course seems not to suffice for planting on it machines of the necessary strength for lifting such masses[1]. The third pyramid (see Pl. I.) has been built in steps or stages diminishing towards the top, the angular spaces being afterwards filled up, so as to complete the pyramidal slope, and perhaps this may have been the mode in which the other pyramids were raised[2]. These successive projections would be "the

---

[1] Vyse, 2, 105.   [2] Bonomi in Gliddon's Otia Ægyptiaca, p. 33, 42.

steps like those of an altar" on which Herodotus[1] represents the machinery to have been planted.

The stones used in the construction appear to have been finally prepared on the rock to the north of the pyramid, where are rows of holes, which may have served for inserting the machinery by which they were raised and turned. Diodorus[2] asserts that no chippings of the stone were to be found, but this is not true. They were thrown over the face of the rock, and remain there in large heaps.

Neither the inscription mentioned by Herodotus[3], commemorating the sum expended on vegetables for the workmen during the erection of the Great Pyramid, nor those of which Abdollatiph[4] speaks, now appear upon the surface. Though the casing-stones can be traced in the buildings of Fostat and Cairo, they bear no marks of ever having been inscribed. It is probable, however, that the *traced* hieroglyphics were then to be seen in greater numbers than now.

Among many exaggerations of which the pyramids have been the subject, one, repeated by several ancient writers[5], represents the shadow as never falling beyond the base. It is true that during a part of the year the shadow at noon does fall within the base, but throughout the whole year, for a longer or shorter time, before or after midday, it falls on the surrounding earth. This carelessness in report-

---

[1] Vyse, 2, 45, 73.
[2] 1, 63. Οὐδὲν ἴχνος οὔτε τοῦ χώματος (the inclined mound up which he supposed the stones to have been moved) οὔτε τῆς τῶν λίθων ξεστουργίας ἀπολείπεται.
[3] 2, 125.
[4] Vyse, 2, 342. "The inscriptions are so numerous, that copies of those alone which are to be seen on the two pyramids would fill ten thousand pages." Several other Arabian writers speak of these inscriptions.
[5] Descr. de l'Eg. 9, 451.

ing a fact so notorious may make us distrust their statements respecting Syene, on which such large inferences have been built respecting the antiquity of astronomical observation in Egypt.

Three small pyramids stand near the south-eastern angle of the Great Pyramid, and are mentioned by Herodotus, who tells a marvellous tale of the means by which one of them, the centre of the three, was erected by the daughter of Cheops[1]. The base, according to him, was 150 feet, which corresponds pretty well with the measurement of Col. Vyse, who makes it 172 feet. They have all inclined passages, beginning either at the base, or a little above it, and leading into a subterranean chamber, but nothing has been found in any of them by which the original occupant could be identified. A few casing-stones remain at the base of the central one, and by their resemblance to those which covered the Great Pyramid, may be thought to afford some countenance to the tradition that it was the tomb of the daughter of Cheops[2]. They are all much degraded, but appear originally to have been about 100 feet in height.

The SECOND PYRAMID stands about 500 feet from the Great Pyramid; its orientation is precisely the same. As the rock rises to the westward, it was necessary to level it for the base, throughout the greater part of its area, but it remains at the south-western and north-western angles, and is stepped up in horizontal layers to correspond with the courses

[1] 2, 126. It is marked D in Wilkinson's plan of the Pyramids, M. and C. 3, 398.
[2] Vyse, 2, 70

of the masonry. Its dimensions are little inferior to those of the Great Pyramid, the original height being 454 feet, and the length of the sides 707; and from standing on more elevated ground, in some positions it even appears higher. It has had two entrances, one at about the same relative height as that in the Great Pyramid, and descending at the same angle; the other from the pavement at the base[1]. The latter becomes first horizontal, and then inclining upwards, again meets the former and proceeds in a horizontal line to the sepulchral chamber, called, from its rediscoverer, Belzoni's, 46 feet in length, 16 in breadth, and 22 in height. It contained a sarcophagus of red granite, imbedded in the floor, rather larger than that in the King's Chamber of the Great Pyramid, being 8 feet 7 inches in length on the outside, and 7 feet within, without sculpture or hieroglyphics. It contained, when rediscovered, no mummy, but some bones which on examination proved to be those of an ox[2]. It appeared, however, from an inscription, that the pyramid had been opened by the Caliphs, so that no argument can be drawn, as to its destination, from the state in which Belzoni found it. Both passages were originally closed up with a portcullis, at the point where they take a horizontal direction; and beneath the lower one, beyond this point is a chamber, excavated in the rock, resembling the Queen's Chamber in the Great Pyramid, 34 feet in length, 10 in breadth, and 8 in height, under the centre of

---

[1] Herodotus does not mention this subterranean entrance of the Second Pyramid, but notices its existence in that near the Labyrinth. 'Οδὸς δ' ἐς αὐτὴν ὑπὸ γῆν πεποίηται (2, 149).

[2] Belzoni, 1, 426.

its angular ceiling. Its destination is supposed to have been sepulchral, but it contained only some loose stones.

According to Herodotus, the first course of this pyramid on the outside was variegated Ethiopic stone[1], *i.e.* granite of the Cataracts; and this still remains in loose blocks at the base. From hence to the summit it appears to have been cased with the same fine limestone from Mokattam as the Great Pyramid. The casing still remains, for about 130 to 150 feet from the summit. Its smoothness and projection over the part which has been stripped render the ascent to the summit difficult, but it may be accomplished by means of holes which have been cut or worn in the stones. The masonry of the interior, with the exception of the passages, is less perfect than that of the Great Pyramid, and it even appears that only certain parts are solid, the intermediate spaces being filled up with rubble. There are remains of a building, probably a temple, at a short distance from the eastern face, and a row of excavated tombs in the rock on the western side. On the rock on the northern side is a row of hieroglyphics of the age of Rameses III.

The THIRD PYRAMID, called by Herodotus that of Mycerinus, is of much smaller dimensions than the others, the base being 354 feet, and the perpendicular height originally 218: its area was about three acres; but it was the most elaborately finished. The site has been made level, not by lowering the rock, but by a substruction of ten feet in height on the eastern side, composed of two tiers of immense

---

[1] 2,127.'Υποδείμας τὸν πρῶτον δό- μον λίθου Αἰθιοπικοῦ ποικίλου. The granite of the Cataracts is called *pyropœcilus* by Pliny, N. H. 36, 13.

blocks. No tradition existed of its having been opened, nor any vestige of an entrance, till the operations begun by Caviglia and concluded by Col. Vyse in 1837. It then appeared that it had been entered like the rest in the time of the Caliphs[1]. The entrance (Pl. I.) was found on the north side, and 13 feet above the base: the passage descends at an angle of 26° 2′ for 104 feet, 28 of which are lined with granite, when it reaches an ante-room, the walls of which are panneled with sculptured partitions. Beyond this are the usual portcullises of granite, and a horizontal passage terminating in a large apartment, 46 feet long and 12 broad, lying nearly under the centre of the pyramid. At one end of it is a depression in the floor, designed for the reception of a sarcophagus, but nothing was found in it. Fragments of red granite, however, were strewed about in the chamber[2], which have been taken for the remains of a sarcophagus, broken to pieces by some early violators of the pyramid; but appear to have been rather chippings of the granite portcullis. Two passages led from this room: one, near the top of the side-wall, returns towards the exterior, and probably reached it, but has been closed again by the builders themselves. The pyramid having been enlarged from its original dimensions, by additions in lateral extension as well as height, the mouth of this passage was closed up by the added stone-work, and the lower passage was cut *from within outwards*[3]. The other passage, the entrance of which appears to have been originally concealed

---

[1] The irregular lines in the Plate mark the forced entrance, and the interior pyramid, the *supposed* original extent.

[2] Vyse, 2, 81. Perring's note.
[3] Perring, 2, 79.

in the floor, descends for about 30 feet, and ends in a sepulchral chamber, 21 feet in length, 8 in breadth and 11 in height, lined with granite, in which a sarcophagus of basalt was found. It was without inscriptions or hieroglyphics of any kind, but was sculptured in slender and graceful compartments, and had the deep cornice which is characteristic of the Egyptian style[1]: with its lid it was a very little smaller than the passages through which it had been introduced. The lid was broken, and found near the entrance of the inclined passage. The mummy had been removed by some previous visitor of the tomb[2]; but in clearing the rubbish from the larger apartment mentioned before, a portion of a wooden case was found, inscribed with a shield which has been read *Menkera*, and near it some woollen mummy cloth, remains of a skeleton, and the resinous gum in which it had been embalmed. The sarcophagus, which weighed nearly three tons, was with great difficulty got out, and sent to England; but the vessel in which it was embarked was lost off Carthagena in 1838. There is yet another sepulchral chamber, into which seven steps descend from the bottom of the last-mentioned inclined passage. It is 17 feet in length, 6 in breadth and height: there are four niches in the wall on one side, and two on the other, designed perhaps for the reception of mummies, which were placed upright in them.

---

[1] Vyse, 2, 84. This chamber is not represented in the Plate.

[2] Edrisi (A.H. 623) says that "the Red Pyramid had been opened a few years before, and that in the sarcophagus the decayed body of a man had been found, with golden tablets beside him, inscribed with characters which no one could read." (See Vyse, 2, 71.)

The name of the Red Pyramid, used by the Arabian writers for the Third, is derived from the courses of red granite with which the base was covered, Herodotus says to half its height[1]. Diodorus describes the first fifteen courses, and Strabo half the height, as covered with *black* stone[2], both probably from misunderstanding the vague expression of Herodotus, who merely says *Ethiopic* stone. The casing has been removed from the part above the first twelve courses, and thus the construction of the mass has been more distinctly shown. It was built in steps or stages, gradually diminishing; the angular spaces being afterwards filled up, so as to complete the pyramidical form. The Third Pyramid had, like the Second, a temple, at a short distance from its eastern face.

A small pyramid which stands to the south of the Third exhibits the same construction, and apparently has never been reduced to a regular slope, by the filling up of the vacant spaces. This has also been explored by Col. Vyse, and in the sepulchral chamber a sarcophagus was found, of small size, with fragments of bones, apparently those of a female; so that this has probably been the tomb of a queen[3]. Two other small pyramids stand in the same line to the south of the Third: one of them has been unfinished; the other contained a granite sarcophagus (six feet two inches long) imbedded in the ground, like that in the Second Pyramid, but with-

---

[1] 2, 134.
[2] Diod. 1, 64. Strabo, 17, 808. If really black and Ethiopic, it must have been of basalt, which however is not found among the fragments. Grobert (Denon, vol. 1, 82, 4) speaks of remains of black marble, of which subsequent travellers make no mention.
[3] Vyse, 2, 45.

out hieroglyphics or sculpture; and a shield, with the same characters as the mummy-board of the Third Pyramid, was painted on one of the slabs of the roof. The smaller pyramids of which Diodorus speaks, and which he says were erected for the queens of the three kings by whom the great pyramids were built, are probably those which have been already described, near the First Pyramid. He says their base was 200 feet; and though this does not exactly correspond with their present state, it suits better with them than with the dimensions of those near the Third, whose base scarcely exceeds 100 feet. Thus the whole number of pyramids on the hill of Gizeh amounts to nine. The construction of the smaller ones closely resembles that of the larger; the sepulchral chamber is in the rock, and it is reached by a passage, of which the entrance is near the surface. The late researches of the Prussian Commission, of which Lepsius was the chief, have ascertained the existence of numerous pyramids in the same region of Egypt, the traces of which had escaped all preceding travellers. No detailed account of their discoveries has yet been published, but it is understood that the number amounts to thirty. Thirty-nine had been previously known. Supposing the pyramids to have been all royal sepulchres, it will still be difficult to estimate the number of the kings of Egypt, from Uenephes[1], who is first mentioned as a builder of pyramids, the third from Menes, to the end of the eighth, the last Memphite dynasty.

The SPHINX is, next to the Pyramids, the most

[1] Manetho, Dynast. 1, No. 4.

remarkable object which the hill of Gizeh exhibits[1]. It is near the eastern edge of the platform on which they stand, and its head is turned towards the river. It is nearly in a line with the southern side of the Second Pyramid, but on somewhat lower ground, and has been excavated out of one of the faces of the Libyan chain. Its elevation of forty feet above the present level of the soil serves as a measure of the extent of rock which has been cut away to build the pyramids. Neither Herodotus, nor Diodorus, nor any ancient author before the Roman age, mentions it; and as it is now known from its inscription to be at least as old as the reign of Thothmes IV. we learn the hazard of relying on negative arguments merely, in proof of the non-existence of monuments of antiquity. In its present state, with only the head and shoulders visible above the sand, which is accumulated by the western winds in the hollow space around it, the original form and dimensions of the Sphinx cannot be recognized. But a few years ago, by the exertions of Caviglia, the sand was cleared away, and some important discoveries made. Approaching from the Nile when all was uncovered, a sloping descent cut in the rock for 135 feet ended in a flight of thirteen steps and a level platform, from which another flight of thirty steps descended to the space between the Sphinx's feet. This gradual approach, during which the figure of the Sphinx was kept constantly in the spectator's view, rising above him as he descended, was well adapted to heighten the impression made by its colossal size, its posture of repose, and calm

---

[1] Howard Vyse, Pyramids of Gizeh, vol. 3. Appendix, p. 109-119.

majestic expression of countenance. The height from the platform between the protruded paws and the top of the head is 62 feet[1]; the paws extend 50 feet and the body is 140 feet long, being excavated from the rock, excepting a portion of the back and the fore-paws which have been cased with hewn stone. The countenance is now so much mutilated that the outline of the features can with difficulty be traced; but there is no reason to believe that they exhibited more of the negro conformation than belongs to the Egyptian physiognomy generally. The head has been covered with a cap, the lower part of which remains, and which probably terminated when entire in an erect *uræus*[2], such as is seen in the figure of the Sphinx on the tablet which represents the offerings of Thothmes and Rameses[3]. It had originally a beard, fragments of which were found below. The space between the protruded paws appears to have served as a temple, in which, at least in later times, sacrifices were performed to the mysterious deity. Immediately under the breast stood a granite tablet, and another of limestone on either side resting against the paws. The first contains a representation of Thothmes IV. or V., offering incense and making a libation to the Sphinx, with a long inscription in hieroglyphics containing the usual pompous ascription of titles to the king[4]; but nothing, as far as it has been interpreted, which

---

[1] Perring (Plates, P. 1, p. 5) says the Sphinx is about 70 feet high.

[2] Vyse, 3, 109.

[3] Pliny, N. H. 36, 12, 77, speaks of Armais as being interred in the Sphinx. The name of Rameses has undergone a similar change into Armæus, or Armais, in the account which Manetho gave of the expulsion of Ægyptus and Danaus. Diodorus, 1, 64, makes Armæus to be the builder of the Great Pyramid.

[4] Birch in Vyse, 3, 113.

throws any light upon the origin of the Sphinx itself. A shield occurs, however, in the fractured part of the tablet, which appears to be the same as that of the founder of the Second Pyramid, with which by its position the Sphinx is more immediately connected. The side tablets represented a similar act of adoration on the part of Rameses III. No inference however can be drawn from these inscriptions as to the age of the Sphinx, which has no hieroglyphics in any part of it, and from its state of decay is probably coæval with the pyramids themselves. On the paws are many inscriptions of the Roman times, expressive of acts of adoration to the Sphinx, or to Egyptian deities. The wall of crude brick which surrounded the whole and checked the accumulation of sand was repaired under Antoninus and Verus, and a small building on the steps is inscribed to the honour of the Emperor Severus and his sons[1]. No opening has been found anywhere to the interior of the Sphinx, which is probably of solid rock; nor anything which indicates that it was itself a place of sepulture, or had any communication with the Pyramids. Remains of red colour it is said may be traced on the features[2] as well as on the lions which were found in the temple between the paws; but it is doubtful whether these belong to the same age as the Sphinx itself.

The design of carving a rock which broke the view of the Pyramids into a gigantic Sphinx was worthy of the grandeur of Egyptian conceptions in architecture and sculpture. It was probably the work

---

[1] Severus visited Egypt A.D. 202 (Dion, 75, 13). The name of Geta is effaced from the inscription.

[2] Rubrica facies monstri colitur (Plin. N. H. 36, 12, 77).

of the same age as the Pyramids themselves. A Sphinx is the representative of the monarch whose name it bears; and as the name of Shafre (Chephren) is found upon the tablet before mentioned[1], it is most natural to suppose that it was fashioned in his honour. The Greek mythology has accustomed us to speak of the Sphinx as a female, and the artists who carved in the Roman times those figures of Sphinxes from which antiquaries derived their first ideas of Egyptian antiquities sometimes represented them as female. But in the genuine works of the Pharaouic times, it is most rare to meet with a female Sphinx; and in these exceptional cases, a female sovereign is represented, as in the Sphinx of the Museum at Turin, published by Champollion in his Letter to the Duc de Blacas[2]. The junction of the human head with the body of a lion denotes the combination of sagacity with strength required in the administration of a king[3]. The *pyramidion* of the obelisks usually exhibits the king by whom they were erected in the form of a Sphinx, doing homage to the god to whom they were dedicated.

Besides the monuments already described, the hill of Gizeh is full of tombs of various ages. A few of them only had been examined, as that called Campbell's and the Tomb of Trades, before the Prussian Expedition under Lepsius, by whom more than 100 have been opened. Their walls are covered with paintings and hieroglyphical inscriptions,

---

[1] Birch in Vyse, 3, 115.
[2] Rosellini, Mon. Civ. 2, 177. No stress, however, can be laid on the use of the word ἀνδρόσφιγγες by Herodotus, in which the first part (as in ανδροφόνος, ἀνδρόκμητος and others) denotes *human*, not *masculine*, being distinguished from κριόσφιγξ.
[3] Clem. Alex. Strom. 5, p. 671 (Potter). Ἀλκῆς μετὰ συνέσεως σύμβολον ἡ σφίγξ.

which give us as clear an insight into the manners and opinions of the Egyptians under the Fourth dynasty as those of Thebes under the Eighteenth and Nineteenth. Hitherto no drawings or detailed descriptions of them have been published, and we only know in general that they prove the high civilization to which Egypt had attained in this early age.

Herodotus[1] describes the preliminary labour of the people of Egypt, in preparing for the erection of the pyramids, as not less than that of building them. To bring the stones from the Mountain of Mokattam, whence all the finer parts were derived, it was necessary that a causey should be constructed across the valley and the plain, rising with a gradual slope to the height of the hill on which the pyramids stand. Ten years were occupied in its construction; it was five stadia in length (3000 feet), 60 feet in width, and in its loftiest part 48 feet in height; built of polished stones with figures carved upon them. There must be some mistake as to its greatest height, since it crossed the valley at the foot of the hills, which is from 80 to 100 feet lower than the site of the pyramid. A causey remains which begins near the Great Pyramid and stretches for a considerable distance across the plain in the direction of the Nile. It can still be traced for 1400 to 1500 feet, being then lost in the alluvial soil which the waters of the inundation have deposited. The polished stones covered with carved figures are no longer to be seen; and hence it has been supposed, that it is not the causey which Herodotus describes, but one constructed by the Ca-

[1] 2, 124.

liphs, when they stripped the pyramids, to convey the stones to Cairo. The size of the blocks of which it is composed, however, suits with ancient Egyptian rather than with Saracen workmanship, and the removal of the casing and its figures would be effected when the pyramids underwent a similar operation. It has been erroneously supposed that Diodorus describes the causey as having disappeared in his time; but he is speaking of the mounds which he supposed to have been erected on the hill itself, as vast inclined planes to raise the stones to the upper courses of the pyramids[1]. That the present causey points towards Cairo, and not towards the quarries whence the stone was brought, is no proof that it is the work of the Caliphs. To have carried it obliquely across the plain in the direction of the quarries would have increased its length; a line direct from the Great Pyramid to the Nile would be nearly in the direction of Cairo, and the stones might be easily conveyed by water to the commencement of the road. There are no remains of a causey opposite to the Second Pyramid; but that which exists opposite to the Third is pronounced by Sir G. Wilkinson to be certainly of Egyptian, and not Arab workmanship. It is shorter than the North causey, but runs in a parallel direction[2].

On the Eastern bank of the Nile, and about nine miles S. of Cairo, the traces of another causey may be perceived, which appears to have served for conveying to the Nile the stones which had been quarried out of the limestone hills of Tourah and Masa-

[1] Diod. 1, 63. [2] Mod. Eg. and Thebes, 1, 359.

rah. Tourah is supposed to represent the Troicus pagus of the ancients—a name which they referred to the captives whom Menelaus brought with him into Egypt[1]. Tourah lies to the north and Masarah to the south. The face of the hill is not cut away according to the more common mode of quarrying, but excavated in spacious chambers, whose openings resemble those of a line of sepulchral grottos. Besides the quarry-marks of the workmen, there are inscriptions recording the sovereigns under whom the quarries were wrought, and the buildings erected or repaired by them. The earliest is that of Amasis of the 17th or 18th dynasty, but it cannot be doubted that the same quarries were wrought for the erection of the pyramids, though no shield corresponding with the names there inscribed has yet been found. The ancient cemetery of the workmen employed in the quarries has also been discovered. It is a sandy hill, between the cultivated land and the Desert, extending about two miles from Masarah to beyond Tourah[2]. Above 150 sarcophagi of limestone were found here, and fragments of wooden coffins, in which the bodies had been enclosed. They appear not to have been embalmed, but protected against rapid decay, by being steeped in common salt, and the wrappers in which they were enveloped were not of linen, but of woollen. Other bodies were found in tombs constructed of slabs of stone, and these were wrapped in linen[3].

The northernmost of the pyramids is that of

---

[1] Strabo, p. 809. *Etjour* in Coptic meant a strong place (see Peyron, Lex. 393), connected in root with צור, τύρσις, *turris*, Tor.

[2] Perring in Howard Vyse, 3, 90.

[3] Perring in Vyse, 3, 93.

Abouroash, about five miles north-west of Gizeh : it is very much degraded and contains nothing of importance. It lies too far from the ruins of Memphis to have been a part of its necropolis, nor is it clear to what ancient city it belonged; but the site of a considerable town may be traced in a sandy plain between it and the Nile. The Pyramid of Reegah, a little to the south of Gizeh, is also very much ruined. A block has been found in it, inscribed with the name of a king, which has been read *Ousrenre* or *Raseser*, and which has been found at Abouseir and at Wadi-Magara near Mount Sinai[1]. But it affords no clue to the age of the pyramid, both because the place of this king is unknown in the chronological series[2], and because the block itself appears to be a fragment of some older building. The name of *Abouseir*, now borne by a village seven miles south-east of Gizeh, probably represents that of the ancient Busiris, the inhabitants of which, according to Pliny[3], used to climb the Gizeh pyramids for the amusement of visitors. But this circumstance proves that Busiris must have stood nearer to them than Abouseir. The pyramids of Abouseir are four in number, besides a fifth unfinished, and stand on an elevation of about eighty feet above the plain, into which two causeys descend. The largest pyramid has been originally 274 feet long and 171 feet high[4]. Their casing-stones have been stripped off, and they are consequently much decayed; and their general structure is loose; but the sepulchral cham-

---

[1] Birch in Vyse, 3, 12. Bunsen, Ægyptens Stelle, B. 2, p. 69, Germ.
[2] Lepsius and Bunsen suppose him to belong to the third dynasty of Manetho, and to answer to the Rauosis of Eratosthenes.
[3] N. Hist. 36, 12, 75.
[4] Perring in Vyse, 3, 12.

bers at the base have been constructed with great care, and the roofing blocks are even larger than any at Gizeh. In one of them they were thirty-five feet long and twelve feet thick; in another forty-five, and in another forty-eight; yet these enormous masses had been unable to resist the means of destruction employed by those who had forced an entrance into the pyramids in search of treasure, and broken or carried off the sarcophagi and mummies which they once contained. In the most northern of the Pyramids of Abouseir a royal name has been found, which has been read *Amchura* by Bunsen and *Shoure* by Birch[1]. The same name is found in the sixth place of the upper line of the tablet at Karnak.

At Saccara, two miles further to the south, in the immediate neighbourhood of the remains of Memphis, a space of about four miles in length is covered with sepulchral monuments of the most various kinds. In the northern part are many excavated tombs and pits, some of the depth of seventy feet, which have served for the deposit of mummies. In others are found those of oxen, sheep, ibises, and dogs; and jars which have been filled with eggs, beetles and serpents. They have been all ransacked to gratify curiosity or avarice, and the plain is strewed with the relics of the dead, and the fragments of the wood and linen in which they have been enclosed. The same plain contains also eleven stone pyramids, from their size the next in importance to those of Gizeh. That which is called the Great Pyramid of Saccara is not built with a

---

[1] Birch in Vyse, 3, p. 22. Bunsen, *u. s.* p. 78. He supposes him to be the same as the Biures of Eratosthenes.

regular slope from the base to the summit, but consists of six stages or degrees, each retiring within the other, and diminishing in height as well as breadth, the lowest being thirty-seven feet high, the uppermost twenty-nine. The face of each story makes an angle of 72° 36' with the horizon. The present height above the base is 196 feet; much of the lower part has been carried away, but it seems originally to have covered an area of more than 15,000 square yards. It is not built in horizontal courses, but a pyramidical nucleus of rubble is enclosed by a series of inclined walls, about nine feet thick, eleven in number on each side of the central mass, with an additional one on the north and south sides. These walls are composed of rudely squared stones, set to the angle of the face. Instead of corresponding exactly with the cardinal points, like all the other pyramids of Egypt, it deviates 4° 35' to the east of north: it has four entrances, and contains hieroglyphics in some of its chambers. Its principal internal peculiarity is, that immediately under the centre of the pyramid there is an excavation seventy-seven feet in depth, twenty-four by twenty-three in width, entirely in the rock. Its upper end was originally covered in by a ceiling of wood,—a material, the use of which is peculiar to this pyramid: this has perished, and its roof is now the rubble-work of the nucleus, which hangs together by the tenacity of the mortar. The bottom of this excavation is floored with blocks of granite, and beneath is an apartment ten feet long and five feet high, the opening into which had been carefully closed with a stopper of granite of four tons weight.

The purpose of its construction does not appear from its contents. Its position renders it wholly unfit for an oracle, the conjecture of Minutoli, who first in modern times opened this pyramid[1]; nor is it much more probable that it was intended as a treasury. As every thing else connected with these structures has a reference to interment, this chamber was probably designed for the deposit of a mummy, though no trace of one has been found. Passages leading to apartments open at different points from the deep excavation, the arrangement of which could not be intelligibly described. The doorway of one of them is bordered with hieroglyphics in relief, among which we find the standard, but not the name, of a king, unknown from any other source[2]. The sides of these apartments had been ornamented with rows of convex pieces of bluish green porcelain inscribed on the back with hieroglyphics. Other passages, leading from these apartments were found nearly filled with broken vases of marble and alabaster, fragments of sarcophagi, and stars, which had probably been the ornaments of ceilings. In a gallery connected with another entrance, and which appeared not to have been ransacked, like the rest of the pyramid, thirty mummies of an inferior description were found, not enclosed either in coffins or sarcophagi, but in wrappers of coarse linen with pitch and bitumen, and only three or four having any painted decorations. Even when Minutoli entered the pyramid in 1821, the only relique which he could find of mummies of an elaborate kind, was a scull strongly gilded and two gilded

[1] Reisen, 232, 403. Taf. 26-28.   [2] Perring in Vyse, 3, 41.

soles of the foot. It is probably of much later construction than the pyramids of Gizeh, and if destined for a royal sepulchre has been used for very miscellaneous interments[1]. Some of the adjacent tombs contain the shields of kings of the third dynasty, the *Tetkera* of Lepsius and Bunsen, and the *Raseser* whose name has been found at Abouseir. Another pyramid at Saccara, called by the Arabs the *Throne of Pharaoh*, is composed of very large stones, but is only two stories high and has obtained its name from its broad top and small elevation. It was not opened before the Prussian Expedition. This and three other of the pyramids of Saccara stand in a transverse valley which leads through the Libyan chain into the Fyoum. The pyramids of Dashour[2], the next in order to the south, and about three miles from Saccara, are not further from the probable limits of ancient Memphis in one direction than Gizeh in the other, and may therefore have belonged to it. They may also have been the necropolis of the town of Acanthus, the ruins of which are about three miles distant. The Acacia (Mimosa Nilotica), from which it derived its Greek name, still grows abundantly in this district. The pyramids are four in number, two of stone and two of brick—a material not elsewhere employed for this purpose, except at Illahoun and Howara in the Fyoum. To the northernmost of the brick pyramids a temple and portico have been prefixed, as to those of Meroe, inscribed with hieroglyphics of which fragments are found, though the buildings themselves can only be traced in their foundations. The bricks, which are crude, are about sixteen inches long, eight wide, and four and

[1] Perring, 3, 38. Bunsen, 2, 351.   [2] Perring, in Vyse, 3, 56.

a half to five and a half thick, some with and some without straw, and the whole mass has been laid with such skill, that in the course of ages not a single brick has slipped from its place. This is the more remarkable, as the pyramid is literally built on the sand. The sand of the Desert has been collected, laid perfectly level and confined by walls, and on this foundation the building has been raised. The exterior has been cased with blocks of the Mokattam stone, not inferior in size or finish to those employed in the Great Pyramid. On some of the blocks sculptures have been found representing funereal offerings, and from the style it is inferred that this pyramid belongs to a considerably later age than those of Gizeh; and the same inference may be more decisively drawn from the occurrence among the fragments of hieratic characters, which were not used for inscriptions till a comparatively late period. From the excellence of the brickwork it has been conjectured that this is the pyramid which Herodotus mentions (2, 136) as being built by Asychis, a successor of Mycerinus, with a boastful inscription, challenging for his work a comparison with the pyramids of stone. No name has been found in any of the inscriptions by which the builder or his age can be fixed, nor is it known whether any chambers exist in the interior. The northern stone pyramid of Dashour had a base of 720 feet, only forty less than the Great Pyramid, but its height was only 342. It had three subterranean chambers, one beyond another, exhibiting a peculiarity of construction. The stones which line the sides project before each other as they rise towards the ceiling, so that one of the chambers which at the floor is twenty-seven feet by twelve, is narrowed at the roof to one foot and two inches. The southern stone pyramid is remarkable for being built in two inclinations, consequently with an obtuse angle at about half the height, giving it the appearance of a truncated pyramid supporting a pointed one. A subterranean chamber eighty feet in height is contracted in the manner just described from twenty feet by sixteen at the bottom, to about a foot at top. Some hieroglyphics have been found traced on the side of the northern entrance, but their meaning is doubtful, and they throw no light on the original construction.

The pyramids of Lisht, about nine miles south of Dashour, with their tombs and mummy pits, represent probably the necropolis of the town of Peme, which stood in this part of Egypt, and of which the name is preserved in Bemha. They are in a state of ruin, so as scarcely to have kept the pyramidal form. At Meydoom[1], twelve miles south of Lisht, is a pyramid resembling in external form the Great Pyramid of Saccara, but consisting only of three stages. Its internal structure is unknown. From hence the range of the Libyan hills trends away to the entrance of the Fyoum. The pyramid of Illahoun stands just where the narrow valley begins by which the Bahr Jusuf passes into the Fyoum, and on the northern side of it. In its present state it is 130 feet in height, about forty feet being a nucleus of native rock. The interior, which is of brick, is strengthened by diagonal walls of stone, and it has been cased on the outside with stone. Nothing has been found in it, by which any light can be thrown on the circumstances of its erection,

[1] Perring, 3, 78, 81.

The pyramids of Howara and Biahmu have been mentioned in the account of the Fyoum.

No reasonable doubt can any longer exist respecting the destination of these groups of pyramids. Not only is it evident that they have been places of interment, the only rational purpose that was ever assigned to them, but where any inscriptions have been found, they concur with tradition in showing them to have been the sepulchres of kings. Further, these inscriptions belong to the earliest dynasties of Egypt, to the kings whom Manetho places before the invasion of the Shepherds, and of whom, besides the founders of Memphis, five dynasties are expressly called Memphite. Around the larger structures which received the bodies of the kings are grouped smaller pyramids in which queens were deposited, and the chief officers of state and religion were buried in excavations, near the remains of their masters. The animals whom the Egyptians most reverenced had also a place assigned them near the highest personages of the land, as we find that at the Labyrinth the bodies of the kings and the sacred crocodiles rested together in the subterraneous chambers[1].

This mode of interment was confined, with trifling exceptions, to the vicinity of Memphis and the Fyoum. There is a pyramid of stone at El Koofa, between Esneh and Edfu in Upper Egypt, and some of brick among the sepulchres in the western hills at Thebes; they were also the ordinary mode of interment in Meroe, but none of the monuments of that country belong to the Pharaonic times.

[1] Herod. 2, 148.

CHAPTER VII.

THEBES.

THE Nile, which just before has flowed in an unbroken stream more majestic[1] than in any other part of Egypt, divides itself as it passes Thebes into several channels separated by islands. They contain no ancient buildings, nor does the Nile leave on them any fertilizing deposit; but they probably existed in the times of the splendour of the city and facilitated communication between the opposite banks. Both the Libyan chain, which is here the more abrupt, and the Arabian recede; the plain of Thebes lies between them, above five miles in length and three in breadth, the widest expansion of fertile land in Upper Egypt and the fittest site for a great capital[2]. The Libyan hills return towards the river at the northern end, and at Qoorneh are almost close to it. The inundation spreads far over the plain on both sides, but especially on the west, and for many weeks insulates the colossal statues of Amenophis. Its depositions have permanently raised the soil, so that the base of every monument within its reach is buried in an alluvial deposit.

---

[1] Descr. de l'Egypte Antiq. 2, 2.
[2] The name *Thebes* is said to be derived from the Coptic *Tape*. Lepsius, Lettre à Rosellini, p. 33. Wilkinson, Mod. Eg. and Thebes, 2, 136. The resemblance to the Bœotian city is probably accidental, Θῆβη being a purely Greek word signifying *a hill*, an etymology well-suited to the locality of the original Thebes, the Cadmea. Varro R. Rust. 3, 1. "Lingua prisca et in Græcia Æoles Bœotii sine afflatu vocant *Tebas*, et in Sablnis, quo e Græcia venerunt Pelasgi, etiam nunc ita dicunt."

An excavation made at the foot of one of the colossal sphinxes at Karnak, where there was no building, and consequently no accumulation of fallen materials, shows a deposit from the Nile of eighteen feet[1]; at this depth is found the layer of rubbish which serves universally as a foundation for the ancient buildings in Thebes, and elsewhere near the banks of the river[2]. Beneath this again lies an alluvial deposit of unknown depth. The rate of deposition varies, diminishing as the stream descends from the cataracts to the sea; at Thebes it can be fixed with tolerable approximation. There is an inscription of the age of the emperor Antoninus[3], on the pedestal of the statue of the vocal Memnon, and the soil has risen seven feet[4] since it was written, *i. e.* in about 1700 years. Assuming the secular increase of five inches to be uniform, and there is no known reason for its being otherwise, we should be carried back to about 2250 years before Christ for the time when the substructions were laid, which must have been the first step towards the building of Thebes. The time of the erection of the obelisk of Luxor was fixed by the calculations of the French Commission, on the same grounds, to the beginning of the 14th century B.C., a date which corresponds very well with the age of Rameses II. whose name the central line bears. How long the valley of the Nile had been peopled before the foundation of the earliest buildings of Thebes is entirely uncertain, and even the inferences which have been drawn from the accumu-

---

[1] Ritter, Africa, p. 843, quoting Girard.
[2] Descr. 2, p. 171, note 2.
[3] Descr. de l'Eg. Ant. 2, 213, 14.
[4] Wilkinson, Manners and Customs, 1, 9.

lation of the soil cannot be received with confidence, without more accurate and continued investigations.

The existing monuments of Thebes are partly on the eastern, partly on the western side of the river; as no continuous wall can be traced on either side, its extent cannot be exactly ascertained. The French Commission estimated its circuit at about eight miles[1], including the breadth of the river. Sir Gardner Wilkinson makes the length five miles and a quarter, the breadth three[2]. Memphis was nearly of the same size as Thebes according to Diodorus[3]. The principal traces of habitations are on the eastern bank, which was peculiarly the city of the ram-headed god Ammon or Kneph, whom the Greeks called Jupiter. Hence the names of No Ammon given to it by the Hebrews, and Diospolis by the Greeks. The western bank was probably less populous, though the remains of temples and palaces show that it was not merely the cemetery of the metropolis. In the Ptolemaic times it bore the name of Memnoneia, and then appears to have been less esteemed as a residence than Diospolis[4], and occupied by those whose trades were offensive to the rest of the community.

Beginning our survey on the western side, where the hills approach the Nile at Qoorneh, the northern limit of the plain, we find, at the distance of about three-quarters of a mile from the river, raised on an artificial elevation, the remains of an edifice

---

[1] More than 14,000 and less than 15,000 metres. Descr. 3, 234.
[2] Mod. Eg. and Thebes, 2, 165, note.
[3] 1, 45. The circumference of Memphis exceeded by ten stadia that of Thebes (ib. 52).
[4] Peyron, Papyri Græci, 2, 41.

built by Setei-Menephthah[1] and Rameses II., to which Champollion has given the name of *Menephtheion*[2]. It was approached by a dromos of 128 feet in length and two pylons, and appears to have comprised both a temple and a palace. The pillars belonged to the oldest style of Egyptian architecture, with the exception of the protodoric of Benihassan. Its dimensions are small compared with other Theban edifices, but the basreliefs, both of Setei-Menephthah who founded, and Rameses who completed it, are remarkable for their fineness.

Following the edge of the cultivated land, in which many fragments are buried by the deposit of the inundation, we reach, at the distance of about a mile, another palace, the most remarkable of all on the western bank, the Memnonium of Strabo, the tomb of Osymandyas of Diodorus, named by Champollion the *Rameseion*, from the evidence which its own sculptures furnish. It is one of the most extensive as well as the most beautiful of the Theban monuments, and its remains are still so considerable, that we can ascertain the general distribution of its parts. It stands on the first rise of the hills from the plain, and flights of steps from one court to another are adapted to the different levels of the ground. Two pyramidal towers form the entrance, beyond which is an hypæthral court of the breadth of eighteen and length of 140 feet, surrounded by a double colonnade. On the left

---

[1] Champollion, Lettres, 380. Wilkinson, Modern Egypt and Thebes, 2, 138. Descr. de l'Eg. 2, 354.

[2] Wilkinson says, begun by Osi- rei. This difference is owing to Champollion's considering the epithet " Men-Pthah," " established by Pthah," as the name, and a different reading of the first character.

of the steps leading to the second court is still seen the pedestal of the enormous granite statue of Rameses, the largest according to Diodorus of all that existed in Egypt. The court around is filled with its fragments; the foot, of which parts still remain, must have been eleven feet long and four feet ten inches broad; the breadth across the shoulders twenty-two feet four inches; the height has been calculated at fifty-four feet, and the weight at $887\frac{1}{4}$ tons[1]. The labour and skill necessary for extracting such a mass from the quarry, polishing it to the most perfect smoothness, and transporting it from Syene, fill us with astonishment; we might have supposed that refined mechanical science was required for its erection, had not its overthrow, which was certainly the work of barbarians, been a task of nearly equal difficulty. The interior face of the wall of the pylon represents the wars of Rameses III.; other sculptures of the same events are found on the walls of the second court, which is of rather smaller dimensions than the first. In one of them he is seen, making war against a city surrounded by a river; and this circumstance, mentioned by Diodorus[2], serves to identify these remains with his monument of Osymandyas. The Osiride pillars of the second court are no doubt the "monolithal figures, sixteen cubits in height, supplying the place of columns," of which

---

[1] Wilk. Mod. Eg. and Thebes, 2, 144. Descr. de l'Eg. 2, 243. It is described by Diodorus, 1, 47. The decisive correction of Salmasius (see Wesseling), τεμνομένους for Μέμνονος, has been overlooked by succeeding writers, who still speak of "Memnon of Syene" as the artist.

[2] 1, 48. This identification has been questioned by the late eminent French philologer and antiquary Letronne; but as it appears to me, on insufficient grounds.

the same author speaks[1]. At the foot of the steps which led from this court to the hall beyond it were two sitting statues of the king. The head of one of these, of red granite, known by the name of the *young* Memnon, was removed with great labour and ingenuity by Belzoni[2], and is now a principal ornament of the British Museum[3], and one of the most perfect specimens of genuine Egyptian art. The height of the whole statue, which was entire in Norden's time, was rather more than twenty-two feet[4]. Beyond this are the remains of a hall 133 feet broad by 100 long, supported by forty-eight columns, twelve of which are thirty-two feet and a half in height and twenty-one feet three inches in circumference. The dedication of this hall, according to Champollion, declares that it was used for public assemblies, or panegyries. On different parts of the columns and the walls are represented acts of homage by the king to the principal deities of the Theban Pantheon, and the gracious promises which they make him in return. In another sculpture, the two chief divinities of Egypt invest him with the emblems of military and civil dominion, the scimitar, the scourge and the *pedum*. Beneath, the twenty-three sons of Rameses appear in procession, bearing the emblems of their respective high offices in the state, their names being inscribed above them. Nine smaller apartments, two of them still preserved and supported by columns, lay behind

---

[1] 1, 47.
[2] Belzoni, Researches, &c. 1, 63, 68, 205.
[3] Gallery of Antiquities, by Birch and Bonomi, p. 104.
[4] Descr. de l'Eg. Antiq. 2, 253.

the hall. On the jambs of the first of the smaller rooms are sculptured Thoth, the inventor of letters, and the goddess Saf, his companion[1], with the title of "Lady of Letters" and "President of the Hall of Books[2]," accompanied, the former with an emblem of the sense of sight, the latter of hearing. There can be little doubt that this was the Sacred Library of which Diodorus speaks, inscribed "Dispensary of the Mind[3]." It had an astronomical ceiling, in which the twelve Egyptian months are represented, with an inscription from which important inferences have been drawn respecting the chronology of Rameses III.'s reign. On the walls is a procession of priests, carrying the sacred arks; and in the next apartment, the last that now remains, the king makes offerings to various divinities. The circle of 365 cubits, each answering to a day of the year, with the rising and setting of the stars and the indications which they afforded, had been carried off by the Persians, and could only be described from rumour by Diodorus, or Hecatæus of Abdera whom he followed. It can hardly have found a place within the present building, in which there is no trace of the name of Osymandyas, and it may possibly be an exaggerated description of an astronomical ceiling. The Prussians have discovered not one, but a multitude of sepulchres, excavated in the rock under that part of the edifice which is nearest to the hills, and a great number of brick vaults, of the age of the Rameses, also destined to sepulchral uses[4]. If this were the residence of the

[1] Wilk. M. and C. 5, 51.
[2] Champollion, Lettres, p. 285, 9.
[3] Diod. 1, 49. Ψυχῆς ἰατρεῖον.
[4] Letter of Lepsius to Letronne, Rev. Arch. Jan. 1845.

king, he must have contented himself with apartments of very moderate number and dimension for his private use, those of greater size and splendour being evidently designed for public solemnities. The whole area was enclosed by a brick wall, composed of double arches, within which, besides fragments of other temples, there are ranges of low vaults. To the north-west of these remains, at El-Assaseef, almost enclosed among the Libyan hills, stands a very ancient temple, founded by a sovereign, whose singular inscriptions, exhibiting a mixture of masculine and feminine forms, leave it doubtful whether they proceeded from a queen exercising kingly prerogatives, or a king consort speaking in the name of his wife. They are preceded by a dromos of not less than 1600 feet in length, and in which more than 200 sphinxes formerly stood. Not much remains, but some polygonal columns are still seen, according in their archaic form with the high antiquity of the inscriptions, which belong to the early part of the eighteenth dynasty[2]. The whole neighbourhood is filled with tombs, some excavated, some of brick, and the north-western extremity of the building approaches so nearly to the Valley of the Royal Sepulchres, that some subterraneous communication has been surmised to exist between them.

Returning to the edge of the plain, we find, at about the distance of one-third of a mile to the south, the ruins of a palace or temple which has been called the *Amenophion*, as having been built by Amunoph

---

[1] Descr. de l'Eg. Ant. 2, 268. 2, 195. Descr. de l'Eg. Ant. 2.
[2] Champ. Lettres, p. 292 foll. 341.
Wilkinson, Mod. Eg. and Thebes.

III., the Memnon of the Greeks. It was dedicated to Sokaris-Osiris[1], whose name appears on the fragments still existing, along with that of Amun-re. The ground on which it stood is called the *Kom-el-Hettan*, or Mountain of Sandstone, from the accumulation of rubbish which its fall has produced. In the direction of the river and separated from the ruins by a space of 1200 feet, are the two colossal statues, called by the natives *Tama* and *Chama*[2], of which the most northern is the vocal Memnon. They tower above the plain, apparently unconnected with any building. But such a state of insulation would not agree with the practice of the Egyptians, and it appears from inspection that they are exactly in the line of the front of the Amenophion; the fragments of two statues of gritstone and another colossus of crystalline limestone are found in the intermediate space[3]. Hence it is probable that the vocal Memnon and its companion formed the commencement of a dromos, extending to the palace of the king whose name they bear.

These statues, including the pedestal, are sixty feet in height; the pedestal is thirteen feet, but more than half of it is buried in the alluvial soil. The material is a coarse hard breccia, in which agatized pebbles or chalcedonies are intermixed, found above the limestone in the Mokattam hills at Gebel-Ah-

---

[1] Rosellini, Mon. Stor. III. 1, 222. Pliny, N.H. 36, 11, represents the vocal Memnon as placed in the temple of Serapis. He was not one of the old Egyptian gods, but he corresponded nearly in his attributes with Sokaris.

[2] They are also called by the Arabs *Selamat*, "the greeting," as if in allusion to the tale of Memnon's saluting Aurora.

[3] Wilkinson, M. Eg. and Thebes, 2, p. 163. See also his great Map of Thebes.

mar[1]. The southern is formed of one entire block; but the northern had been already broken in the time of Strabo[2], either by an earthquake in the year 27 B.C. or by the Persians[3], and in this state it remained till after the age of Domitian, when Juvenal refers to its mutilated state[4]. It was subsequently repaired, probably in the age of Severus, by five separate pieces of sandstone; but there is no inscription to record by whom the reparation was made. The lower part of the body, the arms which are resting on the knees, and the legs and feet, are of the original material. A line of hieroglyphics at the back contains the name of the king Amunoph; on the right side, attached to the throne on which he sits, stands his mother, *Mautemva*; on the left, his wife, *Taia*; and the traces of a smaller figure of the queen are also seen between his feet. The thrones are ornamented with figures of the god Nilus, who is binding up the stalks of water-plants. Though the material, from its irregular structure, was even more difficult to work than granite, it is evident from the remains that it had a most perfect polish.

That the northern statue was the vocal Memnon is attested by a multitude of inscriptions on the legs, some in the Greek, some in the Latin language. They are chiefly of the time of Adrian, who with his empress Sabina visited the statue;

---

[1] Russegger, Reisen, 2, 1, p. 140. Trans. Roy. Soc. Lit. 4to. 2, 456.
[2] Lib. 17, p. 816.
[3] Pausan. Att. 1, p. 101. An inscription on the left leg asserts the mutilation by Cambyses.
[4] Dimidio magicæ resonant ubi Memnone chordæ,
Atque vetus Thebe centum jacet obruta portis.
Sat. 15, 5.

some few of that of Nero, Vespasian and Domitian; one on the pedestal, of the thirteenth consulship of Antoninus[1]. The sound was commonly heard at the first hour of the day, sometimes a little later; a few, among whom were Vibius Maximus and two other præfects of Egypt, were honoured with its repetition[2]; while others came three times before their curiosity was gratified. The Sophist Callistratus adds a circumstance, no doubt of his own invention, that at sunset the statue uttered a mournful sound, as a farewell to the light[3]. How the effect was produced we can only conjecture. It resembled, according to Pausanias, the breaking of an overstretched musical string; according to Strabo, the noise produced by a slight blow[4]; an inscription quoted by Sir G. Wilkinson assimilates it to the sound of brass. This was confirmed by a curious experiment[5]. He ascended the statue and struck with a small hammer a sonorous block which lies in its lap, and inquiring of the Arabs who stood below what they heard, they replied, "You are striking brass." The French Commission, having observed that about the hour of sunrise sounds issued from the ruins of Thebes, conjectured that they might be produced by the sudden change of temperature in the stone; but the fact must be better ascertained before an explanation can be built upon it. If fraud were practised, it belonged to the times when the Egyptian

---

[1] The fullest collection of the inscriptions has been made by Letronne, La Statue vocale de Memnon. Paris, 1833.

[2] Desc. de l'Eg. 2, 215, 218, 221, 227.

[3] Statuæ ap. Philostr. Ed. Lips. 1709, p. 891.

[4] Ψόφος ὡς ἂν πληγῆς οὐ μεγάλης ἀποτελεῖται. Strabo, u. s.

[5] Trans. Roy. Soc. Lit. 4to. 2, 447.

character had been debased by conquest and oppression, and the diffusion of its corrupt superstition through the Roman empire had degraded its ministers into jugglers. There is no proof that the statue was supposed to utter any sounds, even in the Ptolemaic times[1]. The name of Memnon might be affixed to it from its dark colour—from the tradition of Ethiopian conquest—an historical fact attested by the names of Sabaco and Tirhakah inscribed at Thebes—or from the title Meiamoun, borne by several sovereigns of the same dynasty.

Still keeping to the south-west, at the distance of about one-third of a mile from Kom-el-Hettau, the traveller reaches the high mound of ruins on which stands the village of Medinet Aboo, the site of the largest of the western temples of Thebes. There remain two distinct masses of building. That which is furthest from the Libyan hills is a temple of small dimensions, consisting of a sanctuary surrounded with galleries and eight apartments. It was begun by Thothmes I. and carried on by several of his successors of the same name. In front of this building, towards the river, are additions of the most various ages; the enclosure and the propylæa bear the name of Antoninus Pius; a lofty pylon beyond it exhibits the offerings of Ptolemy Soter II[2]. Nectanebus, the last king of the last

---

[1] Eusebius (Χρον. Λόγ. πρ. p. 16. ed. Scal.) says, "Amenophis, who is thought to be Memnon and the speaking stone." But it is evident that he or Africanus mixes his own remarks with what he found in Manetho, inserting the ministry of Joseph, the Exodus, and the capture of Jerusalem by the Assyrians. Syncellus, on the authority of Polyænus, says that Cambyses broke it, thinking there was magic (γοητεία) in it, which seems to imply that even then the statue was vocal. But this is not confirmed by any other author. Sync. Chronogr. p. 151.

[2] Champ. Lettres, 322.

independent dynasty of Egypt, appears on the bas-reliefs of a small chapel, nearly leveled; and the name of Tirhakah, though chiseled out when the Saitic dynasty was established, after the expulsion of the Ethiopian, may still be traced on an elder building which adjoins it. The name of *Thothmeseion* has been given to this edifice, in honour of its founder. Rameses (III.) IV. united it, by a pylon and dromos, to the far more splendid palace which he erected, nearer to the foot of the hills, not in the same line, but a little to the south, and which Champollion calls the Southern Rameseion. The part which is nearest to the Thothmeseion has been called by the French Commission, the Pavilion[1]. It is of a character different from any of the other remains of Egyptian architecture[2], is of two stories, with windows more numerous and larger than are commonly seen in other monuments; and the walls of the apartments are decorated with representations of the private life of the king in his harem and the amusements of his hours of relaxation. The exterior walls exhibit Rameses in the attitude of a conqueror, smiting the chiefs of the foreign nations, leading them into the presence of the god Amunre, or receiving from him a commission to go and make war upon them. The dromos which succeeds to the pavilion is 265 feet in length; the pylon at the end is covered with sculptures relating to the coronation of Rameses and his victories over the nations of the South. Beyond is a hypæthral court, 135 feet long by

[1] Antiquités, 2, 58.
[2] Henry, Eg. Pharaon. 2, 227. It is composed of three pieces, of which the axis is the same, but the size regularly diminishes; so that the section resembles that of an eye-glass with its three tubes drawn out.

110 feet broad, adorned with Osiride pillars twenty-three feet in height; both sides of the towers of the pylon exhibit the wars of Rameses with an Asiatic nation. Through a second pylon a second court is entered, of rather inferior dimensions, but remarkable for the massive proportions of its columns, which have only three diameters, their height being twenty-four feet and their circumference nearly twenty-three. The spaces of intercolumniation are unequal, and the cornice, which is double the architrave, is heavy. All beyond this hall is a mass of ruin. The walls, internal and external, are covered with sculpture. The architrave represents the dedication of the palace; the north-east wall, the coronation of the king and religious processions. The triumphs of the king are continued; heaps of the hands and other members of his conquered enemies are thrown down before him, and their number counted and inscribed. In one of the battle-pieces a lion is represented as running by the side of the king. This circumstance, and one or two others mentioned by Diodorus as to be seen in the tomb of Osymandyas, do not at present appear in the sculptures of the building which we have identified with it; his authorities therefore had probably blended in one description their recollections of two distinct buildings. The western wall is covered with a record of the offerings made by Rameses in the different months of the year[1].

To the south-west of this temple is a low plain, whose limits are marked by high mounds of sand and alluvial soil. It is 7300 feet in length and 3000

[1] Champollion, Lettres, 361.

in breadth, consequently exceeding sevenfold the area of the Champ de Mars at Paris[1]. The French Commission have described it under the name of a hippodrome; Champollion considers it as a fortification; Minutoli and Wilkinson as a receptacle of water, and the latter specifically as the lake on which was performed the ceremony of conveying the embalmed body in a boat, so frequently represented in the funeral solemnities of the tombs. For this last purpose it appears far too large.

The whole sweep of the Libyan hills from Qoorneh to Medinet Aboo is full of sepulchres[2], chiefly excavations in the rock, which is calcareous, of a fine grain and moderate hardness. They appear to have been made expressly for sepulchral purposes, and not to be old quarries, converted into sepulchres[3]. In the quarries of Silsileh and Mokattam no graves have ever been found. This was the Necropolis of the whole city, no tombs existing on the eastern side. For a space of five miles and to the height of from 300 to 400 feet, the face of the hills is pierced with rectangular openings, from which passages lead into the heart of the rock, sometimes horizontally, sometimes with an inclination and interposed staircases and landings. These terminate in chambers, succeeded by other passages and other chambers; or are interrupted by pits, from twenty to forty-five feet deep, communicating by apertures in their bottom or sides with chambers and pits beyond. Their length varies; the whole extent of the tomb of Petamunop is 320 feet in a

---

[1] Description de l'Egypte Ant. 2, 138.
[2] Descr. de l'Eg. Ant. 3, 8.
[3] Rosellini, Mon. Civ. 1, 119.

straight line, and 862, reckoning in the cross-passages and returns; its area is 22,217 square feet, or an acre and a quarter of ground[1]. The most magnificent have an open vestibule before the entrance, and the entrance itself is adorned with sculpture; others open at once from the face of the hill. Where the loose nature of the soil threatened a fall, they are arched with crude brick. The sides of the passages and chambers are often covered with sculptures and paintings, to receive which they have been elaborately prepared. As pebbles and fossils sometimes occur, they have been taken out with the greatest care and the space filled up with another stone or cement. In general the sculpture does not project from the surface of the wall; in a few instances figures have been carved in high relief, but they are usually in niches towards the end of the galleries. Commonly the walls are smooth, without any attempt to imitate by carving the members of architecture. They were covered with a fine stucco, on which the designer drew his figures in red, and the painter laid on his colours like an illuminator. They are usually divided into rectangular spaces, ornamented with chequers, arabesques and various graceful patterns, in which far more freedom is shown than in the religious buildings[2]. The subjects are infinitely varied; scenes of every-day life are perhaps the most numerous in the tombs of private individuals; but acts of adoration to the gods, funeral ceremonies, historical events, are all delineated, besides a profusion of mystical groups, whose meaning cannot be expounded till their

[1] Wilkinson, Mod. Eg. 2, 220.   [2] Descr. de l'Eg. Ant. 3, 40.

legends have been more fully interpreted. The minuteness and delicacy of the hieroglyphic characters is astonishing; it has been calculated that there are 1200 on a space of between forty and fifty feet[1].

The sepulchres at Qoorneh being excavated in a looser stratum than those which are more remote and higher up, have fallen into great decay; but as they were generally unsculptured, they probably were not occupied by the wealthier classes[2]. The hills above the Menephtheion and northern Rameseion abound with the sepulchres of priests and individuals of the higher ranks, who selected the firm strata which they offer, and adorned the walls with a variety of paintings and sculptures which make them inferior only to the tombs of the kings. This distinction generally prevails, that the tombs of the higher classes occur in the most solid part of the rock, but we can trace no strict separation of castes; nor any gradual extension in chronological order, the two extremities of the hills, at Qoorneh and beyond Medinet Aboo, having been occupied apparently as early as the central portion. Besides the excavated sepulchres, many are found constructed of brick, and some pyramids of the same material. The mummies are piled on each other in the pits, or laid down in rows, but never erect against the walls. The tombs of the lower orders contain mummies of bulls, cows, rams, jackals, cats, crocodiles, fishes, ibises, and other birds held sacred by the Egyptians[3], and a small valley in the

[1] Descr. Ant. 3, 43.
[2] Belzoni, 1, 350, 261.
[3] Belzoni, 1, 261.

south-west has received the name of The Apes' Burial-place, from the multitude of embalmed *cynocephali* which have been found there.

The Royal Sepulchres are chiefly in a valley which bears the Arabic name of Bab-el-Melook, 'Gate of the Kings[1].' It is not far from the Thothmeseion already described, but is usually approached by a circuitous and more level route from Qoorneh, from which it is distant about two miles. Before reaching it, another valley branches off at a short distance to the right, called the Western Valley, which contains, besides the tomb of Amunoph III. near the entrance, those of several kings of a foreign dynasty; and another, the remotest, of a predecessor of Rameses II., whose name is uncertain[2]. Immense heaps of rubbish have accumulated, and make research difficult; it is here perhaps that we have to look for the tombs of Amunoph I. and II., and the four Thothmes, the predecessors of Amunoph III. in the eighteenth dynasty.

The Bab-el-Melook is well adapted by solitude and seclusion to be the burial-place of kings. It is enclosed by perpendicular scarps of limestone rock, equally devoid of the traces of animal and vegetable life, and appears originally to have been a basin among the hills, without any outlet. A narrow passage has been cut through the rock at the lower end, whence the name of *gate* has been derived. It divides itself into branches nearly at right angles to the principal valley, and twenty tombs at least

---

[1] *Bab* in Coptic signifies *antrum, spelunca.* See Peyron *s. voc.*
[2] Champollion (Lettres, 247) calls him *Skai*; Wilkinson, *Oeesa* or *Eesa.*

have been ascertained to exist in it. The ancients, who describe these excavations under the name of *Syringes* or tunnels, reckon them originally at forty-seven[1]; seventeen were known in the days of the first Ptolemy, and of these fourteen have been identified by the inscriptions, in which Greeks and Romans have recorded their visits; Strabo speaks of forty; twenty-one have been numbered by Sir Gardner Wilkinson. They are all of monarchs of the eighteenth, nineteenth and twentieth dynasties, which were Theban. No order is observed in their distribution through the valley; each monarch appears to have selected the spot which pleased him, and prepared his own tomb, as at Memphis he raised his own pyramid. It has been observed that the most spacious and highly-finished are those of monarchs who enjoyed a long reign and could devote many years to the excavation and ornament of their future resting-place; and after all death generally overtook them before their work was finished; for only those of Amunoph III., Rameses Meiamun and Rameses III. are complete in all their parts.

The sepulchre of Rameses I.[2] (Ramesu) consists of two long corridors without sculpture, and a chamber containing a sarcophagus. The entrance is nearly choked with ruins. That of Setei-Menephtah, the builder of the Menephtheion of Qoorneh, discovered by Belzoni, is adjacent to it, and is the most splendid of them all, being 320 feet in length—not all in the

---

[1] Diod. 1, 46. Strabo, lib. 17, p. 816. Belzoni himself discovered six.

[2] Marked 16 in Wilkinson's Survey.

same line or on the same level, but descending by steps and inclined passages to 180 feet. At the distance of about 100 feet from the entrance, Belzoni's further progress appeared to be stopped by a pit 30 feet deep and 14 feet by 12 wide. A small aperture, visible on the opposite side, suggested the idea that there might be something beyond, and on trial an entrance was obtained into a corridor succeeded by other stairs and passages, and ending in a coved saloon 37 feet by 27, filled with paintings, in the centre of which stood the beautiful sarcophagus of alabaster which is now in the museum of Sir J. Soane. It was entire, but Belzoni was not the first who had made a forcible entry into the tomb; the mummy was gone, and the cover of the sarcophagus broken to pieces. Immediately under the place on which it stood was an inclined passage, with a staircase, the entrance concealed by the pavement, extending 300 feet further through the rock. One of the apartments contains an astronomical ceiling in which the firmament is a brilliant azure and the stars white[1]. All the walls of the passages and chambers, as far as the saloon of the sarcophagus, are so covered with figures and hieroglyphics, that hardly a foot square is left vacant. Their subjects are very various, but none relating to the occupations of common life; the most remarkable is the procession of the four nations, who were supposed to be prisoners made by Necho in his warlike expeditions, when the sarcophagus was referred to his son Psammuthis or Psammis, but more

[1] Belzoni, Researches, New Plates, III.

probably explained by Champollion of the different nations of the earth.

The tomb which the inscriptions of the Roman times call that of Memnon, is really that of Rameses (V.) Meiamun[1], or his successor, as Champollion asserts. Everything, according to this author, refers to the soul of the defunct king, which being mystically identified with the Sun, is represented as passing successively through the twelve hours of the day and of the night. The same idea is astronomically exhibited on one of the ceilings. A female figure, bent so that the body, legs and arms occupy three sides, is a symbol of the heavens; twelve divisions in the upper and as many in the lower part represent the day and night. During the day the Sun is accompanied by various divinities, changing in each horary division; at night his bark is towed by them. Adjoining to these are tables of the influence of the stars on different parts of the body, during each of the twenty-four hours[2]. The hall which precedes that in which the sarcophagus is found, is cousecrated to the four genii of *Amenthe*, the Egyptian Hades. In the most complete tombs it exhibits the appearance of the king before the forty-two judges, or assessors of Osiris. In that of Rameses V. there are forty-two columns of hieroglyphics, containing the laudatory sentences which the judges pronounce[3], with a picture of the constellations and their influences on different parts of the human body for every day of the year. The tomb called the Harpers'[4], as being that whence Bruce derived

---

[1] No. 9 in Wilkinson's Survey.
[2] Champ. Lettres, 239.
[3] Champ. Lettres, 242.
[4] No. 11 in Wilkinson's Survey.

the picture of two harpers playing[1], belongs to Rameses IV., and is remarkable for the number of scenes and objects of domestic life painted on the walls. In the small apartments of this tomb are pits, in which the chief officers of the king may have been deposited, the subjects on the walls referring to their several functions, as cook, armour-bearer, superintendent of the royal boats, &c.[2]

A separate place of interment was allotted to the queens. It lies about 3000 feet to the north-west of the temple of Medinet Aboo. They are the consorts of the kings who were buried in the Bab-el-Melook; twenty-four have been counted, and about twelve are known to have been those of queens, but the sculptures are much destroyed, with the exception of that of Taia, queen of Amunoph III. They are supposed to be what Diodorus calls the Tombs of the *Pallaces,* or concubines of the Theban Jupiter, their position corresponding pretty nearly with the distance of ten stadia[3] from the tomb of Osymandyas. The confusion of characters seems strange, but may be accounted for from a circumstance mentioned by Champollion[4], that they all bear the title of *Wife of Amun.*

We return to the eastern bank of the river, the true Diospolis, where the two villages of Luxor (El-Uksor) and Karnak contain monuments of Egyptian grandeur, even more remarkable than those which we have already described. The ruins of Luxor stand close to the river; a stone jetty, prolonged

---

[1] Travels, vol. 2, p. 29.
[2] Wilkinson, Mod. Egypt and Thebes, 2, 206. Rosellini, Mon. Stor. 4, 102.
[3] Diod. 1, 47.
[4] Lettres, p. 286. Lepsius, Einleitung, p. 307.

by an addition of brick[1], served at once as a landing-place and a protection against the encroachments of the current. The entrance to the ruins is at the point the most remote from the river, looking to the north-east, and the most conspicuous object on approaching was the pair of obelisks sixty and seventy feet in height, erected by Rameses II. One still remains; the other has been removed to France, and set up in the Place de la Concorde. The architect had endeavoured to hide their inequality by placing them on unequal bases, and advancing the smaller somewhat nearer to the eye. The hieroglyphic characters are wrought with the highest degree of perfection; their depth in many instances exceeds two inches, and the Arabs contrive to climb them by placing their feet in the excavated part. Behind these obelisks are two sitting monolithal statues of the same king, of the red granite of Syene; including their cubical bases, they were thirty-nine feet above the level of the ancient soil, but are now buried in deposits of earth and rubbish from the bust downwards. The pylon, fifty-one feet in height, and the pyramidal wings contain representations of the battles of Rameses in the fifth year of his reign, and therefore of the same campaign which is recorded on the walls of the temple at Aboosimbel[2]. The court to which this pylon gives entrance is 190 feet long and 170 broad, and surrounded by a peristyle of double columns. A pylon, built by Amunoph III., opposite to that of Rameses,

---

[1] According to Champollion, the original part is brick, joined with a cement of extraordinary hardness; the reparations, stone taken from buildings of no very high antiquity.

[2] Champollion, Lettres, 217.

opens upon a colonnade, which leads to a second court of somewhat smaller dimensions, terminating in a portico with a quadruple row of eight columns. Beyond this are a multitude of apartments; among them may be distinguished a sanctuary and a chamber, on the walls of which are represented the birth of Amunoph and his presentation to the tutelary god. Everything southward of the second pylon is the work of Amunoph, and this edifice might properly be called the *Amenophion* of Eastern Thebes[1].

Returning to the north-east entrance, we find an interval of about 6000 feet to the remains of Karnak. The space, right and left, appears to have been covered with buildings, and a dromos bordered with *andro-sphinxes*[2], to have connected the two quarters in which the sacred edifices were placed. If they extended through the whole space, they must have amounted to 600; but at present they remain only at the end nearest to Karnak, where the dromos divided, one part turning to the right, the other, with only a slight deviation, to the left. If we follow the former, we find, at the distance of about 600 feet, the commencement of another dromos of *crio-sphinxes*, the largest which exist among the ruins of Thebes. The head is that of a ram, the body of a lion; the fore-paws are protruded, the body rests upon the hind-paws; a drapery in numerous folds descends from the back of the head over the shoulders and the breast. There must have been between sixty and seventy in a double row, at the distance of eleven feet, between this point and the south-western entrance of the palace of Karnak.

[1] Champollion, Lettres, p. 208.   [2] See p. 137, note 2.

This stupendous mass of buildings stands within a circuit wall of brick, 1800 feet long and somewhat less broad. Its principal approach seems to have been by the dromos which we have just described. Five lofty pylones and four spacious courts intervene, between the end of the dromos and the main body of the building; the first gateway of the pylon is entirely of granite, beautifully wrought; on the outer side were two colossi of granite, on the inner two of crystalline limestone. For some reason not easily divined, the pylones have not been placed in the same line, which must have detracted from the effect which their number and size would otherwise have produced. From the last court the palace is entered nearly in the middle; the portions which lie on the right and left are of very different character, that to the right being occupied by a multitude of smaller apartments, while the left contains only two, the hypostyle hall and the grand court in front of it. These smaller apartments, however, were the nucleus of the whole pile, according to an analogy elsewhere observed in the great Egyptian buildings, which expanded themselves from a centre by subsequent additions, and were not planned from the first in their actual order and relation.

In the court first entered are two obelisks of Thothmes I., one erect and perfect, the other broken to pieces; in the next to the right, two formerly stood, and one still remains, ninety-two feet in height,—the loftiest known, except that of St. John Lateran at Rome. To this succeeds the sanctuary, approached by a granite gateway, and composed itself of the same material. Around it are a multitude of small apartments of doubtful use, and behind, some columns, which both by their polygonal form and the shield of Sesortasen I. mark this as the earliest portion of the building. The most important additions in this portion of the enclosure were made by Thothmes III. In one of the chambers built by him, he is represented sacrificing to his ancestors, the kings of Thebes. This document, called the Karnak Tablet, and hereafter to be more fully explained, is one of the most important records of Egyptian chronology[1].

If we return to the point at which we entered this pile of buildings, and take the opposite direction, we pass from the court in which stands the obelisk of Thothmes, by a gateway bearing sculptures of the victories of Rameses III., into the hypostyle hall, which next to the pyramids is the most impressive and wonderful of all the remains of ancient Egypt[2]. Its dimensions, 170 feet by 329, are such, that according to the observation of the French Commission, the Cathedral of Notre-Dame at Paris might stand within it and not touch the walls[3]. The columns of the central row, twelve in number, are sixty-six feet in height without the pedestal or abacus. They are composed of assizes, each three feet two inches in height, and are eleven feet in diameter, equaling therefore in their solidity the dimensions of the *hollow* columns of Trajan and the Place Vendôme.

---

[1] Hieroglyphics of the Egyptian Society, No. 96.

[2] "Aucun peuple ancien ni moderne n'a conçu l'art d'architecture sur une échelle aussi sublime, aussi grandiose, que le firent les vieux Egyptiens; et l'imagination qui en Europe s'élance bien au-dessus de nos portiques, s'arrête et tombe impuissante au pied des 140 colonnes, de la salle hypostyle de Karnak." Champollion, Lettres, p. 98.

[3] Descr. de l'Eg. Ant. 2, 436.

It would require six men with extended arms to embrace their circumference. On either side are seven rows, containing 122 columns, forty-one feet nine inches in height, and nine feet in diameter. Above the capitals is an abacus, four feet in height, on which the architraves of the ceiling rested; those of the central avenue were of course the widest, and as the space between the columns was seventeen feet, and the architrave extended from centre to centre, their width could never be less than twenty-eight feet. The shorter columns have a cornice above the architrave, to bring them somewhat nearer to an equality with those of the central row; but even this has not sufficed; and above the cornice a kind of *attic* has been constructed of upright stones, reaching to the same height as the architrave of the loftier pillars, and supporting the stones of the ceiling. Light and air were admitted into the hall through openings above the side rows, which thus answer to the clerestory of a Gothic middle aisle. The whole height from the floor to the ceiling is eighty feet.

The destination of this magnificent hall, built by Setei Menephtah, is uncertain; most probably it served for the celebration of the *panegyries* or public religious assemblies, which were periodically held in Egypt, or for the administration of justice. Champollion even thinks that the hieroglyphic character for panegyry is a section of one of these hypostyle halls or *manoskhs*[1]. Such a grove of columns, however impressive by their architectural effect, must have interfered greatly with the

[1] Lettres, 273.

purposes of sight and hearing; and of the apparent area, a very large proportion must have been occupied by the bases of the pillars. Though so much of the imposts has fallen, a great number of the columns are still left standing. But the water of the inundation penetrates by infiltration to their bases, and loosens the soil; they lose their perpendicular position, and one after another falls prostrate. The walls have been adorned with historical bas-reliefs both within and without, partly by Setei, the founder, partly by his son Rameses II. The latter added to the hypostyle hall a vast open court, on the northwest side and towards the river, 275 feet by 329, having a covered corridor on either side, and a double row of columns down the centre[1]. The passage from the hall into this court was by a lofty pylon and propyla, the lintels which covered the entrance between them being forty feet ten inches in length. But the symmetry of the court is greatly injured by a temple built by Rameses III., which interrupts the line of the southern colonnade, projects fifty-four feet into the area, and is continued for about double that length on the outside. The principal gateway towards the river is exactly opposite to that which communicates with the hypostyle hall; there are others on the eastern and western sides. On one of these, the nearest to the grand hall, are seen the names of the cities and nations conquered by Sheshonk in his expedition. An avenue of criosphinxes led up to the principal gateway, and two granite statues, probably of Rameses II., stood immediately before it.

[1] Wilkinson, Mod. Eg. and Thebes, 2, p. 247, and his Map of Thebes.

Besides the buildings we have now described, the wall of enclosure comprised others of inferior magnitude. The dromos which unites Luxor with Karnak divides itself into two branches, and in our survey we followed that which led to the south. The eastern branch, which is almost in a line with Luxor, led through a dromos of rams[1], majestically couched upon their pedestals. Judging from those which remain, there must have been a double row of fifty-eight in a space of about 500 feet. At the end of the dromos stands a gateway, the loftiest of all that remain in Egypt, sixty-four feet in height, not flanked as usual by pyramidal propyla, but standing alone, like the triumphal arches of the Romans. This deviation from the established practice of the Egyptians[2] might alone have excited a suspicion that it was the work of later times; the inscriptions prove that it was constructed by Ptolemy Euergetes I. It now stands completely insulated, but apparently in the line of the brick wall which enclosed the whole area. Another dromos behind the gateway conducts to a temple founded by Rameses IV. and continued by Rameses VIII. and others. There was within the enclosure a lake, and exterior to it, on the east, south and west, ruins of a number of temples, some of the Pharaonic, others of the Ptolemaic age. Remains of a Ptolemaic[3] temple are found at Medamoud to the north

---

[1] Descr. de l'Eg. 2, 509, not *criosphinxes*, as Sir G. Wilkinson says. The σφίγξ (σφίγγω, to grasp and pierce) must have the body and claws of a lion.

[2] There is a similar instance at Denderah; but Denderah is not of the age of the Pharaohs.

[3] Wilkinson, Mod. Eg. and Thebes, 2, 133, mentions some blocks of the age of Amunoph II. and Rameses II. found here, but they may have been transported.

of Karnak, where the Arabian chain, returning to the river, terminates the plain of Thebes on the eastern side; but it is not probable that it was ever included within the limits of the ancient city.

Besides the spaces which we have described as covered with ruins, many others bear evident marks of having been once occupied with buildings. They may be traced by the coarse grass called *halfeh*, the *Poa cynosuroides* of botanists, which flourishes in a soil composed of rubbish[1]. But nowhere has the antiquary been able to discover any remains of the hundred gates which Homer attributes to Thebes, through each of which issued two hundred men with horses and chariots[2]. That these are meant of the gates of a city, not of the pylones of the palaces and temples, nor of the royal stables[3], is evident; the exaggeration may be regarded as a proof how little the Greeks knew, in the Homeric age, of Egypt, and what scope was thus afforded to the imagination of the poet.

[1] Wilkinson, Mod. Eg. and Thebes, 2, 246.
[2] Il. *i.* 381. ......Θήβας
Αἰγυπτίας, ὅθι πλεῖστα δόμοις ἐν κτήματα κεῖται,
Αἵ θ' ἑκατόμπυλοί εἰσι, διηκόσιοι δ' ἀν' ἑκάστην
Ἀνέρες ἐξοιχνεῦσι σὺν ἵπποισιν καὶ ὄχεσφιν.

[3] Diod. 1, 45. Τοὺς ἱππῶνας ἑκατὸν γεγονέναι κατὰ τὴν παραποταμίαν τὴν ἀπὸ Μέμφεως ἄχρι Θηβῶν τῶν κατὰ Λιβύην, ἑκάστου δεχομένου ἀνὰ διακοσίους ἵππους, ὧν ἔτι νῦν τὰ θεμέλια δείκνυσθαι. It is hardly necessary to observe that no trace is to be found of the wonderful tunnel of which Pliny speaks, 36, 20. "Legitur et pensilis hortus; imo vero totum oppidum Ægyptiæ Thebæ, exercitus armatos subter educere solitis regibus, nullo oppidanorum sentiente.

CHAPTER VIII.

AMOUNT OF POPULATION.

IN a country which had been so accurately measured as Egypt in the time of Sesostris[1], we cannot doubt that exact returns of the population had been made. Amasis towards the end of the monarchy compelled every man to appear before a magistrate and declare his mode of life, and this if fully carried out must have afforded an estimate of the number of adult males. The results, however, have not been recorded in ancient authors, nor discovered on monuments. Herodotus gives no account of the population; Diodorus[2] says that in ancient times it had amounted to seven millions and was not less in his own. Agrippa, in the speech attributed to him by Josephus[3], estimates the inhabitants of Egypt at seven millions and a half, besides Alexandria which contained 300,000 more. As his object was to dissuade the Jews from entering into a contest with the Romans, who had so easily conquered Egypt, he would rather overrate than underrate its population. No satisfactory conclusion can be drawn from the statement of Herodotus, that in the time of Amasis there were 20,000 inhabited towns, or of Diodorus, who says that 18,000 were entered in the registers[4]. The numbers are startling from their

[1] Herod. 2, 109, 177.
[2] 1, 31.
[3] Jos. Bell. Jud. 2, 16.
[4] Her. 2, 177. Diod. u.s. Theo-critus (17, 85) increases the numbers of Herodotus by more than one-third, for the glory of Ptolemy Philadelphus.

magnitude, and we are not informed of the amount of population in each inhabited place. The estimates of modern writers, made before Egypt had been surveyed and measured, varied from the four millions of De Pauw to the twenty-seven millions of Goguet[1].

Jomard, availing himself of the great map prepared by the engineers attached to the French Expedition, has endeavoured to solve this problem on statistical principles[2]. He traced on this map the sites of the ancient cities of Egypt, which amount to 200 whose names are ascertained. To Thebes he allots 700,000 inhabitants; to Memphis and Heliopolis together 400,000; to forty-seven chief towns of nomes 470,000, and to 150 other towns 750,000. Following a proportion which has been observed to prevail in other countries, he assumes that the small towns of 1000 inhabitants were three times as numerous as the larger; the villages of 500, nine times as numerous as the small towns; the hamlets of 200, thirty times as numerous as the villages, and hence obtains a total of 5,420,000. By means of the same map he has estimated the extent of land capable of culture in ancient Egypt, and finds that the population of each square league was 2077 (not including in this average the dense population of the great cities), while that of France in 1818 was only 1082 in the same area[3].

Tacitus relates that when Germanicus visited Thebes he was shown the monuments of the reign of Rameses-Sesostris, and informed by the priests

---

[1] Origin of Laws, vol. 2, p. 12, Eng. Tr.
[2] Description de l'Egypte, Ant. Mem. vol. 9, 103 foll.
[3] Jomard, *u.s.* p. 199.

that Egypt had formerly contained 700,000 men of the military age[1]. We are not told what was the military age in this country; at Athens it extended from eighteen to sixty; at Rome from seventeen to sixty. We may assume it at eighteen to sixty in Egypt, with whose customs those of Athens had a close analogy. Now the analysis of the census of 1821 shows that in a population of 20,160 persons, the males from eighteen to sixty were 4644[2]. This is more than one-fifth, and estimated by these data the whole population of Egypt would be scarcely 3,500,000. If we assume eighteen to forty as the military age, we shall have a free population of 4,500,000, and slaves may have swelled the amount to more than five millions.

The great works undertaken by the Egyptian monarchs lead us to form an exaggerated conception of the population. They imply two things: a large amount of disposable labour, that is, of labour not essential to procuring the means of subsistence, and the power to compel the employment of it upon unproductive objects[3]. In no country of the ancient world was subsistence so easily obtained as in Egypt[4]; in none was less required for the mere support of life. According to Diodorus, twenty drachmæ sufficed for the annual maintenance of a child till he grew up[5]. The climate was salubrious,

---

[1] "Jussus è senioribus sacerdotum patrium sermonem interpretari, referebat, habitâsse quondam septingenta millia ætate militari." Ann. 2, 60. Comp. Strabo, 17, p. 816, who is evidently less accurate, as he speaks of obelisks *in* the Theban sepulchres.

[2] See Fynes Clinton, Fasti Hellenici, 2, 387; 3, 459. At Athens the period of *foreign* service began at twenty and ended at forty; at Rome foreign service ended at forty-six.

[3] Arist. Pol. 5, 9, 4.

[4] Her. 2, 14.

[5] Diod. 1, 80. I presume this to be the annual cost, though the words of Diodorus may seem to imply the *entire* cost. Ἀνυποδέ-των τῶν πλείστων καὶ γυμνῶν τρεφομένων διὰ τὴν εὐκρασίαν τῶν τό-

and the human species increased rapidly[1]; yet these alone would not have produced such a numerous population, but for the cheapness of food. Left to themselves, the people might have spent in inactivity the leisure which the facility of acquiring subsistence gave them; but the absolute power of the king and the priests enabled them to exact their labour for the execution of public works, designed for the honour of the sovereign or of religion. Another cause of the proneness to believe that the population of ancient Egypt exceeded anything that has been known in modern countries, is the opinion that large tracts formerly susceptible of cultivation have been covered by the Desert sand. It has been already observed that this opinion is incorrect, and that in fact, by the operations of the Nile, the extent of productive soil is constantly on the increase[2].

The population of modern Egypt was estimated two centuries ago at four millions, probably on no very accurate grounds. It was computed from measurement and taxation by Jomard at two millions and a half[3], during the French occupation of the country. Sir G. Wilkinson reduces its present amount to 1,800,000[4]; a sufficient proof, that under the government of Mahomed Ali, though order has been enforced and commerce increased, no real improvement has taken place in the general condition of the people.

πων τὴν πᾶσαν δαπάνην οἱ γονεῖς ἄχρις ἂν εἰς ἡλικίαν ἔλθῃ τὸ τέκνον οὐ πλείω ποιοῦσι δραχμῶν εἴκοσι.

[1] Aristotle, Hist. Anim. 7, 5, says that births of five children at once were common in Egypt, which Trogus increased to seven. Plin. 7, 3. Strabo, 16, 695. These statements may be received as evidence of the reputation for fecundity which the Egyptian women enjoyed.
[2] See p. 80 of this vol.
[3] Jomard, u.s. p. 139.
[4] Mod. Eg. and Thebes, 1, 256.

CHAPTER IX.

AGRICULTURE AND HORTICULTURE.

IF we may believe Diodorus (1, 43), the Egyptians originally lived only on such plants as the marshes produced, and especially on the *agrostis*; they next advanced to a fish diet, thence to the use of flesh-meat, and only after a long time began to use grain and fruits for food. This is evidently a speculation in the form of history, to which the gradual emersion of Egypt from the waters naturally gave rise. The oldest historical records agree with the monuments in exhibiting them as already an agricultural people.

The remark of Virgil[1], that Jupiter had made the art of cultivating the earth difficult, in order that the faculties of men might be sharpened, is certainly not applicable to Egypt. Its occupants found no forests to be felled or rocks to be cleared away, but a deep, light and fertile alluvial soil. If in the lower part of its course the Nile was bordered by marshes, there was an ample space in Middle and Upper Egypt, through which the fall of the river was sufficient to drain the waters of the inundation when it subsided, and leave a surface which the wind and sun prepared speedily for cultivation. From the account of Herodotus it would seem as if all labour of man had been unnecessary, beyond

---

[1] ....Pater ipse colendi
Haud facilem esse viam voluit, primusque per artem
Movit agros, curis acuens mortalia corda.—Georg. 1, 122.

casting the seed upon the earth, in the region below Memphis. "They obtain the produce of the soil, says he, more easily than any other Egyptians, or indeed any other men. They neither undergo the labour of opening furrows with the plough, nor breaking the clods with a hoe, nor any other of the operations which all others perform upon corn land; but when the river, having spontaneously covered the lands, has supplied them with moisture and retired again, then each man having sown his own field turns in swine upon it, and having trampled the seed in by means of the swine awaits the harvest, and having trodden out the corn by means of the swine carries it off[1]." In this, as in some other instances, the contrast which struck Herodotus between Egypt and all other countries, especially Greece, has led him to make his statement of the difference stronger and more absolute than the fact warrants. The hope of the husbandman depended primarily indeed on the season, which sometimes withheld the necessary amount of rain in Ethiopia, and sometimes poured it down in excess. But if the river rose to its standard height, the care of the cultivator was necessary to enable him to derive the greatest benefit from the inundation. He had to admit the rising water to the fields on which he meant to raise a crop, to exclude it from those in which crops were still growing, and to provide for its distribution by a system of minutely ramified canals. As it retired, he had to detain it by dams till it had deposited all its fertilizing mud. It was not true, therefore, even of Lower Egypt generally,

[1] 2, 14.

that the harvest was raised with no other labour than that which Herodotus describes.

The simplest of their agricultural instruments was the hoe, which probably in some soils supplied the place of the plough by tracing a shallow furrow, or completed its work by breaking the clods. The form of the hoe was nearly that of the letter A, if one side be supposed to be slightly curved and elongated into a tooth. The curved part was generally of wood, as well as the handle. The plough, as represented in the pictures of Gizeh[1], was little more than an enlarged copy of the hoe, the curved side, turned downwards, having become the share, resembling in form the coulter of a modern plough, the handle having been lengthened into a pole, and two curved pieces of wood added at the point of junction, by which it was guided. It is doubtful if metal were ever used for the share; no such instrument has been found in Egypt, but from its colour in some of the paintings, Rosellini infers that brass has been used. The parts of the plough were merely tied together in some representations, and the whole structure of the instruments hows how light was the duty which it had to perform. The ploughmen only in a few instances appear to be using their strength to force the share deep into the soil. A sower followed the plough, carrying a bag or satchel of matting, from which he scattered the seed broadcast. It does not appear that the ground was subsequently harrowed to cover it in; Herodotus speaks of the employment of swine for this purpose; Diodorus with more probability describes cattle as

[1] Rosellini, M. Civ. 1, 289, 296. Pl. xxxii. 2.

being used[1], and he is confirmed by the monuments, in which flocks of goats appear in fields which have been just turned up by the hoe or the plough[2]. The oxen or cows by whom the plough was drawn were sometimes yoked by the neck and sometimes by the horns. From the time of the scattering of the seed till harvest, it seems to have been left to the genial influences of the sun and air, which ripened wheat in about five months, barley in four; at least the Egyptian monuments exhibit no traces of those labours which the Roman agriculturist had to undergo[3], in order to secure his crop. When ripe, the corn was reaped with the sickle, the grain trampled out by oxen, winnowed by being thrown into the air from baskets, and stored up in granaries. The form of one of these is exhibited in a painting of the tomb of Rotei at Benihassan. It consists of a double range of structures resembling ovens, built of brick with an opening at the top and a shutter in the side. A flight of stairs gives access to the top of these receptacles, into which the grain, measured and noted, is poured till they are full. The mode of emptying them was to open the shutter in the side, which discharged all above it, after which it was easy for men to enter, and throw out through

---

[1] Diod. 1, 36. Τὸ σπέρμα βαλόντας ἐπάγειν τὰ βοσκήματα. He appears to have thought that the ploughing was dispensed with altogether.

[2] Rosellini, u. s.

[3] ....Subit aspera silva,
Lappæque tribulique, interque nitentia culta
Infelix lolium et steriles dominantur avenæ.
Quod nisi et assiduis terram insectabere rastris,
Et sonitu terrebis aves, et ruris opaci
Falce premes umbras, votisque vocaveris imbrem,
Ileu magnum alterius frustra spectabis acervum.
                                    Virg. Georg. 1, 152.

IX.]   AGRICULTURE AND HORTICULTURE.   187

the opening the contents of the lower part[1]. In another representation from a tomb at Thebes, the opening of the oven-shaped receptacle is at the bottom. In a tomb at Kum-el-Ahmar we see the sheaves of corn thrown into a hollow conical receptacle. Besides wheat and barley, the monuments show, that the *dhorra* (Holcus sorghum) was also grown extensively in Egypt, and Rosellini mentions that among the various seeds which he has found in the Theban tombs, some have been recognized by a skilful botanist as unquestionably belonging to this plant[2]. The grain was obtained, not by treading out, but by drawing the head through a set of spikes which entirely separated it. Whether this were the *olyra* or *zea* on which Herodotus represents the Egyptians as living, while they despised wheat and barley as ignoble food[3], or the *rye* which is mentioned in the book of Exodus as destroyed by the hail, is uncertain[4]. There must be some exaggeration in the statement of Herodotus respecting the contempt of wheat and barley by the Egyptians, seeing in what large quantities they were grown.

Nature has not only given to the soil and climate of Egypt an uncommon aptitude for the production of crops of grain, but has placed it in the neighbourhood of countries to which the same advantage has been denied. On the West it is bordered by sandy

---

[1] Rosellini, Mon. Civ. 1, 328, tab. xxxv. Wilkinson, M. and C. 2, 136.
[2] Wilkinson, M. and C. 2, 397. Rosellini, M. Civ. 1, 364.
[3] Herod. 2, 36.
[4] The Hebrew word כֻּסֶּמֶת *Kusemeth* (Exod. ix. 32) is rendered by the Septuagint here ὄλυρα, in Is. xxviii. 25, ζέα. It is supposed to be the grain which furnished the *far* or *adoreum* of the Latins: Pliny, 18, 11. Far in Egypto ex olyra conficitur.

deserts; on the East by a rocky region equally incapable of culture. Palestine is not a corn country, except in its most northern district, Galilee; and the sands of the Arabian Desert intervene between it and the fertile plains of Mesopotamia. To Egypt therefore the inhabitants even of distant countries naturally came[1], when visited by famine, to supply themselves from its superabundant produce, which not being perishable, might be stored up for many years. The long ranges of granaries were, no doubt, intended to receive more than one harvest.

Another object of cultivation in Egypt was flax, which was grown chiefly in the Delta, in the neighbourhood of Tanis, Pelusium, and Buto; but also at Tentyra in Upper Egypt; it was a source of great wealth to the country, though the fibre had less strength than that produced in some other regions[2]. It was plucked up by the hand, the linseed stripped off and then steeped and heckled. These operations are represented in the paintings at Benihassan and elsewhere, with very little variation from modern practice. The cultivation of cotton is not represented on any monument, a circumstance which would conclude strongly against the opinion that the byssus of Herodotus was cotton cloth, even had not the examination of the mummy bandages proved that they are linen. Rosellini, however, says that he has found the cotton seed in an *unopened* tomb, and we know from Pliny that it was cultivated in

---

[1] Gen. xii. 10; xxvi. 1; xlii. 57. "All countries came into Egypt to Joseph to buy corn, because the famine was sore in all lands." Πυροφόροι δὲ κατ' αἰγλήεντα κάρ- που Νῆές ἄγουσιν ἀπ' Αἰγύπτου, μέγιστον πλοῦτον. Bacchyl. Fr. 27.
[2] Pliny, 19, 1. Ægyptio lino minimum firmitatis, plurimum lucri.

Upper Egypt in his time, and that the priests made their garments from it[1].

The culture of the esculent plants and roots which formed a large part of the diet of the Egyptians, must also have been a principal feature in their husbandry. Of these the ancients particularly mention the leguminous class, the bean[2], the vetch, the lentil, to the growth of which the climate and soil were so favourable that they appeared above ground on the third day after sowing, with the exception of the bean[3]. Cucurbitaceous plants, such as the cucumber[4], gourd and melon[5], so grateful and salutary in hot climates, grew also in Egypt in great abundance; and it was equally celebrated for the excellence of its onions, leeks and garlic, which with us serve only as the condiment of food, but in Egypt supplied a considerable nutriment to the body of the people, their flavour being much milder than when grown in northern climates. The lands nearest to the Nile, or to the canals which did not require the inundation to fill them, would naturally be appropriated to this kind of cultivation, which demands a frequent supply of water during the growth of the crop. A very simple mode of raising it by the bucket and pole is figured in one of the tombs, by a succession of which with reservoirs it might be laboriously brought to the needful elevation[6]; but before the Greek and Roman times the use of water-

---

[1] Pliny, *u. s.* Rosellini, Mon. Civ. 1, 360.
[2] Herodotus (2, 37) says the bean was not much cultivated. The ancients use *faba* and κύαμος of the seed of the lotus. Diod. 1, 34. Pliny, 18, 10, 2.
[4] According to Herodotus, an inscription on the Great Pyramid recorded the amount of money spent in food of this description, radishes, leeks and onions; and the account, if not historical, is at least characteristic of Egyptian customs.
[5] Numbers xi. 5.
[6] Rosellini, M. Civ. tav. xl. 2.

wheels was not known[1]. The language of Moses in Deut. xi. 10, " the land, whither thou goest in to possess it, is not as the land of Egypt, from whence ye came out, where thou sowedst thy seed, and wateredst it with thy foot, as a garden of herbs," is supposed to allude to the use of a water-wheel of which the moving force was supplied by the foot; but we find no trace in the monuments of this or any other hydraulic mechanism.

An important supplement to the cereal food of the Egyptians was found in the lotus and the papyrus, which though spontaneous products were multiplied and improved by culture[2]. The *ciborium* or capsule of the lotus contained a number of seeds resembling beans; these ground and kneaded with water or milk[3] furnished a bread, which, if eaten warm, was very wholesome. The root of the same plant was sweet, and was eaten by the ancient Egyptians, as it still is in the districts which do not produce corn. The root and lower part of the stalk of the papyrus was either chewed raw or boiled or roasted.

Herodotus says that the inhabitants of the corn-growing region (ἡ σπειρομένη Αἴγυπτος) used wine made from barley, because there were no vines in their country[4]. The same soil seldom serves for grain

---

[1] The wheel which was in use in the time of Diodorus was the κοχλίας, or spiral, of Archimedes (1, 34); one of these, which raised water from the Nile to supply the garrison of the Memphite Babylon, was worked by 150 men. Strabo, 17, 807.

[2] Her. 2, 92. Theophr. H. Plant. 4, 9. The Greeks despised the Egyptians as eaters of the papyrus. Βύβλου δὲ καρπὸς οὐ κρατεῖ στάχυν. Æsch. Supp. 768.

[3] Pliny, 22, 28 (21).

[4] 2, 77. St. Cyril, quoted by Rosellini, observes that no wine or corn was produced in the marshy districts of Egypt. He adds, " alii habent terram arabilem et fœcundissimam et vitium sunt cultores studiosissimi." But eight centuries had intervened between the two writers.

and for vineyards, which thrive best on the sides of hills[1]; and in later times it was in the district of Fyoum, on the borders of the lake Mareotis and at Plinthine, at the extremities of the cultivated land, that wine was grown[2]. The monuments prove, however, that from the earliest times its cultivation and manufacture have been known in Egypt, in accordance with the accounts in Scripture[3]. In one of the oldest tombs, that of Eimai at Gizeh, the whole process is represented. The vines appear to have been supported by notched poles, and trained upon espaliers; elsewhere they are seen in low bushes, such as the vine countries of Europe exbibit[4]. The fruit is gathered in baskets and conveyed to a large vat, where it is trodden by men who take hold of a rope fixed above them, by which they raise themselves a little to increase the force of their treading. In another representation the grapes, already deprived of their first running, are enclosed in a bag of matting, which is then violently twisted by sticks inserted in the ends, so that the juice streams through the interstices. Here, too, we see that everything in Egypt was accomplished by mere manual force, without any mechanical contrivance. The must was then placed in vessels to ferment, and finally the wine poured off into the oblong jars in which it was preserved. These, like the Roman amphoræ, had sometimes a pointed foot, so that they would not stand of themselves, but were pre-

---

[1] ....apertos
Bacchus amat colles.—Virg. Georg. 2, 113.

[2] Strabo, 17, 799. Athen. Ep. l. p. 33. Wilkinson, M. and C. 4, 121. The wine of Coptos in Upper Egypt was very thin. Athen. *u. s.*

[3] Gen. xl. 10. Numb. xx. 5.

[4] Wilkinson, M. and C. 2, 147.

served upright in wooden frames. Both red and white wines were made in Egypt, and the group of characters which represents wine is followed sometimes by others which apparently discriminate the quality, but the meaning of which is unknown.

Lower Egypt contained extensive marsh-districts which were unfitted for cultivation, but from their luxuriant herbage well-adapted for the pasturage of cattle. The districts in which this was carried on lay remote from the civilization of the *cultivated* Egypt, and the herdsmen were a rude and lawless race[1]. They dwelt in huts constructed of reeds, and used the roots of the lotus for bread. To this cause, rather than the remembrance of the evils inflicted on Egypt by Asiatic nomads, that prejudice against the feeders of cattle is probably to be attributed, which shows itself in the history of Joseph. In a portion of Lower Egypt, eastward of the Pelusiac branch, the country of Goshen appears to have lain, which was assigned to the Israelites as the most suitable to the pasturage of their cattle[2]. The higher parts of the Nile, that is Middle and Upper Egypt, can have afforded little scope for pasturage; but the representations in the tombs of Gizeh and Kum-el-Ahmar prove that the care and tending of cattle was carried on in these districts also. Even the necessities of agriculture must have led to the maintenance of oxen and cows in the cultivated Egypt, no other animal being used in ploughing

---

[1] Strabo, 17, p. 802. Diod. 1, 43.

[2] Gen. xlvii. 6. "In the best of the land make thy father and brethren to dwell; in the land of Goshen let them dwell." *The best of the land* must here be understood as "best adapted for their purpose."

and treading out the grain. The Nile supplied by its main stream and its canals ready means of conveyance; but where water-carriage was impracticable and human power not available, cattle were employed in draught. Cows are represented drawing the slide or low cart on which the mummy was conveyed to the tomb, and the blocks of stone which were brought from the quarries of Mokattam for the repair of the Memphian temple are drawn by three pair of oxen. Herds of wild cattle may also have been found in the desert regions on the eastern side of the Nile, which contains spots producing pasture; for among the pictures in the tombs of Upper Egypt is a representation of a huntsman who is shooting them with arrows, and another catching them with a noose[1]. The monuments give ample evidence of the care with which the domesticated cattle were tended. Large yards were attached to the farmhouses, provided with sheds for sheltering them, and rings to which they were tied while feeding[2]. During the inundation it was necessary to withdraw them from the fields and collect them in the villages and towns which usually stood on elevated ground; if overtaken by the waters they were rescued in boats. They were branded with their owner's mark and numbered; when sick, medicine was administered to them by a person who bears the title of *attendant*[3]. Such was the spontaneous luxuriance of vegetation after the waters had retired, that if the land were left unsown it produced an abundant crop

---

[1] Wilkinson, M. and C. 3, 18, from Beni Hassan, Ibid. 15.

[2] Wilkinson, M. and C. 2, 134, from Alabastron.

[3] Rosellini, Mon. Civ. 1, 270, Tav. xxxi. The word is *Renen*. See the Lexicon in Bunsen, 1, p. 579.

of natural herbage. The culture of artificial grasses could not be unknown to a people whose soil and climate were so well suited to their production.

Egypt was especially favourable to the growth of sheep, the ewes according to the ancients bringing forth lambs and yielding wool twice in the year[1]. The flesh of the sheep was little esteemed, and was forbidden food in the Theban nome, as the ram was sacred to the great god of Thebes. No example of its slaughter for food or sacrifice appears in the paintings, though that of oxen is so common[2]. Upper garments of wool[3] were generally worn by the Egyptians and even by the priests, though religious motives forbade their being carried into a temple or used in interments; but the wool of Egypt was coarse and of a short staple. Large flocks of goats were also kept, which are represented in the paintings as browsing upon the branches of the thorny *Mimosa* which grows very abundantly in Egypt[4]. Besides these we find from the paintings that the ibex, oryx and others of the antelope tribe were tamed, and notwithstanding the wildness which they naturally exhibit, as completely domesticated as the sheep or the goat[5]. From the same sources we learn how important a place the breeding and care of cattle held in the economical system of the Egyptians. The kings had herds on their own demesnes, for in the tomb of Menophres at Saccara[6],

---

[1] Diod. 1, 87.
[2] According to Strabo (17, p.803), it was only in the temple of Serapis at the Natron Lakes, that sheep in his time were offered in sacrifice. This district was hardly in Egypt. Comp. Her. 2, 18.
[3] Herod. 2, 42. 2, 81. Yates, Textrinum antiquorum, p. 23. Pliny, N. H. 8, 73.
[4] Rosellini, M. Civ. 1, 260.
[5] Wilkinson, M. and C. 4, 140.
[6] Rosellini, Mon. Civ. 1, 250.

two bulls are represented with the inscription *royal house*, with the number on one 86, on the other 43. In the tomb of Ranni, a military man, at Eilethya[1], is represented a visit of inspection paid by a proprietor to his farm. He is distinguished by an ornamented collar and a long garment, and has in one hand a sceptre or mace, in the other the staff which among the Egyptians marked the higher classes. Two servants follow him, one carrying his bow and quiver and a stool, the other his slippers. Before him goes a writer with a roll and writing instruments; two herdsmen bring in the cattle, one of whom throws himself prostrate before his master, and the other is evidently repeating to the writer the tale of cattle, sheep, goats and swine which are under his charge. An inscription above records the numbers of each—cattle 122; rams 300; goats 1200; swine 1500. In a tomb near the Pyramids, 860 asses, 974 sheep, 834 oxen, 220 cows and 2234 goats are numbered as the property of the occupant[2]. The minuteness of these registers in such a place is a singular proof how far the Egyptians carried the notion that the tomb should be the counterpart of the house; the record of his own wealth while living was to be kept under the cognizance of its inhabitant.

The ass was the ordinary beast of burden in Egypt; the horse never appears in use either for husbandry or draught or riding; its sole employment was in the war-chariot, either in actual service, or in the processions in which the king ap-

---

[1] Rosellini, Mon. Civ. 1, 262, Tav. xxx. [2] Champollion-Figeac L'Univers, p. 185.

peared in military state[1]. The wagons which Joseph sent to bring his father down into Egypt do not appear to have been drawn by horses[2]; the sight of a wheel-carriage, unknown among the patriarchs, was sufficient of itself to convince him that the narrative of his sons was true. That the horse was at this time bred in Egypt is however implied in the same history; as the intensity of the famine increased, the people brought " their horses and their flocks and their herds and their asses[3]" to exchange for food; and when the Israelites quitted the land, Pharaoh pursued them with a large body of chariots. Egypt was probably the country from which neighbouring nations gradually learnt the use of war-chariots and purchased war-horses; for if Arabia in this age produced a breed of horses, it does not appear that then or since it has ever broken them to harness. We know that when the Jews, contrary to the injunction of their legislator, began to multiply horses, Egypt was the source from which they derived them[4]. The earliest mention of Egypt in Grecian literature is in reference to the multitude of its war-chariots[5], and Diodorus is probably correct when he says that the horses were kept in numerous stables along the banks of the Nile, from Memphis to Thebes. That we never see them in the landscapes which mingle Egyptian scenery with the occupations of Egyptian life may be owing to this

---

[1] Wilkinson, M. and C. 3, 179, gives a drawing from a tomb at Thebes, of a plaustrum drawn by oxen, in which an Ethiopian princess rides. It is very like a chariot, but closed at the sides, and shaded by an umbrella.

[2] Gen. xlv. 27.
[3] Gen. xlvii. 17.
[4] Deut. xvii. 16; 1 Kings, x. 28.
[5] Hom. Il. i. 381.

circumstance. They were not turned out to graze, but fed, as the Arab horses are now, on barley and straw. But though Egypt, by its abundance of food, was well adapted for their maintenance and multiplication, it is not the country in which we should expect to find a native breed of horses, for it is not productive of the food on which they would subsist in the wild state, and the fierce animals of the adjoining deserts would speedily have destroyed them. If the race was introduced from Arabia by the Shepherds, it was multiplied and prepared for war-chariots by the Egyptians. Their forms are light, and their action very spirited. What was their prevailing colour it is difficult to say; in the paintings they are always red, but so are the men, whose real colour was dark. It is remarkable that in the hieroglyphical inscriptions the mares are called by the Semitic name of *Ses*[1] (Heb. *Sus*), the horses by the name of *htar* (Copt. *hto, htor*). War-chariots are the most costly of all the varieties of military force; and that the Egyptians should have maintained so large a body of them, for no other purpose than war and state, gives a high idea of the ancient wealth of the monarchy. They do not appear, however, in any monument prior to the eighteenth dynasty.

The art of horticulture is closely connected with that of agriculture, and indeed in Egypt, from the large quantity of vegetable food that was raised and the system of minute irrigation that prevailed, the distinction between the culture of the field and the garden was less than in other countries. The land

[1] Hierogl. of Egyptian Society, Pl. 42. l. 51. c. 19. k.

was watered "as a garden of herbs[1]." We see in one representation men carrying water in earthen jars to be poured upon the beds, in another raising it by a bucket tied to a beam, to the other end of which a large stone is appended[2]. Fruits of various kinds, the date, the pomegranate, the fig, the sycamore, the persea, are recognised in the paintings, and some of them have been found in the tombs. The paintings refute the statement of Diodorus[3], that the Persea was introduced into Egypt from Ethiopia by Cambyses. Others said from Persia; and both appear to be founded on false etymology. Other fruits, as the peach and the almond, are described as growing in Egypt by ancient authorities. Of all these none was so important in Egyptian economy as the date, which is an article of food, not of luxury, in the countries in which it is produced[4]. Oriental exaggeration reckoned up 360 uses to which different parts of the tree might be applied[5]. The ancient Egyptians derived from it uses not less various, as appears from the numerous articles found in the tombs[6]; and a wine was extracted from the fruit, which was used in the process of embalming, and probably also as a beverage. The fruit produced in the Delta was of inferior quality[7]; the best grew in the Thebaid. Both the *Doum* palm (*Cucifera Thebaica*), of which the stem divides, and the *Dachel*

---

[1] Deut. xi. 10.
[2] Rosellini, M. Civ. xl.
[3] 1, 34.
[4] Gentium aliquibus panis; plurimis etiam quadrupedum cibus. Plin. 13, 6.
[5] Strabo, 16, 742. Dr. Clarke, Travels, 5, 409. See p. 88 of this volume.
[6] Wilkinson, M. and C. 2, 180.
[7] Strabo, 17, p. 818. Though it requires a plentiful supply of water and by its presence marks those spots in the Desert in which water is found, it thrives best in a sandy and saline soil.

(*Palma dactylifera*), which grows up with a single trunk, are found, distinctly characterized, in the paintings of the tombs[1].

Horticulture among the Egyptians, however, was not merely an economical, but an *æsthetic* art. A garden laid out with walks, shaded with trees and refreshed by canals and reservoirs of water, appears to have been the usual appendage to a house of the higher order, and a painting of a royal garden has been fortunately preserved in a tomb at Thebes, belonging to a military chief in the reign of Amunoph II.[2] The river, or a large canal, runs beside it, and the broad walk which intervenes between it and the entrance is planted with a row of trees. A flight of steps leads from the bank to the lofty gateway, which bears a hieroglyphic inscription and the shield of the king. The centre of the garden itself is occupied by a vineyard, enclosed by a wall, in which vines covered with ripe fruit are trained on a trellis-work. Within the wall which surrounds the whole garden, the two species of palm before-mentioned are planted in symmetrical alternation, trees of a different growth and thicker foliage being placed between them. A row of the Dachel palm also surrounds the enclosure of the vineyard. There are four reservoirs of water symmetrically disposed, in which waterfowl are playing, and the lotus grows beside them. Opposite to the entrance and beyond the vineyard is a summer-house of three stories, with windows opening on the garden, in the apart-

---

[1] Rosellini, Mon. Civ. 1, 386, xl. 2, 8. Wilkinson, M. and C. 2, 141, where a vignette is given.
[2] Mon. Civ. 2, 386, Tav. lxix.

ments of which are flower-stands with vases, and altars or tables on which fresh-gathered flowers are laid as if for offerings. No great variety of flowers was cultivated in the Egyptian gardens[1]. The lotus and papyrus appear again and again in the form of wreaths, nosegays, offerings upon altars, ornaments of sculpture and painting. Beside two of the reservoirs are painted wooden arbours. From other paintings we find that the reservoirs were also fish-ponds; in one of these an Egyptian is represented seated in his chair, angling beside a pond; his dress and posture sufficiently indicating that he pursues an amusement, not an occupation[2]. Such were the gardens of pleasure in which the kings and great men of Egypt took delight in the days of the splendour and luxury of the Theban monarchy. They were probably the model of the gardens of Solomon, who is represented as saying (Eccl. ii. 5), "I made me gardens and orchards: I planted trees in them of all kinds of fruit: I made me pools of water to water therewith the wood that bringeth forth trees." They were artificial and formal; but a garden which is an appendage to a palace, naturally imitates the stateliness and regularity of architecture rather than the freedom and variety of nature. The taste for landscape gardening is of very recent growth.

---

[1] Comp. Plin. 21, 7. In Egypto minime odorati flores, quia nebulosus et roscidus aer est a Nilo flumine.

[2] Wilkinson, 3, 52.

CHAPTER X.

THE CHASE.—FISHERIES.

THE nature of the country in Egypt seems not to have allowed of the formation of parks or *paradises*, which the Persian monarchs planted with all kinds of trees and stocked them with wild animals for the chase[1]. The Egyptians may, however, have brought the game which they had taken alive in the open country into preserves, where they were kept till needed for food. Egypt did not abound with wild animals[2]. It is probable that the hills on the Arabian, not on the Libyan side of the Nile, are the scene of those hunting-pieces which are found in the tombs both of Lower Egypt and the Thebaid; one of the most remarkable of these is in the tomb of Rotei at Benihassan[3]. We learn from it that it was the custom of the Egyptians, as of the Greeks and Romans, when a herd of wild animals harboured in a spot which might be easily enclosed, to carry a line of nets supported on poles around it, in which they might be entangled when they endeavoured to escape[4]. Being roused from their haunts by the dogs and hunters, they were pierced by the arrows of the sportsman, or pulled down by the dogs. Among the animals represented in the tombs are

---

[1] Xenoph. Hell. 4,1,8,14. Curt. 8, 1, 11. (2. Ed. Zumpt.)
[2] See p. 91 of this volume.
[3] Rosellini, Mon. Civ. 1, 191, Tav. xv.
[4] Virg. Æn. 4, 121. Saltus indagine cingunt.

not only wild cattle, antelopes, oryxes, and hares, but foxes, porcupines, hyænas, wolves and jackals, showing that a large tract of country had been enclosed by the net, and that the objects of the chase were not merely the animals suitable for food. The painter has also in one instance indulged his imagination by introducing some which belong only to a mythical zoology[1]. We know from the accounts of Herodotus, that the Egyptians, like other ancient nations, believed in the existence of animals which have no prototype in nature, and the desert is the appropriate haunt of such fantastic creations. The dogs are of various breeds, greyhounds to run down the feebler and swifter animals, and those of greater strength and fierceness to attack the wolf or the bull[2]. Amidst all the neglect of perspective which characterizes Egyptian art, there is wonderful spirit and character in the drawing of the dogs and the animals which they are attacking, abundantly proving, that the stiffness and monotony complained of in the treatment of religious subjects, did not arise from want of talent in the artists, but from the restraint imposed by authority and tradition. In this mode of hunting, the sportsman generally appears ou foot; at other times, when the chase is in more open ground, he is mounted in his chariot, the game being driven by the attendants and the dogs within the reach of his arrows.

To a people who lived so much upon and in the

---

[1] Rosellini, M. Civ. 1, 191, xxiii. 2, 4, 5. One has the head of a serpent, another of a hawk on the body of a quadruped. The third has the head of a bird, and is winged.

[2] Wilkinson (M. and C. 3, 16) gives a drawing from Beni Hassan, in which a tamed lion appears to be used in hunting.

X.] THE HIPPOPOTAMUS AND THE CROCODILE. 203

river as the ancient Egyptians, the hippopotamus and the crocodile must have been objects of hostility. Both of them no doubt were found in ancient times through the whole course of the Nile[1], though now the hippopotamus is not seen except by accident below the Second Cataract, and the crocodile rarely below 27° N.L.[2] No representation of the chase of the hippopotamus has been found in Lower Egypt, but in the tombs of the Thebaid it is not uncommon. If discovered on land, where it did much mischief in the fields and plantations near the bank, it was assailed with barbed weapons; if in the water, it was attacked from boats, and the lances had ropes fastened to them, so that like a harpooned whale it was tracked beneath the surface, and when it rose again to breathe was pierced with new weapons till it was exhausted by loss of blood[3]. Its flesh was tough and indigestible, but its skin was valuable from its excessive hardness as a covering for shields and for the thongs of whips[4]. The flesh of the crocodile was equally worthless, but it was pursued in most parts of Egypt for its voracity and in others from a religious feeling, while in some parts, as at Ombi, in the neighbourhood of Thebes and on the Lake Mœris, it was tamed and worshiped. Herodotus[5] describes a mode of catching it by a hook baited with the back of a young pig; Diodorus by nets: the Tentyrites encountered it in the water and thrust a piece of wood into its open jaws which

---

[1] Diod. 1, 35.
[2] See p. 94 of this volume.
[3] Wilkinson, M. and C. 3, 71.
[4] Wilkinson, 3, 69.
[5] Herod. 2, 68.

prevented them from closing. In a painting at Kum-el-Ahmar it is represented as being speared from a boat[1], and it was sometimes killed by blows on the head from heavy bars of iron.

The chase of wild animals can never in a country like Egypt supply any important part of the susteuance of the people. It was otherwise with the arts of fishing and fowling. Many of the inhabitants of the marshy districts of the Delta in which grain could not be raised lived wholly upon fish[2], which they caught and dried in the sun; but throughout Egypt fishing was a profitable branch of industry and a productive source of food[3]. The paintings represent the various modes of catching them, with the line, the net and the barbed spear, as well as the processes of drying and salting[4]. The fish were caught in the greatest numbers, not in the branches of the river, but in the pools and lakes which were dry during the low state of the Nile, and filled as the inundation proceeded. This remark of Herodotus, however, must be considered as applicable to the smaller kinds of fish, which even now swarm in such places; the larger must have been taken chiefly in the rivers or those lakes which have at all times of the year a communication with the Nile. The fishery of the Lake Moeris and the canals which connected it with the river was the most productive; during the time that the water flowed inward, it produced under the Persian kings a talent of silver (£250 if an Attic talent is

---

[1] Rosellini, M. Civ. 1, 24.
[2] Herod. 2, 92.
[3] Isaiah xix. 8.
[4] Rosellini, Mon. Civ. 1, 221, xxv. Wilkinson, M. and C. 3, 53.

meant) daily for the royal treasury; during the remainder of the year, a third part or twenty minæ. By placing nets at the openings of the dams by which the water flowed from the Nile or into it, the Egyptian fishermen would have the same advantage as ours by placing their nets in the mouths of tide-rivers[1]. The simple apparatus of the fisherman is nearly the same in all countries, and that represented in the Egyptian monuments hardly differs from our own[2].

Fish are among the least changeable part of the zoology of a country, and those for which the Nile was celebrated in ancient times are now easily recognised among its inhabitants. The genus *Silurus* was the most abundant; *Perca, Cyprinus, Labrus* and *Salmo* are also found[3]. The general character is sufficiently distinct in the paintings, but the Egyptian artists have not given the figures either of their fish or their birds with such minute accuracy as to enable the zoologist to determine their species. They are said by those who have eaten them to be rather insipid[4]; and as affording an attenuating diet they were forbidden to the priests; but they are well suited to a hot climate, the languid appetite in the height of summer relishing no other kind of animal food[5]; and the Israelites in the Desert,

---

[1] Our version of Isaiah xix. 10, speaks of "*sluices* and ponds for fish," as if artificially constructed, but this is scarcely a correct translation. See Gesenius *ad loc.*

[2] See the description given by Abdollatiph of the fishing as practised under the Caliphs, quoted by Rosellini, M. C. 1, p. 230.

[3] Clot Bey (Russegger, Reisen, vol. 1, p. 300) reckons fifty-two species of fish inhabiting the Nile. Their real number is probably not ascertained.

[4] Athenæus, 7, 312, says on the contrary, φέρει ὁ Νεῖλος γένη πολλὰ ἰχθύων καὶ πάντα ἥδιστα.

[5] Harmer's Obs. on Scripture, 2, 327.

"when their soul was dried away," regretted the fish as well as the vegetables of Egypt[1]. When salted they were exported, at least in later times, to foreign countries. Sea-fishing appears not to have been practised by the Egyptians; their religious prejudices kept them from venturing on the element which represented Typhon; and the shallow and muddy waters of the coast are not suited to this occupation, which is not much carried on at the present day.

The great extent of marsh in Egypt and the long continuance of the inundation caused it to abound in waterfowl beyond most other countries. The paintings represent the modes in which they were taken and preserved for food. Most commonly they were enclosed in a net which was let down over the space in which the birds were known to be, and suddenly drawn together. Frequently the sportsman is represented as going in his boat of papyrus among the aquatic plants in which the birds harboured, and knocking them down by the throwstick[2]. In other instances they are caught in traps, and it is evident that the use of decoy-birds was not unknown to the Egyptians. Most of those which are represented as being taken for food are of the duck and goose tribe. The quail is also mentioned by Herodotus[3] as being first slightly salted and then used without cooking. These birds came in vast flocks from the sea, and furnished the criminals who were banished to Rhinocolura, on the coast between Egypt and Palestine, with a considerable

---

[1] Numbers xi. 5. [3] 2, 77.
[2] Wilkinson, M. and C. 3, 39.

portion of their food[1]. They abound also in the Desert of Sinai[2].

An important branch of rural economy in Egypt was the hatching of poultry by artificial heat. It is not mentioned by Herodotus, nor does it appear in the paintings; and it is described by Diodorus, as an example of a practice recently added to those which had been perfected by long experience and handed down by tradition[3]. Indeed it is doubtful whether our domestic fowl was known in Egypt before the Persian Conquest. It cannot be identified on the monuments, though there is a hieroglyphic character commonly called a chicken. The modern Egyptians hatch eggs by the regulated heat of ovens; the ancients buried them in the ground, covered up with dung[4].

[1] Diod. 1, 60.
[2] Lepsius, Tour to Mount Sinai.
[3] Diod. 1, 74.
[4] Ar. Hist. An. 6, 2. Ἐκπέττεται τὰ ᾠὰ ἐπωαζόντων τῶν ὀρνίθων· οὐ μὴν ἀλλὰ καὶ αὐτόματα ἐν τῇ γῇ ὥσπερ ἐν Αἰγύπτῳ, κατορυττόντων εἰς τὴν γῆν ἐν τῇ κόπρῳ. Hist. Aug. Script. Saturninus, 8.

CHAPTER XI.

NAVIGATION AND COMMERCE.

THE sea was regarded by the Egyptians with the dislike and apprehension natural to a people whose original dwelling was inland, and who were not compelled to become familiar with its dangers in order to supply themselves with food. They looked upon it also with horror; as first corrupting and then swallowing up the sweet waters of their beneficent Nile; and gave it the name of the principle of evil[1]. In their early history we find no traces of maritime navigation; they avoided the sea themselves and discountenanced the visits of foreign vessels. This was a prudent precaution; for the earliest navigators, Phœnicians, Carians, Greeks, were all pirates and kidnappers[2]. The distant military enterprises of the kings of the eighteenth and nineteenth dynasties led to the construction of fleets, both on the Red Sea and the Mediterranean. If the Shepherds, who held Lower Egypt so long under their sway, immediately previous to these dynasties, were Phœnicians, they must have been acquainted with maritime navigation, though Phœnicia itself had not yet attained that rank as a maritime state which it afterwards assumed. At no period however was Egypt a great naval power. Inland navigation, on

---

[1] Plut. Is. et Osir. p. 363.
[2] Hom. Od. γ'. 71, o'. 459. Thuc. ι. 6, 7. Joel, 3, 6. Her. 2, 54.

the contrary, was one of the most characteristic features of Egyptian life. The waters of the Nile in their lowest season are never so shallow as not to be able to carry the vessels of light draught with which it was navigated. The inundation answered the same purpose as spring-tides in our rivers, and extended the benefit of water-conveyance far beyond the ordinary limits. Whatever might be the object for which change of place was desired, the Nile furnished the means of its accomplishment. The gentle and equable fall of the river, which does not much exceed two feet in a mile[1] in its medium state, makes it not difficult to ascend against the stream by oars or towing, and as the N.W. winds blow steadily during the inundation, they counteract the effect of the increased current. In Egypt the Nile has no rocks in its bed, and though a sudden squall may drive a sailing vessel on a shoal or against the bank, the shock is not dangerous from the softness of the mud. The shrines of the gods were conveyed by water in solemn procession and in richly ornamented barges from their chief temple to the lesser sanctuaries of the nome. Royal personages and eminent functionaries traveled in the same way, and with equal splendour, from one part of the kingdom to another. Egyptian pilgrims to oracles and other holy spots did not toil along rocky or sandy roads, but embarked on boats, floated down the Nile, with music and dancing, and halting at each town on the bank, summoned the inhabitants to join them in their festivities[2]. The dead were conveyed to their

---

[1] Russegger, Reisen, ii. 1, 545, gives it 2·3 Paris F. in a geographical mile.

[2] Her. 2, 60.

last resting-place across the same stream, which during life was for ever before their eyes, and the scene of so much of their occupation and amusement.

Herodotus has described only one kind of Egyptian vessel, the large *Bari*[1], which was employed for the transport of goods. It was built of the Sont (Acanthe), the hardest wood that Egypt afforded, and without ribs, tree-nails of great length supplying their place; the seams were caulked with papyrus, and the sails were made of the same material. These arks floated down the stream, and were towed up if the wind were not strong enough to impel them against it. They were very numerous, and the tonnage of the largest amounted to several thousand talents[2]. The smallest vessels were made, like a canoe or pirogue, from a single trunk[3]; others again were constructed with ribs and a keel, which is usually very shallow, to allow of the easy extrication of the vessel if it should take the ground; and both the bow and the stern were high out of the water. The sails, which were square, were either of papyrus or canvas, and were hoisted or lowered by means of rings, blocks being apparently unknown to the ancient Egyptians. The mast, which is single, might be struck to prevent the action of the wind upon it as the vessel floated down the stream. We sometimes see as many as forty rowers sitting or standing in a large river-boat, but they are always ranged on the same level. When their

---

[1] 2, 96. The name is generally derived from *bai*, in Coptic a palm-branch, but this tree was not used for ships. The Coptic *phai* or *bai*, " to carry," seems a more probable etymology.

[2] The talent was probably 75 lb.

[3] Rosellini, M. C. 2, p. 41.

number was so large, a man standing near the midship gave the time for the stroke. The steering was performed by one or more large oars at the stern, and a man stationed at the bow sounded with a long pole[1].

As the Nile had no bridges, communication between its opposite banks must have been kept up by means of boats in the ordinary state of the river; and during the inundation, when the whole country, with the exception of the banks, is under water, this mode must have superseded all others. For ordinary purposes the Egyptians used boats of a very simple construction, narrow and sharp like a bean-shell (*phaselus*), made of papyrus rendered watertight by bitumen[2], or paddled themselves in large vessels of earthenware[3]. The tombs of Benihassan contain representations of boats of larger size, in one of which Amenemha, the tenant of the tomb, is conveying the females of his family upon the Nile. It has a partial covering, like that of a gondola or a modern Egyptian *cangia*[4]. The tomb of Rameses IV. at Thebes gives an idea of the splendour of these barges when used for the conveyance of royal personages. The whole body, the pavilion, the masts and the rudder, are painted of the

---

[1] Wilkinson, M. and C. 3, 195–209.

[2] Rosellini, M. Civ. 6, 1. Plin. N. H. 13, 22. Comp. Exod. ii. 3. Lucan, 4, 136. In Minutoli's Travels, plate 25, the Barabras of Elephantine are represented crossing the river astride on floats of reed.

[3] Juvenal, 15, 129, makes them row and *sail* in such boats.

Parvula *fictilibus* solitum dare vela phaselis,
Et brevibus pictæ remis incumbere *testæ*.

[4] The enclosed chamber was called by the Greeks θάλαμος, and such boats σκάφαι θαλαμηγοί, Strabo, 17, 800. In such a vessel Cæsar would have ascended the Nile with Cleopatra to the Cataract, if his army had not refused to follow. Suet. Cæs. 52.

colour of gold, the sails are fringed, and chequered in various brilliant colours, and the figure of the vulture and the phœnix are embroidered upon them. The eye of Osiris is painted on the prow or the rudder, the handles of which represent the royal emblems of the Uræus and the *pschent*, or the head of a divinity[1].

All that has been written on the subject of the commercial voyages of the Egyptians in the times of the Pharaohs is entirely conjectural; neither history nor the monuments afford us any evidence of their existence. We have seen[2] that as early as the fourth dynasty they had communication with the Red Sea, at Suez and Kosseir, and under the eighteenth an attempt at least was made to carry a canal from Lower Egypt to the head of the Gulf. By these channels they might receive the productions of Arabia and India; but it does not appear that they ever made voyages to these countries in the times of their native princes. They received no doubt by land the productions of the nations which surrounded them, but even in this traffic Egypt seems to have been passive. The Midianites who were carrying spicery and balm and myrrh exchanged them probably for the corn and the manufactures of Egypt. Abounding as it did both in the productions of the soil and in those of industry and art, and placed between countries which neither grew corn nor excelled in manufactures, it could not fail to attract a large inland commerce, from Arabia and Palestine, Libya and Ethiopia. We do

[1] Rosellini, Mon. Civ. tav. 107–110. Wilkinson, M. and C. 3, 209.
[2] Chap. II. of this volume.

not however find that the Egyptians quitted their own country to engage in this commerce; and with the exception of the short period, during which Greek and Roman habits prevailed, such has always been their relation to their neighbours. Like India and China, Egypt has been sought by more enterprising commercial nations; but its natives have seldom been seen in foreign harbours or caravans. Their characteristic has been patient, sedentary industry employed in agriculture and manufactures. The productions of the East have been deposited in Egypt, and from thence distributed over the West; but strangers have brought them and strangers have carried them away.

CHAPTER XII.

MECHANICAL AND INDUSTRIAL ARTS.

Of the perfection to which the finer kinds of mechanical art had arrived in Egypt, the remains which have been brought to light from the catacombs and which fill our Museums, afford the most satisfactory proof. The polishing and engraving of precious stones must have been practised in very early times[1], since the signet of Taia, the queen of Amenophis III., is still in existence in the Egyptian Museum of the Vatican[2]. The skilful engraving of the Jews at the time of their Exodus[3], must have been learnt during their residence in Egypt, if it be not rather attributable to Egyptian artists who had followed the people in their migration. Their ornaments and articles of household luxury prove that they were acquainted with the art of enameling and with the manufacture of glass in all its varieties. Their porcelain, which more nearly resembles glass in its quality than the substance which we call porcelain, is remarkable for the brilliancy of its colours and the delicacy with which they are blended. Their common pottery was inferior, both in fineness of

---

[1] I do not mention the supposed seal of Cheops (Shufu), said to be in the possession of Dr. Abbot at Cairo, nor the collar of Menes. The former I am convinced is a forgery; the latter certainly not contemporary with Menes, though it may be made up, in some measure, of genuine Egyptian work. See an engraving of it in M. Prisse d'Avennes, Suite des Monumens, &c., pl. 47.

[2] Rosellini, Mon. Stor. iii. 1, 261.

[3] Exod. xxviii. 15.

material and tastefulness of design, to the Greek and Etruscan, yet some of their vases have considerable elegance. We find vases figured on the walls of a tomb of the age of Amunoph I., and they exhibit those graceful decorative borders, the invention of which has generally been attributed to the Greeks. The manufacture of porcelain, glass and pottery could not be carried on without a knowledge of the properties of the metallic oxides by which they are coloured. This involves an acquaintance with chemistry, an art which appears to have derived its name from the native name of Egypt (*Chemi*), and to have been preserved in that country through all the changes of empire and diffused in the Middle Ages by the Arabian Conquest. We are led to the same inference by the skill in dyeing and printing which the ancient Egyptians possessed. Their linen was celebrated in the earliest times[1]; it was not only dyed but richly embroidered, and rivaled the productions of the Babylonian needle. The specimens which have come down to us are almost entirely mummy-cloths, and cannot therefore be expected to represent the fineness of the most perfect manufacture, in which kings and great men were clad. The linen corslet which Amasis (about the middle of the sixth century B.C.) sent to the shrine of Minerva at Lindus, had according to Herodotus[2] 360, according to Pliny[3] 365 threads twisted together, in each single thread of which it was composed; and though these astronomical numbers may excite suspicion as to their literal truth, there can be no

---

[1] Prov. vii. 16. אֵטוּן, the word here used for *linen*, is the ὀθόνη of the Greeks.
[2] 3, 47.
[3] 19, 1.

reasonable doubt of the wonderful fineness with which the threads were spun. The corslet sent to the Lacedemonians[1] had figures worked in it of gold and cotton. Cotton appears to have been of later cultivation in Egypt, the mummy-bandages being all of linen, as their examination by Bauer's powerful microscope has shown[2]. In Pliny's time, however, cotton had become much more common, and he describes the cloth made from it under the name of *lina xylina*[3]. It had probably been introduced from Ethiopia, for a late traveller[4] informs us that it grows wild on the banks of the White River above Khartoum.

The machinery for spinning and weaving used by the Egyptians appears from the paintings to have been very rude; yet we know from the cotton fabrics of India that the dexterity acquired by long traditionary practice may rival the perfection of machinery. In the grottos of Benihassan, both men and women are represented spinning[5]. The operation is performed by the spindle, which is of the same form as the women of Egypt use at the present day. To obtain the advantage of a longer cast, the spinner is raised upon a stool, or the thread is passed over a forked stick. Some are drawing a single thread from the tow; others uniting two or more threads into one. The processes of weaving are represented on the same monuments, with cloths of a plain and also of a checked pattern. Both the horizontal and the perpendicular loom were in use,

---

[1] Herod. *u. s.*
[2] Her. 2, 86. See Thomson, in Philos. Mag. Nov. 1834. Wilkinson, Manners and Customs, 3, 115.
[3] Pliny, *u. s.* Jul. Poll. 7, 75.
Yates, Textrinum Antiquorum, 1, 261, 468.
[4] Werne, Expedition to discover the Sources of the true Nile.
[5] Rosellini, Mon. Civ. 2, 16.

and the weaver sometimes pushed the woof upwards, sometimes downwards, not always in the latter direction, as the words of Herodotus seem to imply[1]. The shuttle, properly speaking, does not appear to have been used, and instead of it a stick, hooked at each end, was employed to pass the thread of the woof. The use of treadles also was unknown, and the threads of the warp are kept apart by sticks[2]. Both sexes are engaged in weaving, but the women who are so employed are evidently of a low class and working at a trade. Rosellini observes that he has not in a single instance found the mistress of the house or her daughters engaged at the loom, a strong contrast to the manners of Greece, and one of those which induced Herodotus to say that the Egyptian customs were the opposite of those of the rest of the world[3].

Various processes of metallurgy are represented in the tombs and grottos. Egypt, the soil of which belongs to a very late formation, does not itself produce any metals; but copper and gold were found in the primitive regions near the Red Sea[4]. Gold-dust was brought by caravans from the interior of Africa; silver and gold in ingots and rings are among the tribute paid by African and Asiatic nations. Iron ore is found in the same region near Mount Sinai, which abounded in copper[5]; these mines were wrought in the times of the kings who erected the Pyramids, and Col. Howard Vyse has found a piece of iron in an internal joint of the

---

[1] Her. 2, 35. Ὑφαίνουσιν οἱ μὲν ἄλλοι ἄνω τὴν κρόκην ὠθέοντες, Αἰγύπτιοι δὲ κάτω.
[2] Wilkinson, M. and C. 3, 134.
[3] Her. u. s.
[4] See Chapter II. of this volume.
[5] Lepsius, Journey to Mount Sinai.

218   ANCIENT EGYPT.   [CH.

Great Pyramid, where it could only have been placed at the time of its erection[1]. Herodotus supposed that a large quantity of iron was employed in building the Pyramid, and therefore must have had evidence of its use[2], and he says also that an iron instrument was employed in embalmment[3]. The difficulty of working granite, even with tools of the best-tempered steel, is so great that it appears incredible that any combination of copper should have the hardness requisite for this purpose. The weapons represented in the tomb of Rameses IV. have a blue colour like that of steel[4]. These considerations leave no doubt of the use of iron from very early times in Egypt. There is still a difficulty in explaining the almost entire absence of iron tools and instruments among the remains of Egyptian antiquity—a difficulty not wholly removed by the circumstance that this metal is very easily destroyed by oxidation. It probably became more scarce in later times in consequence of the loss of the metalliferous region near Mount Sinai, which the Egyptians do not seem to have possessed after the nineteenth dynasty.

The traces of ancient operations at Syene show, that in order to detach the shaft of an obelisk, the Egyptian quarry-men made a groove through the entire length, into which wedges of dry wood were inserted. These being wetted, expanded themselves

---

[1] The Catalogue of Passalacqua (Nos. 547, 548) contains arrows pointed with iron from the catacombs of Thebes, and other instruments of the same metal.

[2] Her. 2, 125. Having mentioned that 1600 talents of silver were expended in onions and other vegetables for the workmen, he says, Κόσα εἰκὸς ἄλλα δεδαπανῆσθαί ἐστι ἔς τε σίδηρον τῷ ἐργάζοντο καὶ σιτία, καὶ ἐσθῆτα τοῖς ἐργαζομένοισ;

[3] 2, 86.

[4] Rosellini, Mon. Civ. tav. cxxi.

so powerfully, yet so uniformly, that the whole was separated in one piece. If metal wedges had been employed, it would hardly have been possible to strike them along a line of 100 feet, without the risk of fracturing the stone. The pickaxe and the chisel must have been used, with an incalculable amount of labour, to detach the mass of rock required for a shrine or a colossal statue. M. de Rozière thought that he could detect at Syene the exact space of 500 square feet, from which the colossus of the Rameseion in Western Thebes had been hewn.

The remains of Egyptian carpentry comprehend every article of domestic luxury. Their tools were nearly the same as the modern artificer employs, though less perfect as mechanical instruments, and leaving more to his acquired dexterity. The saw, of which the Greeks attribute the invention to Dædalus, appears in some of the oldest Egyptian tombs. The hatchet and the adze are used for splitting and finishing; in the use of the latter, which has a bent handle, the Egyptian workman must have had great skill, as it supplied the place both of the plane and the lathe, neither of which were known. With these they fashioned the legs of a couch or the pole and wheels of a chariot[1]. Chariots were exported; and if we may trust the numbers in 1 Kings x. 29, the price of one in the time of Solomon was 600 shekels of silver, which reckoning the shekel at two shillings, would be sixty pounds; a great price certainly for a work so simple compared with a modern

[1] Rosellini, Mon. Civ. 2, 44.

carriage, unless we suppose that as royal chariots they were elaborately painted or covered with plates of metal.

For the coarser kinds of carpentry the wood of the sycamore was chiefly used, which is soft but durable. The acacia furnished those articles in which hardness and polish are required, as the shafts of military weapons or the handles of tools, as well as various kinds of furniture. For articles of luxury, as the splendid chairs or thrones on which the Theban monarchs are seated, they employed foreign woods, whose origin is the evidence of an extensive commerce—the ebony of Ethiopia, the mahogany (*Swietenia febrifuga*) of India, the firs and junipers of Syria, the cedar of Lebanon[1]. The arts of veneering and inlaying with the more precious woods were also known. Ivory was wrought into various objects of taste, as boxes and caskets; the tusks of the elephant appear among the articles of tribute which the African nations bring to the Egyptian sovereigns. The accuracy of the workmanship is not less remarkable than the variety of the material; with wooden pegs for nails they were able to join their work together with entire compactness[2].

[1] Rosellini, Mon. Civ. 2, 31. [2] Wilkinson, M. and C. 3, 167.

CHAPTER XIII.

MILITARY EQUIPMENT, ARMOUR AND WARFARE.

In the division of the Egyptian people into castes, military service was the duty of the two classes of Calasirians and Hermotybians, whose relation to the rest of the community will be considered when we come to treat of the Constitution and Laws of Egypt. They were distributed in the time of Herodotus chiefly through the nomes of Lower Egypt. Their numbers (410,000 men) exceeded the ordinary demands of the government for permanent duty, and it is probable that from time to time enrollments took place, either of those who had arrived at military age, or were about to be called into actual service; or of those who were to form in turn the body-guard of the king. Such an enrollment appears to be represented in a tomb at Qoorneh, of an individual of the military caste, where nine men, followed by one holding a cane in his hand, present themselves before a scribe who records their names[1]. In the same tomb are seen a company, also of nine recruits, who are evidently undergoing the process of drilling, and are learning to march, under the instruction of a sergeant. The tombs of the military chiefs Amenemhe, Rotei, Nevothph and others at Beni-Hassan contain many groups of wrestlers, who are engaged with each other in the

[1] Rosellini, Mon. Civ. cx.

most varied exercises[1]. It is supposed that the gymnastic training of the soldiers is here represented, and we may thus reconcile the monuments with Herodotus, who denies that such contests were in use among the Egyptians, except in the town of Chemmis, where they were practised in honour of Perseus. It is evident that he is speaking of solemn games, like those of Olympia[2]. Diodorus also tells us that the palæstra was disapproved by the Egyptians[3], as tending to give only a transient strength to the body; but this objection, which might be justly applicable to the high training of a Grecian school, does not apply to the simple exercise which is represented in these paintings.

With the exception of mounted cavalry, every description of force known in ancient warfare appears in the military scenes represented on the monuments of Egypt. Their armies were chiefly composed of infantry armed with shields and lances or bows; but they had also light troops, answering to the ψιλοί of the Greeks and the *velites* of the Latins, who used light darts and the sling or the throwstick, a weapon which even now is found very effective in African warfare[4]. The body-armour of the Egyptian infantry was much less perfect than that of the Greeks. The feet were either wholly bare or covered only with the ordinary sandal; the legs and thighs were not protected by greaves or cuisses. Coats and cuirasses of mail were sometimes worn, formed of small plates of metal joined so as to allow

---

[1] Mem. de l'Eg. 4, 344. Rosellini, M. Civ. cxi–cxvi.

[2] Herod. 2, 91. Γυμνικὸν ἀγῶνα διὰ πάσης ἀγωνίης ἔχοντα.

[3] 1, 81.

[4] Wilkinson, M. and C. 1, 329.

the free movement of the body¹; but the infantry soldier in general had only a quilted tunic, or a cuirass of the same kind, without any metallic covering. The helmet also was only a quilted cap, descending over the back part of the neck and shoulders. Kings usually appear in battle, with a conical helmet of metal. The shield, the common form of which was curved at the top and straight or slightly converging at the sides, was made of wood² and often covered with leather or hide. They were usually half the height of the body³; but the light troops carried them of smaller size and probably lighter material, as wickerwork. The shield, in close fight, could be slung round on the shoulders. The side-arm was either a straight sword, with two cutting edges and a point like a dagger, or a falchion with a curved blade. Besides these we often see the kings armed with a battle-axe (*schopsch*) with a curved blade: a mace bound with metal and having a heavy metal ball at the end is also a common weapon. The Egyptians depended chiefly in battle on the bow; unlike the Homeric heroes, the kings and warriors mounted in cars never appear hurling javelins, but always discharging arrows. The bow was between five and six feet long, the arrow from twenty to thirty inches⁴, and as the bow was raised, so as to bring the arrow to a line with the eye, it was drawn with the greatest force and the arrow discharged with the surest aim⁵. Javelins for casting, and spears and pikes

---

¹ See cuirasses in Rosellini, M.R. tav. ciii. Coats of mail with sleeves, M.C. cxxi.

² 'Οπλῖται σὺν ποδήρεσι ξυλίναις ἀσπίσιν (Αἰγύπτιοι δὲ οὗτοι ἐλέγοντο εἶναι). Xen. Anab. 1, 8. 2, 1.

³ Wilkinson, M. and C. 1, 298.

⁴ Wilkinson, 1, 308.

⁵ 'Αρχαϊκὸν τὸ τὴν νευρὰν πελάζειν τῷ μαζῷ· ὃ καὶ 'Αμαζόνες ἐποίουν· τὸ δὲ μέχρι καὶ ἐς τὸ δεξιὸν οὖς αὐτὴν ἐντανύειν νεώτερον. Eust. ad

for thrusting, were also used; and when a fortress was attacked we see a pike of extraordinary length, raised by several men, who are sheltered under a shed of boards, to assail the defenders on the walls[1]. Sappers appear armed with hatchets for destroying the foundations of walls, with large shields for their defence while carrying on their operations.

The use of the war-chariot was of remote antiquity in Egypt[2]. Homer describes Thebes as having a hundred gates, through each of which marched out 200 men with horses and chariots[3]. Rightly interpreted this only means that the military array of Thebes amounted to 20,000 men, and that horses and chariots were a part of the force; the original does not justify the conclusion of Diodorus, that it could send forth 20,000 chariots[4], and indeed affords no clue to their number. The account of the Exodus describes Pharaoh as pursuing the children of Israel with "600 chosen chariots, even (not *and* as in our version) all the chariots of Egypt," a moderate and probable estimate. The monuments give us a perfect idea of the construction of the war-chariot. The body is lightly framed, sometimes with open sides, and fixed so that the part on which the warrior stood was between the axle and the pole, an arrangement

---

Il. 4, 118. What he calls the modern practice was ancient in Egypt. The Greeks raised the javelin to a level with the ear. Hippol. Eur. 220.

[1] Rosellini, M. R. tav. c. ci. cii. There is a round hole in the upper part of these shields, with a contrivance for opening or closing, which seems designed to afford the soldier the opportunity of reconnoitring under cover.

[2] Of the use of the horse in Egypt, see p. 195 of this volume.
[3] Il. i, 383. See p. 178 of this volume.
[4] 1, 45. Eust. ad loc. Hom., who naturally asks, εἰ τοσαῦται μυριάδες ἱππέων τῇ πόλει, οἱ λοιποὶ στρατιῶται ὅσοι; The poet appears to speak according to Greek ideas of military force, as if the whole population of Thebes of a certain age were military.

which made his posture easier than if he had stood immediately over the axle. It was curved in front, open at the back, without a seat, and low enough to be mounted without a step. A royal chariot was usually richly ornamented at the sides, but the ornaments were of a light open work; quivers were fixed transversely on the outer side from which the warrior supplied himself with arrows, or short spears for close fight. Each chariot held two persons, one of whom guided the horses while the other fought. The king very generally appears alone, having the reins fastened round his body, so as to leave both hands free for the use of the bow; but as he would thus lose all power of guiding the horses, and as he is generally without defensive armour, it is probable that he was accompanied by a charioteer, although the artist has represented him as filling the chariot alone[1], to enhance his dignity and give space for exhibiting him in colossal proportions. The wheels, which were never more than two, have six spokes, rarely four; the pole proceeded from the middle of the axle and was bent upwards at a short distance from the body of the carriage; the yoke was fastened to the end of the pole, and each horse attached to the car by a single trace, extending on his inner side from the base of the pole to the saddle. The heads of the horses were borne up tight by a rein, made fast to a hook in front of the saddle, and the long reins passed through a ring or loop at the side. The heads of the horses were adorned with lofty plumes, and sometimes defended by a head-piece of metal; their harness was covered with ornaments

[1] Wilkinson, M. and C. 1, 337.

of metal, serving also for protection especially at the shoulder-joint, and their bodies with housings of various and splendid colours. In short, as all the essential principles which regulate the construction and draft of carriages are exemplified in the war-chariots of the Pharaohs, so there is nothing which modern taste and luxury have devised for their decoration to which we do not find a prototype in the monuments of the eighteenth dynasty[1]. Their construction, however, was so slight, that though well fitted for the level and smooth roads of Egypt, it is difficult to conceive how they could be used in such rocky countries as Palestine. The want of shoes for the horses must also have been severely felt in such a country. The horse is not found at all in Egyptian monuments prior to the invasion of the Shepherd kings. It is probable therefore that the Egyptians learnt the use of this animal from their nomad conquerors.

Mounted cavalry never appear in monuments of any age among the Egyptian forces. Rosellini[2], who has examined them with special reference to this subject, observes that he has found only eight examples in which men are seen on horseback, and that six of these are evidently foreigners; two only Egyptians, who are no part of a military force, nor engaged in any military act, and their introduction into a battle-piece only shows, that the art of riding was not unknown. A difficulty has been created by the supposed mention of cavalry in the history of the Exodus. In the " song

---

[1] A splendid example is seen in the chariot of Rameses III. at Aboosimbel. Rosellini, Mon. Reali, lxxxi.

[2] Mon. Civ. 3, 242.

of Moses and the children of Israel" it is said[1], "Jehovah hath triumphed gloriously: the *horse and his rider* he hath drowned in the sea." But the word here rendered *rider*[2] is equally applicable to one who rides in a chariot, or on horseback, and is used of both, Jerem. xxii. 4. In the preceding chapter of Exodus indeed, in the narrative of the pursuit of the Israelites, it is said that the Egyptians followed " with horses and chariots and horsemen;" and the word there used is one that in the Old Testament always denotes a mounted horseman[3]. In the 19th verse of the 15th chapter, where the historian no longer quotes the song of Moses, but speaks in his own person, the same word is again used. In the later books of Scripture the existence of large bodies of cavalry in the Egyptian armies is evidently taken for granted[4]. The destruction of the host is more intelligible, if we suppose it to have consisted only of chariots. The horses entangled in their harness, the men oppressed with armour and perhaps embarrassed by the reins which they often fastened round their bodies, might be overwhelmed by a sudden reflux of the waves and " sink into the

---

[1] Exod. xv. 1.

[2] רכב. It is used 1 Kings, xxii. 34, of the driver of the chariot.

[3] פרש. The etymology of this word, all whose senses flow from the idea of *dividing*, proves that it means a man *astride* on a horse. The Septuagint render both רכב and פרש by the same word, ἀναβάτης, a mounted rider.

[4] 2 Chron. xii. 3, Shishak is said to come up with 1200 chariots and 60,000 horsemen. In the corresponding passage in 1 Kings xiv. 25, there is no mention of chariots or horsemen. Rosellini endeavours to make it appear that פרשים signifies, not horsemen, but horses covered with housings; but there is no authority for such a rendering, nor would it suit other passages. He might have found an easier solution of his difficulty in his own explanation of the mention of cavalry in the army of Sesostris: " Lo Storico scriveva qui, come in molti altri luoghi, le cose egizie secondo le idee de' suoi tempi e del suo popolo." M. Civ. 3, 257.

bottom as a stone and like lead into the mighty waters;" but a body of cavalry could not have been so entirely destroyed; a considerable part would have saved themselves by swimming.

The tomb of Rameses IV. in the valley of Bab-el-Melook, contains, along with representations of arms, a number of military ensigns, which are either the figures or emblems of the gods. Anubis is represented by his jackal, Phre by his hawk, Thoth by his ibis, Seb by his crocodile, and twelve other gods by their usual figures. They served to distinguish the several corps, probably according to the tutelary divinity of the nome in which they dwelt. Among the various fictions, to account for the worship of animals in Egypt, one was that originally the Egyptians had no ensigns, and being consequently defeated by their enemies, to preserve better discipline in future they placed figures of animals on spears, and so discriminated the corps of the army; and being thus victorious honoured these animals ever afterward as a mark of gratitude. We see accordingly that bodies similarly armed are placed together and march in step. But although so many monuments remain exhibiting battles, it is difficult to deduce from them any inference as to the progress which the strategic art had made. We do not commonly see the armies drawn out in line or performing evolutions, but engaged in the *melée*; and the leading object of the artist has evidently been to aggrandize the king. He is represented of colossal size, trampling down hosts of his enemies under the feet of horses as exaggerated in their proportions as himself, or piercing them with showers of arrows. Their battles are epic rather than strategic. The Egyptians appear to have been provided with no military engines, either for the discharge of weapons in battle, or the attack of fortified places. Where the attack of a fortress is represented, the defenders are taken off by a flight of arrows, or a spear is brought up by several men, placed under cover, of sufficient length to reach to the battlement of the wall. Scaling ladders were also used in assault.

The Egyptian camp does not appear to have been entrenched, but simply surrounded with a palisade. In the representation of the wars of Rameses III. at Thebes and Aboosimbel, the king's tent is placed opposite to the entrance, and surrounded by the tents of his officers[1]. The horses, unyoked from the chariots, are ranged together in one part, the chariots in another; the asses which carried the baggage are placed by themselves, and their pack-saddles and panniers in another part; one part of the camp was appropriated as a hospital for the soldiers and also for the sick animals; in another we see drilling and flogging going on. Without the camp the infantry and charioteers, partially armed, are exercising themselves in peaceful evolutions[2]. This single monument gives us an insight

---

[1] Rosellini, M. R. cvii.

[2] In the middle of this camp lies a lion, having his forepaws bound; his keeper, with an uplifted cane, stands near him. Rosellini supposes it introduced here symbolically. It seems, however, from Diodorus (1, 48), that on the monument of Osymandyas, which was really the Rameseion of Thebes, the king was represented fighting with a lion by his side, συναγωνιζομένου τοῦ θηρίου καταπληκτικῶς. Some of the expounders of this monument said that he really carried with him a tamed lion; others that he wished by means of this animal to express the qualities of his own character. The former seems most probable; only we need not believe,

into the military system of the Egyptians, which we could never have obtained from the written histories, and shows a minuteness of arrangement and organization which could only be the result of long experience in war[1].

A single monument remains, from which we can learn anything of the naval warfare of the Egyptians. It is preserved on the walls of the palace at Medinet Aboo, and represents a combat of the ships of Rameses IV. with those of a nation of western Asia, whose name has been read by Rosellini Fekkaroo (supposed by others to be Philistines), and the Shairetana, in whom some see Sidonians[2]. It is not clear whether the engagement takes place at sea or in a river. The vessels have a single mast and sail; they are impelled by single benches of rowers, who are protected by bulwarks at the side of the decks; on the top of the mast is a kind of basket in which an archer is stationed, or a watchman to make signals. The Egyptian vessels have a lion's head at the prow; those of their enemies the head of a waterfowl. Both are manned by soldiers, the Egyptians armed with bows and arrows, their enemies with round shields and swords; the vessels are driven against or alongside of each other by the rowers, and the soldiers fight fiercely from the decks.

what Diodorus adds, that this tame lion put the enemy to the rout. No doubt the prominence given to the king in every Egyptian representation of a battle is in great measure artistic flattery; a tame lion would have been a useless companion to him in the furious career which he is represented as running against the enemy.

[1] Sir Gardner Wilkinson has ascertained, by researches among the ruins of Semneh, that the Egyptians had carried the art of fortification to a high degree of scientific perfection; but no detailed account of his observations has yet been published.

[2] Rosellini, Mon. Reali, cxxx., cxxxi.

The Egyptians have possession of the shore or the bank, from which the king and a body of archers are discharging their arrows; so that the enemy are placed between two fires. The vessels appear slight for the navigation of the sea; and the water-plants near the border rather indicate a river. In this case we must suppose that the Nile is the scene of the conflict, and that the Egyptians are defending their country against foreigners, who have established themselves within its borders, and built a navy there. According to Herodotus, Sesostris was the first who built ships of war. His Sesostris was probably the Rameses III. of the monuments, and if so, he preceded by three reigns the king under whom this naval battle took place.

CHAPTER XIV.

DOMESTIC LIFE AND MANNERS.—AMUSEMENTS.

The Pyramids, temples and palaces of Egypt have been secured by their massive strength against entire destruction; but the houses were built of perishable materials, and no such fortunate accident as that which preserved Pompeii has enabled us to look into the interior of an ancient Egyptian town. We search in vain even for foundations in many places, where the former existence of a considerable population is clearly proved by extensive cemeteries. The houses were built in general of crude brick, and they have either fallen to decay or been destroyed that their materials might be applied to other purposes. At Thebes, the blackened remains of the foundations bear traces of the conflagrations to which from the time of Cambyses downward the city was exposed. But from these, though we may discover the strength of the walls and the size of the lowest apartments, we could gain no information respecting the interior disposition of the inhabited part, or the height to which the house was raised; and little respecting the arrangement of the streets. Fortunately the paintings of the sepulchres, which so generally relate to domestic life, have preserved some views of the houses in which the scenes represented are carried on. Sir Gardner

Wilkinson[1] has explored the remains of an ancient town near Tel-Amarna, which he believes to be Alabastron; and though they may not belong to very remote times, they serve to enlarge the scanty information which we derive from other sources.

Diodorus, speaking of the second Busiris, whom he represents as the founder of Thebes, says that he built the houses of private persons some with four, some with five stories[2]. In the historian's age, great part of Thebes had been long in ruin, and certainly no houses existed there to prove what had been the style of architecture in the mythic reign of Busiris. His statement is probably one of those exaggerations by which the glory of this ancient capital was magnified. That the houses should have been of that height, would be inconsistent with what Diodorus himself tells us, of the indifference of the Egyptians to the magnitude and splendour of their dwellings; it is contrary to the practice of the East in all ages, and to the evidence of the paintings. From these we may conclude that the ordinary plan of an Egyptian house comprehended only a single story besides the basement, with a terrace on the roof, open or covered, surrounded by a balustrade or battlement[3]. In hot climates, two great objects in the arrangement of houses are, to admit air and exclude heat. To attain the latter, the Egyptians made their windows small and their apartments lofty; and for ventilation it is probable that they had a contrivance in

---

[1] Manners and Customs, 2, 106.   [3] Rosellini, M. Civ. 2, 380, lxviii.
[2] 1, 45.

the roof, similar to that which is now used in Egypt[1]. Houses which stood detached and enclosed within a wall of their own, had an ornamented garden around them, such as we have already described. Their villas were still more spacious, comprehending a variety of apartments, and had frequently the appendage of a farm-yard[2]. The walls of the principal rooms were covered with stucco and ornamented with paintings. These have generally perished; but from the tombs it is evident that the Egyptians in very early times had made great advances in house decoration. Their walls and ceilings are painted in a variety of patterns, combining elegance of form with richness of colouring. Many of them, even of very early kings, exhibit a remarkable resemblance to those which we see in the mosaics of the Romans, and which have been imitated in our carpets and floorcloths. What is called the mæander, or Greek border, appears in a tomb of the eighteenth dynasty[3]. The resemblances are so numerous and so striking as to leave no doubt that the Greeks and Romans derived from Egypt these combinations, the artistic excellence of which is attested by the circumstance, that they please as much at the present day, as in the remote age when they made their first appearance.

The tombs contain a considerable number of specimens of Egyptian furniture, but they are usually of an uncostly kind; the luxury which

---

[1] See it described in Wilkinson, M. and C. 2, 121.
[2] Wilkinson, 2, 132, from the sculptures at Alabastron. It is to be regretted that he has not given more precise information as to his authority.
[3] Rosellini, M. C. tav. lxxi.

prevailed is however sufficiently attested by the paintings. Compared with modern houses, those of Egypt indeed would seem scantily furnished: they had neither curtains, nor carpets, nor mirrors, nor the elegant apparatus of book-shelves, chiffoniers and writing-desks, which literary habits have introduced among us. Musical instruments too were not with them part of the furniture. Stands for flowers, vases of perfume, and even altars for the reception of offerings which were not to be consumed by fire, appear frequently in representations of the interior scenes of Egyptian life[1]. Besides these, tables, chairs and couches were the principal articles which their rooms contained, and these in wealthy houses were made of costly materials, elaborately wrought and polished. Their forms display freedom and elegance, some of them, as the imitation of the legs and feet of animals, have been perpetuated to the present day in the workmanship of the corresponding pieces of furniture. The thrones or chairs of state, which are pictured in the tombs of the kings, were richly gilt and painted, and luxuriously cushioned; the back bends with an easy and graceful curve; the head of a lion, or the entire figure, forms the arm; the sides are occupied with emblematical devices, or the representation of captives bound beneath the throne of the sovereign. The footstools and seats are also richly carved and covered, and exhibit the enemies of Egypt in the same humiliating posture[2]. When the Egyptians

[1] Rosellini, M. Civ. 2, 469, tav. lxxxviii. 1, 2.
[2] Rosellini, M. Civ. tav. lxxxviii–xcii.

reclined on couches which had no back or scroll at the end for the support of the head, its place was supplied by a semicircle of polished wood upon a stand, on which the head was rested. In that climate the contact of the head during the day with a soft pillow would have been intolerable[1], and this substitute continues to be used among the Nubian tribes. Whatever may be said of the stiffness and uniformity of Egyptian style when employed on sacred subjects, the artists displayed a sense of beauty and grace, where they were not fettered by religious or conventional restrictions, which places them above all ancient nations except the Greeks.

The Egyptians, like the Greeks in Homer's time and the Israelites till a late period of the monarchy[2], sat at meat instead of reclining. The Greeks sat in chairs, but the Egyptians on the ground, with the legs bent beneath them, or on a very low stool, sometimes only a mat or a carpet. The dishes therefore would be placed on a table slightly raised above the floor, as now practised in the East[3], or served round to each guest. Neither knives nor forks were in use, but spoons for eating and ladles for helping have been found. At entertainments, the guests, who were of both sexes, were anointed

---

[1] Rosellini, M.Civ.2,407,tav.xcii. It is called in hieroglyphics *ols*, answering to the Coptic *ouols*, to recline.

[2] Amos ii. 8, is the earliest passage in which allusion is made to reclining, and here it is not a domestic meal which is spoken of, but a feast in an idol's temple.

[3] In the tombs we sometimes see the deceased, with his wife sitting beside a table, on which are meats, bread, vegetables and fruit. In the great picture of a banquet (Rosellini, M. Civ. tav. lxxix.) we see in one part food placed on a low table, before a person sitting on a low seat; in another on the ground, the guests sitting on their heels. Sometimes each couple of guests appear to have had a table between them.

by the attendants before the feast began, and flowers were placed on their head, around their necks and in their hands. From the history of Joseph we learn that at Pharaoh's court, it was the business of a chief of the culinary department to prepare pastry for the monarch's table; and the monuments prove that it was made with great care and fashioned into a variety of elegant forms[1]. Except in this respect the Egyptian cookery appears to have been simple, fish, beef, and goose being the chief articles of food. Gazelles and kids are also seen in the hands of the cooks, preparing for the table. The wine and water were placed in porous jars, and the process of evaporation by which they were cooled was promoted by their being fanned. The water of the Nile was purified probably by mixing paste of almonds with it, according to the present practice[2]. Music accompanied the feast; and the Egyptians, like the Greeks, appear to have amused themselves with gymnastic performers and jugglers and the antics of dwarfs and deformed persons[3]. With what religious rites their more solemn feasts were inaugurated we do not know; in the Ptolemaic times royal banquets appear to have been introduced by prayers for the welfare of the king and the prosperity of the kingdom[4]. At the close of feasts among the wealthier classes, according to Herodotus[5], a figure of a mummy elaborately painted

---

[1] Rosellini, Mon. Civ. 2, 464, tav. lxxxv. Gen. xl. 17.
[2] Rosellini, M. Civ. 2, 467.
[3] Rosellini, M. Civ. xciii. 3, 4. Xen. Symp. cap. 2.
[4] Joseph. Antiq. 12, 2, 11.
[5] 2, 78.

and gilded, a cubit in length, was carried round by an attendant, who thus addressed the guests: "Looking on this, drink and enjoy thyself; for such shalt thou be when thou art dead." This sounds like an Epicurean exhortation to the enjoyment of life; the same exhibition, however, was susceptible of a moral turn, such as Plutarch[1] gives it. "The skeleton," says he, "which the Egyptians appropriately introduce at their banquets, exhorting the guests to remember that they shall soon be like him, though he comes as an unwelcome and unseasonable boon-companion, is nevertheless in a certain sense seasonable, if he exhorts them not to drink and indulge in pleasure, but to cultivate mutual friendship and affection, and not to render life, which is short in duration, long by evil deeds." This by no means implies that the Egyptians applied it to such a purpose, and he elsewhere speaks of the custom, like Herodotus, as designed to exhort the guests to the enjoyment of life[2].

An Egyptian custom, which appeared to Herodotus[3] very remarkable, was that of singing a song in honour of Maneros. As he introduces the mention of it immediately after the carrying round of the image, and as Plutarch expressly says that it was used at their banquets, it is probable that it was one of their festive customs. Who Maneros was is variously explained. According to Herodotus he was the only son of the first king of Egypt (by whom perhaps Osiris, not Menes, was originally intended),

---

[1] Sep. Sap. Conviv. p. 148, B. [3] 2, 79.
[2] Is. et Osir. p. 357, F.

and had died an untimely death. As the same strain, under the name of Linus[1], was sung by the Greeks, and under some other name by the Phœnicians in their own country and in Cyprus, it is evident that the custom of singing it cannot have originated in the death of the only son of Menes. A mythic origin, from some circumstance which was equally interesting to the feelings of all those nations, is much more probable. Plutarch says Maneros was the son of the king of Byblos, involuntarily killed by Isis[2]; and Linus was reputed to have been either the son of Apollo killed by Hercules, or of Urania killed by Apollo. Sappho[3] conjoined Adonis and Linus in one lamentation, whence it is probable that both were personages of the same mythic character. The mourning rites which made a part of all the ancient religions have a primary reference to autumn and winter, when the sun appears to decline in vigour and be preparing for extinction, and vegetative power to be buried in the earth[4]. As the song of Maneros was the most ancient and universal among the Egyptians, it was natural that its origin should be referred to the history of their first king[5]. As the Maneros was a mournful strain, its use at banquets harmonized well

[1]   Λίνον......
'Ου δὴ, ὅσοι βροτοί εἰσιν ἀοιδοὶ καὶ κιθαρισταὶ
Πάντες μὲν θρηνοῦσιν ἐν εἰλαπίναις τε χοροῖς τε
'Αρχόμενοι δὲ Λίνον καὶ λήγοντες καλέουσι.
                               Gaisf. Frag. Hes. 1.

[2] Is. et Osir. p. 357, E. Some said that Maneros was the inventor of music; some that it was not a name, but meant αἴσιμα ταῦτα παρείη.
[3] Pausan. 9, 29.
[4] Plut. Is. et Os. 378, F.

[5] According to Jul. Pollux, Περὶ ᾀσμάτων ἐθνικῶν (4, 54), Maneros was the inventor of husbandry and a pupil of the Muses. He enumerates several other songs, all of the same character, and apparently the same or nearly the same origin.

with the exhibition of the skeleton or mummy—one reminding the guests of the transitory life of man, and the other of the short-lived beauty of the external world[1].

It has been generally thought that common life had a very grave and melancholy aspect among the Egyptians, who were oppressed and impoverished by the predominance of the priesthood. The insight which we have gained into their interior life, by means of the monuments, has shown that this was by no means the case. It is true that they had no theatre like the Greeks, no circus like the Romans; and that their public religious ceremonies were not diversified by exhibitions of strength and skill, of musical taste and literary ability like the great panegyries of Greece. But the life of the people was not so monotonous as it has been supposed to be. We find in the grottoes of Benihassan not only representations of bodily contests which were probably a part of the military training, but games carried on both by men and women, which are evidently the amusement of the people. In these paintings we see women, generally distinguished by a cap, from the back part of which two or three strings of twisted ribbon depend[2], playing with balls, sometimes as many as six at once, and engaged in trials of strength, which exhibit flexibility

---

[1] Huc vina et unguenta et nimium brevis
Flores amœnos ferre jube rosæ,
Dum res et ætas et sororum
Fila trium patiuntur atra.—Hor. Carm. ii. 3.

It is evident from other passages of the same author, that such contrasts were supposed to give a zest to festivity.

[2] This kind of head-dress indicates females of the menial class. In the representation of a female banquet or assembly (Ros. M. Civ. lxxix.) the attendants have caps with such pendent ornaments.

of the limbs in the most extraordinary degree. They make an arch of their inverted bodies, touching the ground with the feet and the back of the head, or stand on the head with the heels in the air. One couple are performing an evolution which is still common with children, locking their arms together behind and lifting each other, or rising from the ground, by bringing the feet and hands to meet. In these feats the women are dressed in tight pantaloons. Among other exercises and contests two men are seen playing at single-stick, their left arms being guarded by shields of wood fastened with straps similar to those which are worn in Italy at the present day, by the players at *pallone*. Another game is exhibited which is still in use; a man is stretched with his face on the ground, and two others kneeling over him strike him with their fists; he is required to guess which strikes him, and if he names the right person, the striker takes his place upon the ground. Others appear to be trying which can fling a pointed knife, so as to enter the most deeply into a block of wood, or raise a bag of sand and sustain it the longest with the uplifted arm. We know that in later times it was a common recreation of the Egyptians to go in boats upon the branches of the Nile in the Delta, or the lakes which it forms as it approaches the sea, and spend the day in festivity under the shade of the Egyptian bean, which grew to the height of many feet[1]. Another amusement which they practised on the river was to man boats, and rowing them rapidly, to hurl or thrust javelins without points against

---

[1] Strabo, 17, 823.

each other as they passed. Such a scene is represented in one of the oldest monuments of Egypt, the tomb of Imai at Gizeh[1], and one of the parties has been thrown into the river by the shock. In another tomb at Kum-el-Ahmar, we see tables with refreshments spread upon them for the use of the parties engaged in the mimic contest[2]. The young men of London in former times amused themselves with similar encounters on the Thames.

Dice have been found at Thebes, marked in the modern manner, but their age is uncertain[3]. Their use must have been common in the time of Herodotus, since the priests represented Rhampsinitus as playing at dice with Ceres; and we may presume that they would not have given their mythe this form, had they known that the game was of very recent introduction. We do not, however, find any representation of it among the monuments. The account which Plutarch gives, of Mercury playing at dice with the moon and winning from her the five odd days of the year, is evidently a fiction of later times, and therefore furnishes no evidence of an ancient usage. But it appears from the monuments that a game answering to our draughts was in use in very remote ages. Plato attributes the invention both of dice and playing-tables to the Egyptians[4]. In one of the grottoes of Benihassan two men appear seated on the ground with a low table between them, on which

---

[1] Rosellini, Mon. Civ. tav. civ.
[2] Rosellini, M. C. 3, 114, tav. cv.
[3] Wilkinson, M. and C. 2, 424.
[4] Phædr. 274 D. Eust. ad Il. β′. 308. Οὐ παικτικὴ ἀλλὰ φιλόσοφος ἡ Αἰγυπτιακὴ πεττεία λέγεται. The game was that which the Latins called *duodecim scripta*, and the Egyptians may have found in it some analogy to the divisions of the ecliptic. Salm. ad Hist. Aug. Script. 2, 749.

are arranged six green and six yellow pieces, all of the same form, with which they are evidently playing; in one instance the greens and yellows are arranged in lines before the respective players, in the other they are intermixed alternately through the whole length of the board[1]. How the board was divided is not shown either here or in the palace of Rameses IV. at Medinet Aboo, where the king appears seated, and playing at this game with a female, probably a royal concubine, who stands before him[2]. The game of *mora*, played by the ancient Romans[3], and with such passionate eagerness by the modern Italians, was practised in Egypt. The tricks of the juggler also afforded them amusement; we see two men seated, with four inverted cups placed between them, and it is evident that the game consisted in guessing beneath which of the cups some object was concealed[4].

The vast difference between ancient and modern times, produced by language, religion, the art of war, the improvements in mechanics, cause them at first sight to seem separated by a gulf, in which all transmission of manners and customs is lost. This is especially the case in regard to ancient Egypt, whose peculiarities made it, even to the Greeks and Romans, a world apart from their own. The middle ages produced a similar apparent disruption between the Greek and Roman world and ours. The discovery of so much in Egyptian life, as revealed by the monuments, which closely re-

---

[1] Rosellini, M. Civ. ciii.
[2] Rosellini, M. R. cxxii.
[3] Cic. Off. 3, 19. Cum fidem alicujus laudant, dignum esse dicunt, quicum in tenebris *mices*.
[4] Rosellini, M. Civ. civ.

sembles our own, restores the continuity of ages, and shows that the great revolutions which change the opinions and institutions of mankind and transfer power and civilization to distant regions, leave untouched and unchanged a great mass of the human race, among whom the customs of daily life are perpetuated, and by whose mediation the most distant times and countries are united.

CHAPTER XV.

DRESS.

THE ordinary dress of the Egyptians consisted, according to Herodotus, of a tunic of linen fringed at the legs, which he calls *calasiris*, and a loose upper garment of wool, which from its material being impure, was neither worn within a temple nor buried with the wearer[1]. This does not correspond with the representations on the monuments, which are in general much older than the days of the historian; we rarely find in them either the fringed tunic or the woollen cloak. The lower classes, when engaged in their operations, are very lightly clad, the whole of the upper part of the body being bare, and only a piece of cloth fastened around the loins[2]. Those of a higher class, whose employment did not require that their limbs should be so much at liberty, wore a similar apron, descending to the knee, the midleg, or the ankle. Instead of a girdle round the waist it was sometimes supported by a strap, crossing the shoulder. Children of both sexes, even among the higher classes, appear to have gone without clothing, at least in the house[3]. Sometimes a short pair of close drawers was worn, reaching to the middle of the thigh[4], either alone or beneath the covering just

---

[1] Herod. 2, 81.

[2] *Lumbare* vocatur quod lumbis religetur. Hoc in Ægypto et Syria non tantum feminæ sed et viri utuntur. Isidor. 19, 22, 25.

[3] See Rosellini, Mon. Civ. tav. lxviii. The children here represented appear to be eight or ten years old.

[4] See the figure of Menephthah, Birch, Pl. 43, fig. 163. Exod. xxviii. 42.

described. A calasiris without fringe, with sleeves tight or loose descending to the elbows, was frequently worn; it was of ample dimensions[1] and formed into many folds, both above and below the waist, where it was gathered by a girdle or tied by a sash with long ends, if worn by women. It might be worn alone, or over the dress before described, and it was common to both sexes. The ordinary dress of women, however, was a close-fitting robe, which began under the breast and descended below the knees, being held up by two straps which crossed the shoulders. That these garments were of linen is evident from the multitude and minuteness of the folds; the material is fine, often to transparency, and the colour varied in rich and elegant patterns. Lightness was the general characteristic of Egyptian drapery, even in the highest rank; the heavy and costly stuffs which form our robes of state, or those of Assyrian monarchs, would have been intolerable in that climate.

Dress was evidently the symbol of rank, and studiously diversified according to its gradations. When Joseph was made next in authority to Pharaoh, he was "arrayed in vestures of fine linen and a gold chain placed about his neck." The king is not only distinguished by the amplitude of his robes and fineness of the material of which they are composed, but by the peculiar form of the short garment or apron worn around the loins. It is often gathered into a point projecting in front[2], and a broad strip depended from the centre of the girdle ornamented with the royal serpent or *uræus*. On

---

[1] Καλασίρις· χίτων πλατύς· οὕτως Αἰγύπτιοι. Suidas in voc.

[2] See Birch, Egypt. Ant. Pl. 33, fig. 133, Pl. 42, fig. 160.

solemn occasions he wore a crown composed of two parts; the inner is a high conical cap, terminating in a knob[1], supposed to be the special emblem of Upper Egypt, which when colours are used is painted white; the outer, painted red, represents Lower Egypt[2]. It surrounded, but did not enclose the head, and the top of the conical cap was visible above it. Each part, however, is often worn separately. The king also wears in battle, and sometimes in peace, a close-fitting helmet cap; and when engaged in religious rites, sometimes a head-dress resembling that of the god whom he is worshiping. Queens have very generally on their heads a cap or bonnet in the form of a gallinaceous bird or a vulture, the emblem of the goddess Maut, the great Mother, or of Isis, who wears this among other head-dresses[3]. The princes of the blood-royal are distinguished by a single plaited lock of hair, left on the head which is elsewhere shaven, and falling down over the ear. The youthful god Horus has his hair arranged in the same way, to indicate his relation to the royal pair, Osiris and Isis[4]. The kings' heads are sometimes covered with a wig of artificial hair, and at others with a large cap, of some striped material, which not only enveloped the whole skull, but descended on the shoulders and breast[5]. The head and beard

---

[1] Τοὺς βασιλεῖς χρῆσθαι πίλοις μακροῖς ἐπὶ τοῦ πέρατος ὀμφαλὸν ἔχουσι καὶ περιεσπειραμένοις ὄφεσιν οὓς καλοῦσιν ἀσπίδας. Diod. 3, 3. The Ethiopians had borrowed it from the Egyptians, not *vice versâ*, as he supposed.

[2] The crown of Upper Egypt was called *ouabsh* (white), that of Lower Egypt *teshr* (red), and both united *Pschent*, a name preserved in the Rosetta Inscription. See Pl.iii.D.4.

[3] Horapollo, 1, 11, 12.

[4] Birch, pl. 19.

[5] See the statues of Rameses the Great and Menephtha the Third, in the British Museum. Birch, pl. 39, 43. Rameses the Third, in the same collection, has this cap (called *klaft*) in addition to the double crown (Birch, pl. 40). The priests often wear it.

were universally shaven by the Egyptians[1] when not in mourning, but they commonly used some artificial covering, a wig or a cap[2], with the exception of the priests, who appear with naked heads[3], unless they wear some symbolical head-dress. An ornament resembling a tuft of the beard plaited, was worn beneath the chin, being fastened by a strap; its size and form discriminating the ordinary mortal, the king, and the god . Women wore their hair long, and arranged in elaborate curls. Gloves were unknown among the Egyptians, and in the monuments are the characteristics of nations belonging to the northern climates. Persons of all ranks frequently appear walking barefoot; the sandal was commonly made of papyrus, and fastened over the instep and between the toes; those worn on solemn occasions were turned up in front like a skate. Leather, however, was also employed, and the manufacture of sandals from this material is one of the operations represented in the tombs of Benihassan[5]. A long staff carried in the hand appears to have marked the class above the necessity of manual labour.

The dress of the Egyptians was usually of an uncostly material, wealth and luxury displaying themselves rather in the ornaments with which the person was decorated; our museums abound with them in every variety of form and costliness. The collars or necklaces worn by the kings were of great size,

---

[1] Herodotus (3, 12) attributes to this practice the hardness by which the Egyptian *cranium* could be distinguished on a field of battle.

[2] See a large collection of these coverings for the head in Wilkinson's M. and C. 3, 354.

[3] Her. 2, 36; 3, 12. Is. xviii. 2, where מורט appears to signify *depilis*.

[4] The end of the beard in gods was slightly turned up. See Birch, pl. 1, fig. 2; pl. 6, fig. 13.

[5] Rosellini, M. Civ. tav. lxv.

covering the upper part of the breast, made of gold, and enriched with precious stones and enamel. That of Thothmes V., represented in his tomb, appears from its form to have been designed to hang on the breast instead of being fastened round the neck: it resembles an elongated horse-shoe, and at the lower end are two lions with the shield of the king between them, and a disc with two *uræi*[1]. Putting ou the collar of office appears to have been the principal ceremony of investiture[2], and one who was specially honoured wore several at once. Neck ornaments of less costly materials and smaller size were worn by women of almost all ranks, beads of gold and silver, precious stones, glass and enamel being strung together, and symbolical figures, serving probably as amulets hung to them, such as the scarabæus and the vulture, the sacred eye of Osiris, or small images of the gods themselves. Rosellini has found cowrie shells strung together in a necklace[3]. Armlets worn above the elbows and bracelets at the wrists with a similar ornament for the ankles were common to both sexes; the wearing of earrings appears to have been confined to women. Rings were worn by both sexes, and by all ranks; the signet-rings of Thothmes III. and Amunoph III., one of gold, the other of silver, have been preserved, bearing their shield; rings were also placed on the fingers of the mummies. According to the wealth of the wearer they were of the most various materials, most frequently gold, sometimes silver and

---

[1] Rosellini, M. Civ. tav. lxxx.
[2] Wilkinson, M. and C. pl. 80. Purpura illa et aurum cervicis ornamentum apud Ægyptios et Babylonios insignia erant dignitatis (Tertull. Idol. 18).
[3] Mon. Civ. tav. lxxxi. 24.

brass, gems, cornelian, ivory, and a blue glass or porcelain [1]. They bear either on the metal, or on the stone which is set in it, the names and images of the gods, especially the great gods of Upper and Lower Egypt, Ammon and Ptah, a sphinx, a lion, or a sacred serpent, and various ornamental or symbolical devices. They sometimes consisted of a scarabæus of stone or porcelain, hooped with metal, and bearing the name of the wearer and some mystical characters; others have been found (but of uncertain age) with a small square box, instead of a stone, apparently intended for holding a concentrated perfume [2].

The custom of burying in the tombs the favourite objects of use during life has preserved to us many articles of female ornament, pins, combs, and brooches of wood or metal, and especially mirrors. When represented in painting, the mirrors are coloured red-brown, the usual colour of bronze, and such is the material of which they are generally composed. The handle was most commonly of wood, and has perished. In one remarkable instance it was preserved entire. Rosellini, in exploring the tomb of the nurse of a daughter of Tirhakah at Thebes, found beside the mummy in a case of wood a bronze mirror, with a cover which protected it from the air and turned aside on a pin to allow of its being used. The polished surfaces of the mirror retained enough of their brightness when discovered to reflect the face [3].

---

[1] Wilkinson, Manners and Customs, 3, pp. 374, 377.

[2] Rosellini, M. Civ. tav. lxxxi. 3. The "Cannarum vindex et tanti sanguinis ultor Annulus," in which Hannibal carried poison, must have been of this construction.

[3] The mirror, when represented

In the tombs are also found many of the little cases which the Egyptian women used for the purpose of holding the *stibium*, with which according to Oriental custom they darkened their eyebrows and eyelashes, increasing the brilliancy and apparent size of the eye. They are sometimes made of stone, sometimes of wood, most frequently of the hollow of a reed, are of a tubular form, and are accompanied with a little pencil, shaped like a pestle at one end, for the purpose of lævigating the stibium, and small at the other for its introduction under the eyelid[1]. Men as well as women appear to have used it[2], and it was not only placed under the eyelids, but a long streak was drawn with it from the corner of the eye towards the temple, as seen in many painted heads. The nails, and even the hands and feet of the mummies, are sometimes coloured with *henneh*, which was therefore probably used by the Egyptians to give these parts an orange hue.

---

in painting, is sometimes preceded by a group of characters which signify "revealer of the face." Rosellini, M. Civ. 2, 429, tav. lxxxi. fig. 37.

[1] It is written in hieroglyphics *stm* with an eye. *Stem* is the Coptic name for it, from which $\sigma\tau\iota\mu\mu\iota$, *stibium*, have evidently been derived. It is prepared from various substances, chiefly plumbago.

[2] Rosellini, 2, 431.

CHAPTER XVI.

ARCHITECTURE.

The remains of Egyptian architecture, if we except the Pyramids, are chiefly temples or palaces, whose style differs little from that of temples. The scarcity of timber in Egypt, and the abundance of easily wrought quarries of limestone and sandstone, for which the Nile afforded the means of ready conveyance, caused the employment of stone for architectural purposes from the earliest times. Nothing indicates that the different members and ornaments of Egyptian architecture originated, like those of the Greek, from structures of wood. Since the names of the monarchs who had inscribed themselves on the monuments have been deciphered, we have been able to form a chronology of Egyptian architecture and discriminate its styles on certain grounds. The temples and palaces of Meroe, which was once regarded as the cradle of Egyptian art, we have seen to be of the late Ptolemaic and Roman times. With few exceptions the great temples of Nubia are excavations, in which the characteristics of architectural style are not so clearly marked as in buildings. There is, however, no reason to suppose that excavation preceded construction in the history of Egyptian art; a notion which appears to have originated in the belief, that the primitive population of the valley of the Nile were Troglodytes.

On the contrary, there is an evident imitation of architectural forms in the grottoes of Benihassan, which are older than any of the Nubian excavated temples. Their columns, architraves and vaults are unnecessary in excavations, and can only have been adopted in order to please the eye which had already become accustomed to them in building. Temples have stood in front of the Pyramids, and from the use to which they were destined, we may presume that they are of equal antiquity with those monuments themselves. As they have disappeared to their foundations, and the edifices of Memphis have even more completely perished, we are left to infer the character of the earliest Egyptian architecture from the fronts of the grottoes of Benihassan, and Kalabsché in Nubia[1]. The columns which form the exterior façade are cut out of the face of the rock, and consequently are of one piece, not composed of assizes. The shaft is always polygonal, with eight or sixteen facets, or sixteen slight flutings, or a mixture of both. It either rises immediately from the ground or rests on a round base of small elevation. There is no capital, properly so called, no cord round the neck, but a slight diminution towards the top. A simple square abacus rests on the top of the column, connected with the architrave, and projects just as much from the summit as is equal to the diminution. The proportions vary from five diameters at Benihassan to two and a half at Kalabsché. The columns of this order appear to have originated from pillars; the four angles

[1] Champollion, Lettres d'Egypte, p. 75; Wilkinson, Mod. Eg. and Thebes, 2, 250.

being cut, an octagon would be produced, and by a further cutting a column of sixteen facets[1]. They approach nearly to the early Doric, and probably gave rise to it. The only specimen of an erection in this earliest style is in the oldest portion of the temple of Karnak, of the age of Sesortasen, built into a subsequent construction[2].

Of constructed temples, Soleb in Nubia and Thebes present the earliest specimens from which any inference as to style can be drawn. They are of the sixteenth century before Christ, and from this time to the termination of the twenty-first dynasty, a space of four centuries and a half, we have a succession of monuments, which though broken in many places still enables us to trace the progress of the art. Two species of column chiefly prevail. In one, which is the older, the capital appears to have been imitated from a flower-bud not yet expanded, and narrower at the top than on the sides. The sides of the capital are sometimes divided into separate faces, by deep indentations, or striated with a continuation of the lines which mark the sides of the shaft. In the second the capital is shaped like a bell with its mouth upwards, the reflexed edge being an imitation of the opened flower of the lotus, or of the head of the papyrus, and the sides formed of the leaves and flowers of plants and trees indigenous to the country. The abacus in columns of the first form projects boldly beyond the capital, and often bears the shield of the monarch by whom the building was erected; in those of the

---

[1] Lepsius, Annali dell' Istituto, 9, 67. 1837.
[2] Wilkinson, u. s.

second it is nearly hidden by the expanded upper edge. There is a third form of capital in which a parallelopiped, or sometimes a solid of the favourite converging form, is interposed between the top of the column and the architrave, as at Denderah, exhibiting the face of a divinity or the representation of a shrine. To this class belong the columns of what have been called *Typhonia*. The solid before spoken of exhibits the figure of a dwarfish god, with gaping mouth and enormously disproportioned head. It is generally found in the small dependent temples, *mamisi*[1], which, according to Champollion, were the birthplace of the offspring of the god and goddess to whom the larger adjacent temple was dedicated. Possibly the motive for placing so unsightly an object in so prominent a position was to frighten away anything inauspicious to the birth of the youthful god. In the temples of the Ptolemaic age, as at Apollinopolis Magna and Latopolis, we find a great variety of capitals, combining parts of the lotus, the papyrus and the palm; but rich and graceful as they are, they are far from producing the same impression as the severe simplicity and uniformity of the Pharaonic architecture. As the columns of Benihassan gave rise to the Doric, so those which imitate plants and flowers appear to be the origin of the Corinthian. The Ionian volute is found in the columns of Persepolis[2], but in no Egyptian monument. It was probably of Assyrian origin, as it has been found in the remains of Nineveh.

---

[1] From the Coptic *ma*, locus, and *misi*, puerperium.

[2] Niebuhr, Voyage, 2, 110.

The shaft bears in Egyptian architecture no definite proportion to the capital; nor the height to the diameter; five to six is the usual number of diameters in the height. It is commonly of the same thickness throughout, though occasionally with a slight diminution. The weight to be sustained required massive proportions, and architects seem slowly to have arrived at the knowledge of the load which a perpendicular column will support: hence in all countries heaviness is the characteristic of the earliest style of public building. With the exception of the very early style already mentioned, Egyptian columns are not fluted; but their massiveness is relieved by being striated, and the appearance thus given to them of being composed of united stems is increased, by the horizontal bands which tie them together under the capital and in the middle. The shaft generally stands on a round or square plinth of little depth; just above the plinth the base of the shaft itself is sometimes rounded and adorned with leaves, so as to give it the appearance of growing up from the plinth. If the surface of the shaft was plain it was often covered with hieroglyphics, especially in the Ptolemaic times.

On the abacus rested a broad but simple architrave, generally sculptured with hieroglyphics; and upon that, without the intervention of a frieze, a cornice of deep curve without *fasciæ*, equal in height to one-eighth or one-ninth of the whole building. The upper edge is often occupied by a row of the sacred serpent, *uræus*. A triglyph after the Grecian pattern is only found in Roman and

Ptolemaic buildings, but something resembling it, consisting of parallel striæ at intervals, is seen in works of the Pharaonic age. The boldness of this member, the cornice, in some measure supplies the want of a pediment, which is never found in Egyptian architecture, flat roofs being naturally used in a country where rain is a prodigy and snow unknown. The portico was composed of a double or even triple row of columns; but the Egyptians, in Pharaonic times, never placed them, as the Greeks did, *around* their temples, and seldom even continued them to the extreme ends of the front, which were occupied by a return of the side-wall. Sometimes, as at Denderah, a wall of half the height of the columns closed up the space between them, and was covered with hieroglyphics. No extant temple of the Pharaonic times has this appendage, and should it appear on further examination that it has never existed, it will be probable that it was added after Egypt became subject to the Greeks, in order to conceal the rites of religion from the curious and hostile observation of foreigners[1].

No rule appears to have been observed in regard to the width of the intercolumniation; but the columns are generally placed nearer to each other than in Greek and Roman buildings. The great weight of the entablature required a solid support below, and the desire to preserve the massive character of their buildings appears to have led the Egyptian architects to crowd their columns more closely than was necessary for security. The rules of classic architecture required that each portion of

[1] This is the conjecture of an able Egyptologist, Mr. S. Sharpe.

a building should exhibit only columns of the same order. The Egyptian architect allowed himself more variety, at least in the capitals. Still symmetry was not neglected, the columns on opposite sides corresponding, and the same form being repeated at regular intervals in the line of the colonnade. In the hypostyle halls no uniformity is observed in the row which stretches away in perspective from the eye, while the side-rows, which are perpendicular to the central one, usually exhibit a correspondence among the pillars of which they are composed. For columns are sometimes substituted on the front of walls colossal figures of Osiris, or of sovereigns with the attributes of Osiris, the pedum and scourge. They resemble in appearance the *Atlantes* and *Caryatides* of Greek architecture, but, unlike them, do not bear any portion of the superincumbent weight. Such was no doubt the Hall of Apis[1], built by Psammitichus at Memphis, in front of the propylæa of the temple of Vulcan[2]. Colossal figures of this kind are found at the Rameseion at Thebes, and within the grotto-temple of Aboosimbel.

The walls of the Egyptian temples and of their edifices generally are perpendicular on the inside, but sloping on the outside; and as the gateways and other openings follow the same principle, there is a general convergence of the upward lines of the architecture, as if the pyramid had been its

---

[1] Her. 2, 153. Αὐλὴν τῷ Ἄπι οἰκοδόμησε, ἐναντίων τῶν προπυλαίων, πᾶσάν τε περίστυλον ἐοῦσαν, καὶ τύπων πλέην· ἀντὶ δὲ κιόνων ὑπεστᾶσι κολοσσοὶ δυωδεκαπήχεες τῇ αὐλῇ.

[2] See a restoration of such a building in the frontispiece to Wilkinson, Manners and Customs, vol. i. The Rameseion at Thebes, p. 162 of the present volume.

type. This gives to the temple or palace that expression of self-reposing and immoveable stability, which belongs to the pyramidal form. A spurious species of arch, produced by the overlapping of stones, is found in buildings of great antiquity in Egypt, but the oldest true arch of stone is found in a tomb at Saccara, of the age of Psammitichus[1]. It appears, however, that the principle of the arch with a keystone was known to the Egyptians when the buildings of Thebes were erected, brick arches being found there[2].

It is hardly possible that architecture, when its scale is colossal, should not be sublime, unless it has destroyed the effect of its own masses by injudicious subdivision or the undue prominence of art. The temples of India and Mexico, even the simple structure of Stonehenge, bear an impress of power, which, independently of all association of time and religion, at once subdues and elevates the mind. This feeling is pre-eminently produced by Egyptian architecture, the scale of which is so vast, that the sculptures by which the walls, columns, and entablatures are covered, do not interfere with the grandeur of the whole effect. The heaviness which its massive proportions might have been expected to produce, disappears, according to the testimony of travellers, when it is seen through an Egyptian atmosphere, with the contrast of deep shade and brilliant light[3]. Yet when we compare it with the Greek, its probable offspring, we see

---

[1] Vyse on the Pyramids, 1, 218.
[2] Wilkinson, Manners and Customs, 2, 117. P. 156 of the present volume.
[3] Descr. de l'Egypte, 2, 586.

the difference between the art which has developed itself from instinctive feeling, and that which has received its laws from the reflecting intellect. The Greeks were not inferior to any nation that has cultivated art in liveliness of feeling; but their intuitive perception of grandeur and beauty was regulated by philosophy, which from the principles of the human mind deduced the laws of unity, harmony and proportion. We shall be sensible of their superiority, if we compare the Parthenon, for example, with an Egyptian building of the same magnitude; the union of perfect beauty in the Attic temple heightens instead of impairing the effect of its majestic proportions. Hence a taste formed wholly on Greek models could not relish Egyptian architecture. Herodotus was too simple and natural to be fastidious; but Strabo in the Augustan age, speaking of one of the grand hypostyle halls of Memphis, says that it had nothing graceful or picturesque, but betrayed an idle waste of labour[1]. In the Greek temples the æsthetic, in the Egyptian the religious feeling predominated, all the subordinate and accessory parts being calculated to bring the worshiper into the immediate presence of the god, with an increasing impression of awe[2]. The approach was frequently by a *dromos* or double row of sphinxes, mysterious compounds of the human form with a lion or a ram, denoting the union of strength and intellect in gods and kings. Colossal figures, in attitudes of profound repose and with a

---

[1] Strabo, 17, 806. Οὐδεν ἔχει χάριεν οὐδὲ γραφικὸν ἀλλὰ ματαιοπονίαν ἐμφαίνει μᾶλλον.
[2] Description de l'Egypte, 2, 570 foll., which contains a commentary on the words of Diodorus and Strabo.

grave and serious aspect, or obelisks of granite placed in pairs, stood before the entrance. The sacred enclosure was approached through a lofty gateway or pylon, on each side of which was a wing (pteron) of pyramidal structure, the residence of the porters or the priests. Through this gateway, on which the emblem of the Good Genius, Horhat, a sun supported by two asps with outspread wings, was inscribed, entrance was gained to a spacious court open to the sky and surrounded by colonnades; and on the opposite side a second gateway admitted to a second hypæthral court; or to a hall, lighted by small openings near the top of the walls, the roof of which was supported by thickly placed columns. In this court or hall, the *naos*, probably the great body of the worshipers assembled on occasions of great solemnity: beyond it lay the proper temple, cell, or *sekos*, approached by a portico, enclosed in walls without colonnades, and sometimes divided into several small apartments, in the remotest of which, behind a curtain[1], appeared the image of the god in his monolithal shrine, or the sacred animal which represented him on earth. An artifice was employed to increase the apparent distance of the adytum, the doorways being made to diminish in height as if by the effect of a lengthened perspective. Even the exterior walls were covered with hieroglyphical sculpture. Such were the larger temples; others had a more simple arrangement. Those which have been called Typhonia, of which an example is seen in the island of Philæ, are simple rectangular buildings having

[1] Clem. Alex. Pædag. 3, 2.

the entrance on the shorter side, without interior columns, but with a colonnade on all sides of the exterior, like the Greek peripteral temples, only not continued round the angles. This of course precludes the inward slope of the walls, which is seen in the larger temples.

Like the Greeks, the Egyptians applied colour to their architecture, to the different portions of the columns and to the intaglios of the obelisks. In colouring those objects which have an original in nature, they by no means aimed at exact imitation, but sacrificed correctness to the richness and harmony of the general effect. The transparent atmosphere and cloudless sky of Egypt give brilliancy to all the colours of nature, and seem to have influenced the taste of the inhabitants, as in other southern countries, leading them to delight in a brightness which we think glaring, and contrasts which to us seem harsh.

CHAPTER XVII.

SCULPTURE AND PAINTING.

SCULPTURE had arrived among the Egyptians at a high degree of mechanical perfection. The hardest materials, granite, serpentine, breccia and basalt[1], were wrought by them with a precision and finish which the modern artist admires without being able to explain. This branch of the art had already been perfected at the early period of the erection of the Pyramids, the sarcophagi which they contain being of granite or basalt elaborately polished. The earliest obelisks, at Heliopolis and in the Fyoum, though their figures are neither so deeply engraved nor so accurately drawn as those of the age of Thothmes and the Rameses, show an art already far advanced. The characters which are sculptured upon them, consisting of minute objects of nature or art, detached portions of the human figure, or conventional figures, do not betray that imperfection of design which is so obvious in the Egyptian painting and statuary, and their sculpture on a larger scale. Everywhere the infancy of art is characterized by the rudeness of the attempt to delineate the human form, the want of life and movement,

---

[1] What is called *basalt* by writers on Egyptian art, is not, however, commonly the igneous rock which mineralogists so denominate. It is of a dark, dull green colour, with large specks of white feldspar, and is more easily worked and polished. The greater part of the monuments of the age of the Psammitichi and the Roman imitations are almost wholly of this material. See Rosellini, Mon. Civ. 2, 153.

the stiffness and deficiency of grace in 'draperies, and the absence of character and expression in the countenance. But it was the peculiarity of Egyptian art, that these characteristics of its infancy were perpetuated through all the stages of its existence. The artists were fettered by strict rules and forbidden to indulge their inventive genius, and hence art became unduly mechanical. Diodorus says[1] that they did not, like the Greeks, judge of the proportion of statues by the eye, but divided the whole body into $21\frac{1}{4}$ parts. Thus the relation of every part to the whole was fixed, and when it was once determined what should be the size of the whole, the size of each part was known, and the artists working separately, their labours might afterwards be combined into one statue. The remains of Egyptian sculpture exhibit no marks of this mode of putting statues together, as even the largest are commonly of a single piece; but it is probable that such a canon may have been employed in fixing their proportions. Plato praises the wisdom of the Egyptians who had established a standard in ancient times for the forms which painters and other artists were to use, and forbade all innovation upon them; in consequence of which, through a period of ten thousand years, the merit of the works of art had never varied[2]. When the remains of Egyptian sculpture and painting are chronologi-

---

[1] Diod. 1, 98.
[2] Leg. 2, p. 656. Πάλαι δήποτε ἐγνώσθη παρὰ τοῖς Αἰγυπτίοις ὅτι καλὰ μὲν σχήματα καλὰ δὲ μέλη δεῖ μεταχειρίζεσθαι τοὺς ἐν ταῖς πόλεσι νέους. Ταξάμενοι δὲ ταῦτα ἄττα ἐστὶ καὶ ὁποῖ᾽ ἄττα ἀπέφηναν ἐν τοῖς ἱεροῖς καὶ παρὰ ταῦτ᾽ οὐκ ἐξῆν οὔτε ζωγράφοις οὔτ᾽ ἄλλοις ὅσοι σχήματα ἀπεργάζονται καινοτομεῖν, οὐδ᾽ ἐπινοεῖν ἀλλ᾽ ἄττα ἢ τὰ πάτρια.

cally studied, this appears not to be strictly true. The tombs near the Pyramids contain some of the oldest and some of the most recent works executed under the independent dominion of the Pharaohs, and the difference is very perceptible to a practised eye. Yet it is a difference in execution and style, not in the forms of art, which were nearly the same in the reign of Psammitichus as in that of Cheops.

The regulations to which artists were subject had their origin, no doubt, as Plato intimates, in the connexion of art with religion, whose symbolical forms could not be varied without introducing uncertainty and doubt into the minds of the worshipers; and their influence extended to every other branch of art. Religion also impeded taste, by prescribing many incongruous combinations of human and bestial forms, and dresses and costumes repugnant to the natural sense of grace and beauty. In the representations of animals, with which religion did not interfere, they showed that they could at once copy and embellish nature, and some of their lions in particular are admirable for their spirit[1]. Their statues are chiefly of gods and kings, to whom a sitting posture, or at least one of perfect rest, was considered appropriate. They are hardly in any instance detached and free, but either are fixed to a wall or pillar, or else retain the traces of such a destination in the square slab which forms the back. The faces are of monumental gravity, neither enlightened by intellect nor animated by passion, nor

---

[1] Description de l'Egypte. Ant. 2, 108. Winckelmann, Hist. de l'Art, 1, 83, note. His observations on Egyptian art were made at a time when its true chronology was not understood.

varied by the expression of character; the limbs are ill-fashioned and stiffly placed, with little attempt to indicate the action of the muscles, and the hands are executed with entire disregard of nature. It appears to have been a rule of courtly art, that a Pharaoh should never be represented with any mark of age; indeed an old man is hardly to be found in all the remains of Egyptian art. The type of the race, which gods and mortals equally exhibit, deviated widely from the standard of Grecian beauty. The forehead is low and retiring; the ears are placed too high up in the skull; the nose is broad and round; the cheek-bones strongly prominent; the eyes long, with a slight obliquity. The lips are full, with an approach to the negro expression of a predominance of the sensual over the intellectual element[1]. Yet notwithstanding these imperfections, there is an impressive harmony, between the character of Egyptian sculpture and that of the people, at once the oldest and the most unchangeable in history; and in looking on its remains we are conscious of feelings which are not excited by the most perfect specimens of imitative or ideal art.

The fondness which the Egyptians display for the colossal in sculpture is characteristic of a people who possessed an unlimited command of material and labour, but were ignorant of the source from which sublimity in art arises. As they placed their figures on a level with the eye, they gave full effect to their gigantic size; but the effect thus produced is akin to that of exaggeration in style. The sense is astonished by a statue forty feet high; but after

[1] Schnaase, Geschichte der bildenden Künste, 1, 434.

the first startling impression has subsided, its incongruity with all around it is forced upon the mind, and the effect is lessened by repetition. This applies more to colossal statues, forming a portion or an appendage of buildings, than to those which are detached. The statues of Amenophis, standing alone on the plain of Thebes, or the Sphinx on the solitary hill of the Pyramids, seem in harmony with their adjuncts, and never cease to be sublime.

It is natural to suppose that carving in wood, from its facility, must have preceded carving in stone, or the hammering and casting of metals to represent the human form. It was certainly of high antiquity in Egypt. Herodotus[1] relates that he was shown the wooden statues of 345 high-priests, who had succeeded each other by lineal descent. He also saw at Sais a number of similar statues, said to represent the harem of Mycerinus, the builder of the Third Pyramid. They were of such antiquity that the hands had decayed and dropped off. Amasis sent two wooden images of himself to the temple of Juno at Samos. Hardly any large statues in wood have been preserved; the largest which Rosellini had seen was only half the size of life; but small images of sycamore and other woods are very common. They usually represent funereal subjects and accompany the mummies. Their execution varies; some are painted and gilt with care, but in general they are coarse and rude[2]. Other figures of wood appear to have been memorials of persons deceased, and preserved in their dwellings.

[1] Herod. 2, 130, 143, 182. Gallery of Brit. Mus. pl. 46, 47,
[2] Rosellini, Mon. Civ. 2, 155. 53.

Had the Egyptians possessed a varied, poetic and anthropomorphic mythology, its influence must have been perceived in sacred art, which among the Greeks, as in Christian Europe, has called forth the highest powers of painting and sculpture. But the genius of the Egyptian religion was adverse to such a free exercise of the fancy on religious subjects; art was the handmaid of theology, not of poetry. The highest powers of the Egyptian artists were put forth in the historical sculptures and paintings with which the walls of the temples and palaces are decorated and the scenes of common life represented in the sepulchral chambers. The temples of Nubia and Thebes contain battle-pieces of the reigns of Thothmes, Amenophis and the Rameses, in which combats of infantry and cavalry, naval engagements and sieges are represented with great spirit and variety[1]. These qualities, no doubt, abundantly compensated to the Egyptians for the defects which an eye trained by the rules of modern art perceives in them. The superior dignity of the king or victorious general is indicated by proportions many times exceeding those of the other warriors; and his actions are as much exaggerated as his stature—grasping a whole detachment of his enemies by the hair, and crushing them under his feet or his chariot-wheels. There is no unity of time or action in the scenes represented, no observance of perspective or even the simplest laws of vision, distant objects being lifted

---

[1] See what the French Commission say, Ant. 2, 110, of a figure of Rameses in a battle-piece:—"On ne trouve plus ici cette pose immobile et sans action qui paraît avoir été de rigueur dans les bas-reliefs sacrés; toute la figure est animée et pleine de mouvement; son action est bien sentie: elle est aux sculptures égyptiennes ce que l'Apollon du Belvédère est aux statues Grecques."

up that they may not be hidden by the interposition of the nearer; by which means, however, the artist avoided the too severe simplicity which limitation to a single line of objects has produced in the Greek bas-reliefs and paintings. Two right or left hands are sometimes given to the same figure. On the propyla of the temples and palaces kings and warriors are represented in corresponding postures and actions on either side, and consequently left-handed on the right side. To give an idea of a canal, planted on each side with palms, the canal is raised up and its surface turned perpendicularly towards the spectator. Yet even in this strange mode of representing a horizontal surface, the painter has not forgotten to diminish the size of the trees on the opposite side of the canal[1]. Even in the representation of single figures, the laws of vision are sometimes neglected. Though presented in profile, the eyes and shoulders are given with the fullness of a front view, and objects which must necessarily have intervened between the spectator and the principal figure are thrown behind, that the view of him might not be broken by any crossing line. In the scenes of common life portrayed in the grottoes, though the drawing is generally incorrect and the laws of perspective neglected, there is a freedom and even playfulness which we should not otherwise have known to belong to the Egyptian character. Their humour even runs into caricature. In one of the royal sepulchres at Thebes we see an ass and a lion singing, and accompanying themselves on the phorminx and

[1] Wilkinson, M. and C. 2, 145.

the harp. Another is a burlesque of a battle-piece. A fortress is attacked by rats and defended by cats who are mounted on the battlements. The rats bring a ladder to the walls and prepare to scale them, while a body armed with spear, shield and bow protect the assailants, and a rat of gigantic size, in a chariot drawn by dogs, has pierced the cats with his arrows and swings round his axe in exact imitation of Rameses dealing destruction on his enemies. In a papyrus of the Museum of Turin, a cat is seen with a shepherd's crook watching a flock of geese, and a cynocephalus playing on the flute[1].

We see from the monuments that the Egyptians painted on wood, but except the hieroglyphics of mummy-cases, we have scarcely any other remains of their painting than the colouring of sculpture or on walls. The porous sandstone or fossiliferous limestone in which the tombs were excavated was covered with stucco[2], previous to its being painted, and even works in granite and other hard stone were treated in the same manner. Their colours were few—red, green, blue, yellow, and black, but being chiefly composed of metallic oxides, they were brilliant and durable[3]. They were laid on without intermixture or degradation; without any attempt, by light and shade, to give the roundness of nature to a plain surface. It could hardly be otherwise when the chief use of painting was to colour the outlines of sculpture. Even in this branch of art, religion interfered

---

[1] Champollion-Figeac, L'Egypte, pl. 54.
[2] Descr. de l'Egypte, 3, 45.
[3] Rosellini, Mon. Civ. 2, 183.

to limit the taste and fancy of the painter, certain colours being prescriptively used for the bodies or draperies of the gods.

The mechanical process of painting among the Egyptians did not differ much from the modern practice of distemper. The wall or board destined to receive the picture, if its own surface was rough and coarse, was covered with a coating of lime or gypsum-plaster. The outline was then sketched in with red chalk, and afterwards corrected and filled up with black. The same mode was adopted preparatory to sculpture. The painter lævigated his colours and mixed them with water, then placed them on a pallet hung from his wrist and applied them to the surface on which he was at work. *Fresco* painting, in which the colours are laid upon the plaster before it dries, was not practised by the Egyptians. Some traces are thought to have been found of *encaustic* painting, by means of wax dissolved in naphtha[1], but it is doubtful if they belong to the Pharaonic times.

The knowledge of anatomy among the Egyptians was confined to the results of the practice of embalming. Neither they nor the Greeks, who carried the design of the human figure to perfection, and imitated with exquisite skill the varied action of the muscles, ever traced them beneath the skin to their connexion with the skeleton. The Egyptians did not enjoy the same advantage as the Greeks for the study of the naked figure; they had neither

---

[1] Rosellini, Mon. Civ. 2, 205. Wilkinson, Manners and Customs, 3, 312.

the exercises of the palæstra[1] nor annual public games. But they were not strangers to a simpler kind of gymnastics. In the tombs of Benihassan entire walls are covered with representations of pairs of combatants engaged in wrestling and locked together in every possible variety of attitude. There is not perfect accuracy in the design, but in general the character of each action is justly discriminated.

The profusion with which the Egyptians employed sculpture and painting in their temples, palaces and tombs, has no parallel in the history of art. Elsewhere they were subsidiary to architecture; in Egypt they were a part of it. The pylon, the column, the ceiling, the external and internal wall, were covered with sculpture. Had this, like the bas-relief of the Greeks, projected from the surface and cast a shadow over it, the continuity of the architectural lines must have been broken and their effect destroyed. But the Egyptian bas-reliefs unite the qualities of a cameo and an intaglio[2]; they rise from within the hollow traced for the outline of the figure, but this rise is given by cutting into the stone of the pillar or the wall, not by cutting away its surface. Thus nothing projects; the figure is protected from injury, and the shadow of the prominent part falls within the hollow. The colours, which if laid on figures in real relief would have been too glaring, are softened by their retiring below the surface, and indeed become necessary to

---

[1] Herod. 2, 91. Diod. 1, 81.
[2] Wilkinson, Manners and Customs, 3, 303. Schnaase, Geschichte der bildenden Künste, 1, 430.

bring them forward to the eye. Real bas-reliefs are also found, but rarely in the older style.

The progress of the fine arts in Egypt appears to have followed very exactly that of civilization and power, during the period of its independence. The Pyramids themselves, while they bear ample testimony to the mechanical skill with which their materials were wrought and put together, throw no light on the state of the arts of design and colouring. Tombs near the Pyramids, however, which must be of nearly the same age with the First and Second, as the names of the same kings occur in them, contain sculptures and paintings representing the ordinary occupations of the people, in which the inferiority of execution to similar delineations at Benihassan of the age of Sesortasen, and still more those of the 18th dynasty at Thebes, is very manifest. In the age of the erection of the pyramids, Egypt bears no traces of extensive dominion or foreign conquest; the shields of their builders have not been found in Ethiopia. But in the age of Sesortasen, from causes lost to us, through the want of continuity in Egyptian history, we find the monarchy in a much higher state of splendour and power, his conquests over the Ethiopian nations being commemorated in the temple of Semueh[1]. The dynasties of the sovereigns who took refuge in the Thebaid during the invasion of the Shepherds, have left no memorials in works of art; but it immediately revived after their expulsion. The reigns of the three Thothmes exhibit the power of Egypt

[1] See page 21 of this volume.

gradually rising, as manifested in the extent of country occupied by their arms, and the great works which they undertook. The obelisk of St. John Lateran remains as a proof of the high perfection to which both sculpture and design had arrived under the third sovereign of that name. In the reign of Rameses-Sesostris the power of the monarchy had risen to its greatest height, and this is also the point of culmination of Egyptian art, as attested by the obelisks of Luxor, the palace of the Memnonium, the excavated temple of Aboosimbel, and numerous remains of sculpture. It remained without any marked change through the reign of his successor, but after this we have little means, except the royal tombs of the 18th and 19th dynasties, of judging what was the state of art. Under the 20th and 21st even this fails; but the spirit of conquest revived under Sheshonk in the 22nd, and his victories are commemorated on the walls of Karnak. There does not, however, remain enough to characterize the state of art. The sceptre was lost by the dynasties of Thebes, and fell into the hands of families of Lower Egypt. Civil dissensions, the Ethiopian conquest, and the usurpation of Sethos followed; and it was not till the power of the monarchy was again consolidated under Psammitichus, that art revived. The great works which he and his successors executed at Sais have perished, or are buried under its ruins; but the obelisk of Monte Citorio at Rome, and many smaller works, dispersed through the museums of Europe, show that neither skill nor taste had greatly degenerated.

The obelisk is of such excellent workmanship, that Zoega had referred it to the age of Sesostris[1]; but when compared with ascertained works of the 18th dynasty, its inferiority in boldness of execution is evident[2]; and that of Apries, in the Piazza of the Minerva at Rome, falls still more below the standard of the age of the Rameses. There are few remnants of the splendid works with which Amasis adorned Memphis and the royal residence of Sais; but the prosperity of Egypt and the general diffusion of the elegances and luxuries of art is attested by the tombs of private individuals, which in their costliness and extent rival the royal sepulchres of earlier times[3].

With Amasis the period of the native cultivation of art in Egypt ceases. The invasion of the Persians soon followed. Cambyses destroyed the temples of Thebes, Memphis, Heliopolis and Sais with fire, carried off their treasures to Persia, and transported thither the most skilful of the Egyptian artificers to adorn Persepolis and Susa. During the continuance of the Persian rule, the country was disturbed by frequent insurrections, very unfavourable to the cultivation of art. But every short interval of independence appears to have been marked by the erection or repair of monuments. Some remain of Amyrtæus, under whom a native government was re-established for six years; more of Nectanebus, who maintained himself for eighteen

---

[1] De Obeliscis, p. 642. The inscription placed on it by Pope Pius VI., who set it up, calls it *Obeliscum Sesostridis.*

[2] A frieze in the British Museum, figured in the Hieroglyphics of the Egyptian Society, pl. 7, is of the age of Psammitichus, and in a very good style.

[3] Wilkinson, Manners and Customs, vol. 3, 306.

years, and was the last sovereign of independent Egypt. It was not long before it passed under the power of the Ptolemies. Without renouncing their own religion, they constituted themselves patrons of the faith of their subjects, and renewed the temples which had suffered from age and Persian bigotry. If the works of architecture executed by them did not rival in magnitude those of the Pharaohs, they were so entirely Egyptian in their character as to have been long attributed to the ancient monarchs of the country. The discovery of the inscriptions, in Greek or phonetic hieroglyphics, has enabled us to assign to each building or portion of a building its true age. The erections under the Ptolemies, as those of Hermopolis, Esneh and Edfu, were of great extent and magnificence; but they betray no influence of Greek art, and their architecture and sculpture is only a new development of Egyptian style. There is greater variety and perhaps more elegance in the capitals of the columns; the inferiority of Ptolemaic art is chiefly seen in the sculpture, which is less pure in design and elaborate in execution; and as we approach the Roman times becomes coarse and careless. The emperors continued to build and repair in Egypt, and the architecture of Denderah, though florid and overloaded with ornament, retains the genuine characters of Egyptian style. One of the latest erections, a temple to Cnuphis, Sate and Anouke, the divinities of the Cataracts, at Syene, built in the reign of Nerva, shows the extreme of the declension of art. The name of Geta[1] is the last that is read in hieroglyphics on an Egyptian

[1] Champollion, Lettres d'Egypte, p. 200.

monument; it can still be traced on the pronaos of Esneh, notwithstanding its erasure by his brother Caracalla[1].

[1] The progress and decay of Egyptian art may be studied in the obelisks of Rome. Those of St. John Lateran and the Piazza del Popolo exhibit its perfection; those of Monte Citorio and the Minerva, its intermediate state; those of the Piazza Navona and Monte Pincio, its extreme decline, in the reigns of Domitian and Hadrian.

CHAPTER XVIII.

MUSIC.

The influence of music on the character was considered so important even in Greece as to be the subject of legislation and the grave discussions of philosophers[1]. It is not wonderful that it should not have been left free to change with taste and fashion in Egypt, where law extended its control over all the habits of life. According to Plato, the Egyptians, having perceived that melody, as well as the plastic arts, was capable of exercising a powerful moral effect upon the young, and that there was great danger in allowing individual caprice and fancy an influence, established in very early times such music as was favourable to virtue, and allowed no innovation to be made upon it, through love of variety. He adds, that to his own time this law continued in force[2]. It appears from his language, however, that it was to religious music that it applied. Isis was the reputed author of these sacred strains. Music formed no part of the general education of the Egyptian youth, any more than the exercises of the palæstra; one being considered as rendering the mind effeminate, the other as procuring a transient strength at the expense of permanent weakness[3].

---

[1] Arist. Pol. 8, 4.
[2] Leg. 2, tom. ii. p. 657. Ἐκεῖ φασὶ τὰ τὸν πολὺν τοῦτον σεσωσμένα χρόνον μέλη τῆς Ἴσιδος ποιήματα γεγονέναι. He calls them in the context, τὴν καθιερωθεῖσαν χορείαν.
[3] Diod. 1, 81.

This remarkable contrast to Greek manners may explain the little notice of Egyptian music which occurs in the Greek authors. Most of the persons who appear in the monuments, either singing or playing, were evidently hired performers or slaves.

No musical notation has been found on the Egyptian monuments. As Pythagoras, who had long resided in Egypt, entered deeply into the science of music and its mathematical relations, it has been concluded that his knowledge was derived from the Egyptian priests; but what is true of geometry may be applied to the mathematical principles of music, that if the facts were known to the Egyptians, the theory has probably been discovered by the Greek philosopher.

The variety of instruments of which we find representations, and the uses to which they are applied, show that the Egyptian music must have been a much more comprehensive art than the accounts of the ancients would have led us to suppose. As instruments of different kinds are employed in one concert, they must have understood the laws of harmony. Time was kept by beating the hands. In the mechanism of the art they far exceeded all other nations of antiquity. Their harps were furnished with numerous strings of catgut, from three to thirteen, and in one instance, mentioned by Rosellini[1], even twenty-two. The lyre also, of which the Greeks attributed the invention to their own divinities, and the improvement to Orpheus or Amphion, had been in use in Egypt for centuries prior to the commencement of Greek civilization,

[1] Mon. Civ. 3, 13.

and along with it a multitude of other stringed instruments of various power and tone. The guitar appears in early monuments[1]. Its construction is a proof of the musical knowledge of the Egyptians, as from its three cords a perfect melody could be educed, by the application of the fingers to shorten the strings[2]. The use of a *plectrum* to touch the cords is rare, and is found chiefly in connection with the guitar. Of wind instruments, the single, double, and oblique flute were employed for festive, sacred and funereal purposes; the noisy music of the cymbals, castagnettes and tambourine, was chiefly used in festivity, or to excite the fanaticism of the votaries when they flocked in myriads to the temple of some popular divinity[3], or went through the villages with bacchanalian processions. The *sistrum*, so much used in the worship of Isis or Athor, can hardly be called a musical instrument; but the rattling of its wires appears to have served, like the sound of the cymbals, to excite the feelings of the worshiper. Another instrument of the same unmusical kind was in use —two sticks of metal, which were struck against each other. The drum, which was used in ceremonies and festivities, was also the principal instrument of warlike music among the Egyptians, and appears in monuments of a very early age[4]. It was of a more oblong form than ours, and was struck only with the hand. The metallic sticks before mentioned were also a part of the military band;

---

[1] Rosellini, Mon. Civ. tav. xciv–xcix.

[2] See the representations in Wilkinson, M. and C. 2, 299 foll. This superiority of the Egyptian stringed instruments over the Greek lyre, was observed by Dr. Burney, Hist. of Music, vol. 1, p. 197.

[3] Herod. 2, 48, 60.

[4] See Wilkinson, M. and C. 2, 269–304.

and the trumpet, which was of comparatively late introduction among the Greeks, is found in the earliest representations of Egyptian campaigns.

Great care was bestowed on the embellishment of their musical instruments by the Egyptians. Some have been found made of a wood brought from India or Senegal; others are painted, inlaid, or covered with coloured leather. Two of the most remarkable representations of harps are found in the chambers of the tomb of Rameses IV. at Thebes[2]; one of them has thirteen, the other eleven cords; they are covered with painting of the richest colours and graceful patterns; on the lower extremity is figured a human head with the uræus on the forehead and the two parts of the *pschent*, the emblem of royalty[3]. The shaved heads of the performers show that they are priests[4], and they appear to be performing in honour of two funereal divinities who are seated near. The larger instruments are rested on the ground, or on a stand; the smaller are borne in the hand, or suspended by a band from the neck like the *phorminx* of the Greeks.

Music appears to have been used in Egypt, not only on solemn and festive occasions, but as a recreation in the labours of domestic life[5]. Champollion thinks that he has discovered, in the tomb of a high-priest at Eilithya, the song which the

---

[1] Homer alludes to it, Il. σ´, 219, but, as the Scholiast observes, κατὰ πρόληψιν. Feithius, Ant. Hom. 519.

[2] See p. 170 of this volume.

[3] Rosellini, Mon. Civ. tav. xcvii. See also the Frontispiece to Wilkinson, M. and C. vol. 2.

[4] We find in the sepulchres the title of "Musician to the King" (Ros. Mon. Civ. 3, 83. Birch, Gallery of Ant. 171) and "Minstrel of the Hall of Amun."

[5] Rosellini, M. Civ. 2, 416.

peasants used while the oxen were treading out the corn[1].

The dance, as far as it formed a part of religious worship, was subject to the same strict law of adherence to ancient forms as music and the arts of design[2]. More freedom may have found a place in the pilgrimages to the temples or the festivities which followed the sacrifices. It was a frequent accompaniment of funereal rites, and a favourite amusement at feasts. The postures of the dancers are varied, and often closely resemble those of the modern art[3]. Both sexes are engaged, sometimes separately, sometimes together. Besides the more refined and graceful dance, the *motus incompositi* of the lower classes are also represented in the monuments; but they do not exhibit those voluptuous and licentious performances which the Asiatics practised, and which disgust travellers in modern Egypt[4]. We may regret that the restrictions placed by religion upon the fine arts should have checked their free development, among the ancient Egyptians, but the same cause prevented their perversion into the instruments of moral corruption.

---

[1] Champollion, Lettres d'Egypte, p. 146, 196. He gives these as the words of the song—

"Battez pour vous (*bis*), O bœufs; battez pour vous (*bis*)
Des boisseaux pour vos maitres."

[2] Plato, Legg. 2, ii. 656.   [4] Rosellini, Mon. Civ. P. 2, t. 3,
[3] Rosellini, M. C. tav. xciv-viii.   p. 94.

CHAPTER XIX.

ART OF WRITING.

THE monuments and other antiquities of the Egyptians show that the art of writing was practised by them more extensively than by any contemporary nation. They seldom raised an edifice without covering it with inscriptions; there remain obelisks, statues, funereal tablets in great numbers, which appear never, except through accident, to have been left uninscribed: even articles of domestic and personal use frequently have characters impressed or engraved upon them. The workman's tools, when buried with him, are found to bear his name; cattle were numbered and marked with the name of the owner; garments are described having one or two hieroglyphic characters woven or worked with a needle into the border after the manner of modern housewives[1]. Fragments of manuscripts on papyrus exist of the earliest Theban dynasties, perhaps even of the times preceding the invasion of the Shepherds. Although the pyramids externally no longer exhibit any inscriptions, the stones of the interior have hieroglyphics traced on them, and that too in a linear form, which shows that their origin was not recent. Even if we had not these tangible and extant evidences of the prevalence of the art of writing from near the commencement of history, it would be sufficiently attested by the pictures of

[1] Rosellini, M. Civ. 2, 241.

Egyptian life and manners which the tombs preserve. We not only find sacred functionaries, who from a written roll rehearse the praise of the god, or direct the ceremonial of a coronation; or see the fate of the deceased in the funeral judgment recorded with the pen; but the same instrument is perpetually in use in the ordinary transactions of life. Scribes are employed in noting down the quantity of grain deposited in a granary, numbering the cattle on a farm, or recording the weight which has been ascertained by the public scales[1].

From all this, however, it would be hasty to infer anything like a general diffusion of the art of writing in the times of the Pharaohs. Those who are employed in the offices above described have the air of being professional scribes, such as even now supply in the South of Europe and the East, the want of education among the people at large. No books ever appear among the furniture of a house; no one is ever represented reading, except in some function; no female is ever seen reading or writing. The inscriptions relating to religion, which are beyond comparison the most numerous, would be explained, as far as their explanation was deemed expedient, by the priests and ministers of the temples to the people; and those which accompany the paintings and sculptures which record the exploits of the kings, by persons of the same order[2]. The composition and preservation of the sacerdotal

---

[1] Rosellini, Mon. Civ. 3, 184.
[2] " Mox visit (Germanicus) veterum Thebarum magna vestigia; et manebant structis molibus literæ Ægyptiæ, priorem opulentiam complexæ: jussusque e senioribus sacerdotum patrium sermonem interpretari, referebat," cæt. Tac. Ann. 2, 60.

and royal genealogies and annals belonged also to the priesthood. All the books which Clemens Alexandrinus[1] enumerates were either sacred or scientific, and as such would not only be in the custody of the priests, but would receive their interpretation from them. It seems indeed from his account as if the knowledge of the system of hieroglyphics belonged not to the entire priesthood, but only to the *hierogrammateus*. There was a time when in Europe the knowledge of theology, science, and in great measure law, was attainable only through the medium of the Latin, which the common people could neither speak nor read, nor even all the priests. This was a state of things very analogous to that of Egypt; it gave a monopoly of knowledge to the priesthood, yet was by no means devised for that purpose.

The earliest ancient author by whom the Egyptian writing is spoken of is Herodotus, who says that they write and calculate, carrying the hand from the right to the left, and that they use two kinds of letters, one sacred and the other demotic[2]; but he enters into no explanation of either system. Plato, however, who attributes the invention of letters to Theuth, plainly implies that he knew them to be alphabetical, since he describes this god or dæmon as dividing vocal sounds into vowels, consonants and semivowels[3]. Diodorus in his account of Egypt says that "the priests teach their children two

---

[1] Strom. 6, 4.
[2] 2, 36. What he says of their writing from right to left, is true only of the hieratic and demotic characters.
[3] Phileb. 2, 18. Comp. Fisch. ad Weller. 1, 25.

kinds of letters, those called sacred and those which are more generally learnt[1];" and towards the end of the same paragraph, that " the people of Egypt generally, as distinguished from the priests, learn from their fathers or their kinsmen the training that belongs to each special mode of life; but letters[2] only to a small extent, and not all, but chiefly those who practise some of the arts." He gives a fuller account of the system in the third book of his history (c. 3). The Ethiopians, who claimed to be the source of the population and arts of Egypt, alleged that the Egyptians had two[3] modes of writing; one demodic, learnt by all, the other called sacred and learnt by the priests alone, secretly from their fathers; but that among the Ethiopians all indiscriminately used the latter. In the following section he explains more fully the nature of the Egyptian hieroglyphics. "These characters," he says, " resemble all kinds of animals, and the extremities of man, and moreover instruments, especially those of carpentry[4]. For among them the art of expression by writing[5] does not furnish the sense by means of the putting together of syllables, but from the metaphorical significance of the objects copied, memory lending its aid[6]. For they represent a hawk and a crocodile and a serpent, and of the parts of the human body, the eye, the hand, the face, and

---

[1] Τά τε ἱερὰ καλούμενα καὶ τὰ κοινοτέραν ἔχοντα τὴν μάθησιν. 1, 81.

[2] Διδάσκουσι, which is usually changed into διδάσκονται, should be omitted, and the ellipsis supplied from μανθάνουσι.

[3] ΔΙΤΤΩΝ for ΙΔΙΩΝ is an obvious correction which has been made by several authors.

[4] The hatchet, the pincers, the mallet, the chisel, the square, the saw, all appear among the hieroglyphics. See Champollion, Dict. no. 651 foll.

[5] Ἡ γραμματική.

[6] Ἐξ ἐμφάσεως τῶν μεταγραφομένων καὶ μεταφορᾶς, μνήμῃ (r. μνήμης) συνηθλημένης.

others of the same kind. Now the hawk signifies all things which are rapidly done; for this is nearly the most rapid of all birds, and by a natural metaphor the expression is transferred to all rapid things and things analogous to them, just as in speech[1]. The crocodile denotes all badness; the eye is the observer of justice and guardian of the whole body: and of the extremities, the right hand having the fingers stretched out, denotes the giving of sustenance; the left, closed, the preservation and guardianship of money. The same mode applies to the other figures derived from the body, and mechanical instruments and all the rest. For following out the significations which exist in each, and exercising their minds by long practice and memory, they read readily everything that is written."

In this passage, by far the fullest which any classical author has left respecting the Egyptian writing, it will be observed that no notice is taken of any alphabetical use of the hieroglyphic characters. They are all supposed to be used symbolically, *i. e.* to denote qualities by visible objects naturally associated with them. Even of these, few are found to correspond in the hieroglyphical writing with the senses assigned by Diodorus. The hawk represents royalty and divinity, and especially the gods Horus and Phre or the Sun, possibly from its rapidity of flight, but more probably from the brilliancy of its eye; but not all rapid things. The crocodile denotes darkness, but not badness of every kind; the

---

[1] Παραπλησίως τοῖς εἰρημένοις. This is the translation of Zoega, p. 430, but perhaps it means as before mentioned, i. e. by metaphorical significance.

outstretched hand and arm express the act of *giving*, or more exactly the Egyptian verb T, to give; but the closed and expanded palm are measures of length[1]. Believing, on the authority of Diodorus, that hieroglyphics were in the main symbolical, those who sought for their meaning in recent times set out in a wrong direction, and bewildered themselves in the mazy regions of conjecture. Ammianus Marcellinus also[2], though he correctly stated the use of hieroglyphics to be " ut ad ævi sequentis ætates patratorum perveniret vulgatius memoria," and thus contradicted the notion of a secret character, misled inquirers by his description of their nature, which he distinctly declares not to be alphabetical[3]. They were confirmed in their errors by the only systematic work on Egyptian hieroglyphics which has come down to us, the Hieroglyphica of Horapollo[4]. This book, according to its title, was written in Egyptian by Horapollo and translated by Philippus; but the age of both is unknown. If the author be the Horapollo mentioned by Suidas, he was an Egyptian grammarian, who taught at Alexandria and Constantinople in the reign of Theodosius; if the name has been falsely assumed, the composition of the work must be placed considerably later. The explanations which he gives are wholly symbolical; in general fanciful and false, both as re-

---

[1] Champollion, Dict. nos. 54, 55.
[2] Lib. 17, c. 4, p. 119, ed. Wagner.
[3] " Non ut nunc literarum numerus præstitutus et facilis exprimit, quidquid humana mens concipere potest, ita prisci quoque scriptitarunt Ægyptii; sed singulæ literæ singulis nominibus inserviebant et verbis; nonnunquam significabant integros sensus."
[4] The best edition is that of Leemans, Amstelod. 1835. It has been translated into English, and illustrated by Cory.

gards the analogies on which the symbolical use is supposed to be founded, and the actual practice of hieroglyphical writing. The sixth section of the first book may serve as a specimen. "What the Egyptians express by delineating a hawk. They delineate a hawk when they wish to denote a god, or height, or depression, or pre-eminence, or blood, or victory. *A god*; because the animal is prolific and long-lived; and, moreover, because it seems to be an image of the sun, being able, beyond all other birds, to look steadily at his rays; whence physicians use the plant hawkweed (*Hieracia*) to cure the eyes; whence also they sometimes represent the sun as of the form of a hawk, as being the lord of vision: *height*; because other animals, aiming to soar, go obliquely round about, not being able to go straight; but the hawk only soars straight upwards: *pre-eminence*; because it appears to excel all other animals: *blood*; because they say that this animal drinks not water, but blood: *victory*; because it conquers all birds; for when it is in danger of being mastered by another, it lays itself on its back in the air and fights with its claws turned up and its wings and rump downwards; and is victorious, because its antagonist cannot do the same thing." The only part of this which is true is that the hawk is an emblem of divinity and of the sun. A few coincidences are found between the explanations of Horapollo and the real meaning of the hieroglyphics, but they are exceptional, and his authority as an interpreter is in itself worth nothing[1]. It is evident

---

[1] See Champollion, Précis, p. 348. He says he has found only thirteen of the characters mentioned by Horapollo, which really bear the meaning he assigns to them.

that the power of reading a hieroglyphical inscription was not possessed by him, if it existed in his time; that only an imperfect traditional knowledge of a few symbols remained, and that boundless scope was given to the fancy in explaining their origin.

The Latin writers throw no light upon the system of hieroglyphics. Tacitus[1], speaking of the Egyptians, says that they first expressed ideas (*sensus mentis*) by the figures of animals; and declared themselves to be the inventors of letters—a glory which the Phœnicians had usurped in consequence of their extended navigation, by which it had been diffused through Greece. Lucan[2], on the other hand, claims for the Phœnicians to have known alphabetical letters before the Egyptians had invented the papyrus, and while they only cut magic figures of birds and beasts in stone. This shows that he supposed the written and monumental characters of Egypt to be entirely distinct, which is contrary to the fact. Pliny[3] speaks of the sculptures on Egyptian monuments as being letters; yet we cannot hence infer that he knew them to be alphabetical. Plutarch[4] more distinctly speaks of twenty-five Egyptian letters, assigning as the reason of this number that it is the square of five. As, however, he elsewhere says that the Ibis, the bird of Thoth, was the first letter[5], though this character

---

[1] Ann. 11, 14.
[2] Pharsalia, 3, 221.

      Phœnices primum, famæ si creditur, ausi,
      Mansuram rudibus vocem signare figuris.
      Nondum flumineas Memphis contexere byblos
      Noverat; in saxis tantum volucresque ferasque,
      Sculptaque servabant magicas animalia linguas.

[3] Hist. Nat. 36, 14 (8 al.), 7, 57 (56).
[4] De Is. et Os. 2, p. 374.
[5] Sympos. 2, 738.

has no alphabetical sound, he could only mislead one who endeavoured to ascertain the true nature of Egyptian writing.

Ammianus Marcellinus, in the passage before quoted, in which he describes the transport of an obelisk by Constantius and its erection at Rome, gives a translation by Hermapion of the inscription on that which stood in the Circus Maximus. It furnished no assistance, however, in the discovery of hieroglyphics; for it was not known which of the obelisks once erected there was meant, the Lateran or the Flaminian. The name of Thothmes, not Rhamestes, has since been found on the Lateran obelisk, and the inscription on the Flaminian, which does contain the name of Rameses, cannot be read into any close conformity with the translation. Yet the phrases "King Rhamestes Son of the Sun, living for ever;" "the beloved of Apollo and the Sun," "founded upon Truth," "Lord of the Diadem," &c., are of constant recurrence in hieroglyphical inscriptions, and prove that at least their general sense was understood when Hermapion wrote. No obelisk, however, has been found at Rome with an inscription so exactly agreeing with this of Ammianus that it can be identified as the original.

The only ancient author who has left us a correct and full account of the principle of the Egyptian writing is the learned Alexandrian Father, Clemens, who wrote towards the end of the second century after Christ. In his *Stromata*[1] he says, "Those who receive education among the Egyptians learn

[1] Lib. 5, c. 4, p. 657, Potter.

first of all the method of Egyptian writing which is called *epistolographic*; secondly the *hieratic*, which the hierogrammats use; and last, and as the completion, the *hieroglyphic*. Of this one kind is direct, by means of letters, the other symbolical. And of the symbolical, one expresses directly by means of imitation, another is written as it were tropically, and another runs into downright allegory[1] by means of certain enigmas. For example[2], when they wish to represent the sun they make a circle, and the moon a crescent, in the way of direct imitation. But in the tropical way they engrave characters, using them metaphorically according to their affinity, and sometimes changing them and sometimes transforming them in a variety of ways. Handing down, for example, the praises of their kings in mythological fables, they record them by means of the sculptures. Of the third kind, which uses enigmas[3], let this be a specimen; they likened the other heavenly bodies to serpents, on account of their oblique course, but the sun to a beetle, because having made a round ball of cow-dung he rolls it with a retrograde movement."

When we come to relate the history of the discovery of hieroglyphics, we shall find that every part of the system is described by Clemens, and may wonder that his words had not served as a guide to the truth. They are, however, a little ambiguous,

---

[1] Ἀντικρὺς ἀλληγορεῖται. For this use of ἀντικρὺς in the sense of *plane, omnino*, see Suid. s. voc. Ἀντικρὺς, διόλου ἢ παντελῶς ἢ φανερῶς. Plut. 370 D.

[2] This is the sense of γοῦν, both here and below. It often introduces an illustrative or confirmatory statement. See Hartung, Gr. Partikeln, 2, p. 15.

[3] Plutarch, *u. s.* Οὐ δι' αἰνιγμῶν οὐδὲ συμβολικῶς, ἀλλὰ κυρίοις ὀνόμασι.

and their meaning was rendered more perplexed by the preconceived opinions with which learned men translated and expounded them. They are ambiguous, inasmuch as Clemens seems to make the *hieratic*, which is only a running-hand of hieroglyphics, a distinct species, and thus led his commentators to seek for some essential difference where none existed. Even the expression διὰ τῶν πρώτων στοιχείων, "by means of letters[1]," which is now so clearly seen to mean an alphabet, was variously interpreted. Again, we commonly use the word *symbolic* as equivalent to *emblematic*, and understand by it something which does not represent things directly, but by allusion and analogy; whereas Clemens includes under it the making pictures of objects to represent those objects, as well as to suggest certain analogous qualities to the mind, which he afterwards distinguishes as the *tropical* use. The confusion was increased by the endeavour to harmonize with this passage another in Porphyry's 'Life of Pythagoras[2],' in which he says that there were three modes of writing among the Egyptians—the epistolographic, the hieroglyphic, and the symbolic; thus making the two last distinct species, and the hieroglyphic *direct* in its mode of expression[3]. The consequence was, that those who after the revival of archæological studies engaged in the problem of interpreting hieroglyphics, attached themselves generally to the discovery of the symbolical and enigmatical characters; and as Horapollo was their guide, they necessarily went astray.

[1] Not *initial letters*, but simply letters, the *prima elementa* of the Romans. See Lepsius, Lettre à Rosellini, p. 44. Hor. Sat. 1, 26.

[2] Vit. Pyth. c. 11, 12.

[3] Κοινολογουμένων κατὰ μίμησιν, where κοινός is equivalent to κύριος in Clemens.

This accorded with the view generally adopted, that hieroglyphics were devised by the priests to conceal their mystical doctrines[1]. Warburton, the most sagacious of them, abandoned the notion of an occult character and recognised the existence of an alphabet; but he confined it to the epistolographic and hierogrammatic, expressly excluding the hieroglyphic[2]. Zoega, in many respects so meritorious, entirely misapprehended the meaning of πρῶτα στοιχεῖα in the passage of Clemens, and rejected the opinion of De Guignes, who thought he had perceived alphabetical characters among the hieroglyphics[3]. Indeed it was scarcely possible that any sagacity should have discovered from the words of Clemens the real fact that the alphabetical, the direct symbolical and the tropical were not three distinct systems, used by different classes of men and kept separate, but only three different modes, all of which might be employed jointly in the expression of a single sentence[4].

Probably we should have had to the present day only a similar succession of hypotheses, but for an event connected with the French Expedition to Egypt in 1798. A French engineer, in digging the

---

[1] The Christian Fathers inculcated this view of hieroglyphics. See St. Cyril, quoted by Zoega, p. 23.

[2] Divine Legation, B. 4, sect. 4, v. 2, p. 97.

[3] Deguignius, dum in monumentis Egyptiis inter hieroglyphicas notas invenisse sibi visus est characteras aliquos alphabeticis similiores quam imitativis, opinioni indulsit nullo idoneo argumento firmatæ, p. 441. De Guignes' paper is in the Mém. de l'Ac. des Insc. 34, 3.

[4] The signification of the *tau* or *crux ansata* (Pl. iii. b. 3) as *Life*, had been preserved in consequence of its resemblance to the cross. Sozomen (Hist. Eccl. 7, 15) relates that when the Serapeion of Alexandria was destroyed by the order of Theodosius, a hieroglyphical character resembling a cross was found on some of the stones, and explained by those who understood such things, to mean ζωὴ ἐπερχομένη.

foundation of a fort near the Rosetta mouth of the Nile, found a *stele* or tablet of basalt, on which was an inscription in three different characters. One of these being Greek, it was soon ascertained that the purpose of its erection was to acknowledge, on the part of the high-priests, prophets and other sacred functionaries assembled at Memphis in the year 196 B.C., at the coronation of Ptolemy Epiphanes, the services rendered to the sacerdotal order and to Egypt generally by the young king, and to decree him certain honours. The Greek contains a command that the decree should be inscribed " in the sacred letters, and letters of the country and Greek letters[1];" and it was obvious from the inspection of the characters that the first are what we call Hieroglyphic, and the second what Herodotus and Diodorus call Demotic or Demodic[2], and Clemens Epistolographic. It was natural to conclude that each of the inscriptions was substantially the same; and as the numerals for *first, second* and *third* were found in the same relative position at the end of the hieroglyphic and demotic as the corresponding words in the Greek, it became probable that there was even a literal agreement. Various attempts were accordingly made to decipher the other two by the aid of the Greek. They were rendered difficult, partly by the circumstance that the hieroglyphic portion is much mutilated, and partly by the first inquirers, Akerblad and Young,

---

[1] Τοῖς τε ἱεροῖς καὶ ἐγχωρίοις καὶ Ἑλληνικοῖς γράμμασιν.

[2] Dr. Young and his followers have adopted the name *enchorial* from the inscription; but *demotic* is more definite, as " letters of the country" are here evidently opposed to " Greek letters," not " sacred letters."

directing their attention rather to the demotic than the hieroglyphic part. The earliest publications of the latter, in the 'Archæologia' and 'Museum Criticum[1],' relate to the attempts to read the demotic into Coptic. Having convinced himself that the demotic was not alphabetic, he turned to the study of the hieroglyphic, and in 1818 circulated among his friends a hieroglyphical vocabulary in which about 200 characters were explained. These were afterwards published in the Supplement to the 'Encyclopædia Britannica' in 1819[2]. Many of his interpretations have been confirmed by subsequent inquirers, as the character for *year*, *month* and *day*, the system of numeration, the hieroglyphic for *god*, *priest*, *land*, *shrine*, *give*, *name*, and others; in the majority of his conjectures, however, he was not successful, and especially in those cases where there is no decided visible resemblance between the sign and the thing signified. Two very important points, however, were ascertained by him; that the oval rings on the Egyptian monuments contain proper names[3], and that female personages, both human and divine, are discriminated from the male by the addition of an egg and a semicircle (Pl. III. C. 7, 8). At the end of his list he gives, with a quære, *Sounds?*, thirteen hieroglyphical characters, to which he assigns the values BIR, E, ENE, I, KE, M, MA, N,

---

[1] Arch. 18, 61. May 19, 1814. Mus. Crit. vol. 2, p. 154, 331. 1826. The correspondence with De Sacy and Akerblad, contained in this paper, is of the years 1814, 1815. The letter to the Archduke John of Austria, 1816.

[2] Vol. 4, Art. Egypt, pl. 74-78.

[3] Champollion and others have represented this as *known* from the work of Zoega (Précis, p. 22). But in both the passages referred to, Zoega speaks doubtfully, and rather rejects than adopts the opinion that these rings contain proper names. Pp. 374, 475.

OLE, DS, P, T, O. This was the first glimpse of the great discovery of the *phonetic* use of hieroglyphical characters, but Dr. Young himself had not a clear conception of his own discovery. He had arrived at the deciphering of the hieroglyphic names through the medium of the demotic, and having convinced himself that the demotic was not alphabetical, he formed the same conclusion respecting the hieroglyphic. The characters which he fixed were derived from the two names Berenice and Ptolemæus (Pl. II. C. 1, 2); and he was confirmed in his opinion that they represented things, and phonetically the names of those things, by the resemblance between the first character in the group Berenice and a basket, which in Coptic is *Bir*. This first error threw him wrong in his subsequent analysis; for he naturally supposed the second character, which really represents R, to be an E. The N and I, which are the third and fourth, he interpreted correctly, but erred again in supposing the fifth, which is K, to be redundant; and the sixth, which is an S, to be KE[1]. So in the name of Ptolemy he correctly ascertained the P, S and T, but supposed the M to be MA, the L to be OLE, and the O to be superfluous. It may well surprise us, that having ascertained several of these characters to represent single sounds he did not conclude them all to do so; in other words, to belong to an alphabet instead of being pictures of things whose names were used to express the sounds of proper names. The conclusion, that as several of the characters represented

---

[1] This last letter is not found in some of the shields of Berenice, and is not in that copied in the Plate.

letters, all must do so, would have been irresistible in regard to our own language, in which it never happens that a single letter is itself a name; but in the Coptic a single letter is frequently a word. How imperfect his discovery was appears evident from the fact, that he did not succeed in deciphering the name of a single ancient Pharaoh except Thothmosis. Here it happened that the first syllable was not spelt alphabetically, but expressed by means of the Ibis, the bird consecrated to Thoth (Pl. II. C. 9). In all the rest he failed entirely. Thus the name of Psammitichus (6) he read Sesostris; that of Sesortasen, Heron; that of Amenoph (8), Tithous. An accident prevented him from availing himself of a monument which would have shown him that the phonetic characters were a real alphabet. An obelisk had been found in the Isle of Philæ and transported to London by Mr. W. J. Bankes, on which Ptolemy appears written precisely as on the Rosetta stone, and also another royal name. Now the Greek inscription on the base[1] mentions, along with Ptolemy, Cleopatra, and it was an obvious inference that the second hieroglyphic name was to be read Cleopatra, especially as it terminated with the two characters which Dr. Young had already assigned as the distinction of the female sex. All the letters which form the name Cleopatra occur either in Ptolemy or Berenice, and if the same characters were again found in their proper places in this new combination, the evidence of their true nature would be conclusive. Unfortunately, by an

---

[1] Letronne, Recherches pour servir à l'histoire de l'Egypte, p. 297–303. Lepsius, Denkmäler, taf. xvii.

error in the lithographed copy of the hieroglyphics on the obelisk, the first letter of the name of Cleopatra was expressed by a T instead of a K, and Dr. Young too hastily allowing himself to be discouraged by this circumstance[1], a more recent labourer in the same field carried off the larger share of the honour of the discovery.

There can be no doubt that Champollion, who did not publish his *Lettre à M. Dacier* till 1822, had seen the Hieroglyphical Vocabulary of Dr. Young, or that he had derived from it the idea, unknown to him before, of a phonetic value in the hieroglyphical characters enclosed in the oval shields. But he saw more than Young himself; he saw that instead of representing words they represented letters, and, aided by a suggestion of Letronne, he brought this to the test, by means of the obelisk of Philæ, whose evidence had escaped from Young. The combination of this with the Rosetta stone gave him an alphabet of fifteen letters, and the evidence of their sound was increased by a comparison with the name of Alexander (ALKSNTRS), found with a Greek inscription at Karnak (Pl. II. 4). The rapidity with which he proceeded to read names occurring on monuments of the Ptolemaic and Roman times, showed that the true key was in his hands; the buildings on which they were found had generally Greek inscriptions, fixing the reigns in which they were erected. Ascending to the times of the Persian conquest and the Pharaohs, who lived before it, and applying the same alphabet which he had derived from the Ptolemaic and Roman inscriptions, he was soon able to read the names of Cambyses

[1] Discoveries in Hieroglyphical Literature, p. 49.

(Kenbot) (5), Psammitichus (6), Tacelothis, Osorchon, Amunmei-Sheshonk (7), Amenophis (Amenotp) (8), Thothmes[1] (9), Amunmei-Rameses (11), Cheops (Shoufou) (10), and others, known, either from the classical historians or from Manetho, as ancient sovereigns of Egypt. Nor was this the limit of his discovery. He soon ascertained that parts of the hieroglyphical inscriptions which are not included in the oval shields, could be resolved by the same phonetic alphabet into words of the Coptic language, and that this use extended backwards to the very earliest ages of the monarchy. In the dispute which arose respecting their respective shares in this great discovery, neither Young nor Champollion showed himself perfectly candid. Young did not acknowledge distinctly the imperfection of his own analysis, and the important difference in principle between his method and Champollion's. Champollion on the other hand concealed the fact, that he had derived from the works of Young the first idea of a phonetic use of the hieroglyphics. The discovery of Young, however, in the state in which he left it, would have been productive of little benefit; as amended by Champollion, it has unlocked the long-closed chambers of Egyptian archæology.

When we analyse a hieroglyphical inscription, we find that its characters are used in three different ways. First, that which Champollion calls the *figurative*, but which we prefer to call the *pictorial*, since figurative in English has the meaning of *tropical* or *symbolical*. In this case the delineation of an object is designed to convey to the mind the

---

[1] Two of the characters in the shield of Thothmes, the guitar and the beetle, are not phonetic.

idea of that object and nothing more; and were the whole inscription made up of such delineations, it would be a picture-writing like that of the Mexicans. It is one of the circumstances in the description of Clemens, which prevented the nature of Egyptian writing from being understood, that he includes this in the general appellation of *symbolical*, as in the case of a disk for the sun and a crescent for the moon, distinguishing it as "that kind of the symbolical which produces its effect directly by imitation." This pictorial representation sometimes stands instead of a phonetic name for the object; but the most common use is to make the phonetic group of characters more intelligible, by being subjoined to them. Thus to the names of individuals the figure of a man is subjoined; to the characters which express the words for *name, wine, eagle, grapes, egg, statue, ear, wall, ass, milk*, and others (Pl. III. A.), figures are added, forming what Champollion calls the *determinative* of that group of characters. To *ran*, name, is subjoined the shield or ring in which proper names are commonly enclosed; to *erp*, wine, two jars, &c.[1] In a similar way a man dancing is subjoined to the verb signifying that act; a woman on her knees with a child, to the verb signifying to nourish or bring up; a man erect with outstretched hand, to the verb which signifies to call upon[2]. Sometimes the figure is only partially given, the head or the limbs being substituted for the whole

---

[1] Lepsius, Lettre à M. Rosellini, pl. A.

[2] The determinative was sometimes fixed by the sound rather than the sense. Thus a spindle was used as the determinative of *singing*, *hos* in Coptic signifying both a spindle and to sing. See Dr. E. Hmcks, Tr. of R. I. Academy, v. 21, P. 2.

body. This mode of fixing the sense of a particular group of characters was especially convenient in a system of writing, which did not mark either by points or intervals the commencement of one word and the termination of another.

The second use of the hieroglyphical writing is the *symbolical*, in which the object delineated is not meant to convey to the mind simply the idea of itself, but of something associated with and suggested by it. Thus a crescent is used to denote a month (Pl. I.), because no doubt, originally, the Egyptian month was lunar; the palm to denote a year, because (it is said) the tree puts forth a branch every month[1]; the vulpanser or goose of the Nile, a son, because the bird is remarkable for its filial affection[2]; the bee, a people obedient to their king[3]; the vulture, maternity (Pl. III. B. 5); the bull, strength, or a husband; a stretched-out hand, the action of giving (Pl. IV. F.); two legs, verbs of motion; a hand holding a club, force; an ostrich-feather, truth, from the equality of all the filaments; a lotus, Upper Egypt; a head of papyrus, Lower Egypt—as their characteristic productions (Pl. III. D. 5); the conical cap, Upper Egypt; the exterior diadem, Lower Egypt, as the insignia of their respective sovereignties (Pl. III. D. 4), the character for *land*, four roads crossing, being subjoined to each; a writing-case, a scribe (*ib.* B. 7); a palace (D. 8) is represented by a rectangular enclosure, with a large court and pylon; a temple, by a similar

---

[1] Horapollo, i. 3. See Pl. III. D. 1.
[2] Horapollo, i. 53. See Pl. III. B. 1.
[3] Horapollo, i. 62. See the character which precedes the shield of Ptolemy (Pl. IV. No. 4), in the copy from the Rosetta Stone.

enclosure, with a sacrificial hatchet, the symbol of a god (7); a priest (B. 6), by a figure with uplifted hands and a vessel of libation. These are instances of obvious and simple association; in other cases the reference is more obscure. We do not know the reason why *life* was represented by the *crux ansata* (III. B. 3), or *worlds* by two parallel lines (*ib.* 2), or *wife* by a figure resembling a shield (*ib.* 4). We may conjecture that the *crux* is a key, which gives entrance into life; that the parallel lines denote unlimited extension; but we can offer no proof that this was the origin of their application. The meaning, however, is not doubtful.

Of that more deep and far-fetched symbolism, which constituted what Clemens calls the enigmatical kind, modern research into the hieroglyphics has revealed very little. The examples which he himself gives, the representation of the course of the stars by a serpent, and of the sun by a scarabæus[1], are not confirmed by the monuments. Plutarch[2] tells us that on the propylon of the temple at Sais were inscribed, a child and an old man, a hawk, a fish and a hippopotamus; that the hawk denoted a god, the fish, hatred, and the hippopotamus, impudence; and that the whole together was to be read, " Ye who are being born and ye who are about to die, the god hates impudence." Such a condensation of symbolical meaning would approach the enigmatical, and we cannot pronounce that the Egyptians never expressed themselves in this way; but we do not find examples of it in their

---

[1] It seems rather to denote *the world* (Champ. Lex. No. 174).

[2] Op. 2, p. 363. Compared with Clem. Alex. Stromat. 5, 7.

monuments, and it is very foreign to the character of the hieroglyphical writing. As far as it has been hitherto explained, there are in it very few symbols for the expression of abstract conceptions and propositions connected with them by material objects. We may turn page after page of Champollion's Dictionary of Hieroglyphics, and find no signs but such as are pictorial or phonetic.

The last-mentioned class, the *phonetic* (the first in the enumeration of Clemens) is really by far the most extensive. The greater part of the characters of which a hieroglyphical inscription is made up are as truly *letters*, as if it were Greek or English; and as discovery has extended itself, signs supposed to be symbolical have shown themselves to be phonetic[1]. There are, however, two circumstances which distinguish the Egyptian writing from that of other nations. One is that in other alphabets the characters appropriated to express vocal sounds appear to have no resemblance to any material object, but to be arbitrarily or conventionally allotted. It is true that in the Hebrew the names of the letters are significant, *Aleph* meaning an ox, *Beth* a house, and so on; and an ingenious attempt has been made[2] to show that the earliest form of Aleph resembled the head of an ox, of Beth the gable of a

[1] For example, the vulpanser (Pl. III. B. 1) has been explained before symbolically to denote *son*; but it is perhaps the letter *S*, representing the Coptic *Se*, a son. The branch (*ib.* 4, 5) appears not to be a symbol of royalty, but the first letter, *S*, of an old Egyptian (not Coptic) word, *Suten*, king. The first character in the group for Egypt (III. D. 6) was supposed to represent a crocodile's tail; and as this denoted *darkness* (Horap. 1, 70), and the native name of Egypt, *Chemi*, signified *black*, it was supposed to be a symbol of Egypt. It is now considered to be the letter *Ch*, joined with the letter *M*, to spell C*hem*. Many similar instances might be given.

[2] Hug über die Erfindung der Buchstabenschrift. Ulm, 1801.

house; but it is only by great exercise of the fancy that such an opinion can be rendered plausible throughout. In the hieroglyphical writing the majority of the characters are pictures of well-known objects, and the few which have no obvious archetype, as the most common forms of S, P, M, and T, may be concluded from analogy to have had the same origin. Dr. Young supposed the transition from the pictorial to the phonetic use to have taken place, by the adoption of the picture of the object as an exponent of the sound of its name; a basket (*Bir*), for example, to denote the syllable Ber in Berenice, the oval shield being used to show that the image of the basket was meant in this case to suggest, not the object itself or its uses, but the sound of its name. Syllabic characters, however, are the exception, not the rule, in Egyptian writing. Champollion showed that the characters represented letters, not syllables, and were phonetically used without, as well as with, the oval shields. According to him, when the Egyptians wished to represent a sound, they took for its exponent the picture of some object, whose name in the spoken language *began* with that sound. It was even thought that Clemens, when he described the first method as imitating by means of *the first elements*, meant by this *initial* letters[1]. There are, certainly, some remarkable coincidences between the characters and the first letters of the Coptic names of the objects which those characters represent. Thus an eagle stands for A, and its Coptic name is *Ahom*; a leaf of an aquatic plant, Coptic *Achi*, stands

[1] See p. 293 of this volume.

for the same letter; a lion for L, Coptic *Labo*; an owl for M, *Moulad*; a knotted cord for H, *Hahe*, and some others. This may have been the cause of the appropriation, but it cannot be carried through the whole of the phonetic alphabet. The Coptic language, as known to us, affords no reason why A should also be denoted by an arm, OU by a chicken, B by a leg, or K by a patera. While the evidence remains thus imperfect, we can only say that this is an easy way of accounting for the transition from the pictorial to the phonetic use.

The second peculiarity which distinguishes the Egyptian alphabet from those with which we were previously acquainted is, that in them one form is appropriated to the expression of one vocal sound, whereas in Egyptian writing, most of the elementary sounds have more than one sign. These equivalents have been called *homophones* by Champollion, and they were the cause of considerable embarrassment in the early stages of the discovery. Were the origin above assigned to the phonetic use correct, it is evident that any object might be used to denote a letter, whose name began with that letter, and the latitude in the use of homophones would be boundless. But in fact their use is much more restricted. We have first to strike off a considerable number of characters never used phonetically in writing the names of the ancient Pharaohs. Again, in many instances, as was first pointed out by Lepsius, a character which in the symbolical writing stood by itself for a whole word, is used phonetically for the initial letter of that word, but in no other combination. Thus the sacrificial axe stood symbolically for a *god*, in Coptic *Nouter*; and when this word is phonetically written, the axe stands for the first letter N; but never elsewhere. So *life* was represented symbolically by the *crux ansata* or *tau*; and in writing the word *onch*, which is Coptic for *life*, this character stands for O, but in no other. It was a rule to write particular combinations of sounds with certain letters only; A, M and N had each several homophones, but in the name of the god AMuN (Pl. III. C. 1), only one form of the three letters is ever found. In the word *Men*, "established," M is always written with the crenellated parallelogram (Pl. II.), which is never used in *Mai*, "beloved." Where no such traditional rule prevailed, the choice of the homophone appears to have been determined by symmetry, some forms grouping best together. The list of 132 homophones has been reduced by Lepsius to 34 of general use[1]. They represent fifteen sounds; the vowels A and E; I, and the diphthongs AI and EI; O, and the diphthong OO; the consonants B, K, T (which is not distinguished from D), R and L, which were one letter in Egyptian pronunciation and writing[2], M, N, P, S and SH, and three aspirates, F, CH and H. Of these, B, P and F in the general phonetic alphabet have only one sign; O, K, R, S, SH, CH, H, two; A and N three, T and M four. The difficulty of mere reading according to such an alphabet is not great, even when we include the signs which are phonetic only in certain combinations. The

---

[1] See his alphabet, as given in the Lettre à M. Rosellini, in Pl. II. It is copied in Pl. II. G. H. at the end of this volume.

[2] In the demotic character they are always distinguished.

vowels were seldom written, by the Egyptians themselves, except at the beginning and end of words.

In every inscription of any length, we find these three modes of writing, the pictorial, the symbolical and the phonetic, in use together, but with a great predominance of the phonetic[1]. It is natural to suppose that there was a time when the pictorial alone was used; that the symbolical was an advance in the power of abstraction, and that the phonetic was the last stage of progress. We may also conceive that the phonetic analysis began by reducing words to syllables, before it resolved syllables into elementary sounds. These things are hypothetically probable, but have no historical proof. In the oldest remains of Egyptian writing we find the same mixture of the pictorial, the symbolical, and the phonetic as in the latest. Other nations, however, exhibit the art of writing in these several stages. The Mexican writing was in the main pictorial; but it was also in a slight degree symbolical, a tongue denoting "speaking," a foot-print, "travelling," a man sitting on the ground, "an earthquake;" it had even the rudiments of a phonetic system, the significant names of individuals or places being expressed by the objects which the different parts signified[2]. The Chinese system of writing was in its origin pictorial; we can still trace, in the oldest forms of the characters which represent natural objects, the intention to make a drawing of their outline. But from this point it diverged entirely from the Egyptian. The Chinese written

---

[1] See Note at the end of this Chapter.

[2] Prescott's Mexico, 1, 86.

character is a vast system of symbols, so multiform and so ingeniously applied, that by means of it the most complex ideas are synthetically represented, the most abstract connected with the image of something real. The Egyptian, we have seen, is symbolical only to a very limited extent. The Chinese possess in their symbolical writing the means of expressing the whole range of their ideas, yet they used their characters also to express their spoken language; but approached no nearer to the phonetic use of hieroglyphics than by employing them for syllables, not letters[1]. This difference is probably connected with the difference in the genius of the Chinese and Coptic languages. The Chinese consists of a very small number (less than 400) of monosyllabic sounds, which are capable of being varied by intonation so as to multiply them to 1300; but these roots are never inflected or incorporated by composition. The Coptic may be regarded as poor in the number of its roots, and inflexible as regards its grammar and etymology, if compared with the Greek or the Sanscrit; but it admits the principle of modification to express the relations of thought, and composition to express complex ideas. The Egyptian writing, therefore, holds an intermediate place between a purely pictorial and symbolical, and

[1] "Comme tout signe simple ou composé, a son terme correspondant dans la langue parlée, lequel lui tient lieu de prononciation, il en est un certain nombre qui ont été pris comme signes des sons auxquels ils répondaient, abstraction faite de leur signification primitive, et qu'on a joints en cette qualité aux images pour former des caractères mixtes. L'une de leurs parties qui est l'image détermine le sens et fixe le genre; l'autre qui est un groupe de traits devenus insignifians, indique le son et caractérise l'espèce. Ces sortes de caractères sont moitié représentatifs et moitié syllabiques." Abel Remusat, quoted by Champollion, Précis, p. 353.

a purely alphabetical system. The Chinese have 80,000 characters, and their number must increase with every accession of ideas; the Egyptians, according to the enumeration of Champollion's Dictionary, 749; alphabets have varied in number from sixteen to upwards of fifty; but twenty appear sufficient to the analysis of vocal sound. A difficulty adheres to the Egyptian system which is not found in either of the others, from the intermixture of the three modes; when we find a character which represents an object, it is in itself uncertain whether it stand pictorially for the object, or symbolically for some property associated with it, or phonetically for some sound to the expression of which it has been appropriated. This difficulty can only be surmounted by practice.

In hieroglyphical inscriptions the characters are arranged either in horizontal or in perpendicular lines. In the former case they are sometimes to be read from right to left, and sometimes from left to right, but always beginning at the side towards which the heads of the animal figures are turned. Where an inscription is composed of a number of perpendicular columns, the same principle prevails; the reading begins with the column which is outermost on the side to which the heads are turned. Rosellini has noted an exception to this rule in the case of a long inscription at Medinet Aboo, in honour of Rameses IV., in which the columns succeed each other from left to right, though the figures are turned to the right[1].

[1] Mon. Stor. 4, p. 84. He mentions one or two other instances of the same kind, *e. gr.* a sarcophagus of Rameses IV. in the Louvre.

It is important to understand the nature of the evidence for the reading and interpretation which Egyptologists give of hieroglyphical writings. The general values of the phonetic characters are the most firmly established. They are fixed by the Rosetta Stone, the obelisk of Philæ, the inscriptions on the Ptolemaic temples, and the monuments of the Roman times, where the same names occur in Greek or Latin characters, the value of which is not doubtful. Such evidence cannot of course be furnished respecting the Persian times or those of the ancient Pharaohs. But a system which prevailed under the Ptolemies cannot have originated with them, and no reason can be imagined why the same principle of interpretation should not be applied to what has all external marks of identity. When therefore the alphabet which has furnished us with the names of Ptolemy, Cleopatra, Alexander, Cæsar and Trajan, gives us also Kenbot, Nteriush, Chshiersh and Artesheshes, in a country which we know to have been subject to Persian sway, we cannot hesitate to recognise Cambyses, Darius, Xerxes and Artaxerxes. In the line of the old Pharaohs we must rely on the evidence acquired by previous successful identifications, and the striking coincidence with the names which Manetho professed to have derived from monuments and records. A single instance will serve to show the application of this process. The colossal statue of the plain of Thebes, popularly known as the vocal Memnon, we are told by Manetho was really the king Amenophis[1].

---

[1] 'Αμενώφις· οὗτός ἐστιν ὁ Μέμνων εἶναι νομιζόμενος καὶ φθεγγόμενος λίθος. Dyn. 18. The last words are, perhaps, not Manetho's.

Pausanias says the Thebans deny this to be the statue of Memnon, and say that it is a native, Phamenoph[1]. Among the inscriptions of the Roman age which cover the legs of the statue is one in which the writer records that he has heard the voice of Memnon or Phamenoph[2]. In the usual oval ring on the pedestal of the statue is a group of characters, which Champollion by the aid of his alphabet, already established by the evidence which I have mentioned, read Amenothph[3]. *Ph* is the Coptic article, and it is difficult to imagine a more convincing proof than this coincidence affords of the soundness of his principle. The pronunciation of many names not royal has been ascertained by their transcription in Greek. Among authorities of this kind, the bilingual papyrus of Leyden[4] is most remarkable. It is of a late age, and bears traces of having been written after the rise of Gnosticism; but containing the transcription of some hundred names in demotic, hieratic and Greek, it enables us to ascertain the phonetic value of the characters. There must still remain some doubt in regard to characters which do not occur in the spelling of names whose pronunciation is known by their Greek or Latin equivalents. Thus the name which Champollion and others after him have read *Osortasen*, on the obelisks of Heliopolis and the Fyoum, is read by Lepsius and Bunsen *Sesortasen*, and no decisive

---

[1] Attic. c. 42. 'Ἀλλὰ γὰρ οὐ Μέμνονα ὀνομάζουσιν οἱ Θηβαῖοι, Φαμενῶφα δὲ εἶναι τῶν ἐγχωρίων, οὗ τοῦτο ἄγαλμα ἦν.

[2] Ἔκλυον αὐδήσαντος ἐγὼ Πόβλιος Βαλβῖνος φωνὰς τὰς θείας Μέμνονος ἢ Φάμενοφ.

[3] Précis, p. 286. The fourth character is called by Lepsius and Bunsen, A.

[4] Published by Professor Reuvens.

test can be applied to settle the dispute. Some doubt hangs also over cases in which a hieroglyphic character may stand for a whole word or for a letter. Champollion attributes to the ibis the sound of Thouth or Thoth, the name of the god of whom the ibis was the symbol; and this is confirmed by the name Touthmosis given by Manetho to the king, whose name is spelt by an ibis and the letters M, S. In other instances however it is doubtful whether we are to give the whole sound of the name or only that of the first letter. There is a people frequently mentioned in the campaigns of the Egyptian kings, in whose name the figure of a lion occurs. This is considered by Champollion to stand simply for R, and he reads the name *Shari*; while Rosellini[1] makes it to be *Moui*, one of the Coptic words for lion, and reads the name *Sciomui*. The same character, the lute, which in the Rosetta Stone appears to signify grace or beneficence, is supposed to stand phonetically for *nofre*, the Coptic for *good*; and he has read accordingly the shield of the queen of Amasis *Nofre-Are*, and one of the Sesortasens has received on the same evidence the addition of Nofre-ftep; but the phonetic value of this character and others in the names assigned to royal or private personages is still doubtful.

The pictorial signs are commonly such as to carry the evidence of their own meaning with them. It is otherwise with the symbolical characters, whose relation to the ideas which they are meant to express is often obscure, and could not have been divined without some direct evidence. The most

[1] Mon. Stor. iii. 2, 20.

decisive is that of a bilingual inscription; but unfortunately this evidence is applicable only to a very limited extent. The portion of the Rosetta Stone which contains the hieroglyphical inscription is the most injured, nearly two-thirds being broken off, and no other monument of the same kind has yet been brought to light[1]. From the part which exists, compared with the Greek, all our real knowledge of the system has been derived; but even in this the correspondence between the hieroglyphic and the Greek is by no means so exact as to furnish us with the precise analysis of every phrase in the former[2]. It is probable that the decree was originally composed in Greek, and that considerable latitude was indulged in rendering it in hieroglyphics. Other means of interpretation, however, are not wanting. The meaning of a word or phrase may be fixed by its connexion with some visible representation. Thus Amenophis-Memnon at Luxor[3] appears leading in his hand four steers as an offering to Amun, whose colour is respectively pied, red, white and black. Before each is a single character, and as the animals differ in nothing except colour, it is a reasonable presumption that the character denotes the colour. That which is before the white victim is apparently an onion—not ill-fitted for an emblem of this colour. It occurs again elsewhere in connexion with a character, which from being placed over offerings or tribute of gold, or men working in precious metals,

---

[1] A copy of a part of it has been found at Philæ; it will probably be illustrated by Lepsius. See Bunsen's Egypt, p. 594, Eng.

[2] It has been attempted by Salvolini, probably from the papers of Champollion, in his Analyse Grammaticale Raisonnée de différentes Textes Egyptiens, vol. 1, Par. 1836.

[3] Rosellini, M. Reali, tav. xli.

evidently means gold[1], and the combination "white gold," *i. e.* silver, suits very well the place in which it occurs. Further, the inner conical part of the *pschent*, or double royal cap, is painted white, and we find the same character placed beside the representation of it. The character opposite to the black steer is a crocodile's tail, which according to Horapollo[2] was the symbol of darkness. It is used in other combinations to which the idea of black or dark suits well. The character opposite to the red steer is a bird, whose colour no doubt was red. It is found with the representation of the lower part of the *pschent*, which is coloured red. In the absence of such direct indications, recourse must be had to the method of decipherers. Assuming upon merely presumptive grounds a certain meaning, they try it upon various combinations, and by eliminating successively what is shown to be false, arrive at last at the true solution. The nature of the hieroglyphic texts affords the means of ascertaining the sense of doubtful characters. They consist (the funeral papyri particularly) very much of formulary phrases; and when in one of these, the components of which are well known, there appears a variation, the probability is that the new character is only an equivalent or homophone of that whose place it has taken.

It has been already mentioned that in many instances the representations of known objects have groups of characters placed beside them, which are

---

[1] It occurs also on the Rosetta Stone, where it is directed that the statue of the king shall be gilded. Line 8, in Birch's facsimile.

[2] Hierog. 1, 70. Σκότος λέγοντες, κροκοδείλου οὐρὰν ζωγραφοῦσιν.

read by means of the phonetic alphabet into words, which in Coptic denote those objects. The grammatical forms and particles of the Coptic language are also found, in such frequent recurrence, that Champollion has been able to exhibit their hieroglyphical equivalents in a systematic form. So little doubt remains of the phonetic value of most of the characters, that it might have been expected that whole inscriptions might be read into Coptic and interpreted with certainty by the known vocabulary of that language. This expectation, however, has not been fulfilled. Although Champollion and Rosellini affect to write in Coptic characters their translations from the hieroglyphics, it is evident from inspection of them that a very small portion corresponds to any known Coptic words. This cannot be altogether explained by the scantiness of the remains of this language; for in many cases where it furnishes a word to express an obvious idea or a simple object, the hieroglyphic is different. There are indications of the existence of an old or sacred language, differing from that which was in common use, and it may be this, not the vulgar Coptic, into which, if we were acquainted with it, the hieroglyphic character should be read. Manetho, in the passage quoted from him by Josephus, speaking of the Hyksos or Shepherd-kings, says, *Hyk* in the sacred language signifies king, and *Sos* a shepherd, in the common dialect: or according to the reading of another manuscript of Manetho, which Josephus had consulted, *Hyk* or *Ak* meant captive. Now *Shos* is the Coptic for a shepherd; the old Egyptian for king is *Suten*, which is often found phonetically written; but *hyk* is also, though more rarely, used in the sense of ruler[1], while it is not found in the Coptic. We cannot therefore doubt, that in the age of Manetho a distinction already existed between the sacred and the common dialect. Indeed it was hardly possible that it should be otherwise; whatever care the priesthood might exercise, in preventing the corruption of the idiom in which their sacred books were written, it was out of their power to control those natural causes, which introduce changes into the popular speech. Perhaps, when the study of the hieroglyphic texts has been more extended, it may be possible to recover from them this lost language, and thus give complete confirmation to the system which has been adopted for reading them, but at present no such work could be accomplished. Till then, we cannot rely with entire confidence on those interpretations which are not derived from the Rosetta Stone, or do not correspond with the Coptic, or are not certified by such frequency of recurrence as to render their meaning indisputable. The theological and mystical nature of much of the hieroglyphical literature renders its deciphering particularly difficult; in ordinary cases no other proof is required that the process is correct, than that it furnishes a meaning intelligible in itself and suitable to the connexion; but such a test is not applicable to the vague and dreamy contents of the funereal Ritual, or the legends which accompany the figures of the gods. The hieroglyphics which are found with the historical paintings and sculptures

[1] Champoll. Dict. des Hierog. p. 323; Lepsius, Lettre à M. Rosellini, p. 71.

have a more definite subject, and the uncertainty of the philological interpretation is in some measure obviated by the distinctness of the scene exhibited. Yet even of these no such connected rendering has been given, as carries its own evidence with it, and many conjectural meanings are assigned, which it will require the test of varied application to other passages to confirm. This view of the present state of our knowledge of hieroglyphics will explain, why in this work hardly any use has been made of inscriptions in expounding the theological dogmas of the Egyptians, and the sparing and cautious use which will be made of them in the historical portion.

It is clear that the hieroglyphic character is the "sacred letters" of Herodotus and Diodorus and the Rosetta inscription, and that the *enchorial* of the latter is the *demotic* or *demodic* of the two former and the *epistolographic* of Clemens Alexandrinus. The *hieratic* of this Father is that which appears in most of the papyri before the time of the Saitic kings, among others the hieratic canon or Royal List of Turin. We find also in the older papyri linear hieroglyphics[1], in which the figures, instead of being fully drawn and filled up as in painting or sculpture, have only their outlines traced with a pen. These linear hieroglyphics are always disposed in vertical columns, as on the obelisks. The inspection of the hieratic characters would at first sight lead to the supposition that they were entirely

---

[1] An example of linear hieroglyphics may be seen in the publication of the Egyptian Society, Lond. 1823, though there called erroneously "a hieratic MS. of Lord Mountnorris." (Pl. 1–6.)

distinct from hieroglyphics; they are always written in horizontal lines, and appear arbitrary in their forms. A closer examination and comparison, however, shows that they are really derived from the hieroglyphics, with such changes as were necessary to adapt their stiff and angular forms to rapid writing. This will be evident in comparing, group by group, the fac-simile of a portion of the Rosetta Stone, given in Pl. IV., with the hieratical transcription placed below it. In the arrangement of the hieratic characters, following consecutively in horizontal lines, the order of pronunciation is more exactly observed than in the hieroglyphics, which are sometimes disposed with a view to symmetry. The phonetic use predominates more than in the pure hieroglyphics, some of the pictorial and symbolical characters being dropped, as too cumbersome for writing[1]. The hieratic character was not exclusively devoted to such purposes as we should call sacred, *i. e.* religious rituals and treatises, but derived its name from being used for sacerdotal purposes, such as the keeping of the temple accounts, genealogical registers, and the copying of portions of the great funereal Ritual, in cases where a hieroglyphical manuscript would have been too expensive. The oldest extant specimen of this writing is a fragment pasted into the interior of the wooden coffin of a king called Nantef, belonging to some dynasty of the Old Monarchy. It differs in no important respect from that of the papyri of the eighteenth dynasty[2].

[1] Lepsius, Lettre à M. Rosellini, p. 70.

[2] Bunsen, Egypten's Stelle, B. 2, 254; 3, 7.

The demotic character appears from existing remains to have been chiefly used in contracts and judicial pieces; its employment on the Rosetta Stone is a proof, that among the mixed population of Egypt under the Ptolemies, the knowledge both of the hieroglyphic and the hieratic had become more than ever confined to the priests; what was to be generally understood must be in Greek or demotic. According to Lepsius, it exhibits not only the vulgar character, but the vulgar idiom. But the analysis which has hitherto been made of the documents in this character, notwithstanding the advantage of a Greek translation of some of the papyri, as well as the Rosetta Stone, has not been sufficiently complete to allow of our asserting this with confidence. It is evident, however, that the character has been derived from the hieratic, as that from the hieroglyphic, by the necessity of adaptation to still more rapid writing; that pictorial and symbolical characters are more rare, though not entirely banished, and that the language which it represents approaches more nearly to the Coptic.

In the passage already quoted, Clemens says that the Egyptians record the praises of their kings "by means of anaglyphs," and hence a particular kind of writing has been created, called by Champollion[1] *anaglyphic*. But "anaglyph" means only an engraved figure or character[2], and is the appropriate expression for hieroglyphics considered with reference to their mechanical execution, not their

---

[1] Précis, p. 348.
[2] Strabo (17, p. 806), speaking of the Egyptian *pylones*, says, ἀνα- γλυφὰς ἔχουσιν οἱ τοῖχοι μεγάλων εἰδώλων.

import. According to Champollion, this class was composed almost entirely of symbolical characters. "The greater part of the symbolical images indicated in the whole of the first book of Horapollo, and in that part of the second which seems the most authentic, are found in the painted or sculptured pictures either on the walls of the temples and palaces and tombs, or in the MSS., on the bandages and coffins of the mummies, on amulets, &c.—paintings and sculptures which do not exbibit scenes of public and private life, nor religious ceremonies, but which are extraordinary compositions, in which fantastic beings, or it may be real beings, having no relation to each other in nature, are nevertheless united, brought together and put in action. These purely allegorical or symbolical bas-reliefs, which abound on Egyptian constructions, were specially designated by the ancients under the name of anaglyphs, by which I shall henceforward distinguish them." I am not aware that any other passage in the ancients but that of Clemens even *appears* to give the name of anaglyphs to a distinct kind of hieroglyphical writing; and how far he was from using it in the sense which Champollion arbitrarily assigns to it, is evident from his saying that in this way the Egyptians recorded the praises of their kings.

EXPLANATION OF THE HIEROGLYPHICS IN PL. IV.

The lowest compartment of this plate, which is taken from Lepsius' Lettre à M. Rosellini, contains a facsimile of a portion of the Rosetta

Stone, with a transcription by Lepsius in the hieratic character, and the corresponding words of the Greek.

In the Group No. 1, the first character on the right-hand, called by Champollion the *Sistrum*, is explained by him (Dict. No. 336; Gram. 2, 75) as K or S. The Coptic word for *set up* is *Ko* or *Kaa* (Lev. xxvi. 1); the other characters are S and A, with the legs determinative of verbs transitive. Lepsius reads the whole, *Ko-sa*; Bunsen and Birch (Bunsen's Egypt, vol. 1, p. 595) *Sha*, taking the sistrum as an H. The analogy to the Coptic is doubtful, but the sense is clear, as the same group occurs four times in the Rosetta Inscription (1. 6, 13, 14 *bis*), and always in connexion with setting up a tablet or a statue.

No. 2. The first figure, a breast and pair of hands holding a paddle or rudder, is considered by Lepsius as the letter H; the two next, N, T, appear to be connected with the Coptic root *Tntn, to be like*, answering to the Greek εἴκονα. The fourth is the determinative, a royal statue. The crown (3) is N, the sign of the genitive, and belongs to

No. 4, the branch and bee, originally interpreted "King of the obedient people," from a passage in Horapollo (1, 63, λαὸν πρὸς βασιλέα πειθήνιον δηλοῦντες μέλισσαν ζωγραφοῦσι), and another in Ammianus Marcellinus, 17, 4, " Per speciem apis mella conficientis indicant regem : moderatori cum jucunditate aculeos quoque innasci debere ostendentes." The branch was supposed to represent the plant from which the honey was derived. Subsequently Champollion considered the two first characters as phonetic, S, T for *Suten*, king, and the bee as the determinative of the kingly office. Bunsen (p. 595) explains the bee or wasp as an emblem of the Lower Country, and the branch of the Upper.

In the shield No. 5, the characters in the first division are the phonetic name Ptolmais. The second, answering to τοῦ αἰωνοβίου in the Greek, contains the *crux ansata*, the emblem of life. The two following characters are phonetic, T T, which may, perhaps, answer to the Coptic *Tka*, eternity. The straight line denotes the world, Pl. III. B. 2. The fourth division contains, first, the phonetic name of the god Ptah, then the phonetic syllable *Mai*, beloved. This epithet of the king is not translated in the Greek.

No. 6 is the sacrificial hatchet, the symbol of god. No. 7 contains the letters H R, perhaps connected with Coptic *Hra*, face; the legs expressing an active quality, ἐπιφάνους, " that manifests himself."

In No. 8, the hemisphere stands for lord (Pl. III. B. 2), and the three musical instruments either denote symbolically the charm (χάρις, εὐχαρίστου) of music, and hence goodness, grace; or the letter N, the initial of *Nofre*, Coptic for *good*. The triplication of the sign denotes the plural or the superlative.

No. 9 contains the characters *Ko-out*. The Coptic for *dicere* is *Djo*,

XIX.]   EXPLANATION OF HIEROGLYPHICS.   323

but the letter *Djandja* is often interchanged with *K*; *out* is the Coptic participle; and thus the whole would signify *dictus* (Champ. Dict. p. 408). No. 10 contains the shield which encloses names, here used for *ran* (Pl. III. A. 1), name, and the serpent, *ph*, his (Pl. IV. E. 4); the whole answering to the Greek ἡ προσονομασθήσεται. The figure of a man, with the hand raised towards the mouth, is the determinative of verbs relating to the expression of ideas in speech and writing (Champ. Dict. p. 33). The name of Ptolemy follows in the original, with the epithet, " who defends Egypt."

The upper portion of Pl. IV. exhibits the manner in which grammatical combinations and inflexions were represented in hieroglyphics. *Son* (E.) is in Coptic *Sere* or *Shere*, or abbreviated, *Se*, *Si*; it is here expressed pictorially by the figure of a child. Substituting for this the word *Shere*, it is thus varied in combination with the possessive pronouns, the phonetic characters for which are added to it. The Coptic prefixes the definite article P, like the Greek ὁ υἱός μου, inserts a short vowel, and places the possessive *before* the noun.

HIEROGLYPHIC.		COPTIC.
Singular.		*Singular.*
Shere-i,	my son.	P-a-Shere. The *a* is a fragment of *Anok*, Coptic for *I*. Heb. אנכי.
Shere-k,	thy son (male addressed).	P-ek-Shere.
Shere-t,	thy son (female addressed).	P-et-Shere.
Shere-ph,	his son.	P-eph-Shere.
Shere-s,	her son.	P-es-Shere.
Plural.		*Plural.*
Shere-n,	our son (with three strokes, the sign of plurality).	P-en-Shere.
Shere-tn,	your son.	P-eten-Shere.
Shere-sn,	their son.	P-ou-Shere.

The division F. of the same plate exhibits the numbers and persons of the verb *give*. This in Coptic is T, connected with *Tot*, hand. The hand stretched out with an offering may be regarded as a symbol of the act of giving; but it is also used phonetically for T and D. The formation of the persons proceeds thus in the Coptic, again prefixing the pronouns.

HIEROGLYPHIC.		COPTIC.
Singular.		*Singular.*
T-ci,	I give.	Ei-t.
T-k or t,	Thou givest.	K-t.
T-f,	He gives.	Ph-t.
T-s,	She gives.	S-t.
Plural.		*Plural.*
T-n,	We give.	N-t.
T-tn,	Ye give.	Tetn-t.
T-sn,	They give.	Ou-t or Se-t.

The explanations and examples now given will convey an idea of the general principles of hieroglyphic writing. A popular view of the subject, with a very full phonetic alphabet, will be found in Wilkinson's Mod. Egypt and Thebes, vol. 2, p. 582. Fuller information may be sought in Champollion, Grammaire Egyptienne, Paris, 1836–1841; Dictionnaire Egyptien, Paris, 1841; Bunsen, Egypt's Place, &c. vol. 1, 496–600, and the valuable papers of Dr. Edward Hincks, in Transactions of R. I. A. vol. xxi. The two last-mentioned writers have suggested modifications of the system of Champollion, which it does not belong to the scope of the present work to examine.

CHAPTER XX.

SCIENCE.

NEITHER physical nor mathematical science can be attributed to the ancient Egyptians, in the sense in which the word is now understood, as implying that the facts respecting the operations of nature with which observation had furnished them, had been generalized into laws, established on demonstration. They were great observers of all remarkable phænomena under the name of prodigies, and carefully noted all their circumstances and results; but it was for the purpose of predicting similar results, if similar prodigies occurred again[1]. They were acquainted with certain relations of space and number, but neither their geometry nor their arithmetic could be called a science, not being deduced by reasoning from self-evident truths[2]. Such, however, as Egyptian science was, it belonged exclusively to the priests[3]. The education of the people generally was nothing more than a training in the occupation which they inherited from their parents or kinsmen, to which a slight tincture of learning was added in the case of artisans. The

---

[1] Her. 2, 82. Τέρατα πλέα σφι ἀνεύρηται ἢ τοῖσι ἄλλοισι ἅπασι ἀνθρώποισι· γενομένου γὰρ τέραος, φυλάσσουσι γραφόμενοι τὠποβαῖνον· καὶ ἢν κοτε ὕστερον παραπλήσιον τούτῳ γένηται κατὰ τωὐτὸ νομίζουσι ἀποβήσεσθαι.

[2] "Avant l'école d'Alexandrie il n'a point existé chez les anciens peuples de *science* proprement dite." (Letronne, Revue des deux Mondes, 1845, p. 520.)

[3] Diod. 1, 81.

priests carefully educated their own sons, who might pass into the order of soldiers or public functionaries, as well as continue priests, in the knowledge of the hieroglyphical and demotic character[1], and in geometry and arithmetic and astronomy. Geometry appears not to have risen much above the practical art of land-surveying, from which it derived its name. Had we more precise information respecting its transmission from Egypt to Greece, in the seventh century before Christ, we should be enabled to judge of the progress which it had made in the country of its origin. Pythagoras, who was the founder of mathematical science among the Greeks, had been admitted to all the secrets of the Egyptian priests. He is said to have sacrificed to the Muses, on the discovery of the relation between squares of the sides which contain, and of the side which subtends the right angle of a right-angled triangle[2]. If this relation *and its mathematical proof* were known to the Egyptians, they must at least have laid the foundations of geometrical science. According to Plato, Theuth, secretary to Thamus king of Egypt, invented arithmetic and geometry[3]. But this cannot be received as an historical statement; no such name as Thamus appears in the list of kings, and Theuth is evidently the god Thoth, the mythic source of all knowledge preserved by writing.

---

[1] Τὸ δ᾽ ἄλλο πλῆθος τῶν Αἰγυπτίων ἐκ παίδων μανθάνει παρὰ τῶν πατέρων ἢ συγγενῶν τὰς περὶ ἕκαστον βίον ἐπιτηδεύσεις, γράμματα δ᾽ ἐπ᾽ ὀλίγον οὐχ ἅπαντες ἀλλ᾽ οἱ τὰς τέχνας μεταχειριζόμενοι μάλιστα. (Diod. *u. s.*) Plato appears to allow a greater amount of knowledge to the Egyptian laity than Diodorus—Τοσάδε τοίνυν ἑκάστων χρὴ φάναι μανθάνειν δεῖν τοὺς ἐλευθέρους ὅσα καὶ πάμπολυς ἐν Αἰγύπτῳ παίδων ὄχλος ἅμα γράμμασι μανθάνει (Leg. 7, 2, p. 818).

[2] Plut. de Repugn. Stoic. 2, p. 1089. Cic. N. D. 3, 36.

[3] Plat. Phædr. iii. 274, ed. Steph.

Another account makes Mœris[1] to have been the author of geometry, a third Sesostris[2], evidently because these sovereigns engaged in undertakings for which a knowledge of geometry was requisite. Nothing remains in the monuments by which we could ascertain the state of the science in early times; but the belief of the Greeks, that Pythagoras, Thales, Pherecydes, Anaxagoras and Plato had derived their knowledge of mathematics from Egypt, would be inexplicable if this country had not long preceded their own in its cultivation. If Pythagoras learnt there the proposition which is associated with his name, but himself discovered the demonstration, this would be analogous to the relation which in other respects we discover[3] between the Egyptian and the Grecian intellect. The relation between the squares of the sides of a right-angled triangle was known to the Chinese before they became acquainted with European mathematics, but it was proved by measurement, not geometrically[4]. From the measures of the angles of the pyramids it has been concluded[5] that at the time of their construction the Egyptians were not acquainted with the division of the circle into degrees, but that the angles were regulated by the

---

[1] Diog. Laërt. 8, 11. Τοῦτον (Πυθαγόραν) γεωμετρίαν ἐπὶ πέρας ἀγαγεῖν, Μοίριδος πρῶτον εὑρόντος τὰς ἀρχὰς τῶν στοιχείων αὐτῆς, ὥς φησιν Ἀντικλείδης. Mœris was probably fixed upon from the great engineering works attributed to him in the Fyoum. According to Strabo (17, 788), the Roman Petronius made Egypt fertile with a lower rise of the Nile than had been ever known before; so that even in the art of making canals, the Romans excelled the Egyptians.

[2] Herod. 2, 109.

[3] Ὅτι περ ἂν Ἕλληνες βαρβάρων παραλάβωμεν, κάλλιον τοῦτο εἰς τέλος ἀπεργαζόμεθα. — Plat. Epin. ii. p. 988.

[4] Davis, The Chinese, ch. 19.

[5] Perring. See Bunsen, Ægypten's Stelle, B. 2, p. 365, Germ.

proportion between the base and perpendicular of a right-angled triangle. Their astronomical monuments, however, show that under the eighteenth dynasty they had divided the ecliptic into twelve parts of thirty degrees, and this was probably the origin of the division which still continues in use. For there is no reason why the quadrants of a circle should be divided into ninety degrees each, but an obvious reason for dividing the ecliptic by twelve and thirty, these being the nearest whole numbers to the lunations of a year and the days of a lunation. Spherical trigonometry appears to have been wholly unknown in ancient Egypt.

The amount of astronomical knowledge which the Egyptians possessed in the time of the Pharaohs remains obscure, after all the light which recent discoveries have thrown on their condition in remote ages. They enjoyed, equally with the Babylonians, the advantage of a wide horizon at Heliopolis, and a sky free from clouds and vapour, both there and at Thebes, for making constant observations[1], but they had no such commanding observatory as the Tower of Belus afforded to the Chaldæan astronomer. The *horoscopus*[2] who occupied the second place in the procession of the priests, carried in his hand a *horologium* (sun-dial) and a palm[3], symbols of astronomy, and was compelled to

---

[1] Cic. Divin. 1. Plat. Epin. ii. 987. The French astronomer Nouet denies this, and says that the horizon of Egypt is much obscured by haze.

[2] Clem. Alex. Strom. p. 757, ed. Potter.

[3] Horapollo, 1. 3, 4. A palm-tree (φοῖνιξ) was the emblem of a year, because it put forth twelve branches (βάϊς) in the year, one at each new moon. The βάϊς was an emblem of the month. It seems, however, from the hieroglyphics, that the βάϊς was the emblem of the year (Pl. III. D. 1).

learn by heart the four books of astronomy attributed to Hermes-Thoth. One of these related to the distribution[1] or grouping of the fixed stars; another to the conjunction and opposition of the sun and moon; another to their rising. Besides these, the hierogrammat was required to understand the order of the sun and moon and five planets. Such is the account given by Clemens Alexandrinus in the beginning of the third century after Christ. The fact that the pyramids are placed with the centre of their sides exactly facing the cardinal points, shows that in the early age when these structures were erected, they had the means of tracing an accurate meridian line. To accomplish this, however, requires rather time and care than great astronomical knowledge. It is effected by the observation of the shadow of a gnomon, at the time of the solstices, which is nearly of the same length at equal distances from the meridian, the sun then changing his declination very little in the course of a day.

As the hieroglyphic for month is the crescent of the moon, the Egyptian months must have been originally lunar. The division of the seasons was physical, not astronomical. It was threefold (see Pl. I.), the four months of vegetation being originally distinguished by a *flowering plant*; the four of ingathering or harvest by the characters for *house* and *mouth*; the four of the inundation by a cistern and the character for *water*; but when the year became fixed, these characters had ceased to be appropriate, two-thirds of each season having advanced into the neighbouring division. Each month had

---

[1] Τοῦ διακόσμου, Clemens, *u. s.*

a name which has been preserved by Greek and Coptic writers[1], but they do not correspond phonetically to the hieroglyphics. Each month and day had also its tutelary god[2], but this was rather an astrological than astronomical distribution. The hieroglyphics of the months were in use at an early period of the old monarchy, being found according to Lepsius on the pyramids of Dashour.

When the Egyptians established the division into twelve months of thirty days each, they may have reckoned the year at 360 days, but at a very early period they had learnt to intercalate five additional days[3]. When this great correction of their calendar took place is uncertain. Syncellus, in the Laterculus[4], attributes it to Asseth, one of the Shepherd kings; but Lepsius says that he has found traces of the five intercalary days, or *Epagomenæ* as the Greeks called them, in a grotto at Benihassan of the twelfth dynasty, that is before the invasion of the Shepherds[5]. Their introduction

---

[1] They are as follows in the Julian year:—

1. Thoth ....29. August.
1. Phaophi ....28. September.
1. Athyr ....28. October.
1. Choiak ....27. November.
1. Tybi ....27. December.
1. Mechir ....26. January.
1. Phamenoth ......25. February.
1. Pharmuthi ......27. March.
1. Pachon ....26. April.
1. Payni ....26. May.
1. Epiphi...........25. June.
1. Mesori ....25. July.
Epagomenæ ....24—29. August.
(Ideler, 1, 143.)

After the introduction of Julius Cæsar's correction (B.C. 30), the Alexandrians intercalated a day every four years, and then began their year on the 30th of August (Ideler, Hist. Unters. p. 125).

[2] Herod. 2, 82. Lepsius, Einleitung, p. 144, thinks the names of the months were derived from the gods.

[3] Her. 2, 4. Αἰγύπτιοι τριηκονθημέρους ἄγοντες τοὺς δυώδεκα μῆνας, ἐπάγουσι ἀνὰ πᾶν ἔτος πέντε ἡμέρας πάρεξ τοῦ ἀριθμοῦ καὶ ὁ κύκλος τῶν ὡρέων ἐς τωὐτὸ περιιὼν παραγίνεται.

[4] "Asseth first added the five Epagomenæ, and made the Egyptian year, which had previously only 360 days, to consist of 365." Sync. Chron. p. 123.

[5] Einleitung, 146. Mention is there made of a "Festival of the Five redundant days of the year."

into the year was expressed by an ingenious mythe. Thoth (Hermes), the god of astronomy and calculation, plays at dice with the Moon, and wins from her a seventieth (a round number for seventy-second) part of each of the 360 days of which the year consisted, out of which fractional parts $\left(\frac{360}{72}=5\right)$ five entire days are composed. These days are consecrated to five gods whose worship thus seems to be indicated as of later origin; the first to Osiris, the second to Arueris, the third to Typhon, the fourth to Isis, and the fifth to Nephthys[1]. In the astronomical monument at the Rameseion, a vacant space is left between Mesori the last and Thoth the first of the Egyptian months, apparently to represent the intercalated days[2].

But the intercalation of five days was not sufficient to bring the Egyptian calendar into harmony with the heavens. The true length of the solar year exceeds 365 days by nearly six hours. It is evident therefore that there would be an error in defect of a quarter of a day in every year, of a day in every four years, a month in 120 years, and a year of 365 days in 1460 years. Without some further correction the Egyptian year would be an *annus vagus*; its true commencement and all the festivals, the time of which was reckoned from it, travelling in succession through all the days and months, just as our own were doing, but at a less rapid rate, and in a contrary direction, before

---

[1] Plut. Is. et Osir. c. 12. The Epagomenæ are designated as Day of birth of Osiris, Day of birth of Horus, &c.; but as it should seem, only on monuments of later times. Lepsius, p. 146.

[2] Trans. of Roy. Soc. Lit. 4to vol. 3, 2, p. 434.

the alteration of the Style. Herodotus appears not to have been aware that any correction had been applied to the calendar, or indeed required; since he praises the intercalation of five days, as bringing back the circle of the seasons to the same point. Diodorus[1] however represents the priests of Thebes, and Strabo[2] those of Heliopolis as knowing the true length of the solar year, and intercalating five days and a quarter. They furnish no evidence however of the antiquity of the practice, nor of its adoption in civil life. Indeed Geminus of Rhodes[3], who lived in the time of Sylla, expressly says that the priests did not intercalate the quarter day, in order that the festivals might travel through the whole year, and "the summer-festival become a winter-festival and an autumn-festival and a spring-festival." Such a change implies that the original import of the festivals, some of which were closely connected with the season of the year[4], was no longer obvious. It is even said that the priests imposed on the sovereign at his inauguration an oath that he would keep up the old reckoning, and not allow the quarter day to be intercalated[5]. This again points to a time when the priests had become

---

[1] Diod. 1, 50.
[2] Strabo, 17, 806.
[3] Βούλονται οἱ Αἰγύπτιοι τὰς θυσίας τοῖς θεοῖς μὴ κατὰ τὸν αὐτὸν καιρὸν τοῦ ἐνιαυτοῦ γένεσθαι, ἀλλὰ διὰ πασῶν τῶν τοῦ ἐνιαυτοῦ ὡρῶν διελθεῖν· καὶ γένεσθαι τὴν θερινὴν ἑορτὴν καὶ χειμερινὴν καὶ φθινοπωρινὴν καὶ ἐαρινήν. Geminus, Isagoge in Arati Phæn. c. 6, quoted by Ideler, Handb. der Chronologie, 1, 95.
[4] Thus on the 28th day of Phaophi, after the autumnal equinox, they celebrated the festival of the "Birth of the Sun's Staff," in allusion to his increasing feebleness; at the winter solstice they carried a cow seven times round the temple, which was called the "Seeking of Osiris," Plut. Is. et Os. p. 372.
[5] Deducitur rex a sacerdote Isidis in locum qui nominatur ἄδυτος, et sacramento adigitur, neque diem neque mensem intercalandum. Schol. Lat. Vet. in Arat. Germanici, Ideler, u. s.

jealous of the civil power, and wished to perpetuate the confusion of the calendar, as the patricians did at Rome, for their own purposes. The use of a lunar year by the Mahometans, which causes the great Fast of Ramadan to travel through the year, is a proof of the force of ancient custom.

It appears probable, however, that from an early period the true length of the solar year, and the time in which the excess would amount to an entire year, was known to the Egyptian priests, though not applied to the popular calendar. In the Roman times they certainly had a period, called Canicular, Cynic or Sothiac[1], of 1461 years, which is exactly the number of Julian or true years of $365\frac{1}{4}$ days, answering to 1460 of the *vague years* of 365 days[2]. Now among the periods which were assigned for the return of the Phœnix, one was 1461 years[3], and hence we may conclude that the period of the Phœnix was the same as the Sothiac period. The symbol of the Phœnix must have been of long standing in the time of Herodotus, since it was so much misapprehended, that he describes it under the head of zoology[4], though naturally incredulous respecting the tale of the young phœnix bringing his father, embalmed in frankincense, to the temple of Heliopolis. He reckons the intervals of his appearance, however, at 500 years,

---

[1] Bainbridge, Canicularia, Oxf. 1648, a work which still retains its value.

[2] Ægyptiorum annus magnus initium sumit cum primo die ejus mensis quem Thoth vocant Caniculæ sidus exoritur. Nam eorum annus civilis solos habet dies 365 *sine ullo intercalari*, coque fit ut anno 1461 ad idem revolvatur principium. Censorinus de Die Natali, c. 18.

[3] Tac. Ann. 6, 28. De numero annorum varia traduntur; maxime vulgatur *quingentorum* spatium; sunt qui adseverent *mille quadringentos sexaginta unum* interjici.

[4] Ἔστι δὲ καὶ ἄλλος ὄρνις ἱερὸς, τῷ οὔνομα φοίνιξ. Her. 2, 73.

on the authority of the Heliopolitans, and so far throws doubt on the identity with the Sothiac period. Indeed the great variety of periods assigned may lead us to suspect that the Phœnix was a *general* emblem of a Cycle[1]. The most probable etymology of the word is from the Coptic *phenech, sæculum.*

One of these Sothiac periods came to a conclusion in historic times; expiring in A.D. 138–9[2]. Reckoning backward 1460 years we come to 1322 B.C. This does not absolutely prove that it was in use 1322 B.C., or was then first established; but it has been thought that the monuments supply this deficiency. The period is called Sothiac, because the time assumed for its commencement was when Sirius or the Dogstar, called by the Egyptians Sothis[3], and consecrated to Isis[4], rose heliacally on the first day of Thoth, the first month of the Egyptian fixed year, the 20th of July of our reckoning. This phænomenon appears to have been fixed upon, from the brilliancy of the star, which would make it more conspicuous; and its coincidence with the commencement of the inundation, which occurred about this time, made it still more appropriate as the starting-point of an Egyptian period. Now in

---

[1] Horapollo, 1, 35, says the Phœnix was an emblem of one returning home after long absence in a foreign land. The priests themselves (Ælian, H. An. 6, 58) disputed about the expiration of a Phœnix period. Ælian extols the Phœnix as the better arithmetician.

[2] Censorinus, who wrote A.D. 238, says, "anni illius magni qui Solaris et Canicularis et Dei annus vocatur, nunc agi *vertentem annum centesimum.*" Ideler, *u. s.*

[3] Αἰγυπτίοις ἀρχὴ ἔτους Καρκίνος

πρὸς γὰρ τῷ Καρκίνῳ ἡ Σῶθις, ἣν Κυνὸς ἀστέρα "Ελληνές φασι. Porph. Antr. Nymph. c. 24. "Sothis hæc apud Vettium Valentem MS., ex libris Petosiris vocatur Σήθ, masculino genere, τοῦ Σὴθ ἀνατολή." Marsham, Can. Chron. p. 9.

[4] Ὅλον τὸ ἄστρον (the Lion) ἀφιερώκασιν Ἡλίῳ· τότε γὰρ καὶ ἐμβαίνει ὁ Νεῖλος καὶ ἡ τοῦ Κυνὸς ἐπιτολὴ κατὰ ἐνδεκάτην φαίνεται καὶ ταύτην ἀρχὴν ἔτους τίθενται καὶ τῆς Ἴσιδος ἱερὸν εἶναι τὸν Κύνα λέγουσι. Schol. Arat. Phæn. l. 152.

the astronomical monument at the Rameseion[1], in the middle of the vacant space between the months Mesori and Thoth, is a figure of Isis-Sothis. It is inferred that this monument was erected in commemoration of the commencement of a Sothiac period, and the chronology of Egyptian history suits well enough with the date of the work, which belongs to the age of Rameses II. or III. Though the evidence of the monument is not decisive of the year, there is nothing improbable in the supposition that the true length of the year was known, and a period established for bringing the vague and the true year into harmony, in the latter part of the fourteenth century before the Christian æra; and astronomical calculation shows that Sirius rose heliacally at Heliopolis on the 20th July in the year 1322[2]. The same coincidence would take place in the same latitude 1460 years earlier, or 2782 B.C.[3], which Fréret and Bailly supposed to be the time when the cycle was established. Isis-Sothis is called "Star of the beginning of the year," in hieroglyphics of the age of Rameses II.[4], which implies the existence of a *fixed* year, beginning with the rise of that star.

Upon this period of 1461 years, which whenever established was real, was founded an imaginary period of 36,525 years, produced by multiplying it with 25[5]. This was the great year in which all the heavenly bodies were supposed to make a

---

[1] Wilkinson, Modern Egypt and Thebes, 2, 155. Tomlinson, Trans. Roy. Soc. Lit. 3, 2, p. 484.
[2] Ideler, Handbuch, 1, 129.
[3] Ideler, *ib*. 130. Fourier, Mém. sur l'Eg. vol. 7.
[4] Lepsius, Einleitung, 1, 152.
[5] Syncellus, Chronogr. p. 52, ed. Dind.

complete revolution of the heavens[1]. Twenty-five was the number of years, after which, 309 lunations having occurred, the new and full moons returned on the same day and nearly the same hour of the Egyptian calendar[2]. It was also the time after which the moon-god Apis, if he lived so long, was put to death[3].

Herodotus and Tacitus both speak of 500 years as a period assigned to the return of the Phœnix. We know of no astronomical cycle which exactly corresponds with this; the nearest number is 532, produced by multiplying the solar and lunar cycles (19×28), the period after which the new and full moons return on the same days of the week. As the larger cycle of 1461 years is called in round numbers 1000, so 500 might be popularly substituted for 532. The use of such a cycle would imply that the Egyptians reckoned their days by sevens: this is not expressly said by any ancient author. We know, however, from Dion Cassius that the custom of assigning a day of the week to the sun, moon and planets arose in Egypt[4], where the number seven was held in great reverence; and it is more probable that it had prevailed there in ancient times, than that it had been introduced subsequently to the age of Herodotus.

The intercalation of a quarter day is in excess about six minutes, and therefore does not bring the

---

[1] Sync. p. 35. Ἕλληνες καὶ Αἰγύπτιοι ἐν εἴκοσι πέντε (25) περιόδοις ἐτῶν τῶν ἀπὸ αυξα' (1461) τὴν κοσμικὴν ἀποκατάστασιν γένεσθαι λέγουσι, ἤγουν ἀπὸ σημείου εἰς σημεῖον τοῦ οὐρανοῦ ἀποκατάστασιν.

[2] Ideler, Handb. 1, 182. A less accurate reason had been assigned by Marsham, Can. Chron. p. 9, "Est in 25 vagis annis eadem Lunæ ratio quæ in 19 fixis."

[3] Plut. Is. et Osir. 374 B. Plin. 8, 46.

[4] Τὸ ἐς τοὺς ἀστέρας τοὺς ἑπτὰ, τοὺς πλανήτας ὠνομασμένους τὰς ἡμέρας ἀνακεῖσθαι κατέστη ὑπ' Αἰγυπτίων. Dion. Cass. Hist. 37, 18.

reckoning, once in four years, into complete conformity with the heavens; but neither the Egyptians, nor the Greeks who improved upon them, appear to have known the exact length of the solar year. Hipparchus, the greatest astronomer of antiquity, reckoned the tropical year at $365^d\ 5^h\ 55'\ 12''$, which is $6'\ 24''$ too long[1]. This error, adopted by Julius Cæsar into the Roman calendar, rendered necessary the Gregorian reform of the style, by which all future irregularity is precluded.

It has been supposed that the Egyptian astronomers were acquainted with the Precession of the Equinoxes, that is, the gradual increase of the longitude of all the fixed stars at the rate of about $50''$ in a year, or a degree in 72 years, in consequence of which the position of the solstitial and equinoctial colures, in reference to the signs of the zodiac, is perpetually varying[2]. The only passage in an ancient author which can be understood as attributing this knowledge to them is in the second book of Herodotus. Having calculated from the data of the priests that 11,340 years had elapsed from Menes to Sethos, he adds, "In this time they said that the sun had four times risen out of his customary place, and had twice risen from the point where he now sets, and twice set at the point whence he now rises; and that while these things were going on, nothing in Egypt had varied, neither in regard to the productions of the earth, nor the

---

[1] Ideler, Handb. 1, 64.
[2] Their complete revolution is the ἀποκατάστασις τοῦ ζωδιακοῦ, spoken of by Syncellus, *ubi supra*, as taking place in 36,525 years. The true period of the Precession, at the rate of $1°\ 23'\ 40''$ in a century, is about 26,000 years.

effects of the river, nor in regard to diseases or death[1]." Literally taken, this account supposes a double change in the rotation of the earth upon its axis, nothing less being sufficient to cause the sun " to rise where he now sets, and set where he now rises." Eminent critics have seen in it a reference to the change of the tropics, consequent on the precession of the equinoxes[2]. No such meaning, however, can be fairly extracted from the words of Herodotus, and if we endeavour from what he has said, to make out what we suppose the priests to have told him, we enter a boundless field of unsatisfactory conjectures. It is not improbable that they may have discovered a secular variation in the position of the fixed stars, especially of Sirius, which they carefully observed; but being ignorant of its law, its amount, and the effects which, according to the true system of the heavens, it would appear to produce, they made the extravagant statement which Herodotus has recorded. That they considered the phænomenon as a secular variation, not as a prodigy, is evident from their mentioning that no failure of crops, no deficiency of the inundation, no increase of disease or mortality had been the result. We have the strongest ground to conclude that the precession was not known, as an observed and ascertained astronomical fact, to the Egyptians. It was the discovery of the Greek Hipparchus, and the observations, the discrepancy of which with his own revealed the change to him, were not made

[1] 2, 142.
[2] Lepsius, Chronologie der Egypter, Einleitung, p. 190 foll. Boeckh, Manetho und die Hundsternperiode, p. 421. Scaliger and Ideler (1, 138) referred the passage to the recurrence of the Sothiac period.

by Egyptian astronomers, but by the Greeks Aristyllus and Timocharis about 160 years before[1].

Eclipses, the great bases of astronomical chronology, had not been recorded with any extraordinary accuracy by the Egyptians, or Hipparchus and Ptolemy, who both lived in Egypt, would have availed themselves of such materials. The latter author found at Babylon records of lunar eclipses, observed with an accuracy that leaves little to modern science to correct, from the middle of the eighth century B.C.[2] Solar eclipses are said to have been recorded there, as far back as the nineteenth century B.C.[3], but nothing of this kind appears to have been furnished by Egypt. Diodorus[4], indeed, maintains that the Thebans had accurately observed and also predicted both solar and lunar eclipses. Seneca[5] speaks of solar eclipses observed by the Egyptians, and collected by Conon; yet these statements cannot avail to prove that they were scientific observations, when set against the negative evidence arising from the neglect of them by Ptolemy. Still less can we draw any conclusion in favour of the scientific astronomy of the Egyptians from what Diogenes Laertius says[6], that they assigned the number of solar and lunar eclipses between Vulcan and Alexander the Great. As they reckoned this interval at 48,863 years, the eclipses had certainly

---

[1] Ideler, Handh. 1, 27. In favour of its being known to Eudoxus and learnt by him from the Egyptians, Lepsius, *ubi supra*.

[2] Ideler, in the Trans. Roy. Soc. Berlin, 1815, has worked out some of these by lunar tables, and finds them agree within a few minutes.

[3] Simplicius, in his Commentary on Aristot. de Cœlo, quoted by Ideler, Historische Untersuchungen, p. 166.

[4] 1, 50.

[5] Nat. Quæst. 7, 3. Conon lived about 250 B.C.

[6] Prooemium, sect. 1.

not been *observed*. We do not find in the paintings and sculptures of Egypt any representation of instruments for observing astronomical phænomena, nor do we know that in this respect the Babylonians had any advantage over them. The latter people, however, were the authors of two inventions for measuring time—an operation essential to an accurate record of eclipses—the dial, and the division of the day into twelve parts[1]. Recent investigation has shown, that the system of weights and measures adopted in Egypt, originated among the Babylonians[2]; we may hence infer that they surpassed other nations in the management of calculation; and thus they would naturally outstrip them in scientific astronomy. The topography of Egypt was accurately known to the Egyptian priests by the measurement of the land, but they seem never to have applied astronomy to geography by fixing the latitudes of places. This was an invention of the Alexandrian Greeks. They knew, however, the obliquity of the ecliptic, and Pythagoras[3] may have derived from the same source his doctrine that the sun is the centre of the planetary system, the earth a spherical body revolving around it[4].

If the Egyptians were not the founders of scientific astronomy, there can be no question that they were most assiduous observers of the aspect and position of the heavenly bodies, and attributed to them an important influence on human events.

---

[1] Herod. 2, 109.
[2] Boeckh, Metrologische Untersuchungen über Gewichte, Münzfüsse und Masse des Alterthums, 1838.
[3] Diod. 1, 98. Plut. Plac. Phil. 2, 12.
[4] Diog. Laert. Pyth. 81, 25.

We have examples of astronomical monuments in the sepulchral chambers of Sethos and the Rameses at Thebes, placed there, as the later zodiacs of Denderah and Esneh, for astrological rather than astronomical purposes. On the circle of Osymandyas (see p. 155 of this vol.) every day was marked by the planets and stars which rose and set upon it, and the prognostics which these afforded, according to Egyptian astrology[1]. They had an astrological system, attributed to two names of uncertain age, Petosiris and Necepsos[2], according to which they could assign the influence which the day of an individual's birth would have upon his character, fortunes and length of life, and the effects, beneficial or injurious, of the movements and revolutions of the planets. By their science the Egyptian astrologers could foretell years of scarcity and plenty, pestilences, earthquakes, inundations and the appearance of comets, and do many other things surpassing the sagacity of the vulgar. And they represented themselves to have been in these points the teachers of the Chaldæans, whom they claimed as an Egyptian colony[3]. They evidently attributed virtues to particular numbers, 3, 7, 10; and their multiples are of perpetual occurrence. They had made a duodecimal division of the zodiac and allotted constellations to each, but not the figures by which they are commonly distinguished. These are found only on monuments of the latest Ptolemaic or Roman times. Each of these duodecimal

---

[1] Herod. 2, 82. Diod. 1, 81.
[2] Plin. 2, 21. 7, 50.
[3] Φασὶ δὲ καὶ τοὺς ἐν Βαβυλῶνι Χαλδαίους, ἀποίκους Αἰγυπτίων ὄν-τας, τὴν δόξαν ἔχειν τὴν περὶ τῆς ἀστρολογίας, παρὰ τῶν ἱερέων μαθόντας τῶν Αἰγυπτίων. Diod. 1, 81.

divisions was again subdivided into three, making thirty-six *Decans* for the year[1]. The human body was divided into thirty-six parts answering to the Decans, and specially under their influence, a god or dæmon presiding over each. In later times at least, the opinion prevailed that the souls of men entered into life through one of the signs of the zodiac, the six first being favourable in their influence, the six last unfavourable.

The erection of such edifices as the pyramids and temples, and the execution of great works in hydraulics, proves little respecting the scientific knowledge of the Egyptians. Works demanding quite as much skill were executed by the Italian nations before the rise of Rome, or by the Chinese and Mexicans, to none of whom is there any reason to attribute high attainments in mathematical science. The description given by Herodotus[2] of the manner in which the pyramids were constructed, leads us to form no high estimate of their mechanical skill. Machines of wood, apparently simple levers, of strength sufficient to raise a block to the height of one course, were planted on each successive stage, and thus the top was reached. Diodorus[3] supposes a still more inartificial procedure, the construction of inclined mounds, by which the stones were raised to the necessary level. It is not probable that either account rested on historical evidence; but they show that the Egyptians did not believe that their predeces-

---

[1] Lepsius, Chronologie der Eg. Einleitung, p. 66. He has compared the hieroglyphical signs with the Egyptian names which Hephæstion has preserved, and finds a remarkable coincidence. Of the Egyptian horoscopy, see Stob. Eclog. ii. 8, p. 386, 390, ed. Heeren. Orig. c. Cels. 8, p. 416. Salmas. Plin. Exercit. in Solinum, p. 460.

[2] 2, 125.

[3] Τὴν κατασκευὴν διὰ χωμάτων γενέσθαι, μήπω τῶν μηχάνων εὑρημένων. 1, 63.

sors possessed any refined mechanical knowledge, and therefore had not much themselves. We have a representation in one of the tombs of the manner in which a colossal statue was transported, in the age of Sesortasen II. It is accomplished by the main strength of 172 men, arranged in rows, with scarcely any application of mechanical knowledge[1]. Had the pulley or the capstan been used, we should have found some representation of them among the varied pictures of Egyptian life. No such representations, however, occur[2]. The Greeks themselves, a considerable time after their acquaintance with Egypt began, were so poor in mechanical contrivance, that when Chersiphron built the temple of Ephesus, in the reign of Amasis, he was obliged to raise his architraves by surrounding his columns with bags of earth, which served as an inclined plane[3]. Had the Egyptians been acquainted with the mechanical powers, the Greeks would have borrowed them in the interval between Psammitichus and Amasis. Simple machinery, combined with an unlimited command of human power, is sufficient for the greatest works which Egypt exhibits. Belzoni, with a very small number of men, could remove his fractured Colossus to the Nile, by using levers and rollers. The erection of obelisks appears to require more mechanical skill; yet even this might be accomplished by inartificial means[4], without the

---

[1] Atlas to Minutoli's Reisen, Pl. 13. Wilkinson, Manners and Customs, vol. iii. p. 328.
[2] A pulley from an Egyptian tomb is preserved in the Leyden Museum, but its age is uncertain.
[3] Plin. 36, 21 (14). 36, 9.
[4] The process consists in gradually introducing earth beneath the shaft which is to be raised. In this way the *trilitha* of Stonehenge are supposed to have been elevated. Pliny (36, 8) says 120,000 men were employed to raise an obelisk at Thebes.

machinery which the Romans employed to erect, or Fontana to replace them[1].

The Egyptian system of arithmetical notation was simple in principle but cumbrous in detail (see Pl. IV.). In the hieroglyphic writing the nine digits were expressed by an equal number of strokes; *ten* by a specific character, repeated as far as nine to denote the decads, and combined with strokes to denote the intervening digits. A *hundred*, a *thousand, ten thousand*, a *hundred thousand*, were all denoted by specific characters. In the hieratic character and the demotic the strokes are combined for rapid execution, as far as four, which has a specific character; and this is joined with the four preceding to make up the digits as far as nine. *Ten* has an appropriate character; so have the hundreds, thousands, ten thousands and hundred thousands. In its general principles therefore the Egyptian notation is closely analogous to the Phœnician[2], Etruscan[3] and Roman, multiplying strokes for the lower numbers, and using specific characters for the higher multiples; but is opposed to the Hebrew and Greek, which employed the letters of the alphabet. There is a considerable resemblance between the hieratic and demotic form of the characters for the digits, and the Arabic numerals, which renders it not improbable that the Mahometan conquerors of Egypt may have borrowed their system thence. There is no approach, how-

---

[1] See the description in Ammianus Marcellinus (17, 415) of the elevation of an obelisk in the Circus Maximus.

[2] Gesenius, Scripturæ Phœnic. Monumenta, 1, p. 85.

[3] Müller, Etrusker, 2, 317.

ever, to a decimal notation, which is the great excellence of the Arabian system, and though distinct as a record, the Egyptian method must have been very inconvenient for calculation, which was probably performed by mechanical means.

An Egyptian cubit in the Museum at Paris gives 1·707 foot for the length of this measure. We do not know what was the unit of weight; but one of the tombs of Thebes exhibits the weighing of gold and silver. The whole weight is a calf; a half, the head of an ox; a quarter, a small oval ball[1]. It is remarkable, that notwithstanding the high civilization which the Egyptians had attained, they had no coined money in any period of their independence. Their currency was gold and silver rings[2], which were estimated by weight; but it is uncertain how they supplied the want of a copper coinage for small values. It has been conjectured that the scarabæi which have been found in such numbers, served this purpose.

Although the art of medicine was practised by the Egyptian priests and its literature wholly in their keeping, they were not the sole physicians and surgeons of the community, as will be hereafter shown. Egypt was remarkable for the production of medicinal herbs[3]: commerce with Asia[4] and the interior of Africa would greatly increase the number of drugs, and the fame of its physicians was spread throughout the ancient world. Homer de-

---

[1] Wilkinson, Mod. Eg. and Thebes, 2, 34.
[2] Rosellini, Mon. Civ. 2, 286.
[3] Od. δ', 228. Jerem. xlvi. 11. Go up into Gilead, and take balm, O virgin, daughter of Egypt: *in vain shalt thou use many medicines*; *for thou shalt not be cured.*
[4] Genesis xxxvii. 25.

scribes them as " sons of Pæon, skilful above all men[1]." Cambyses sent for an oculist from Egypt[2], and Darius kept Egyptian physicians about him, as the most skilful, though, as the event proved, they were surpassed by a Greek[3]. Every place in Egypt, says Herodotus, is full of physicians[4]. They were required to practise according to certain precepts, established by men of high reputation, and handed down from ancient times in the sacred books. Six of these are enumerated by Clemens Alexandrinus[5], one treating on the structure of the body, another on its diseases, a third on medical and surgical instruments, a fourth on drugs, a fifth on the eyes, and a sixth on female diseases. This division and arrangement, comprehending physiology, pathology, pharmaceutics and surgery, indicates an advanced state of the science. The different branches of practice were minutely subdivided, and each practitioner confined himself to one[6]. Some were oculists, some dentists, some treated diseases of the head, some of the bowels, and some those of uncertain seat. Such appears to be the natural tendency of medical practice, when carried to a high degree of experimental skill, and exercised among a numerous population. Their system was prophylactic[7]. Attention to diet was a leading principle in it; they considered the food as the great source of disease, and endeavoured to counteract its ill effects by frequent fasts as well

---

[1] Od. δ', 229.
[2] Her. 3, 1.
[3] Her. 3, 129.
[4] 2, 84.
[5] Strom. 6, p. 758 Potter.
[6] Her. u. s.
[7] Diod. 1, 82. Τὰς νόσους προκαταλαμβανόμενοι θεραπεύουσι τὰ σώματα κλυσμοῖς κ. τ. λ.

as medicine[1]. Herodotus observes that, except the Libyans, the Egyptians were the healthiest race with whom he was acquainted, and he attributes this to the absence of those extremes which in other countries make the changes of the seasons dangerous. Food was plentiful in Egypt[2], and the materials of clothing cheap; the Nile afforded a supply of water which was most copious during the hottest part of summer, and the Etesian winds which blew during the same period, tempered the heat of an almost vertical sun. Medical science, however, could hardly be progressive under the restrictions to which, according to one account, it was subject. If the patient could not be cured by the application of the precepts contained in the ancient books, the practitioner was exonerated; but if he departed from them he was liable to capital punishment (we must suppose in the event of the patient's death), the legislator thinking that few were likely to improve upon the practice which had been observed from ancient times, and established by the most skilful professors of the art. Such is the statement of Diodorus[3]; but it appears from Aristotle[4], that after three or four days' unsuccessful treatment by the established methods, the physician might adopt others, without incurring responsibility. The extreme subdivision of the profession, unless counteracted by a compre-

---

[1] Her. 2, 77. Συρμαΐζουσι τρεῖς ἡμέρας ἐπεξῆς μηνὸς ἑκάστου. Sea-bathing (ἡ διὰ θαλάττης θεραπεία) was said to be another of their remedies, which had proved successful in the case of Euripides (Diog. Laert. Plat. 7).

[2] Diod. 1, 80.

[3] 1, 82. According to Horapollo, 1, 38, one of these books, treating of symptoms, was called *Ambres*.

[4] Arist. Polit. 3, 10. Κινεῖν is to innovate on existing institutions (Plat. Hipp. Maj. 284 B).

hensive education, must have tended to reduce medical practice to a very mechanical art.

In later ages at least the Egyptian art of medicine was much contaminated by astrology. This mixed science was called *Iatromathematic*[1]. It was the natural result of the opinion, which, as we may infer from the monuments[2], prevailed in very remote times, that the sun and constellations had an influence on different parts of the human body according to the place in the heavens which they occupied.

[1] Zoega de Or. Obelisc. 523. Lobeck, Aglaophamus, 927.
[2] Champollion, Lettres d'Egypte, 239, gives an account of such a table of solar and stellar influence, in a royal tomb at Thebes.

CHAPTER XXI.

RELIGION.

SECT. I.—THEOLOGY.

THE ceremonial religion of the Egyptians is known to us in more complete detail from paintings and sculptures than that of any other nation; but when we endeavour to penetrate into the conceptions which this splendid ritual expressed, we encounter insuperable difficulties. It was not the practice of the ministers of ancient religions to reduce theological belief into precise dogmatic forms; the names by which the deities were to be invoked, the prayers to be addressed and the sacrifices to be offered to them, were fixed by usage or positive regulation; but the ideas attached to the name invoked varied with the worshiper's state of intellectual culture. This is to a certain extent true of all religious conceptions; they are refined or gross, elevated or low, according to the mental state of the believer. Religions, however, established on the authority of Revelation naturally seek to confine this variety within the narrowest possible limits. The Egyptian religion, on the contrary, was even more indefinite than those of the Greeks and Romans, among whom an historical mythology gave an objective reality and fixedness to the religious conceptions, which mere intellectual abstractions, such as Egyptian art symbolized, could not possess.

No work written by an Egyptian priest or theologian remains to reveal the religious system of his countrymen. We know the theological writings of Manetho only partially and at second-hand through Plutarch; Herodotus has preserved some valuable information about the external religion of Egypt, and occasionally a sacerdotal tradition respecting the gods of the temples which he visited. But if he derived from the priests any more abstruse information respecting their religious system, he has not recorded it. He often suppresses what he had been told, from religious scruples, but it is evident that what he shrunk from repeating were tales of the sufferings of the gods, especially Osiris[1], or revolting circumstances connected with religious rites, not the truths of a more profound or spiritual theology. The revelations which they may have made to Pythagoras, in his longer and more intimate acquaintance with them, have nearly all been buried in the same mysterious silence as his own doctrines[2]. It is probable that the familiarity of Plato with their theological system had a great influence upon the form in which he promulgated his conceptions of the divine nature; but we derive little knowledge of this country from his works, beyond an occasioual allusion and a testimony to the high antiquity and unchangeable character of all its institutions[3].

---

[1] 2. 62, 132, 171.
[2] Pythagoras tantum non omnia institutioni sacerdotum Ægyptiorum debet, in iis etiam, ut credo, quæ sibi ipsi ascripsit. (Jablonsky, Proleg. p. xlix.) But the proof of this comprehensive statement is not even attempted by the learned writer. The assertion also that Thales borrowed from Egypt his doctrine "that God was the Intellect which formed all things from water," is made without proof. (Proleg. p. xlvi.)
[3] Tim. iii. 22.

Diodorus gives an account of the Egyptian religion in his first book[1], drawn from different and not always accordant sources; but throughout it is evident that those from whom his information was derived were eager to connect the Egyptian theology with the Greek; and not so much to explain what it was in itself, and in its primary conception, as to find in it analogies to the Greek mythology, favouring the claim of Egypt to be the native country of the Greek gods. The sun, moon and elements, forming the body of the universe, were according to him the original divinities, the two first bearing the names of Osiris and Isis, Jupiter being the vivifying spirit, Vulcan fire, Demeter the earth, Oceanus or the Nile the watery element, and Minerva the air. These were the heavenly and immortal gods; but besides these there were others, some bearing the same, some different names from the immortals, who had been rulers of Egypt, or for some other merit had been placed in the rank of divinity. It is evident that we have here the result of an attempt to combine two different explanations, the physical and the historical; and as the latter finds no countenance in the older work of Herodotus, it was probably devised after the Egyptians became familiar with the Greek mythology. For it was part of this historical system, that these illustrious persons had not only during their lives conferred great benefits on Egypt, but had traversed the world for the same purpose, and had been received as divinities, though under different names, by the inhabitants of other countries. Inscriptions were feigned, to give plau-

[1] Hist. 1, 6–26.

sibility to this opinion. Thus at Nysa in Arabia, according to an account recorded by Diodorus[1], two columns were found, one of Isis, the other of Osiris, on the latter of which the god declared that he had led an army to India, to the sources of the Danube, and as far as the ocean. This, if not immediately borrowed from Manetho, as the words of Eusebius seem to imply[2], was at least derived from him, and shows that even he wrote with the Greek mythology before his mind, and adapted to it his explanation of the Egyptian religion. For there is nothing in history, or in the monuments, which indicates that the gods of Egypt were really deified men.

Under the later Greek sovereigns and Roman emperors, the worship of Egyptian deities spread very extensively beyond the limits of Egypt. The rites and doctrines of this religion, by their solemnity and mysticism, revived for a while the faith which the established system had no longer the power to excite; miraculous cures and other benefits, obtained by the votaries of Isis[3] or Serapis, nourished this faith; the credit which the ancient oracles had lost was transferred to the dreams which they sent to their worshipers, or divinations practised in their temples. Curiosity was awakened to gain some deeper insight into the meaning of the figures and emblems of its gods, and the sense hidden

---

[1] 1, 28.
[2] Γράφει καὶ τὰ περὶ τούτων πλατύτερον μὲν ὁ Μανέθως· ἐπιτετμημένως δὲ ὁ Διόδωρος. (Euseb. Præp. Ev. 3, 2.) He naturally asks, what propriety there could be in giving human names to the parts of Nature: but according to the view which the Christian Fathers usually adopted, he considers the human origin of the gods the true one, the connexion with the elements as a fiction. (Ib. p. 91.)
[3] Diod. 1, 25.

in the dark allegories by which its tenets were rather concealed than expressed. The priesthood no longer possessed any power to prevent the disclosure of their secrets. A philosopher like Plutarch did not disdain to write his learned treatise *de Iside et Osiride*, addressed to Clea, the chief of the Thyades, or female ministers of the Bacchic orgies at Delphi[1]. She had been initiated by her father and mother into the mysteries of Osiris[2]; but Plutarch wished to communicate to her more lofty and philosophical views of the Egyptian theology than those taught by the Isiac priests, who in this age appear to have been selfish impostors, preying on the credulity of the superstitious, and themselves entirely ignorant of the real meaning of the rites into which they initiated others. The Egyptian learning which he has brought together makes his treatise the most comprehensive and valuable of all the ancient writings on this subject, and many curious facts are preserved in it respecting religious usages and doctrines. But when he explains the origin and design of these usages, and the primary meaning of the allegorical and symbolical language in which theology was clothed, it is evident from the variety and uncertainty of his explanations that they are merely the conjectures of ingenious theorists, among which the author chooses that which best accorded with his own views. His knowledge was derived from Greek books, without actual in-

---

[1] There was a temple of Isis, the most sacred of any dedicated by the Greeks to her worship, at Tithorea, near Delphi (Paus. 10, 32).

[2] De Is. et Os. p. 364 E. The genuineness of this treatise of Plutarch has not escaped the scepticism of the German critics, but the name is of no great importance.

spection of Egypt, or power to interpret its monuments. Manetho is the earliest writer whom he quotes, and his chief authority. Plutarch himself explains the mythic history of Osiris, Isis and Typhon, as an allegory of the contest of the two principles in nature. We must therefore receive his essay, not as an authorized exposition of the Egyptian theology, but as an ingenious attempt to extract from it a connected and rational system, in which however much knowledge is incidentally preserved.

The disposition to bring the doctrines of Egyptian theology into harmony with Greek philosophy is more glaring in the later Platonists, and makes such writers as Porphyry, Iamblichus, Proclus, Damascius, little to be depended upon in forming an idea of the original religion of Egypt. In the age in which they lived, the long intercourse of the Egyptians with the Greeks had produced a considerable assimilation between them, and an endeavour mutually to accommodate their systems. These Neo-Platonists or Eclectics had in fact admitted into their philosophy much that had an Egyptian or Oriental origin, besides giving to the doctrines of Plato and Pythagoras such modifications as would adapt them to their purpose of establishing a system which, in doctrine and morals, might be an effectual antagonist to Christianity. The Egyptians themselves knew little respecting the original import of their own theology in this age, and the knowledge of the sacred character was nearly lost[1].

The attempts made between the revival of letters

---

[1] See p. 288 of this volume.

and the discovery of the hieroglyphics, to reconstruct the system of Egyptian theology, were fruitless. Two writers of the eighteenth century advanced as far as it was possible to do, while the key to Egyptian antiquity was wanting. Jablonsky, in his *Pantheon Ægyptiorum*[1], by the careful collection of everything which the ancients have left us on this subject, greatly facilitated the labours of every subsequent inquirer; but the truth was not to be discovered by any comparison or combination of what the ancients had written; and the scantiness of all information from the times when the Egyptian theology was a living system, compelled him to build to an unsafe extent upon the foundation of the later Platonists and Pythagoreans, and the Orphic and Hermetic books. His knowledge of the Coptic language, however, which he justly assumed to be in substance the same with the ancient Egyptian, enabled him to throw some light from etymology, both on the titles and attributes of the Egyptian gods and the names of their early kings, into which the names of the gods frequently enter. Zoega[2], directing his attention primarily to the monuments of Egypt, cleared away many errors of long standing respecting the uses of the obelisks and pyramids, and approximated to a true conception of Egyptian antiquity as closely as it was possible to do, by the combination of learning and sagacity, before the language of the monuments was understood.

The discovery of the Rosetta Stone led to the

---

[1] Francf. ad Viadr. 2 vols. 8vo, 1750.

[2] De origine et usu Obeliscorum. Romæ, 1797, fol.

knowledge of the group of characters expressing the name of the god Ptah[1]; and when the phonetic alphabet was once established, many others were rapidly ascertained. The name of the divinity is frequently written over or beside his sculptured or painted figure, and from these sources Wilkinson[2] and Champollion restored with little uncertainty the Egyptian Pantheon. In some respects it corresponds with the accounts of the ancients, but in many differs from them. In the further progress of the hieroglyphical discoveries, the legends which accompany the figures of the deities have also been interpreted. They appear to contain a declaration of their parentage, their attributes and operations; but, for reasons previously assigned, we have used them sparingly and cautiously, as evidence of the religious system of the ancient Egyptians. Beyond a few formulary phrases, fixed by bilingual inscriptions, or whose frequent recurrence gives some security of their meaning, we cannot place implicit reliance on the interpretations even of the most sagacious writers. The interpretation of the papyri which accompany the mummies is still more obscure, from the mysterious nature of their subject; and had they been more convincingly deciphered, their authority would be doubtful, as they do not represent the public religion of the country.

The distribution of their sovereigns into dynasties seems to have suggested to the Egyptians a similar arrangement of their gods, but in a sense somewhat different; the dynasty of sovereigns comprehend-

---

[1] See Pl. IV., the shield of Ptolemy.

[2] Wilkinson, Materia Hieroglyphica, published at Malta, 1828.

ing several generations, whereas one god reigned through the whole of a dynasty[1]. Vulcan or Ptah is said to have been the first, succeeded by his son, the Sun, Agathodæmon, Cronos, Osiris, Typhon. Horus, the son of Osiris and Isis[2], was the first of those who succeeded the gods, and are called in the Greek of Syncellus ἡμίθεοι, in the Latin of Eusebius *heroes*, by whom the Egyptians understood, not heroes or demigods in the Grecian sense, as beings having one mortal, one divine parent, but gods of an inferior order, Mars, Anubis, Hercules, Ammon being reckoned among them. Herodotus makes the reign of mortal kings immediately to have succeeded that of Horus, the son of Osiris. To the demigods are said by Manetho to have succeeded " dead men," νέκυες, *manes*, whom the Egyptians appear from this collocation of them to have considered as forming the lowest link between the divine and human nature, and therefore as the immediate predecessors of earthly sovereigns. To these dynasties long periods of domination are arbitrarily ascribed, which the Christian chronologers endeavoured to reconcile with the Scriptures by summarily reducing the years of the Egyptian reckoning to lunar months, or even single days[3].

The papyrus called the Hieratical Canon of Turin, shows that in the remote age in which it was written, probably that of Rameses the Great,

---

[1] Herod. 2, 144. Τὸ πρότερον τῶν ἀνδρῶν θεοὺς εἶναι τοὺς ἐν Αἰγύπτῳ ἄρχοντας, οἰκέοντας ἅμα τοῖσι ἀνθρώποισι καὶ τούτων αἰεὶ ἕνα τὸν κρατέοντα εἶναι. But he does not use the term *dynasty*.

[2] Syncell. p. 18.

[3] Euseb. Arm. 1, cap. 19. Suidas, Lex. s. voc. Ἥφαιστος. Αἰγύπτιοι τὴν περίοδον τῆς ἡμέρας ἐνιαυτὸν ἔλεγον.

dynasties of gods were supposed to have preceded Menes, but from its torn condition no exact agreement can be made out. Seb (Saturn), Osiris or Isis, Seth or Typhon, Horus, Thoth, Thmei, are the only gods whose names remain; corresponding nearly with the succession given by Manetho[1].

The dwelling of the gods among men and their personally ruling over them belongs to a natural and widely diffused conception of primæval times, as distinguished for purity, and therefore honoured by the intimacy of superior natures. It has nothing historical. Some motive, however, must have regulated the distribution of the gods into successive dynasties. It was natural that the earliest dominion should be attributed to the greater gods, and that Ptah, who represented the elemental fire, and was the father of the Sun, should be placed at the commencement of the whole series. But we cannot infer anything from this arrangement respecting the successive ascendency of different religious systems in Egypt, or conclude that the worship of Ptah was really older than that of Osiris. There was an obvious physical reason why the god of fire should be made to precede the god of the sun. So in the arrangement of the Greek divinities, Ouranos and Ghe (Heaven and Earth) are naturally placed before Cronos (Time), as Cronos before Jupiter. Yet there is no trace of a period in Greek history when Uranus and Cronos were worshiped, and Jupiter was yet unknown as a deity, or only deemed subordinate to the others, as there is none in Egyptian

---

[1] Le Sueur, Chronologie, p. 307, pl. xi.; Birch, Trans. Roy. Soc. Lit. 1, 203, 8vo.

history of Ptah or the Sun being worshiped while Osiris and Isis had no place in the Pantheon.

The papyrus of Turin, from its mutilated condition, affording us no satisfactory evidence of the manner in which the Egyptians arranged their gods, Herodotus is on this point our oldest authority[1]. He says that there were eight gods originally, and that Pan and Leto belonged to this number; that from these, twelve were produced, of whom he specifies only Hercules; and again a third set from the second, whose number he does not specify, to which Dionysus (Osiris) belonged. No other ancient writer mentions this threefold series of the Egyptian gods; it does not correspond with Manetho's division into gods, demigods and *manes*; nor do we find traces in the monuments of any such classification. Nevertheless we cannot doubt that in the time of Herodotus these three series were distinguished; only we are not called upon to receive the chronology which reckoned 17,000 years from Amasis to the origin of the twelve gods, nor even to admit that there was any real succession among the three groups into which they were divided, or that they represent the ascendency of the different bodies of priests.

Of those who have endeavoured to assign its primary meaning to the Egyptian religion, some

---

[1] 2, 43. Ἀρχαῖός τίς ἐστι θεὸς Αἰγυπτίοισι Ἡρακλέης· ὡς δὲ αὐτοὶ λέγουσι ἐτεά ἐστι ἑπτακισχίλια καὶ μύρια ἐς Ἄμασιν βασιλεύσαντα, ἐπεί τε ἐκ τῶν ὀκτὼ θεῶν οἱ δυώδεκα θεοὶ ἐγένοντο; ὧν Ἡρακλέα ἕνα νομίζουσι. 2, 46. Τὸν Πᾶνα τῶν ὀκτὼ θεῶν λογίζονται εἶναι οἱ Μενδήσιοι· τοὺς δὲ ὀκτὼ θεοὺς τούτους, προτέρους τῶν δυώδεκα θεῶν φασι γενέσθαι. 2, 145, he says that "Pan was a very ancient god, one of the eight who are called the first; Hercules of the second, who are said to be twelve; Bacchus" (Osiris) " of the third"—οἱ ἐκ τῶν δυώδεκα θεῶν ἐγένοντο. 2, 156. Λητώ, τῶν ὀκτὼ θεῶν τῶν πρῶτον γενομένων.

have represented it as simply material, the elements and heavenly bodies being themselves the gods, without any pervading and presiding intellect. "The philosophy of the Egyptians concerning the gods," says Diogenes Laertius[1], "is this, that matter was the beginning of all things; that from it the four elements were separated, and some animals formed; that the Sun and Moon are gods, one called Osiris, the other Isis." Eusebius[2] says that the Egyptians believed the world was God, and that different gods made up its parts, but did not admit any intellectual principle. He quotes Chæremon also as asserting, that the Egyptians had no other gods than the visible universe, the sun, moon and planets. Others sought its explanation in a system of metaphysical conceptions respecting the Divine nature and the manifestations of Divine power. The following passage, from the older Hermetic Books, quoted by Iamblichus[3], will show how the doctrines of Greek philosophy were combined with those of Egyptian mythology:—

"Before all the things that actually exist, and before all beginnings, there is one God, prior even to the first god and king, remaining unmoved in the singleness of his own Unity: for neither is anything conceived by intellect inwoven with him, nor anything else; but he is established as the exemplar of the god who is good, who is his own father, self-begotten, and has only one parent. For he is something greater and prior to, and the foun-

---

[1] Prœm. 12.
[2] Præp. Ev. iii. 3, 9. Αἰγυπτίων ὁ λόγος τὸν κόσμον εἶναι τὸν Θεὸν ᾤετο ἐκ πλειόνων θεῶν τῶν αὐτοῦ μερῶν συνεστῶτα.
[3] Cory's Ancient Frag., p. 283.

tain of all things, and the foundation of things conceived by the intellect, which are the first species. And from this One, the self-originated god caused himself to shine forth; for which reason he is his own father and self-originated. For he is both a beginning and god of gods, a monad from the One, prior to substance and the beginning of substance; for from him is substantiality and substance: whence also he is called the beginning of things conceived by the intellect. These then are the most ancient beginnings of all things, which Hermes places before the etherial and empyrean and celestial gods. But according to another arrangement he places the god Emeph" (probably Kneph) " as leader of the celestial gods, whom he declares to be Intellect conceiving itself, and turning its conceptions upon itself. Before this he places the one indivisible and what he calls the first image[1] and names Eicton[2], in which indeed is the first that conceives and the first that is conceived; on which account it is worshiped in silence only. In addition to these, other rulers preside over the creation of visible things: for the creative intellect, presiding both over truth and wisdom, when it proceeds to production and leads forth into light the secret power of the hidden reasons, is called *Amon* in the Egyptian tongue. And when it perfects all things without falsehood, but according to art with truth, *Ptha*; but the Greeks change Ptha into Hephaistus, attending only to the technical. And as

[1] Πρῶτον μάγευμα, which seems to be here used in the same sense as ἐκμαγεῖον (Suid. ἐκτύπωμα· ἀποσφράγισμα). See Tim. Locr. p. 534 E., where Matter is called ἐκμαγεῖον, as receiving likenesses into itself from the Idea, which is the παράδειγμα τῶν γεννωμένων. Wyttenb. ad Plut. 373 A.

[2] From εἴκω, to resemble.

and has other names in virtue of other powers and operations.

"There is also among them another presidency over all the elements that are concerned in production and their powers, four male, four female, which they assign to the Sun; and another dominion over all nature, as concerned in production, which they give to the Moon. And dividing the heaven into two parts or four, or twelve or thirty-six, or the double of these, they place at the head of them more or fewer, and set over them all one superior to them. And thus from first to last the whole system of the Egyptians, in regard to the beginnings, sets out from one and advances to a plurality; the many again being guided by one, and the nature of the unlimited being everywhere controled by some limited measure, and by the supreme Unity the cause of all."

That the Egyptians, in the age of this writer, expounded their own mythology into the metaphysical system here set forth, is not to be doubted. Whether they had done so before they became acquainted with the Greek philosophy is less certain. Yet the residence of Pythagoras and Plato in Egypt[1] makes it not improbable that the resemblance to their metaphysical doctrines which appears in the foregoing extract may be owing to their communications with its priests. The Pythagorean rules of diet and discipline, so minute and fanciful, bear strong marks of being transferred from the practice

---

[1] See the passages quoted in the notes of Menage on Diogenes Laertius, Pythag. 3. Plat. 7.

of the sacerdotal order in Egypt. It is another question whether the Hermetic doctrines represent the true and primary conceptions of Egyptian theology. There is nothing in the symbols by which the gods are distinguished, to indicate that they denoted such abstract notions, nor in the fragments of their mythological history to show that they stood in such a relation to each other. The ἱεροὶ λόγοι which Herodotus relates, resemble the mythological tales which in other countries were told of the gods, not mystical or metaphysical doctrines. It would have been singular if among the most cultivated people of early antiquity a *theosophy* had not been formed, of which the object was to refine away the gross conceptions in which the primitive legends, symbols and rites of religion originate, and engraft upon traditionary mythology the speculative philosophy of a later age.

A strong presumption against any interpretation, which supposes the Egyptian religion to contain a *system*, whether of physical, metaphysical or other truth, arises from the fact, that it does not appear to have been systematically conceived and projected; but to have been fashioned into a whole by the agglutination of parts, having a separate origin. From various passages in Herodotus it is obvious, that the worship of the different gods was established by the inhabitants of the several nomes[1], and this division of worship goes as far back as the origin of the monarchy[2]. There must indeed have been a certain

---

[1] Ὅσοι μὲν Διὸς Θηβαιέος ἵδρυνται ἱρὸν, ἢ νομοῦ τοῦ Θηβαίου' εἰσὶ, οὗτοι μέν νυν πάντες οἴων ἀπεχόμενοι, αἶγας θύουσι· ὅσοι δὲ τοῦ Μένδητος ἔκτηνται ἱρὸν, ἢ νομοῦ τοῦ Μενδησίου εἰσὶ, οὗτοι δὲ αἰγῶν ἀπεχόμενοι, ὄϊς θύουσι. Her. 2, 42.

[2] Manetho, Dyn. 2, 2.

unity of religious conception in the mind of the nation, otherwise we cannot understand that political unity which belonged to them in the earliest recorded period of history. But this unity of rehgious conception is rather a national agreement in the mode of expressing the religious sentiment which is common to mankind, than the united belief of a theological system, devised by common consent, or imposed on all by some superior authority. So we find one language, with dialectic differences, prevailing along with other circumstances which constitute national unity; it is essential to that sympathy without which the social union could not be formed. It does not however show itself by the existence of a parent language of which the several dialects are the offspring; nowhere can we establish historically the existence of such a language; but in a general conformity of mental conception and vocal expression, characterizing the whole nation, yet differenced at the same time by local or other influences. So the unity of the Egyptian people implies such a degree of accordance in religious conception, that they could all join in a common worship, and receive as divine the deities whom their neighbours specially adored; but by no means that the whole theological system existed in its integrity, previous to the commencement of history, and that different nomes selected from it the gods of their local worship. It seems more probable, that from a multitude of religious conceptions, formed and embodied with a pervading resemblance and community of character, such as one people would naturally exhibit, a system was subsequently constructed, allowing each local deity his separate honours, and the supreme veneration of his original votaries, but also giving to them a subordination of power and division of functions, which they did not before possess.

Such an origin will best explain the extraordinary intermixture and confusion of the characters and functions of the Egyptian gods. In their visible symbols and in their names they appear at first sight to be distinct, and there is usually some office prominently assigned to every one; but on further examination we find that each assumes occasionally the attributes of the others, and that a permanent line of demarcation cannot be drawn between them. Those which appear usually in an inferior rank are at times invested with the titles of supreme divinity. This too was a natural consequence of a local origin; to the people of each nome their own special god would become the chief object of worship; the inhabitant of the Thebais would attribute to his Amun, of Memphis to his Ptah, of Sais to his Neith, the offices and operation of the head of the system. And besides this, reflecting men would naturally endeavour to bring back the diversity of persons and attributes in the popular theology to the idea of a primitive and controling unity. For we find everywhere, in the civilized ancient world, a belief in one supreme power, co-existing with polytheism, either as the result of a primæval revelation of this doctrine, or of that conviction of a unity of purpose and administration which forces itself upon the mind, from its own consciousness of a moral and intellectual unity, and from the observation of the external world.

Still the historical fact remains, recorded by Herodotus, and liable to no doubt, that the Egyptians had a threefold division of their gods, into eight, twelve, and an indefinite number. It is not quite clear from his language, whether the twelve were the offspring of the eight, so that the whole number became twenty, or whether the number twelve included the eight, so that only four new deities were added to the list. It has been generally taken for granted, that the eight were the only original gods, and that in them we have the germ of the theological system of the Egyptians. Thus Jablonsky[1] supposes that this *ogdoad* was made up of the seven planets and Ptah, the supreme intelligence which presided over the universe. But he confesses, that of such a worship of the heavenly bodies he finds no mention in Herodotus, and scarcely any in later writers; and he is compelled to suppose, that some other meaning was substituted to the astronomical in very early times. The monuments give no countenance to this supposition of an astronomical origin.

Others again have supposed that the eight gods formed a system in which a gradual progression from concealment to manifestation in the divine

---

[1] "Septem germanos (in a passage of Martianus Capella) quis non agnoscat totidem planetas, per quos totum mundum gubernari credebant veteres? Fontem vero lucis æthereæ, in totius mundi lumina fusum, non esse ahum quam *Pthan*, sive *Vulcanum*, alio loco docuimus. Hæc est antiquissima Deorum Ægyptiorum ogdoas, quæ primis idolatriæ in Ægypto stabilitæ seculis, diu sola obtinuit, et deos omnes, ab illa gente cultos, uti auguror, complexa est." (Jabl. P. Æg. Proleg. p. lxii.) Others substituted the Sun for Ptah. See Chæremon ap. Euseb. Præp. Ev. 3, 4. Porphyr. ibid. Ἡ τῶν Αἰγυπτίων ἀπόρρητος θεολογία, οὐδὲ ἄλλους πλὴν τῶν κατ' οὐρανὸν ἀστέρων τῶν τε ἀπλανῶν καλουμένων καὶ τῶν ὀνομαζομένων πλανητῶν ἐθεολόγει, δημιουργόν τε τῶν ὅλων εἰσῆγεν, οὐτιναοῦν ἀσώματον, οὐδὲ λόγον δημιουργικόν, οὐδὲ μὴν οὐδὲ θεὸν οὐδὲ θεούς, οὐδέ τινας νοερὰς καὶ ἀφανεῖς δυνάμεις· μόνον δὲ τὸν ὁρώμενον Ἥλιον.

energy is shadowed forth[1], and others have merely selected those which from their importance and antiquity seemed to have the most plausible claim to be reckoned among the eight gods. In all such arrangements and distributions there must be much that is arbitrary; yet the division into eight[2] and twelve no doubt had a motive. The number twelve is clearly astronomical. The Egyptians first allotted a god to each month and day of the year, that is, they assigned to each of the divisions of the sun's path through the heavens, one of their gods or dæmons; and so strongly were they influenced by a desire to connect their theology and their astronomy, that when the five additional days were introduced into the reckoning of the solar year, they distributed the birth-days of the gods Osiris and Isis, Typhon, Aroeris and Athor among them, assigning one to each. These are plain marks, not of an astronomical origin of the Egyptian deities, but a distribution of them according to an astronomical principle. There may therefore have been also an astronomical reason for fixing the number of the oldest gods at eight, this being the number of the spheres of

---

[1] Bunsen, Ægypten's Stelle, 1, 456.

[2] Lepsius (Einleitung, p. 505, note 2) is of opinion that the eight gods were originally only seven. Elsewhere he says (p. 253, note), "The great gods, who as far as I know have never been correctly reckoned up, were, according to the Theban doctrine, *Mentu, Atmu, Mu, Seb, Osiris* [Aroeris], *Set, Hor*; according to the Memphite doctrine, *Ptah, Ra, Mu, Seb, Osiris* [Hor], *Set, Hor*. The exclusion of Aroeris and also at a later time of Set, produced other deviations from this series, in different times and places. In their stead most frequently *Sebek*, sometimes also *Thoth*, the first of the second series, was assumed amongst the greater gods. *Amun* occasionally appears at their head, but did not originally belong there." The evidence of these arrangements has not yet been produced, and they cannot be reconciled with Herodotus.

the planets (including the Sun and Moon) and the fixed stars[1]. Eight was a sacred number in antiquity. The Orphic or Pythagorean maxim πάντα ὀκτώ may probably have had an Egyptian origin[2]. It is the first cube number, and may on that account have been held in mystic reverence among a people who attached sanctity to numbers. The Pythagoreans considered it as the number of justice[3]. The Dii Selecti of the Romans were eight; the Cabiri according to one reckoning eight[4]. An alleged inscription from an Egyptian *stele* enumerates as the gods of Egypt, Wind, Heaven, Sun, Moon, Earth, Night, Day and Love, in all eight[5]. Were the evidence more satisfactory that the Egyptian gods originally represented the elements, the number eight would be the best adapted to it, since they reckoned them four, and supposed them to have a double nature, male and female[6]. According to the view, however, which has been already proposed, it is not likely that the whole system originated in any *one* principle. There appear in it traces of at least three, the worship of the heavenly bodies, the personification of the powers supposed to be engaged in the creation, preservation, and government of

[1] Clem. Coh. p. 44. Ξενοκράτης Χαλκηδόνιος, ἑπτὰ μὲν θεοὺς τοὺς πλάνητας, ὄγδοον δὲ τὸν ἐκ πάντων αὐτῶν συνεστῶτα κόσμον αἰνίττεται. Plat. Epinom. ii. 986. Ἴστε ὀκτὼ δυνάμεις τῶν περὶ ὅλον οὐρανὸν γεγονυίας.

[2] Jabl. Proleg. p. lxxi. An Orphic poet (Eus. Præp. Evang. 3, 9) thus enumerates the eight principles: Fire, Water, Earth, Night, Day, Counsel (Metis), Love, and Zeus, who comprehends them all.

[3] Macrob. Somn. Scip. 1, 5, p. 17.

[4] Euseb. Præp. Ev. 1, 10, from Sanchoniatho.

[5] Jabl. 1, 18. According to the fanciful explanation of Sextus Empiricus (adv. Math. 5, p. 733, Bekk.), the Egyptians reckoned all the celestial bodies as eight, viz. the Sun and Moon, five planets, and the fixed stars.

[6] Senec. Quæst. Nat. 3, 14. Jamblich. de Myster. 8, 3.

the world, and the assignment of personal symbols to abstract qualities. The worship of Ra (the Sun) is clearly an example of the first; that of Khem or Pan (the productive power of Nature) of the second; and that of Thoth (the Reason and inventive faculty of man) of the third.

Whatever may have been the occasion of fixing the number eight, it is probable that it was composed of four male and four female gods; for we generally find that the Egyptian deities were arranged in triads, a god, a goddess and their son. The following arrangement has no positive authority, and only professes to bring together the eight deities who appear to have held the chief place in the veneration of the Egyptians. In some cases the relation of consort existed, in others not.

Amun	Maut, Mut or Buto.
Khem (Pan)	Athor, Leto.
Kneph	Neith.
Ptah	Pasht, Bubastis.

I have placed AMUN (or AMMON) at the head of the system, because the Greek authors are unanimous in considering him to correspond with their Jupiter[1], and this must have been from their relative place in the Greek and Egyptian systems, as there was nothing in their physical attributes to identify them. The meaning of the name appears to have been uncertain to the Egyptians themselves; Manetho *thought* that it denoted concealment; but

---

[1] Herod. 2, 42. Diod. 1, 13. Plut. Is. et Osir. 354 C.

this sense hardly belongs to the Coptic root[1]. Hecatæus of Abdera agreed in the statement that Ammon was a concealed god, inasmuch as he was the first, and denoted the universe, but explained his name as signifying *come hither*, being a common form of compellation. *Amou* or *Amoun*, in fact, in Coptic signifies *veni*[2]; but it is not very probable that the name of the god should have originated in this way. The most obvious etymology is from the Coptic *amoun*, which signifies glory, *celsitudo*, and would be appropriate to the chief of the gods[3].

Amun is usually represented, especially at Thebes, with a human face and limbs free, and therefore not apparently symbolizing a concealed divinity, having two tall straight feathers on his head proceeding from a red cap. In front of these plumes a disk is sometimes seen[4]. The body is coloured of a deep blue. The Greeks and Latins agree in describing Amun as having the head of a ram. Herodotus says[5], "The Thebans and those who, like them, abstain from sheep, say they do it for this reason, that Jupiter (Amun), when Hercules desired to see him, at first refused; but, on his persisting, cut off the head of a ram which he had flayed, and held it before him, clothing himself in the skin, and showed himself to him in this form. And for this reason the Egyptians represent Jupiter with the head of a ram. And once a year, on the

---

[1] The verb *amoni*, from which it is supposed to be derived, means to *detain*, not to *conceal*. See Peyron, Lex. *s. v.*

[2] Jabl. Panth. Æg. 1, 179. Peyron, Lex. Copt. p. 6.

[3] The reference of the name Amun to Cham or Ham is destitute of all probability.

[4] Birch, Eg. Ant. in Brit. Mus. P. 1, p. 2.

[5] 2, 42.

festival of Jupiter, they kill and flay a ram, and clothe the statue of Jupiter in the manner described, and then bring near to it another statue of Hercules." We may conclude from this ceremony that the statue of Amun was not always represented with the head of a ram; and in fact the figures thus distinguished have usually the name of another god, to be mentioned hereafter. But the ancients have been too hastily charged with error in calling Amun ram-headed. The name of Amun is found beside figures so characterized[1]; the temple of Ammonium was dedicated to the ram-headed god[2]; and we have here already an instance of the difficulty of preserving an exact line of distinction between the Egyptian divinities. Jablonsky supposed that Amun represented the Sun in Aries, in accordance with his theory, that the positions of this luminary at the four great seasons of the year had each a symbol among the Egyptian gods, Amun, Horus, Serapis and Harpocrates[3]. The monuments give no confirmation to this opinion; nor do they on the other hand afford us much light as to the primary conception; but the epithet *Ra*, Sun, often subjoined to Amun, seems to indicate an original connexion with the solar god. His worship prevailed in Nubia and Meroe according to the ancients; and this is to a certain extent confirmed by the monuments, the ram-headed god being found there[4]. It has been conjectured that this affinity of the worship of Thebes and the higher regions of the

---

[1] Wilkinson, M. and C. pl. 22.
[2] Minutoli, Reise, Atlas, fig. 8, 9, 19. See p. 72.
[3] Proleg. p. lxx. lib. 2. 2, 3, 4, 5, 6.
[4] Hoskins's Ethiopia, pl. 10.

Nile, gave rise to the story of Jupiter and the rest of the gods annually visiting the Ethiopians, and feasting for twelve days among them[1]. But the custom to which Diodorus and Eustathius[2] allude in explanation of this story was something different; for the statue of the god was carried not *up*, but *across* the river, into Libya, not Ethiopia; and the account given by the priests bears marks of being devised in order to appropriate to Egypt another passage in the Iliad[3].

A remarkable circumstance connected with the name of this god has been noticed by Sir Gardner Wilkinson. On many monuments of Egypt, the hieroglyphics or phonetic name of *Amunra* have been substituted for others, which have been so carefully erased that he was unable to ascertain what the original had been[4]. The *figure* of the god, however, remains unaltered. This substitution has been so systematically made, that it must have been the result of some general order; and as it is confined to monuments erected previous to, and during the reign of the 3rd Amunoph, it is probable that it was done by his authority. Before this time the traces of Amun in the Egyptian theology are few. Ammenemes, in the twelfth dynasty, is the earliest king into the composition of whose name that of

---

[1] Hom. Il. a', 423.

[2] Diod. 1, 97. Eustath. Comment. ad loc. Hom.

[3] Hom. Il. ξ, 346. The carpet of flowers which sprung up under the embrace of Jupiter and Juno was, according to these commentators, derived from the custom of carrying the shrines of the gods to the top of a mountain, and strewing flowers beneath them.

[4] Manners and Customs, 4, 244. As in the statue of Amenophis in the British Museum, and on the obelisk of the Lateran at Rome. See Dr. E. Hincks, in Trans. of R.I.A. vol. 21, P. 1. He thinks that *Amun* has been effaced and re-inserted.

Amun enters. The motive of the substitution has not been explained[1], but it has probably been connected with some change in the religious system of the Egyptians.

The god who has sometimes the ram's head, sometimes the horns of a goat, is in the great majority of instances designated in the hieroglyphical inscriptions as NOUF, NOUB or NUM (Pl. III. C. 3), with the figure of a ram subjoined. His image is of more frequent occurrence in Nubia and Meroe than that of Amun. He is supposed to be also the Κνήφ of the Greeks, of whom Plutarch says that the inhabitants of the Thebaid considered him to be without progenitor and immortal[2], and on that account did not contribute, like the rest of the Egyptians, towards the maintenance and interment of the sacred animals. It is probable that this is the same god whom Damascius calls Καμήφις[3], and who in the text of Iamblichus appears as Ἡμήφ, the ruler of the celestial gods. According to Eusebius the Egyptians called the creator (demiurgus) Kneph[4], though this attribute is more commonly given to Ptah. Strabo says that there was a temple at Elephantine dedicated to Chnuphis[5], which appears to be the same name; and an inscription has

---

[1] According to Major Felix, the obliterated characters were a vulture flying, its body formed by an eye, holding in its claws a signet (Birch, Gall. of Antiq. p. 2, note 12). The flying vulture was the emblem of the goddess of Eilithyia, who corresponded with the Lucina of the Latins. Bunsen supposes that the ithyphallic Khem was the god for whom Amun was substituted (Æg. vol. 1, p. 438). On the obelisk of Karnak it appears to have been Athom or Atmou.

[2] Θνητὸν οὐδένα θεὸν νομίζοντας ἀλλα ὃν κυλοῦσιν αὐτοὶ ΚΝΗΦ ἀγέννητον ὄντα καὶ ἀθάνατον. (Is. et Os. p. 359.)

[3] Cory, Ancient Fragm. p. 321. ΚΑΜΦ, which is a various reading, is not very remote from ΚΝΗΦ.

[4] Præp. Ev. 3, 11.

[5] Lib. 17, p. 817.

been found at Élephantine " to the god Chnoubis[1]." Hence he is called in the legends " Lord of Ebo," the name of Elephantine[2]. We have proof again of the confusion or blending of him with Amun, for a Greek inscription in the oasis El Khargeh declares the temple to be dedicated " to the great god Amennebis," *i. e.* Amun Neph[3]. At Syene an inscription has been found *Jovi Hammoni Cenubidi*[4]. The description which Porphyry gives of Kneph[5], as having a human figure, a dark blue colour, a girdle and a sceptre, and a royal feather on his head, accords with the representations of Amun, not of Kneph. The same author says that from his mouth was produced an egg, out of which came the god whom the Greeks call Hephaistos, and the Egyptians Ptha. The monuments do not confirm this account; but in the temple of Osiris at Philæ he appears, fashioning upon a wheel or lathe the limbs of Osiris, while the figure of the god Nile stands by and pours water on the wheel. Elsewhere he is called the potter, and at Elephantine appears working a lump of clay upon the lathe[6]. We may therefore safely conclude that he was worshiped as the power which reduced all things to order and form in creation; and hence, while the philosophising interpreters of later times made him to be an intellectual principle, he was according to

---

[1] Wilk. M. & C. 4, 238.
[2] Rosellini, M. del C. 94.
[3] Wilkinson, Mod. Eg. & Thebes, 2, 369; or is this *Amun-neb*, Amun Lord?
[4] Wilkinson, 2, 289.
[5] Euseb. Præp. Ev. 3, p. 115.
[6] Rosellini, M. del C. 151. To such a figure Porphyry seems to allude, when he describes a statue at Elephantine, in human shape, of dark blue colour, the head of a ram, the horns of a goat, and a circular disk upon them; Κάθηται δὲ, παρακειμένου κεραμέου ἀγγείου ἐφ' οὗ ἄνθρωπον ἀναπλάσσειν. Euseb. 3, 12.

more material conceptions the element of Water[1], or the Sun. In a statue in the British Museum he wears the disk of this luminary on his head.

Another title which has been given to Noum is Agathodæmon. According to Sanchoniatho, as quoted by Eusebius[2], the Phœnicians represented this god by a serpent; and the Egyptians gave a similar title to Kneph, from which we may infer that his attributes were regarded as beneficent. The serpent, we know, was among the Greeks and Romans the emblem of a beneficent genius, and the author from whom Eusebius derived this statement may have had in view the serpent with the winged globe, placed by the Egyptians over the doors and windows of their temples as a tutelary god[3]. This emblem however belonged not specially to Kneph. The asp, which was a royal emblem, appears to have been appropriate to him, and was the "horned serpent," which according to Herodotus[4] was sacred to Jupiter in the Theban district. Jupiter indeed was in his interpretation Amun; he knows nothing of Kneph; but this is only a fresh instance of the confusion of these two divinities. Antipater of Sidon, in an epigram in the 'Anthologia[5],' calls Ammon "the renowned serpent." The *cerastes* is often found embalmed in the Thebaid, especially in the tombs of Qoorneh.

KHEM or AMUN KHEM is the ithyphallic god, whose representation occurs so frequently among

[1] Birch, Gall. of Ant. p. 9, 10.
[2] Præp. Evang. 1, 10.
[3] See p. 261 of this volume. Ægyptios dracunculos Romæ habuit quos illi *Agathodæmonas* vocant. Æl. Lampr. Heliogabalus, 28.
[4] 2, 74.
[5] Jacobs, vol. 2, p. 6.

the sculptures of Thebes[1]. His head-dress, of long straight feathers, shows his identity or at least connexion with Amun, as the peculiarity of his form is only a coarser indication of creative power. His right hand is lifted up, not *holding* a scourge, but with a scourge bent in an angle over the fingers; the face is human, like that of Amun; the body, including the left arm, is wrapped in bandages. He is supposed to be the Pan of the Greeks, partly from his form, partly from an inscription on the Kosseir road, in which he is called the Pan of the Thebans[2], partly from a passage in Stephanus Byzantinus[3], in which the statue of the god of Panopolis is described with circumstances corresponding with the ordinary representations of Khem. No such name as Khem has been found connected with the figures of this god; when a phonetic name is placed beside him, it is Amun, or Amunra; or a group of characters, whose pronunciation is uncertain, but which includes a bolt. That his name was Khem or Khemmo is inferred from the circumstance that Diodorus says the town of Chemmis in the Thebaid bears the same name as the god and is *interpreted* Panopolis[4]. On the authority of Herodotus[5], it has been supposed that Khem is the god whom the people of Mendes represented with the head and legs of a goat. He adds that both the goat and Pan are called in the Egyptian language *Mendes*. But Khem is

---

[1] Wilkinson, M. & C. 4, 258.
[2] Ibid. 4, 263.
[3] Πανὸς πόλις. Ἔστι δὲ καὶ τοῦ θεοῦ ἄγαλμα μέγα ὀρθιακὸν ἔχον τὸ αἰδοῖον εἰς ἑπτὰ δακτύλους· ἐπαίρει δὲ μάστιγας τῇ δεξιᾷ σελήνῃ ἧς εἴδωλόν φασιν εἶναι τὸν Πᾶνα [οἱ δ' Ἕλληνες εἴδωλόν φασιν εἶναι τοῦ Πανός]. Steph. Byz.
[4] Diod. 1, 18.
[5] Her. 2, 46.

never represented with the head and legs of a goat, nor indeed has any such representation been found on the monuments, and the Coptic for *goat* is not Mendes, but *Baampe*. The goat, however, was evidently consecrated to the god of Mendes, if not employed as his symbol, since the type appears upon the coins of the nome in Greek and Roman times[1]; nor could Herodotus be mistaken as to the honour paid to the goat in the Mendesian nome. The Greeks supposed that the Egyptians called a cat, Bubastis, and a dog, Anubis, from the consecration of the animals to the divinities of these respective names, in both cases incorrectly. Pan, however, was represented with attributes indicating him to be in propensity like Khem[2], and hence the application of the name was natural. Their place in the popular mythologies of Greece and Egypt was indeed very different; the admission of Pan into the list of gods was, according to Herodotus, one of the most recent events in the Greek religion; whereas the Egyptian Pan, in the representation of the Mendesians, was one of the eight original gods. But their functions were not dissimilar; both evidently represented the fertilizing principle; and as Khem is often accompanied by plants and trees, and kings are represented in his presence turning the ground with a hoe[3], it may fairly be inferred that Khem, like Pan, was connected with agriculture and gardening. The description which Suidas gives of

---

[1] Tochon d'Anneçy, Recherches sur les Médailles des Nomes, s. voc.
[2] Κατωφέρης καὶ συνουσιαστικός.
[3] Wilkinson, Manners and Customs, Pantheon, pl. 26. The sceptre of the Ethiopian kings, according to Diodorus (3, 3), was in the form of a plough or hoe. See p. 185 of this volume.

the god whom he calls Priapus, and whom he says the Egyptians named Horus[1], shows that he is the same as Khem, who sometimes is called the victorious Horus, though widely different in his attributes from the god who commonly bears that name. The bull which generally accompanies Khem on the monuments has no doubt an allusion to the productive power; the vulture, the emblem of maternity, sometimes follows. His worship holds a conspicuous place among the ceremonies of the coronation of Rameses Meiamoun, represented on the walls of the palace of Medinet Aboo[2]. The king stands before the shrine of Amun-Khem, and offers him incense and libations; and his statue dismounted is afterwards borne by twenty-two priests on a rich palanquin, in the midst of fans and branches of flowers. The king walks on foot before the god, preceded by the white bull, his symbol, to which a priest burns incense. In another part, the statue of the god having been replaced in his shrine, the king cuts with a golden sickle the ears from a sheaf of corn, and a priest offers them to the god, in allusion it is probable to that connexion of Amun-Khem, as the principle of fertility[3], with agriculture which has been noticed above.

---

[1] Τὸ ἄγαλμα τοῦ Πριάπου, τοῦ Ὥρου παρὰ Αἰγυπτίοις κεκλημένου, ἀνθρωποειδὲς ποιοῦσιν, ἐν τῇ δεξιᾷ σκῆπτρον κατέχον· ἐν δὲ τῷ εὐωνύμῳ κρατοῦν τὸ αἰδοῖον αὐτοῦ ἐντεταμένον, διότε τὰ κεκρυμμένα ἐν τῇ γῇ σπέρματα φανερὰ καθίστησι. The πτερά which he says he bore on his head are the tall plumes of Amun-Khem, which have sometimes, as Suidas describes, the disk of the sun.

[2] Wilkinson, M. and C. pl. 76.

[3] Is. et Osir, 371 F. Πανταχοῦ δὲ καὶ ἀνθρωπομορφὸν Ὀσίριδος ἄγαλμα δεικνύουσι ἐξορθιάζον τῷ αἰδοίῳ διὰ τὸ γόνιμον καὶ τὸ τρόφιμον. From another passage of the same treatise (365 E.), it has been concluded that Osiris, in this form, was called Ἀρσαφής (Jabl. 1, 289), but this does not appear to have been Plutarch's meaning.

Amun-Khem appears to be really the god whom Plutarch describes as a form of Osiris, with whom he might the more easily be confounded, as the scourge or flail which appears above his raised hand is the same, in a slightly different position, as that which Osiris commonly holds. The inscription "Amun-ra," followed by the bull and vulture, is also found over a figure of the god with the head of the ram, so that here we have the three gods Amun, Kneph and Khem united under one form. Another combination is Amun-Hor, with the head of a hawk, the bird especially consecrated to Horus; and on the Kosseir road is a tablet in which the god Khem is represented as a hawk with human legs, holding up the flagellum and with the plumes of Amun[1].

These were the great male deities of Thebes; the chief god of Memphis was PTAH or PTHAH. He was connected with those of Thebes by the legend which Eusebius quotes from Porphyry[2], that Kneph produced an egg from his mouth, from which Ptah was born. But he was probably as much an independent and self-derived god to the Memphites, as Kneph or Amun to the Thebans. The representation of the universe by an egg, however, in the Orphic theology[3], makes it probable that the Egyptians used a similar figure for creation, and at Philæ, in a sculpture of a late date, Ptah is represented as "setting in motion the egg of the sun and moon[4]."

---

[1] Wilkinson, M. and C. 4, 265. It is of uncertain age.
[2] Præp. Evang. 3, 11, p. 115.
[3] Jablonsky, Pantheon Eg. 1, 41. Aristoph. Aves, 695.
[4] Rosellini, Mon. del Culto, p. 146, tav. xxi.

According to Iamblichus, the Egyptians held him to be the divine artificer, a notion which the Greeks may have lowered and popularized to that of a skilful artist, fashioning all objects by means of the element of fire. A figure at Dendera is supposed by Wilkinson[1] to represent him sketching, as preliminary to the act of creation.

On the Rosetta Stone Ptolemy is described as beloved by Hephaistos, and the corresponding shield in the hieroglyphic inscription (P. 322, No. 5) fixed the phonetic group for Ptah. He is commonly represented with a cap, fitting close to the skull; the body is enveloped in bandages from which the hands alone protrude, holding a sceptre or staff. Sometimes he is standing on a pedestal divided in steps, and carries in his hand, or has near him, a graduated pillar or stand, which from its representing on the Rosetta Stone the words *established in perpetuity*[2], is generally called the emblem of stability[3]. A figure with the ostrich feather on her head, supposed to be Truth or Justice, is seen accompanying Ptah, who, according to Iamblichus[4], "perfects everything with truth." He is also found bearing in his hands the scourge and hook of Osiris, as if identified with this god[5]. Perhaps the swathed body and protruded hands may symbolize the first putting forth of a creative power in action, which had been previously hidden and quiescent. The idea of power imperfectly developed may be conveyed by another common mode of representing Ptah[6]. When

---

[1] Manners and Customs, 4, 253. Pantheon, pl. 23, 5.
[2] Hierogl. Text. l. 5. Greek, l. 6. διαμενούσης.
[3] Champ. Dict. p. 261.
[4] De Myst. Eg. 8, 8.
[5] According to Suidas he was identified with Dionusos. Ἄφθας ὁ Διόνυσος.
[6] Her. 3, 37.

Cambyses entered the temple of Hephaistos at Memphis, he greatly ridiculed the statue of the god, which resembled the pygmy images called *Pataikoi*, carried by the Phœnicians on the prows of their vessels; the images of the Cabiri also resembled those of the Hephaistos of Memphis. It is probable that the Pataikoi derived their name, which is certainly not Greek, from the word Ptah. Pygmy figures, with disproportioned heads, phallic, bow-legged, with a physiognomy approaching the Ethiopic, are found in great numbers at Gizeh, in the ruins of Memphis, and especially in the mummy-pits of Saccarah. Though not accompanied by the group of characters denoting Ptah, it seems probable that they represent one conception of him. They have often a scarabæus on the head, an emblem particularly consecrated to Ptah[1]. At Philæ the scarabæus is substituted for the head[2]. These pygmy figures sometimes carry in their hands the ostrich feather, which is the emblem of Truth[3]. The god was also called Ptah Socari. A group of characters which reads thus is found near figures which partake of the attributes of Ptah and Osiris, and the word *Socari* is sometimes joined with the name of one, sometimes of the other, and sometimes of both[4]. The epithets which are added appear to indicate, that in the character of Socari, Ptah was a god of the unseen world[5].

---

[1] Horapollo, 1, 12. The monuments do not confirm what this author adds, that the vulture is also given to Ptah.
[2] Rosellini, M. del C. 152.
[3] Birch, Gall. Brit. Mus. pl. 9.
[4] Wilkinson; pl. 24. The name Παaμύλης was given by the Egyptians to a phallic god, who was also called Σόχαρις. The representations of Ptah Socari are sometimes phallic. Hesychius s. voc. Παaμύλης. Birch, p. 15.
[5] Birch, p. 15.

According to Horapollo, Ptah combined both sexes. The monuments give no countenance to this statement, which however was in accordance with ancient mythology, and especially with the Orphic doctrines, at least in the representations of them by which alone they are known to us[1]. Plutarch says, the scarabæus, which was the emblem of Ptah, had no distinction of sex[2].

In Amun, Khem, Noum and Ptah we have four gods of the highest rank. Each, except perhaps Ptah, had a consort, but these generally fill inferior places in the Pantheon. Amun at Thebes is often joined with a goddess named MAUT, a name which signifies *mother*, and is expressed by a vulture. As Amun was understood to correspond with Jupiter, Maut would be Juno. She is represented with the *pschent* on her head, and has such titles assigned to her as "mistress of heaven," "regent of the world," &c.[3] According to Plutarch[4] *Muth* signifies mother, but he identifies the goddess of this name with Isis. As the divinities of Egypt frequently resolve themselves into one another, and especially into Osiris and Isis, there is no reason to doubt that Muth and Maut are the same. "Mother of the world" is an epithet of the moon; but Isis was the moon. The name Βούτω, Buto, of the Greeks, is nearly allied to Muth, M and B being interchangeable letters; but there is not sufficient evidence to identify these goddesses[5].

The female companion of Noum or Kneph is

---

[1] Ζεὺς ἄρσην γένετο, Ζεὺς ἄφθιτος ἔπλετο νύμφη. Orph. ap. Euseb. Præp. Ev. 3, 9.
[2] Is. et Osir. 355.
[3] Birch, pl. 4.
[4] Is. et Osir. 374.
[5] Wilkinson, Pantheon, pl. 20.

SATE. The Greek and Roman writers have not preserved her name, but from a Greek inscription discovered by Rüppell on a small island near the Cataracts, she appears to be the same as Here[1]. As Kneph has been confounded with Jupiter Ammon, Sate, the consort of Kneph, would naturally be considered as the wife of Jupiter. The name is ascertained by the hieroglyphics which accompany the figure, an arrow (in Coptic *sat*) piercing a banner[2]; the arrow is supposed to allude also to the sunbeams, and *sate* in Coptic is *splendere*.

Khem is joined in worship with a goddess named THRIPHIS, who in Greek inscriptions at Athribis and Panopolis, of the Roman times, is called "most great goddess;" but no representation of her has been identified. Sir G. Wilkinson[3] supposes her to be one of the lion-headed goddesses, whose special names have not been ascertained. Nothing indicates that she stood in the relation of consort to Khem; this office seems rather to belong to a female deity whose name is written AMUNT or TAMUN, and who is often conjoined with him in a triad at Thebes[4]. PASHT, the Bubastis of the Greeks, is represented with the head of a lion or a cat, and frequently accompanies Ptah. In the Pharaonic times the figure has commonly the lion's head; that of the cat is found in later works. The disk on her head, as well as the lion, is supposed to indicate her connexion with the solar deity[5], of whom among the Egyptians this animal was the

---

[1] Minutoli, Reisen, p. 375.
[2] Wilkinson, Pantheon, pl. 21.
[3] M. and C. 4, 265.
[4] Wilk. M. and C. 5, 66.
[5] Æl. Hist. An. 5, 39. Horapollo, 1, 17,

symbol. Neither her attributes nor the inscriptions connect her with the Moon, though the Greeks considered her as the same with their Artemis[1], and Artemis as the Moon. The Moon in the Egyptian theology was a male deity. Pasht appears with the title *Toer-Mouth*, Great Mother, and this has been supposed to be the origin of *Thermuthis*, a name the Greeks gave to one of the goddesses of Egypt[2]. The name of *Merepthah*, "beloved of Pthah," is frequently given to Pasht[3], yet it does not appear that she was properly his consort. She sometimes carries the emblems of life in her hands[4], and has various titles, according to the different forms in which she is represented, which do not, however, give any clue to the original conception of her character. According to Herodotus[5], Bubastis was the Egyptian name for Artemis, sister of Horus (Apollo) and daughter of Osiris and Isis, a genealogy which would refer her to the latest family of gods. Amun and Maut are frequently accompanied by a youthful figure, their son KHONS or KHONSO (Pl. III. C. 6). He is represented under the form of a mummy with protruded hands like Ptah, and carries a staff with the emblem of stability; but he has also a crescent and globe on his head, as if in allusion to the Moon[6]. The author of the Etymologicum Magnum[7] says that the Egyptians called Hercules *Chon*, and the similarity of the sound has

---

[1] Pasht, lion-headed, appears as the tutelary goddess of the *Speos Artemidos* or grotto of Benihassan. (Wilkinson, Mod. Eg. and Thebes, 2, 55.)

[2] Jablonsky, 1, p. 116. Rosellini, M. Stor. iii. 1, 405.

[3] Birch, p. 16.
[4] Wilkinson, Pantheon, pl. 27.
[5] 2, 156.
[6] Wilkinson, Pantheon, pl. 20.
[7] S. v. Χῶνες.

led some authors to suppose that he had Chonso in view; but with the exception of his being the son of Amun, the Theban Jupiter, there is no resemblance between him and the Grecian Hercules. His relation to Amun, the king of the gods, is marked by the manner in which his hair is gathered in a large lock falling over the side of the head. The young princes are distinguished in the historical paintings by this arrangement of the hair; and in the case of the youthful Horus, also, it marks his relation of royal son to Osiris and Isis.

A goddess named ANOUKE appears as the companion of Noum or Kneph and Sate in the monuments of the Thebaid, especially near the Cataracts, and from the usual relation of the deities who are thus grouped together, she may be concluded to be their daughter. In a Greek inscription found by Rüppell[1] on a small island near Philæ she is called Hestia (Vesta), a goddess who was unknown to the Egyptians[2], and who was not believed by the Greeks to be a daughter of Jupiter and Juno, but the eldest child of Saturn[3]. In her dress and general attributes Anouke much resembles Neith, but is distinguished by a head-dress of feathers, arranged in a circular form and placed upon a cap.

Khem or Amun Khem and the goddess Amunt are accompanied by a youthful god, called Harka[4], whose attributes are nearly the same as those of Horus and other deities, who complete the triads

---

[1] "To Chnubis, who is also Ammon, and to Sate, who is also Hera, and to Anoukis, who is also Hestia, and to Petempamentes, who is also Dionysus, and to Petensetes, who is also Saturn, to Petensenes, who is also Hermes, great gods, and to the other dæmons of the cataracts." (Minutoli, Reisen, 375.)
[2] Her. 2, 50.
[3] Apollod. Bibl. 1, 2, 5.
[4] Champollion, Lettres, p. 209.

found in the principal temples. No deity appears to stand in such a relation to Ptah.

We have not found any representative of Leto, whom Herodotus places among the eight gods. In some points she resembles ATHOR, whom the Greeks identified with their Aphrodite[1]. There was a temple at Atarbechis[2] in Lower Egypt consecrated to Aphrodite, and as the termination *bechis* represents the Coptic *baki*, ' town,' it is probable that the first syllable is derived from Athor. At Chusæ, a village in the nome of Hermopolis, the Celestial Aphrodite was worshiped, and a white cow was honoured as her representative[3]. The Celestial Aphrodite was the oldest; her worship prevailed extensively in Assyria, Phœnicia, Arabia and Libya, without our being able to say which of these countries was its original seat. At Momemphis in Egypt, according to Strabo[4], a sacred cow was maintained in honour of Venus, as Apis at Memphis and Mnevis at Heliopolis. And he adds the remark, that these three were held divine, in distinction from the bulls and cows kept in many other temples, which were held sacred, but not divine. In all these cases it is probable that Athor was the goddess really meant. It was so at Tentyra; Strabo[5] says that the Tentyrites worshiped Venus. Now the larger of the beautiful temples which remain at Denderah has the capitals of its pillars composed of heads of the goddess Athor, and is covered with sculptures in her honour. She

---

[1] Etym. M. s. voc. Ἀθύρ. Τὴν Ἀφροδίτην Αἰγύπτιοι καλοῦσιν Ἀθώρ.
[2] Her. 2, 61.
[3] Æl. Hist. Anim. 10, 27. Πεπιστεύκασιν αὐτὰς προσήκειν τῇ δὲ τῇ δαίμονι. Ποίαν γὰρ εἰς ἀφροδίσια ἰσχυρὰν ἔχει ἐκεῖνος βοῦς θῆλυς.
[4] Strabo, 17, 803.
[5] Strabo, 17, 815. See p. 44 of this volume.

is generally represented wearing a head-dress surmounted with horns and a solar disk, and is figured under the form of a cow. In the temple of Aboosimbel she appears in this form, and receives libations and flowers from the king and queen. The representations of Athor at Denderah, Gebel-el-Birkel and Aboosimbel, with a human face and the ears of a cow, as well as those with cows' horns, have been generally given to Isis, but they are discriminated by the name. That of Athor is expressed by the hawk of Horus in a square enclosure (Pl. III. C. 8), the whole being read *Tei-hor* or *Eit-hor*, "habitation of Horus." She appears also in the form of a spotted cow[1].

Athor had very little resemblance to the Greek Aphrodite. It has indeed been remarked, that, setting aside the cow's ears, there is more beauty in the face of Athor than any other of the Egyptian divinities; and she is said to be called the mistress of sports[2], but her ordinary titles are very different, and seem to connect her with the region of the West[3]. Jablonsky endeavoured to assign a cause for this in the character which he supposed the Greek Celestial Venus to have sustained, viz. Primæval Night, the parent of all things[4]. We learn indeed from Hesychius[5] that there was a temple in Egypt to Ἀφροδίτη Σκοτία, but that by this epithet

---

[1] Rosellini, M. del C. pl. 29, 3.
[2] Birch, Gall. B. M. p. 20.
[3] The western part of Thebes was called Pathyris, and the nome Pathyrites (the Pathros of Gen. x. 14, Is. xi. 11), and is supposed to have taken its name from Athor. (Wilk. M. and C. 4, 387. Peyron, Pap. Gr. P. 2, p. 30.)
[4] Panth. Eg. L. 1, c. 1.
[5] Hes. Lex. s. v. Σκοτία. Another explanation was given of the name, Σκοτίας Ἀφροδίτης ἐν Φαίστῳ ἱερὸν εἶναί φασι ὡς Κρυψιπόθου. (Etym. M. voc. Κυθήρεια.)

primæval darkness was intended does not appear. The Orphic Hymn to Night[1] gives her the epithet of Venus, but it would be too bold an inference that this doctrine must have been originally Egyptian. It is not wonderful that Athor should have been so frequently confounded with Isis, and that the Greeks should have referred to Isis the figures with the head or horns of a cow, and have founded upon them the legend of Io and her identification with Isis; for without their respective names it is difficult to discriminate them. A figure in the British Museum[2] with horns and a disk upon her head, placed upon the vulture or fowl (see p. 247), would from its attributes be supposed to be Isis; but the name beside it is "Athor, mistress of heaven." Athor appears combined in a triad with various gods; at Apollinopolis Magna with Hor-hat or Horus, and a youthful god, Hor-Sened-To; at Ombi with Sevek, the crocodile-headed god, and Khonso; the same whom at Thebes we saw as the son of Amun and Maut.

NEITH, the goddess of Sais, is another of great celebrity. Though her principal temple and the chief seat of her worship was at Sais, it is evident that it extended through the whole country; for on the night on which those who had assembled at Sais, to her *panegyry*, lighted lamps in her honour around the houses, the same rite was celebrated in every part of Egypt[3]. Plato, in the Timæus, as-

---

[1] Νύκτα θεῶν γενέτειραν ἀείσομαι ἠδὲ καὶ ἀνδρῶν,
Νὺξ γένεσις πάντων, ἣν καὶ Κύπριν καλέσωμεν.

(Orph. H. 3, 1.) The second line seems out of its place, but it is probably Orphic.

[2] Gall. Brit. Mus. pl. 11, fig. 36. [3] Herod. 2, 59.

sures us that the tutelary deity of Sais was called in Egyptian *Neith*, and this is confirmed by other authors[1]. *Nat* in Coptic signifies a *web*, and as weaving was one of the principal functions of Minerva, according to the Greek conception, it has been thought that it gave origin to the name. It is written NT, and a figure accompanies these letters (Pl. III. C. 4), which has been taken for a shuttle[2]; but it has not the form of the shuttle, as represented in the paintings, nor indeed from its long curved ends does it seem very capable of being applied to such a use. Neith does not appear on any monument exercising the art of weaving, but is sometimes armed with a bow and arrows, corresponding to the warlike Minerva of the Greeks. If the Egyptians really conceived of her as weaving, it was probably in a figurative sense for creating. In the Egyptian theology she held a much higher character than the Greek. According to Plutarch[3] and Proclus[4] her temple at Sais contained this inscription: "I am the things that have been and that are and that will be; no one has uncovered my skirts[5]; the fruit which I brought forth became the Sun." That while she declares her perpetual virginity, she also calls the Sun her fruit, may be

---

[1] See Jablonsky, Panth. Eg. L. 1, c. 3. It is a most improbable notion that *Athene* was derived from *Neith* by inversion of the letters, when the Greek mode of writing was substituted for the Egyptian. Athene was known to the Greeks by her present name, long before they began to write from left to right; nor are languages learnt from written characters.

[2] Wilk. plate 28, 5.
[3] Plut. Is. et Os. 354, with Wyttenbach's note.
[4] Proclus in Timæum, p. 30.
[5] Τὸν ἐμὸν πέπλον οὐδείς πω ἀπεκάλυψεν. Comp. Deut. xxii. 30. Plutarch seems to have mistaken the meaning of the words, referring them to the mysterious nature of the goddess, instead of her virginity.

explained from what Horapollo says, that the Egyptians considered her (and Ptah) as uniting both sexes in themselves[1]. One of her titles is, "the great cow, engenderer of the Sun[2]." She is, however, not always to be distinguished from the other goddesses: Plutarch, in the passage which we have just quoted, calls her Isis[3]; and she is sometimes confounded with Amunt, Athor and Maut. Lower Egypt was the chief seat of her worship, and she wears the crown of the lower country; but her monuments are found also in the Thebaid, and her name, Neith, is of early occurrence in the history of the Pharaohs, as *Nit*ocris in the sixth dynasty of Manetho, and Ase*neth* (worshiper of Neith) in the history of Joseph[4]. The Saites, according to Strabo, paid honour to the ram, like the Thebans; and Proclus says that the constellation Aries and the whole equinoctial circle was consecrated to her; but no trace of such a connection appears in the monuments.

Many of the Egyptian gods are identified with the Sun, as we find that in later times those of Greece and Rome were; but RA or RE was *Helios*, the physical Sun. *Rra* or *Erra* is the Coptic name for "king[5]," appropriated to the Sun, like the names *Baal*, *Melek*, *Adonai*, which in the Syro-Arabian languages denote monarchy, and were also titles of the Sun. That Ra was specifically the Sun, as a

---

[1] Horapollo, 1, 12.
[2] Birch, Gall. Brit. Mus. p. 12.
[3] The hieroglyphic epithets of Neith show her original identity with Isis (Lepsius, Einleitung, p. 310, note 4).
[4] Jablonsky, *u. s.* § 3.
[5] With the Coptic article prefixed, it becomes *Phra* or *Phre*. Jablonsky (Proleg. § ix.) interprets the name of Potipherah priest of On' (Heliopolis), Gen. xli. 45, *Phont phre*, sacerdos Solis.

portion of the astronomical system, is probable from the circumstance that Heliopolis was the chief seat of his worship, and that here solar astronomy was specially cultivated. The phœnix is manifestly a symbol of some astronomical solar period; and it was to the temple of Heliopolis that he was reputed to bring his father[1]. The name which is read *Ra* is not a phonetic character, but a disk symbolical of the Sun, and therefore it is by no means certain, that wherever this character occurs, it is to be interpreted of the god of Heliopolis; on the contrary, it may mean the Sun under some other of the various symbolical characters which he sustains in Egyptian mythology. The same sovereign is found designated as the Sun (Ra), and as "approved by the Sun," showing that such phrases as "born of the Sun," applied to other gods, cannot be considered a proof of filiation from the god of Heliopolis. The name *Ra* does not occur in the Greek authors, but it is probable that they have substituted Apollo for him, whom the later Greeks identified with the Sun. The hawk is his symbol; he often appears with the head of a hawk and the disk of the sun, the uræus-serpent, the scarabæus. His attributes closely resemble those of Horus, and it is only by the subjoined characters that the two can always be discriminated.

In speaking of Noum or Kneph, we have mentioned the god whose symbol is the disk of the sun, supported by two asps and the extended wings of a vulture, so frequently sculptured over doorways, propylæa and other openings of buildings, as to

[1] Herod. 2, 73.

make it probable that it represents a tutelary genius. The temple of Edfou, or Apollinopolis Magna, was especially dedicated to him as HOR-HAT-KAH, or the "Horus of the land of Hat," the name of this region. As Horus, his type is the hawk, also an emblem of the Sun; and the sculptures of the temple of Apollinopolis[1], which represent the progress of the Sun, called Phre-Hor-hat, Lord of Heaven, in his bark or *bari* through the hours, point to the same character. As an emblem of dominion, the hawk has the *pschent*, or crown of Upper and Lower Egypt. He is also represented as of a human figure, hawk-headed. With the addition of *oer* (*ouer* Copt. quantus), *great*[2], the name Haroeris or Aroeris, Horus the Great, seems to have been formed, whom the Greeks identified with their Apollo. He was worshiped at Ombi[3], and there formed a triad with a goddess *Tsenenofre* and a youthful god, *Penebto*. At Edfou, Horbat forms a triad with the goddess Athor and *Hor-sened-to*. These youthful gods, who are represented pointing their finger towards their mouths, all passed, before the discovery of the hieroglyphic character, as figures of Harpocrates, with whom indeed they are closely allied.

SEBEK or SEVEK, the crocodile-headed god, was principally worshiped at Ombi, Silsilis and Crocodilopolis in the Arsinoitic nome. According to Strabo, the Egyptian name of the crocodile, worshiped in this latter place, was *Souchos*[4]; and as

---

[1] Rosellini, Mon. del Culto, p. 240, tav. xxxviii.
[2] 'Αρωήρει θεῷ μεγάλῳ 'Απόλλωνι. (Inscr. at Ombi, Ham. Æg. p. 75. Plut. Is. et Os. 355 E.)
[3] Rosell. Mon. del C. p. 201.
[4] The *zoological* name of the crocodile was χάμψα. Her. 2, 69 (Copt. *msah*).

the Egyptian *b* seems to have been vocalized into *ou*, the name is probably the same as Sebek, denoting the god, or the animal worshiped as the symbol of the god[1]. The disk of the sun, joined to his titles, seems to indicate some relation to this luminary[2]; which may have consisted in this, that the ancients believed the crocodile, when out of the water, to be the most sharp-sighted of all animals[3]. What Ælian and other writers[4] say of the crocodile's laying *sixty* eggs, which are *sixty* days in being hatched, living *sixty* years, &c., as it has no foundation in the natural history of the animal, has probably been invented, because it was supposed to be sacred to the sun, and this was an astronomical number. Tamed, the crocodile seems to have been considered as an emblem of gentleness and justice[5]; in its natural state, of rapacity and cruelty, whence it was the symbol of Typhon[6]. In the former character it seems to have been a natural emblem of the gently swelling and beneficent Nile[7]; and Wilkinson observes after De Pauw[8], that the places in which it was worshiped, and therefore of course tame, were those to which the Nile could only reach by the maintenance of the canals which diffuse the inundation.

ATMOO or ATHOM[9] is one of the manifold deities

---

[1] Str. lib. 17, p. 811.
[2] Wilk. M. and C. 5, 36.
[3] Her. 2, 68. Arist. H. Anim. 2, 10.
[4] Æl. Nat. An. 10, 21.
[5] Damasc. ap. Phot. Bibl. 242. Σοῦχος δίκαιος· ὄνομα δὲ κροκοδείλου καὶ εἶδος ὁ Σοῦχος· οὐ γὰρ ἀδικεῖ ζῷον οὐδέν.
[6] Plut. Is. et Os. 371 C.
[7] Euseb. Præp. Evang. 3, 11.
[8] M. and C. 5, 533.
[9] It is written Atmoo, but according to a remark of Lepsius (Lettre à M. Rosellini, p. 40), the vowel which was *written* at the end was often *pronounced* in the middle, e. g. Anpu, Anubis, Chnsou, Chons. The name is very commonly written only TM.

having reference to the Sun, and as he does not appear to have any particular connexion with the Osirian circle, we place him in the second class. He probably represented the western setting or nocturnal sun, *i. e.* the sun below the horizon, or in Amenthe, the Egyptian Hades. In paintings he is coloured red, and he wears the crowns of the upper and lower region, placed one beside the other[1]. He has sometimes the prefix of *Nofre* or 'the good,' in which case his head is adorned with a lotus or two straight feathers[2].

MONTH or MANDOO appears also to have a reference to the sun, since his name is sometimes followed by the solar disk, or the figure of the god Ra, and he is represented with the head of a hawk. He has been supposed to be the same as the Mendes of the Greeks, but if the names have any connexion, the attributes of the two deities are entirely different. There is a deity, Mandoulis or Maloulis, mentioned in some Greek inscriptions, whose name suggests his identity with Mandoo, but it is written with entirely different characters, nor do their attributes agree. According to Champollion, he appears at Kalabsché or Talmis as the son of Isis by Horus (who would thus be the husband of his mother), and with the attributes and ornaments of Khons[3]. Nor is there anything in the attributes of Mandoo to identify him with Mars, to whom he has been supposed to answer[4]. In inscriptions, however, the kings of Egypt are said to style themselves "Mandoo towards the nations," from which it would seem

---

[1] Wilkinson, M. and C. 5, 25.
[2] Birch, Gall. Brit. Mus. 1, 21.
[3] Lettres, p. 156.
[4] Wilk. M. and C. 534.

SECT. I.—THEOLOGY.

as if the office of protector or avenger belonged especially to him.

Of the direct personification and deification of the parts of nature, we find few traces in the Egyptian theology. We have seen that the Sun was worshiped as Ra; the Moon as a male deity was connected with Thoth, and as a female with Isis, both belonging to the Osirian circle; but neither of them appears to have been primarily or exclusively the representative of the Moon. The starry heavens, in Coptic *Tpe*, were personified, and represented as a female figure, of which the trunk formed a horizontal line, the arms and legs depending parallel to each other, and stars covering the intermediate space. The day and the year also appear to have been represented in a corporeal form. The Greeks, who call Isis Demeter, must have understood her to represent the Earth, but this was not her exclusive nor probably her primary character. Osiris was also said to be the Nile[1], equally without foundation, as regards the primary conception; but the River was certainly personified and received divine honours[2]. A festival called Niloa was celebrated at the time of the first rise of the waters[3], *i. e.* about the summer solstice, with sacrifices and universal rejoicing, the amount of the inundation and consequently the fertility of Egypt being supposed to depend on the performance of these rites in an acceptable manner. A priesthood specially dedicated to him must have

---

[1] Tibull. Eleg. 1, 7, 27. Plut. Is. et Osir. says the Nile was 'Οσίριδος ἀποῤῥοή.
[2] Heliod. Æth. 9, 9. Θεοπλαστοῦσι τὸν Νεῖλον Αἰγύπτιοι καὶ κρειττόνων τὸν μέγιστον ἄγουσιν. Schol. Pind. Pyth. 4, 99. ὁ Νεῖλος παρὰ τοῖς Αἰγυπτίοις τιμᾶται ὡς θεός.
[3] Heliodorus, *ibid.*

existed in several parts of Egypt, since we learn from Herodotus that it belonged to them exclusively to bury the corpse of one who had been drowned in the Nile. It does not appear that any of the existing temples were devoted to his sole worship; but Hecatæus mentions one, in the town called Nilus[1], which stood in the Heracleopolite nome, near the entrance of the Fyoum. Several stelæ in the quarries at Silsilis are inscribed with acts of adoration to the river, who is joined with Phre and Ptah[2]. On the Egyptian monuments, the god is designated by a group of characters, the last of which is a symbol of the waters[3], and is read *Moou*; the others are phonetic and have been read *Hapi* or *Phe*. He is represented usually of a blue colour, of a round and plump figure, sometimes with female breasts, indicative of his efficacy in nourishing vegetable and animal life[4]. Two figures sometimes appear, as on the base of the throne of Amenophis-Memnon at Thebes, similar in other respects, but one crowned with lotus to denote the upper course of the river, the other with papyrus to denote the lower.

The later Greek and Latin writers speak of Æsculapius as one of the gods of Egypt, but he was not identified among the sculptures till a Greek inscription was found at Philæ in which his name occurs.

---

[1] Steph. Byz. s. voc. Νεῖλος.
[2] Rosellini, M. del C. 214.
[3] According to Lucian (Jup. Trag. § 42), the Egyptians sacrificed to the element of Water, and this was not a local but universal worship among them.
[4] Birch, p. 25. In Rosellini, Mon. del Culto, tav. lxxiv., the Nile is represented of a blue colour, *bringing* offerings of aquatic plants, flowers and birds. A female figure alternates with the males, which Rosellini supposes to denote the *regions* of Egypt. The original is in the tomb of Rameses Meiamoun.

SECT. I.— THEOLOGY.

It is written Eimopth[1], and he is called the son of Ptah; his attributes, also, have some resemblance to those of the great god of Memphis[2]; he wears the same close-fitting skull-cap, which probably gave occasion to his being said to be bald[3]. His arms and limbs, however, are free, instead of being, like those of Ptah, involved in bandages. The Greek mythology made Æsculapius the son of Apollo; but according to the Phœnician, Æsculapius was one of the Cabiri[4], whose worship at Memphis and elsewhere was connected with that of Vulcan or Ptah[5]. The Egyptian Eimopth has no attribute which specially refers to the art of healing, and it may have been an arbitrary interpretation of the Greeks which gave him the name of Æsculapius, as some applied the same name to Serapis[6].

The name of SEB was not known from the Greek or Roman writers, but has been found on the monuments and in the enumeration of the gods. He is called "the father of Osiris[7]," and as Osiris was said to be the son of Cronos[8], Seb has been identified with Cronos, but there appears no particular analogy between their attributes[9]. He is also called

---

[1] Salt's Essay, p. 50. ’Ιατρικῆς καθηγητῆς ὁ ’Ασκληπιὸς ὁ ‘Ηφαίστου. Herm. Stob. Heeren, p. 1090, 1092. ’Ασκληπιὸς ὁ ’Ιμούθης, Ἡᾶνος καὶ ‘Ηφαιστοβούλης. Herm. ap. Stob. Hceren, p. 392. Elsewhere (1092) he is made the author of poetry.

[2] Amm. Marcell. 22, 14. From the mention of Memphis as celebrated for his worship, it should seem as if he had confounded him with his father Ptah.

[3] Synesius, quoted by Jablonsky, P. 3, p. 196.

[4] Euseb. Pr. Evang. 1, p. 39.

[5] Kemick, Egypt of Herodotus, p. 254.

[6] Tac. Hist. 4, 84. Jabl. P. 3, p. 197.

[7] Wilkinson, 4, 311. Panth. pl. 31.

[8] Diod. 1, 27. Plut. Is. et Os. p. 355.

[9] "I give you the years of Seb," is said to be a frequent address of gods to sovereigns. Wilk. u. s.

"father of the gods," which may have led the Greeks to call him Cronos, but this title seems to have a special reference to his connexion with the gods of the Osirian circle. NETPE[1] answers to Rhea in the same way as Seb to Saturn, *i. e.* as the mother of Osiris. They form therefore the natural transition to the Osirian mythe.

Herodotus observes that "all the Egyptians do not worship the same gods in a similar manner, except ISIS and OSIRIS, the latter of whom is said to be Dionusos; these all worship in a similar manner[2]." His words do not imply that there was a diversity of belief, but of worship, manifesting itself in the sacrifice of certain animals in some of the nomes, which in others were held sacred to particular gods, and therefore never used for victims. The inference which has been drawn from this passage, that the other deities were *merely* local, Osiris and Isis national, is not warranted by his words, and the difference was probably owing to the later origin of the Osirian worship, which was diffused from some one point with a rapid development and a uniform system. Such an event, though relatively late, still lies beyond the historical times of Egypt; for we find the proofs of his worship on the oldest monuments. "The tombs in the vicinity of the Pyramids," says Sir G. Wilkinson[3], "belonging to individuals who were contemporary with their founders, show that Osiris had at that time the same offices as in the age of the Ptolemies

---

[1] Wilkinson, 4, 312. Pantheon, pl. 32.
[2] 2, 42.
[3] Wilk. M. & C. 4, 323.

SECT. I.—THEOLOGY.

and Cæsars." This remark, however, does not apply to the Typhonian history and phallic rites of Osiris. They appear to have been of decidedly later origin. Herodotus[1] ascribes the introduction of the Egyptian gods into Greece to the age of the Pelasgi; that of Dionusos-Osiris to Melampus, much later. This is good evidence of relative antiquity. With the worship of Osiris was connected that of Isis and Horus, their son; and Anubis, Thoth and Typhon bear part in his mythic history.

The names of Osiris and Isis give us no insight into the primary conception of these divinities; the Greek etymologies possess no authority, nor does the Coptic language furnish any on which we can rely[2]. Herodotus tells us that Isis was the Demeter of the Greeks; and without urging this as a proof that the worship of Dionusos and Demeter originated in Egypt, we may at least infer a marked similarity of attributes. Dionusos, from the variety of his own attributes and the uncertain etymology of the name, affords us no means of fixing the attributes of Osiris; but the name Demeter is " Mother Earth." It is probable, therefore, from the usual relation of male and female divinities, that Osiris had an original connection with the earth. We find a Solar character attributed to Dionusos, but only in later times; and the idea that Osiris repre-

---

[1] 2, 49, 50.
[2] See Pl. III. C. 2, 7. The *throne* in both groups was once considered as a symbol of *dominion*, the *eye* in that of Osiris of *providence*. Now the throne is read phonetically *Hes* (Isis), the eye, *iri* (Osiris or Hesiris). No such word as *Hes* exists in the Coptic; *Oss* is a seat. See Peyron s. voc. Plutarch (Is. et Os. 355 A.) says *os* signifies *many*, and *iri* eye. *Osh* in Coptic does signify 'many,' but *iri* is 'to do.' Hellanicus said the Egyptian priests pronounced the name *Usiris*.

sented the Sun[1], is not supported by the monuments. He is indeed occasionally identified with the Sun, by the titles under which he is invoked; but so are most of the other gods. The Greeks regarded Dionusos chiefly as the giver of the vine; but this seems not likely to have been the original character of Osiris, since the vine was very partially cultivated in Egypt; and there is nothing in his attributes or mythic history to assimilate him to Bacchus, considered in this character. The gift of the vine appears indeed to have been attributed to Bacchus, as representing generally the principle of fertility residing in the earth and manifesting itself in the luxuriance of vegetable nature[2]. Isis again has been identified with the Moon, and the appropriation to her of the cow or heifer as a symbol has been supposed to have a reference to her horned shape. The cow, however, is a very natural emblem of productiveness. Herodotus[3], speaking of the sacrifice of swine by the Egyptians, says it took place only on the day of the full moon, and in honour of the Moon and Dionusos; but as he has elsewhere declared Isis to be the Greek Demeter, it is not probable that he here means the same divinity by the Moon.

If Osiris originally represented the Earth, we can readily understand how he may have acquired the character which is most prominently his in the Egyptian mythology, of a ruler of the unseen world, and judge of the dead. The earth is the repository of bodies from which life has departed, and its deep

---

[1] It was the opinion of the age of Diodorus, 1, 10.
[2] Τῶν ἀκροδρύων καὶ ὅλως τῶν φυτευτικῶν ἡ δύναμις, Διόνυσος ὀνο- μάζεται. Euseb. Præp. Evang. 3, 11, from Porphyry.
[3] 2, 47.

and gloomy caverns realize the idea of a land of darkness and silence. Here the Hebrews placed their *Sheol*[1], in which the dead rested in insensibility; here was the Tartarus of classic and the Hela of northern mythology. The Πλούτων of the Greeks appears to have been the same as Πλοῦτος[2], and to have acquired his name either from the mineral riches of the earth, or more probably from its productive power. The *Dis* of the Latins is contracted from *Dives*[3]. It seems to have been in virtue of his original connexion with the earth, that Dionusos became identified with Pluto[4].

The reserve with which Herodotus always speaks of the gods, and especially of Osiris, makes it difficult to know what conception he had formed of him, or what were the grounds on which the Greeks identified him with Dionusos. It is probable, however, that the chief point of resemblance was the sufferings which each god was said to have undergone and which were set forth in their respective mysteries[5]. What he mentions of Melampus and his doctrines[6], shows plainly that he had introduced into Greece the story of the death of Osiris and the

---

[1] Isaiah, xiv. 9.
[2] See Hesych. voc. Πλοῦτος. Æsch. Prom. V. 806. Aristoph. Plut. 727. The Greek name of Proserpine is explained, as meaning 'the produce of the year.' Hesych. Φερσεφόνεια. The root of Πλοῦτος and Πλούτων is probably φλέω, which signifies 'to be fruitful.' Hes. φλεῖν· εὐκαρπεῖν. Hence φλέων or φλεύς, an epithet of Dionusos. Æl. V. H. 3, 41. Etym. Mag. s. voc. Βασιλεύς.
[3] Cic. N. D. 2, 26. Terrena vis omnis atque natura Diti Patri dedicata est; qui *Dives*, ut apud Græcos Πλούτων, quia et recidant omnia in terras et oriantur e terris. Trophonius (τροφή), the son of Phoronis (φορή), who was the subterranean Mercury (N. D. 3, 22), appears to represent the same idea.
[4] Ὡυτὸς δὲ Ἀΐδης καὶ Διόνυσος. Clem. Alex. Coh. p. 30, ed. Potter.
[5] Ἐν τῇ λίμνῃ ταύτῃ τὰ δείκηλα τῶν παθέων αὐτοῦ νυκτὸς ποιεῦσι, τὰ καλέουσι μυστήρια Αἰγύπτιοι. Her. 2, 171.
[6] 2, 49.

mutilation and discertion of his body[1]. Whatever this might imply, it had a strict analogy in the mythic history of Bacchus, who, under the name of Zagreus, was said to have been torn limb from limb by the Titans[2]. This was an Orphic doctrine[3], and we know from Herodotus, that the Orphic and Bacchic doctrines and usages were really Egyptian[4]. The description of a Roman poet[5] can have little weight in deciding, whether Osiris originally represented the principle of fruitfulness as existing in the earth and manifested in vegetation; but the mode in which he is figured on the monuments gives countenance to this opinion. He bears in his hands two instruments, a flail and a hook, or *pedum*, one connecting him with agriculture, the other with pasturage[6]; or if the former should be considered as a scourge, rather than a flail, the allusion to agriculture will remain, since this scourge appears from the paintings to have been used for urging and guiding oxen in the plough. Possibly the hook may also belong to agriculture, as it appears that the reapers carried such an instrument to collect the ears of corn for the sickle. The mystic *van* of Bacchus was also an emblem of agriculture, being the basket in which the corn was shaken, that the wind might separate the grain from the chaff. The other

---

[1] These were the usual subjects of the mysteries. Min. Felix, c. 21, 195. Considera sacra ipsa et mysteria; invenies exitus tristes, fata, funera miserorum deorum.

[2] Lobeck, Aglaoph. p. 553. Schol. Pind. Isthm. 7, 3.

[3] Macrob. in Somn. Scip. 1, 12.

[4] Her. 2, 81.

[5] Primus aratra manu solerti fecit Osiris,
    Et teneram ferro sollicitavit humum.
    Primus inexpertæ commisit semina terræ,
    Pomaque non notis legit ab arboribus.—Tib. Eleg. 1. 7. 29.

[6] Wilkinson, Pantheon, pl. 33.

attributes of Osiris throw little light upon the original conception of his character. His body is swathed, because in his character of the King of Hades, he is the type of all the deceased. He wears, in coloured monuments, a white crown, which is said to represent the celestial hemisphere. The title which is often given to him in inscriptions, "Manifester of good[1]," suits well with the notion of his originally representing the productive power of the earth; and it is easy to explain how, from such a primary conception, the idea that Osiris was the Nile or the Sun should arise; since each of these is in itself a principle of fertility. Those who philosophized more deeply made Osiris to be not only the Nile, but the humid principle generally, as the source of production[2]. The notion that he represented the Sun was thought to be countenanced by his hieroglyphic containing an eye[3]. The appellations said to be given to him in the hieroglyphic inscriptions, if rightly interpreted, are of that general kind which would be applicable to any chief divinity; one of them, "Lord of *Ebot*" or Abydos, has reference to his worship in this ancient town of the Thebais, which, as the place of his supposed burial, was chosen for their interment by his votaries throughout Egypt. The various legends of his birth or burial here or at Memphis, Philæ, Busiris, Taphosiris[4], have no

---

[1] Ouôn-nofre, "the opener of good." Plut. Is. et Os. 368 B. says Omphis was a title of Osiris.

[2] Plut. Is. et Osir. p. 363 D, 364 A.

[3] "Osirin Ægyptii, ut Solem esse asserant, quotiens hieroglyphicis literis exprimere volunt, insculpunt sceptrum, inque eo speciem oculi exprimunt." (Macrob. Sat. 1, 21.) See note[2] on page 399. The *sceptre* is the hooked staff which is found in the hands of Osiris, but not as a part of the hieroglyphic, as Macrobius erroneously supposed. See also Plut. Is. et Os. p. 371 E.

[4] Plut. Is. et Os. 359 A.

historical significance. The two latter rest on fanciful etymologies; the former indicate only the importance of the sacred establishments in his honour at these places, and the desire of his worshipers to exalt the glory of their respective temples.

The character of Isis must depend on that which we assign to her consort Osiris, since in the ancient religions the male and female divinities who are thus paired together represent usually the same principle, considered in that difference of relation which a difference of sex suggests. If Osiris were the Sun, it was natural that Isis should be the Moon; or the Earth, to which he communicates his fertilizing power; if Osiris were the Nile, the land of Egypt which he overspreads and impregnates would be represented as his consort[1]; while those who made Osiris to be the Reason and Intellect which rules and guides all good things[2], conceived of Isis as the material nature which receives impression and form. According to the simpler view which we have taken of the original conception of Osiris, Isis would represent merely the power of nature, sustaining the part of the female in the work of production, receiving and nourishing the germ of life. The representation of her which is the most common and popular, as nursing the infant Horus, the joint offspring of herself and Osiris, agrees well with this view, and the horns of the cow were placed upon her head[3], probably to symbolize the same conception. Its very vagueness favoured the extension of the worship of these divinities, since

---

[1] Τὸν μὲν Ὄσιριν εἰς ὕδωρ μεταλαμβάνουσι, τὴν δὲ Ἶσιν εἰς γῆν. Origen c. Cels. 5, p. 257.

[2] Plut. Is. et Os. 371 A.

[3] Herod. 2, 41.

every devotee could identify them with what god be pleased. "Some," says Diodorus (1, 25), " think the same goddess to be Isis, some Demeter, some Thesmophoros (the Eleusinian Ceres), some the Moon, some Juno, and some call her by all these appellations. Some think Osiris to be Serapis, some Dionusos, some Pluto, some Ammon, some Jupiter, some Pan." Each could allege some circumstance in favour of his opinion.

But that which made the Osirian worship so popular in Egypt in the times of the Pharaohs, as it served afterwards to diffuse the Isiac religion through the Roman empire, was its connexion with the mysterious subject of the state of man after death. To other gods, as Ptah or Athom, the office of presiding in Amenthe, the unseen world, was attributed only occasionally and by substitution; Osiris was the Pluto of Egyptian mythology, and bore the title of Pethempamenthes, or president of Amenthe[1]. It is in this character that we find him so generally represented in the papyri which accompany the mummies. In these delineations Osiris appears seated on a throne, attended by the goddesses Isis and Nephthys. Near him are the four genii, as they are called, of Amenthe, variously represented, sometimes in the form of mummies, sometimes of short vases, which antiquaries have called *Canopi*, in which the different *viscera* are supposed to have been preserved, embalmed. Each has a different head; one with a human head, called *Amset*, held the stomach and larger intestines; *Hapi*, with the head of a cy-

---

[1] See the Inscription in Minutoli, Reisen, 375, where he is identified with Dionusos.

nocephalus, the smaller; *Smautf* or *Sioutmauf*, the lungs and heart; *Kebhsnauf*, the liver and gall-bladder[1]. It has been conjectured that these genii really represent the god himself, as we find them at Philæ armed with the crook and flail which belong to Osiris[2]. It seems however more natural to consider them as belonging essentially to the scene of the judgement. The intestines had according to the Egyptian notion a very important connexion with the moral qualities of the individual, and upon them the blame was laid of any sin of which he might have been guilty. It is true, that according to Porphyry[3] and Plutarch the bowels were cast into the Nile. But this is certainly inconsistent with the account of Herodotus, who says that the bowels when taken out were washed with palm wine and pounded spices, a process evidently designed for their preservation[4]; and in the paintings which represent the process of embalming[5], these four vases are placed beneath the table on which the dead body is laid. If therefore they did not always contain, they may be considered as representing the viscera in the judgement-scene, and thus the whole body was brought before Osiris. They are frequently placed on the lotus, which grows out of the water over which the throne of Osiris stands[6]. At the opposite end is the deceased, introduced by Horus, or by the goddess of Truth. The centre is occupied by a large scale-beam which Anubis has erected;

---

[1] Wilkinson, Pantheon, pl. 61. Birch, Gall. of Brit. Mus. pl. 22.
[2] Bunsen, 1, p. 501, Germ.
[3] Porphyr. de Abstin. 4, 10.
[4] 2, 86. So Diodorus, 1, 91.
[5] Rosellini, Mon. del Cult. xxiii. xxvi. Mon. Civ. cxxix. Sext. Emp. p. 174.
[6] Rosellini, Mon. Civ. cxxxv. Wilkinson, Pantheon, pl. 87, 88.

in the one scale is a vase, shaped like a heart, and supposed to represent the moral qualities of the deceased; in the other is a figure of the goddess of Truth, with the ostrich-feather on her head, and the emblem of life in her hands. Thoth, standing by, notes the result of the weighing in a tablet or roll of papyrus. Horus then, holding Thoth's record in his hand, advances towards Osiris, who is supposed to pronounce sentence of reward or punishment, according to his report. In some of the judgement-scenes other figures are introduced, representing the assessors[1] who aided in the judgement. Their full number was forty-two, after the analogy of the number of the earthly judges, by whose sentence it was to be determined, whether the deceased should be conveyed to the tomb of his ancestors, or remain in his own house[2]. The figure of some voracious animal, called by the Egyptian antiquaries a *Cerberus*, but not triple-headed, appears in some of the judgement-scenes, keeping watch over the entrance of a sepulchre. It more resembles a hippopotamus, and as Eusebius tells us[3] that this animal represented the West, and was supposed to swallow the Sun, it would be an appropriate symbol of the world of darkness and of the western side of the Nile, in which, with very few exceptions, the Egyptian tombs were placed. We shall have to speak elsewhere of these things in connexion with the Egyptian doctrine of a future life; at present we consider them only in reference to the functions of Osiris.

Osiris is the only Egyptian god who has a de-

---

[1] Οἱ κάτω πάρεδροι. Diod. 1, 49.   [3] Euseb. Præp. Evang. 3, 12.
[2] Diod. 1, 92.

tailed mythic history, similar to the legends of the Greek mythology; and doubtless this analogy to their own religion recommended the Osirian and Isiac rites to the Greek and Roman devotees. It is thus related by Plutarch:—

"Rhea having secretly united herself with Saturn, the Sun, who was indignant, laid upon her a curse, that she should not bring forth in any year or month. Mercury, however, who was also a lover of Rhea, playing at dice with the Moon, took away the seventieth part of each period of daylight, and from these made five new days, which are the *epagomenai* or intercalary days. (Seventy here stands, as elsewhere, a round number instead of the precise one, for seventy-two; five being the seventy-second part of three hundred and sixty.) On each of these five days Rhea bore a child. On the first was born Osiris, the son of the Sun, at whose birth a voice was heard proclaiming that the Lord of all was coming to light; or, according to another version, Paamyles, drawing water in the temple of Jupiter, heard a voice which enjoined upon him to proclaim that the great and beneficent king Osiris was born. This Paamyles received him to nurse, and hence the festival of the *Paamylia*, which was a *phallephoria*. On the second day was born *Aroeris*, son of the Sun, whom they call Apollo, and the Elder Horus. On the third was born *Typhon*, not in the usual course, but bursting out with a sudden stroke from the side of Rhea. On the fourth day was born Isis[1], the daughter of Hermes;

---

[1] According to the text of Plutarch (Is. et Os. 355 E.) Isis was born ἐν πανύγροις (in præriguis locis palustribus). The reading is doubtful, and Bunsen conjectures ἐν πανηγύρεσι.

on the fifth Nephthys, who was called Teleute (the end), and Aphrodite, and according to some, Nike. Typhon and Nephthys were the children of Saturn, and married to each other[1]. In consequence of the birth of Typhon, the third day of the *epagomenai* was a *dies nefastus*, and the kings of Egypt neither transacted public business, nor took the usual care of their persons till night. Isis and Osiris united themselves, even before their birth, and their son was called, according to some, Aroeris, or the Elder Horus. The more common account, however, made the son of Osiris and Isis to be the Younger Horus.

" Osiris being king, instructed the Egyptians in the arts of civilization, teaching them agriculture, enacting laws for them, and establishing the worship of the gods, and afterwards traversed the world for the same purpose, subduing the nations, not by arms, but by persuasion, and especially by the charms of music and poetry, which gave occasion to the Greeks to identify him with Dionusos. In his absence Isis administered the regency so wisely, that Typhon was unable to create any disturbance; but on his return he conspired against Osiris with seventy-two men and the Ethiopian queen Aso; and having secretly obtained the measure of Osiris, caused a coffer splendidly adorned to be brought into the banqueting-room, promising to give it to the guest whom it should fit. Osiris put himself into it to make the trial, and Typhon and his associates immediately pegged and soldered down the case, and set it afloat on the river. It floated to

---

[1] According to the probable reading γήμασθαι for τιμᾶσθαι.

the Tanitic mouth, which on that account the Egyptians held accursed. These things were done on the seventeenth of the month Athyr, in which the Sun enters the Scorpion, and in the twenty-eighth year of the reign, or as some said of the age, of Osiris. The Pans and Satyrs who lived about Chemmis, hearing of these events, and being agitated by them, sudden terrors obtained the name of Panics: Isis cut off her hair and put on mourning, at the place at which she first heard the news; whence it obtained the name Coptos[1]. Meeting some boys, she heard from them to what place the coffin had been floated, and hence the Egyptians deemed the words of boys to carry with them a divine meaning. Osiris had by mistake united himself with Nephthys, and a son had been born to him, whom Nephthys hid immediately upon his birth. Isis sought him out, and found him by the guidance of a dog, who attended her thenceforth, and was called Anubis.

" Meanwhile the chest had been floated to Byblos, and cast ashore; the plant *erica* had grown up about it and enclosed it, and in this state it had been made use of as a pillar to support the palace of the king. Isis arrived, divinely conducted, in search of it, and recommending herself to the queen's maidens, had the charge of the young prince committed to her. She thus obtained possession of the chest, and opening it, carried it to Buto, where Horus was being brought up. The event of her return was celebrated by sacrifices on the seventeenth day of the month Tybi, and the figure of a hippopotamus bound was

---

[1] Κόπτεσθαι, plangere, is the Greek word for 'to mourn for the dead.'

impressed upon the sacrificial cakes, as an emblem of the defeat of Typhon[1]. Here she deposited the body in secresy, but Typhon, hunting by moonlight, found it and cut it into fourteen pieces. Isis, in a *baris* made of papyrus, traversed the marshes, and when she found one of the members, buried it there; whence the number of reputed places of interment of Osiris. In the end she found all the members but one, which had been devoured by the fishes *phagrus* and *lepidotus*. Isis therefore made an emblem of it, whence the honours still paid to it by the Egyptians. (Probably, though Plutarch does not expressly say so, Isis was conceived to have re-composed the body from the limbs thus recovered.) Osiris returned from Hades and gave his aid to Horus, who was preparing to overthrow the power of Typhon. Typhon fell into the hands of Isis, but she released him, at which Horus was so enraged that he plucked his mother's diadem from her head, and Mercury supplied its place by a helmet in the form of a cow's head. Two other battles took place before Typhon was finally subdued. Harpocrates was born from the union of Isis and Osiris, after the death of Osiris, and was consequently imperfect with a weakness in his lower limbs."

Such is the mythe as related by Plutarch, who intimates that there were other portions of it more revolting[2], which he had suppressed, as the discerption of Horus and the beheading of Isis. It has evidently been framed, like many of the Greek mythes, to account for existing religious usages

---

[1] Plut. Is. et Os. 371 D.
[2] P. 358 E. Τῶν δυσφημοτάτων ἐξαιρεθέντων.

and ideas. In the first place, it clearly assumes that the worship of Osiris, in connexion with the other personages of this mythe, is subsequent to the formation of the Egyptian pantheon. "The Egyptians," says Herodotus, "were the first people who assigned every day in the year to the god to whom it was appropriated." Three hundred and sixty days originally composed their year, and the memory of this number was preserved in religious rites; at Philæ 360 cups, which were every day filled by the priests with milk, and 360 priests were employed in carrying daily water from the Nile, to be poured into a perforated cask at Acanthus[1]. The year being thus filled up, it was necessary to find a new time for the new gods. Mercury, that is Thoth, the god of numbers and science, gained this at play with the Moon; the Egyptian months being twelve, all of thirty days, a seventy-second part of each made in the whole five entire days[2]. Though the fiction, however, proceeds upon the assumption that the Osirian circle was later than the rest of the gods, it by no means follows, as an historical fact, that its introduction was coincident with the addition of five days to the calendar. There are other traces of a connexion with astronomy, in the number 72 assigned to the fellow-conspirators of Typhon; and 28, the days of a lunation, assigned as the year of the reign or life of Osiris, at the time of his destruction by Typhon; and in the Sun's entrance into the Scorpion, assigned as the season of the year when this took place, being that at which, after light and darkness have been

---

[1] Diod. 1, 22, 97.   [2] See p. 331 of this volume.

equally balanced at the equinox, darkness appears to triumph through the months of winter. The order in which the different events of the mythe succeed to each other, accords very well with the supposition, that they relate to the disappearance of the sun from the northern hemisphere, and the train of consequences which it produces to the earth. His burial and disappearance took place in autumn; the voyage of Isis to discover his remains in the month of December; the search for them in Egypt about midwinter; and in the end of February, Osiris, entering into the Moon, fertilizes the world[1].

The representation of Osiris, as god of the invisible world, and his being figured as a mummy, naturally produced an explanatory mythe. It accounts for an immortal god being subjected to death, and for the association of Thoth and Horus, Isis and Nephthys with him in his capacity of ruler of Amenthe. The erection of the coffin at Byblos alludes to the use of Osiride pillars in Egyptian architecture. (See p. 258.) The story of the discerption of his body explained the circumstance that the honour of his interment was claimed by so many different places in Egypt, and the ceremony of the *phallephoria* in his honour. The co-operation of a queen of Ethiopia in the plot against his life is significant of the national hostility of that people against the Egyptians, and the prevalence of female dominion. The plotting against him in his absence may have been borrowed from the history of Sesostris, as the account of his expeditions to distant countries for the purpose of civilizing them, betrays its origin in

[1] See Prichard's Analysis, p. 103. Plut. Is. et Os. 43.

times when the Egyptians had become acquainted with foreign nations, and were disposed to glorify themselves as the original source of knowledge and the arts. The story of the dog, who assisted Isis to discover the son of Nephthys, and attended her ever afterwards, explained the form of the god Anubis, who belongs to the Osirian circle: that the animal with whose head this god is represented is not a dog, but a jackal, shows that the mythe was accommodated to the general conception, not to the fact. The respect paid by the Egyptians to the words of children, a feature of their excessive superstition, is explained by the aid which children gave to her in her researches.

Another object of the mythe was to explain the affinity which existed, or was believed to exist, between the worship of Isis in Egypt, and that of the same or a similar divinity in Phœnicia, and especially at Byblos. The identity of these goddesses was believed, and was the foundation of the legend of Io's wanderings. There was at all events a close resemblance between the rites which related to the death and revival of Adonis at Byblos, and of Osiris in Egypt[1]. Some of the people of Byblos claimed to have the sepulchre of Osiris among them, and maintained that all the rites commonly referred to Adonis properly related to Osiris. Their connexion appears from the story related by Lucian[2], that a head formed of papyrus, or a vessel of papyrus containing a letter, was annually thrown into the sea at Alexandria, and floated to Byblos; and by its arrival there informed the women of Byblos that Adonis

---

[1] Mövers die Phönizier, vol. 1, c. 7. [2] De Syria Dea, 9, 89, ed. Bipont.

was found. Now this mourning for Adonis is evidently the same as the mourning for Thammuz, spoken of by Ezekiel (viii. 14), and therefore the Egyptian mourning was probably an ancient custom, not one introduced by the Greeks at Alexandria. Since the papyrus grew in Phœnicia as well as in Egypt[1], it would be easy to keep up this ceremony of the annual exhibition of the head, or the vessel of papyrus at Byblos.

We do not find any representation of the mythical history of Osiris on the older monuments of Egypt, and this confirms the suspicion that, at least in the form in which we have received it from Plutarch, it is comparatively modern. The most remarkable sculptures illustrative of this history are found at Philæ, but in a building which belongs to the latest age of the Ptolemies and the commencement of the Roman dominion. They are preserved on the walls of an interior secret chamber over the temple[2]. Osiris is first seen in his usual form, as god of the invisible world, namely as a mummy with the crook and flail, and with the inscription *Osiris Pethempamentes*. In a succeeding compartment the head of Osiris is represented placed on the short column or stand, called a Nilometer, or the emblem of Stability, and two female figures are before it, probably ministers of the temple. A third compartment exhibits the limbs of the dismembered god, upon which a head is placed, as if to indicate that the life of the entire body is still subsisting in it. Isis and Nephthys stand one at each end. Next comes a mummy,

---

[1] Steph. Byz. *s. v.* Βύβλος. The name Byblos seems to indicate its abundant growth there.

[2] Rosellini, Mon. del Culto, tav. xxi–xxvii.

borne by the four genii of Amenthe, succeeded by the representation of a funeral chest, in which are the lower limbs and *torso* of the god, while two genii stand by and receive in a vessel the fluid which spirts from it. In the following compartment the body appears extended upon its funeral bed, but the motion of the limbs gives evident signs of life[1]. Isis and Nephthys stand by as before. It should seem as if here some transposition had taken place in the order of the scenes, for the next exhibits the mummy in its usual state, with Anubis standing by; and another scene follows in which it lies amidst a bed of twenty-eight lotus flowers[2], while Anubis pours water over it. In the last compartment a goddess with the head of a frog stands at the feet, and the mummy exhibits partial signs of revival[3]. The frog was emblematic of the embryo stage of life[4], and is found at the bottom of the notched palm-branch which represents human life. There was a male as well as female divinity with the head of a frog[5].

It is remarkable that Typhon, who acts such an important part in the mythe of Osiris, as related by Plutarch, does not appear committing violence upon him, nor indeed in any special relation to him, either in this or any other Egyptian monument. It is even doubtful what was his specific representation. The deformed and pigmy god who appears in the sculptures of some temples, which have hence been called *Typhonia*, is now considered to be the

---

[1] The figure is ἰθυφαλλικός.
[2] Wilkinson, 4, 189. See p. 412 of this volume.
[3] It is ἰθυφαλλικός.
[4] Horap. 1, 25. Ἄπλαστον ἄνθρωπον γράφοντες βάτραχον ζωγραφοῦσι ἐπειδὴ ἡ τούτου γένεσις ἐκ τῆς τοῦ ποταμοῦ ἰλύος ἀποτελεῖται.
[5] Wilkinson, 4, 256. Pantheon, 25.

representative of Ptah-Socari, not of Typhon. There is a figure of a god with square ears, supposed commouly to be those of an ass, but by Lepsius of a giraffe, which has been effaced from the monuments in which it occurred, as on the Flaminian Obelisk at Rome, where it forms one of the characters in the shield of the king, whose name has been read *Setei Menephthah*. It remains untouched in the *pyramidion* and in the compartment immediately below[1], apparently because it was not deemed worth while to raise a scaffolding so high for the purpose of destroying it, but wherever it could be reached it was chiseled out and the character of another god substituted. Now this same god appears on other monuments in relations and offices which are inconsistent with the idea that he represented the evil principle and murderer of Osiris. Thus he is seen, in conjunction with Horus[2], placing a crown on the head of Rameses the Great, and elsewhere instructing a young king in archery[3]. From these circumstances combined it has been concluded that a change took place in the Egyptian worship subsequently to the reign of the king in whose shield his name last appears, and that this god became odious to his former worshipers. This however is not the only instance in which the figure of a god has been erased from the monuments. The figure of Amun has been treated in this way on the obelisk of the Lateran[4]; yet Amun retained his high rank among the gods to the latest period of Egyp-

---

[1] See Bonomi's drawing, Trans. Roy. Soc. Lit. 1, 177. The margin shows how the substitution has been made.
[2] Wilkinson, plate 78.
[3] Ibid. plate 39.
[4] See p. 372 of this vol.

tian history. Nor is it probable that a god originally of beneficent attributes should be all at once converted into a representation of the principle of Evil. The name which commonly appears over the head of the god has been read by Sir G. Wilkinson *Obtaut* or *Ombte*, by Lepsius *Nubei*. The same figure, however, is sometimes accompanied by a phonetic group which reads *Set*[1], and as this appears to have been the name of a deity worshiped not only by the Egyptians but by the neighbouring Asiatic nations[2], some circumstance connected with their hostilities may have led to his disfavour. This figure occurs it is true in a group with those of Osiris and Isis, Nephthys and Aroeris, in the same relative position in which Plutarch mentions Typhon[3]. On the other hand, the different names which this divinity bore, according to the explanations of Plutarch, all denoted violence, turbulence and opposition, and therefore indicate that the nature of the god was also conceived of as something antagonistic to the principle of good. The animals which were emblematic of Typhon, the ass, the hippopotamus, the crocodile and the bear, all suggest the same idea of stupidity and malice, cruelty and rudeness. The god with the head of a giraffe, notwithstanding the apparent coincidence of *Set* and *Seth*, must therefore be distinguished from Typhon, who from the first origin of the Osirian mythe denoted hostility to Osiris, the good and beneficent principle.

---

[1] Typhon was called Babys, Bebon, Smu, *Seth*. Plut. Is. et Os. p. 371 B, C. 367. Hellanicus ap. Athen. 15, p. 679 F. *Ses* or *Seth* is Coptic for *pullus asinæ*. Comp. Plut. Is. et Os. p. 362 F.
[2] Osburn's Egypt, p. 91.
[3] Wilkinson, M. & C. 4. p. 415, 416.

This idea is capable of assuming a great variety of forms, according to the aspect under which we view Osiris. And free scope seems to have been given to the fancy by the Greeks and later Egyptians in devising physical and metaphysical explanations of the mythe. So general a contrast between the good and evil principles as that between Ormuzd and Ahreiman in the Zoroastrian mythology does not appear to belong to the Egyptian system, or we should find other gods whose attributes are beneficent assailed by other Typhons. It is probable, therefore, that we are to seek the explanation in some special character of Osiris. Though this god originally may not have represented the Nile, it is certain that he was identified with it in the minds of the Egyptians, as the Nile was with the principle of moisture, to which everywhere, but most obviously in Egypt, vegetable life and fertility are due. The Greek word Typhon denoted a fiery and mephitic blast, a violent wind; "the Egyptian priests[1]," says Plutarch, " call *Typhon* everything that is arid and fiery and dry and hostile to moisture, and the conspiracy and dominion of Typhon is the power of the drought which dissipates the moisture of the Nile, the source of production and increase." The month of Athyr, or November, is fixed upon for the enclosure of Osiris in the *soros* or coffer, because it is in that month that the Nile after the inundation retires within its channel[2]. The general explanation will suit equally well with the supposition that Osiris is the Sun and Typhon the power of darkness, since

---

[1] Οἱ σοφώτεροι τῶν ἱερέων. Plut. Is. et Os. p. 364, 366 C.

[2] See p. 83 of this volume.

the time of low Nile is that in which the influence of the Sun is withdrawn. Other nations represented this luminary as in a state of feebleness and suffering during the winter; the Phrygians thought that he slept at this time, and celebrated his wakening with joyful rites; the Paphlagonians represented him as bound in winter and loosed at the return of spring[1]. Others explained Typhon of the fiery heat of the solar rays, by which the earth's moisture is exhaled and large portions of it made arid and uninhabitable. The opposition of moisture and drought seems likely to have been the primary idea of the mythe. It offered, however, a ready symbol of those antagonist forces which are everywhere found in nature; Plutarch declares it to be his opinion that Typhon was not drought, causing the Nile to shrink, or the sea-water, swallowing it up, or wind, or darkness, absorbing the light of the sun, but whatever in nature was destructive and injurious was a part of Typhon. This was probably an extension of the original conception; and when the same author makes Typhon the principle of Evil generally, which always resists Good, but is always overcome by it, he confesses that he accommodates the theology of the Egyptians to the philosophy of Plato and the doctrines of Zoroaster[2].

Two divinities appear under the name of HORUS, and are connected with the Osirian mythe. The elder Horus was the brother of Osiris, born on the second day of the *epagomenai*. The Greeks identified him with Apollo[3]; and Apollo, at least in

---

[1] Plut. p. 378 F.
[2] Ὡς τὰ ἐπιόντα δηλώσει τοῦ λόγου. τὴν Αἰγυπτίων θεολογίαν μάλιστα ταύτῃ τῇ φιλοσοφίᾳ συνοικειοῦντος. Is. et Os. p. 370, 371.
[3] Herod. 2, 156.

later times, was held to be the same with the Egyptian Aroeris[1]. As *Har* is the Egyptian name for Horus, and *oer* is *great*, it is probable that Aroeris means "Horus the Great." He is represented with the head of a hawk, and being a personification of the Sun (which led the Greeks to consider him as Apollo), it is probable that this bird was chosen as his emblem from the brilliancy of its eye. Many of the titles attributed to Horus in the inscriptions, indicate his relations to the Sun[2]. He is called Horus the son of Isis (*Hor si Esi*), but he was properly the brother of Isis; no consistency is observed in these fanciful relationships. In the judgement-scenes in Amenthe, he appears introducing the deceased or presenting him to Osiris, probably because the Sun, from his wide range and piercing vision[3], might naturally be supposed cognizant of all the actions of mankind. A hawk, as his representative, was often placed in the tombs[4]. He does not appear in the Typhonian mythe, as related by Plutarch, in the capacity of a defender or avenger of Osiris; but he is represented in the monuments as piercing with a spear the serpent Apop, who is connected with the giant Apophis, said to have made war on Jupiter, another version probably of the story of Typhon's attack on Osiris[5]. At Hermopolis, Typhon was represented by a hippopotamus, on which was mounted a hawk, fighting with a serpent[6].

[1] Hamilton, Ægypt. p.75. Ἀρωήρει θεῷ μεγάλῳ Ἀπόλλωνι. Plut. Is. et Os. 355 E.
[2] Birch, Gallery of Antiquities, p. 36.
[3] Eurip. Med. 1247. Soph. Ajax, 845.
[4] Wilkinson, M. and C. 4, 401.
[5] Plut. p. 365. Wilkinson, Pantheon, pl. 42. Diod. 1, 36.
[6] Plut. 371 D.

The avenger of Osiris, the youngest of the gods, and the last of them who reigned over Egypt, was the youthful Horus, the son of Isis and Osiris. He is represented as a boy, naked, having his skull entirely bare, except a single lock which is plaited and worn on the right side. For this, a mystical reason was assigned[1]; but as the princes of the blood-royal were distinguished by this fashion of wearing the hair[2], it probably was only designed to characterize him as a youthful prince. He sometimes appears with the hook and flail to indicate his relation to Osiris, and with the royal cap or *pschent*. His finger is raised towards his mouth, a gesture which the Greeks interpreted as enjoining silence, and called him Harpocrates, the god of Silence[3]. The first syllable of this name, which, notwithstanding its apparent Grecism, must be of Egyptian etymology, is evidently *Har*, Horus, the two last *pechret* (Copt. *hrot filius*), the son[4]. He often appears with his limbs bent, and this the Greeks supposed to be indicative of lameness; and Plutarch accounted for it from the peculiar circumstances under which the union of his parents had taken place. Jablonsky[5], assuming the correctness of the Greek opinion, hence explained Harpocrates, as *Ar-phoch-rat*, lame in the feet, and supposed him to be an emblem of the Sun, weak and just beginning

---

[1] Macrob. Sat. 1, ch. 21. Ægyptii, volentes ipsius Solis nomine dicare simulachrum, figuravere raso capite, sed dextra parte crine remanente. Servatus crinis docet Solem naturæ rerum nunquam esse in operto; dempti autem capilli, residente radice, monstrant hoc sidus, etiam tempore quo non visitur a nobis, rursum emergendi, uti capillos, habere substantiam.

[2] See p. 247 of this volume.

[3] Varro, Ling. Lat. 4, p. 17, ed. Bip. "*St* Harpocrates digito significat."

[4] Bunsen's Egypt, 1, p. 434, Eng.

[5] Panth. Æg. 2, 247.

SECT. I.—THEOLOGY.

to recover his power, at the winter solstice. But this all rests on misapprehension. The finger of Horus pointing to the mouth, is expressive of his having acquired the power of speech; a human figure with the hand raised towards the mouth being the general determinative of verbs which have a relation to the ideas voice, mouth, speech, writing[1]; and a youthful figure in this attitude specifically represents a child[2]. The most common representation of Horus is being nursed on the knee of Isis, or suckled at her breast; she is then frequently figured with the horns of a cow on her head. Sometimes he is seated on an opening lotus, which is supposed to be an emblem of the opening day, or in the sepulchral scenes of the return to life. The Christian fathers speak of a mourning of Isis for the loss of her child, but they mean Osiris, not Harpocrates[3].

NEPHTHYS is another personage who belongs to this series of the Osirian gods, and the last in order of birth. There is a goddess who appears very generally united with Isis, in the judgement-scenes in Amenthe and the representation of the sufferings of Osiris, wearing on her head an emblem composed of a basket and the representation of a house, which is read phonetically *Nebtei*[4]. As a sister of Isis she shared her functions, and is scarcely to be distinguished from her. Thus she appears with the

---

[1] Champ. Dict. Egyptien, p. 33.
[2] Champ. p. 31.
[3] Min. Fel. c. 21. Isiaci miseri cædunt pectora et dolorem infelicissimæ matris imitantur; mox invento parvulo gaudet Isis, exultant sacerdotes. Lactant. Ep. Div. Inst. c. 23. filium parvum, *qui dicitur Osiris*, perdidit et invenit.
[4] Wilkinson, Panth. pl. 35.

cow's-horns and disk and the vulture cap, which are the usual insignia of Isis[1]. According to Plutarch, Nephthys represented that which was unseen and below the earth, and Isis that which was conspicuous and above it[2], thus dividing the earth as it were between them. According to the same author, Nephthys was married to Typhon and was the mother of Anubis. This may be explained from her character as representative of the dark and unseen part of the earth; as Anubis was the guardian and emblem of the invisible world, and Typhon the enemy of the light. Isis represented the beginning and Nephthys the end[3], and when a dead body is introduced, Isis stands at the head and Nephthys at the feet. She appears to have been confounded by the Greeks with Athor or Aphrodite, which is not wonderful, since Isis and Athor have been very generally mistaken by them for the same.

ANUBIS alone remains of the five gods included in the Osirian mythe. He is not mentioned by Herodotus, but among the later Greeks and Romans none of the Egyptian gods attracted more notice. His image formed a part of the ritual processions which accompanied the diffusion of the worship of Isis throughout the Roman world[4]; and those who, either as philosophic theists, or as adherents to the established religions of Greece and Rome, disapproved of the animal worship of Egypt, found an especial subject for their contempt in a god repre-

---

[1] This close resemblance explains what Plutarch relates, that Isis discovered συγγεγονέναι δι' ἄγνοιαν τῇ ἀδελφῇ ὡς ἑαυτῇ τὸν Ὄσιριν.

[2] Plut. p. 368.
[3] Plut. u. s.
[4] Ovid, Met. 9, 689. Apul. Met. 11, p. 262, quoted by Jablonsky, Panth. Æg. lib. 5, p. 13, 15.

sented under the form of a dog[1]. It is indeed doubtful whether the animal whose head forms a mask for Anubis were a dog or a jackal; the nocturnal habits of the latter animal, and its feeding on dead bodies, make it a more natural emblem of a deity, whose seat was the world of darkness and the repositories of the dead. The ancients, however, universally conceived of Anubis as represented by the dog, and we have seen that Plutarch explains the Osirian mythe in conformity with this idea. His name is phonetically spelt Anep or Anepo (Pl. III. C. 5), and his chief function, according to the popular theology, was to bear a part in the embalmment of Osiris, and assist in the judgement of the dead, when he commonly appears along with Thoth, adjusting the balance in which the merits of the deceased are weighed. Some of his titles allude to his funereal functions; thus he is styled "chief of the hills[2]," the dead being usually deposited in sepulchres excavated in the rocky banks of the Nile; and in interment-scenes in the funereal papyri, he appears at the door of the tomb, receiving the mummy in its case from the mourners. He also took charge of the soul in Amenthe and conducted it on the way of its wanderings[3]. Hence it was natural that he should be identified by the Greeks with their Hermes ψυχοπομπός. From the accounts of later writers, it would seem as if Anubis had been represented under a double character, as

[1] Virg. Æn. 8, 698.
   Omnigenûmque deûm monstra, et latrator Anubis,
   Contra Neptunum, et Venerem, contraque Minervam
   Tela tenent.
[2] Birch, Gallery of Antiq. p. 44.   [3] Birch, u. s.

a subterranean and also as a celestial god; and that his images were sometimes black and sometimes of a golden hue, to represent these opposite relations[1]. According to Plutarch, Anubis was the horizon, the line which separates between light and darkness; and according to Clemens Alexandrinus, the two dogs by which he was represented were the upper and the lower hemisphere[2]. These conceptions may seem to derive some support from the monuments in which the jackal of the north and the jackal of the south are distinguished, the former the guardian of the terrestrial world, the latter lord of heaven[3]: but they hardly belonged to the popular religion.

The last personage to be mentioned, as taking part in the judgement-scene in Amenthe, is THOTH, the ibis-headed god, who stands beside the scales and notes the result of the weighing. He is connected with the Osirian mythe as having gained from the Moon the five days in which the gods were born, but he appears in these scenes in his capacity of the god of writing. The Greeks, in their endeavours to find an historical origin for the personages of mythology, represented Thoth as a divine man, if not a god[4], who invented the distinctions of articulate language into vowels and consonants, and fixed the numbers and letters of the alphabet, besides arithmetic, geometry and the game of tables[5], and made his inventions known to the contemporary

---

[1] Apuleius, Metam. xi. p. 775, ed. Elmenh. Ille superûm commeator et inferûm, *nunc atra nunc aurea facie sublimis,* attollens canis cervices arduas.

[2] Jablonsky, Panth. Æg. lib. 5, p. 26.

[3] Birch, Gall. of Ant. p. 43.

[4] Εἴτέ τις θεὸς εἴτε καὶ θεῖος ἄνθρωπος. Plato, Phileb. 2, 18, ed. Steph.

[5] Comp. Plat. Phileb. 2, 18. Phædr. 3, 274.

king of Egypt, Thamus. This Thoth, sometimes called *Tat*, was the same as the Hermes of the Greeks. The fifth Mercury, says Cicero[1], is he who is said to have taught laws and letters to the Egyptians; they call him Thoyth, and the first month of the year among them bears the same name. According to Diodorus, Hermes was the hierogrammat of Osiris, and having invented language, music, letters, the gymnastic art and astronomy, accompanied his master in his progress over the world and communicated these inventions wherever he came[2]. It is evident that Thoth is only a personification of the inventive powers of the human mind; the dispute whether he were Hermes simply or Hermes Trismegistus[3], whether he invented letters or only arithmetic, in what king's reign and in what year of the world he lived, proceeds upon a groundless assumption that he was an historical personage. The name, which the Alexandrians spelt Thoth and the other Egyptians Thouth[4], denotes in Coptic a *column* or *stele*[5]; and the historical fact that the oldest specimens of the art of writing were preserved on stone was expressed by giving this appellation to its supposed inventor. The art of writing is immediately connected with arithmetic and musical notation, with geometry and astronomy; that Hermes was also the inventor of gymnastic was an addition to the Egyptian mythe made by the Greeks, among whom the office of presiding in the Palæstra was assigned

---

[1] N. D. 3, 22.
[2] 1, 16.
[3] Hermes Trismegistus appears to have been specially worshiped at Pselcis (Dakkeh, see p. 26 of this vol.) in Nubia, with the title of *Patnouphis*; but all the inscriptions are of the Roman times. Wilkinson, Mod. Eg. and Thebes, 2, 320.
[4] Philo-Byblius apud Euseb. Præp. Evang. 1, 9.
[5] Peyron, Lex. Copt. s. voc.

to him. Thoth appears to have been especially the symbol of the knowledge possessed by the sacerdotal caste in Egypt, which was comprised in forty-two books of Hermes, and included, besides properly sacred literature, astronomy and geography.

The ibis was consecrated to Thoth, and the figure of this bird stands as a phonetic symbol, with the sound of *Thoth* or *Tet*, in the shield of several kings of the name of Thothmes or Tethmosis[1], though there is no reason to believe that it is the Coptic word for ibis. The name Athothis (*ha-thoth*), interpreted by Eratosthenes Ἑρμογένης, occurs as the second in his list of Egyptian kings, proving that this deity belongs to the oldest period of the monarchy. With a name nearly similar, *Taut*, he appears also in the Phœnician history, and in the same character of the inventor of letters.

Thoth in the Egyptian monuments commonly has the head of the ibis, and holds a tablet and reed pen in his hand, or the notched palm-branch, which is said to be an emblem of the month[2] or of time. Why the ibis was chosen as the emblem of this god is uncertain; various fanciful reasons have been assigned for the selection; perhaps the most obvious may be the most true—that the contrast of black and white, which is remarkable in the plumage of this bird, made it a suitable symbol of writing, and also of the bright and dark parts of the moon. The Cynocephalus or Ape was an emblem of the same god; it appears both holding the tablet and pen,

---

[1] See Pl. II. No. 9, and p. 300 of this volume.

[2] Horapollo, 1, 4, Μῆνα γράφοντες βαῖν ζωγραφοῦσι. According to the same author, the palm put forth a branch every month, twelve in the year.

and with the disk of the moon upon its head; answering to the double character of Thoth. A multitude of reasons, manifestly absurd and having no foundation in the natural history of the ape, have been assigned for this selection[1]. Probably the near approach which this animal makes to the possession of reason, and its power of imitating the actions of man, suggested it as a fit representative of the rational faculty, Thoth being not merely the inventor of writing, but the author and patron of all the exercises of the human intellect. For the connexion of the Cynocephalus with the moon, it is difficult to imagine any special reason; but astronomy belongs naturally to the god who invented arithmetic, and the earliest and simplest form of astronomy is derived from the changes of the moon.

Hermopolis (Eshmoon) was a principal seat of the worship of Thoth, and the ibis and the cynocephalus were among the conspicuous ornaments of the portico of its temple, now destroyed. The name, which in Coptic signifies *eight*, is supposed to allude to some function of Thoth, who is called in inscriptions "the Lord of Eshmoon," but no satisfactory explanation of this title has been given.

The hall in which the judgement-scene takes place is called the "Hall of the two Truths," and the region of the West, Amenthe, "the land of the two Truths[2]." Thmei, the goddess of Truth, is represented by a sitting figure, with an ostrich-plume on her head; an emblem of truth or equity, because

---

[1] They may be seen in Horapollo, 1, 14.

[2] Birch, Gallery Brit. Mus. P. 1. p. 28.

the filaments of the feathers were said to be all of the same length. Sometimes she appears blindfolded, like the image which the chief judge in the Egyptian courts wore around his neck.

We have not attempted to discriminate the gods of the second and third order, but have enumerated those to whom temples were consecrated, or who occupy a prominent part in religious representations. Egypt had also its *Dii minorum gentium*, objects of limited and local veneration, whose nature is usually even more obscure than those whom we have described. Some appear to owe their existence to the custom of matching together a male and female divinity, whose union was supposed to result in the birth of a juvenile god. Others are slight variations of the attributes of the greater deities; others, personifications of towns and districts and parts of nature. Since the number of Egyptian gods was so great, that every day in the year was consecrated to one, and every sign and subdivision of the zodiac had its own genius, we may suppose that there were many who were not even the objects of local and limited veneration, but were introduced for the sake of symmetry and completeness. Their multiplication to supply the demands of poetry, art or superstition is characteristic of the expansion which the simple elements of a popular theology receive in process of time[1].

The Egyptians are commonly said to have had nothing answering to the hero-worship of the Greeks. They did not believe in those unions of gods with

[1] In the earlier books of the Old Testament we find no enumeration of angels and no distinction of their offices, as after the Captivity.

mortals, which, according to the Greeks, gave birth to a race half human, half divine[1]. But they paid religious honours to eminent persons after their decease, not unlike the Greek hero-worship in those ages in which the notion of a divine descent had long ceased, and when Miltiades, Brasidas and Aratus had each his *heroum*[2]. Thothmes III. on the tablet of Karnak presents offerings to his predecessors; so does Rameses on the tablet of Abydos. Even during his lifetime the Egyptian king was denominated " beneficent god."

We have not found among the gods of the Pharaouic times any representative of Serapis, whose worship was introduced from Sinope in the reign of the first Ptolemy, and who became very celebrated, along with Osiris and Isis, in the Greek and Roman times[3]. According to the narrative of Tacitus, derived from the Egyptian priests[4], Ptolemy, when he was adorning Alexandria, then recently built, with temples and other religious edifices, was warned in a dream to fetch from Sinope in Pontus the statue of Jupiter Dis, who was held in great reverence there. He accordingly sent emissaries, who succeeded in bringing off the statue, in spite of the reluctance of the inhabitants to part with their god. When it reached Egypt, Timotheus, the Greek *exegetes*, and Manetho, the high priest of Sebennytus, being consulted by the king, pronounced that the statue represented the god Serapis, arguing from the Cerberus and the serpent which were its

---

[1] Il. μ', 23. Her. 2, 143. The Egyptian priests denied ἀπὸ θεοῦ γενέσθαι ἄνθρωπον.

[2] Wachsmuth, Hell. Alt. II. 2, 105.

[3] Clem. Alex. 1, p. 42, Pott. Τὸν μεγαλοδαιμόνα ὃν κατ' ἐξοχὴν πρὸς πάντων σεβασμοῦ κατηξιωμένον ἀκούομεν τὸν Αἰγύπτιον Σάραπιν.

[4] Tac. Hist. 4, 83. Serapidis dei, quem dedita superstitionibus gens ante alios colit.

accompaniments. It is evident from this that Serapis was a god previously known in Egypt; and according to Tacitus there had been a temple at Rhacotis, the site of Alexandria, of small dimensions, from ancient times, consecrated to him. There was also a still more celebrated temple of the same god, under the title Zeus Sinopites[1], near Memphis, and according to one account it was from this place, and not from Sinope, that the god was transferred to Alexandria. The nature of the god himself was variously interpreted; "some deemed him, from his healing powers, to be Æsculapius; others Osiris, the very ancient deity of the Egyptians; many Jupiter, the chief ruler of all things; but the majority Dispater, arguing from his insignia, or from doubtful indications." The temple appears to be that which Strabo describes under the name of a Serapeum, near Memphis, which in his time was nearly buried in the sand, so that only the heads of the sphinxes in the dromos were visible[2]. Such was its sanctity, that no stranger was allowed to set his foot within it, nor was it visited even by the priests, except for the interment of Apis[3]. This appropriation, and the circumstance that the temples of Serapis were placed without the walls of towns[4], indicate a god who was connected with the invisible world[5], and suggest that Apis may be the last part of the name. It is difficult, however, to refer

---

[1] Dion. Perieg. 255. Eustath. ad loc.
[2] Strabo, l. 17, p. 807.
[3] Pausanias, lib. 1, c. 18.
[4] Macrobius (Sat. 1, 7) says this was owing to the reluctance of the Egyptians to receive a strange god; but he must have been very ignorant of the old Egyptian religion to assert "nunquam fuit fas Ægyptiis pecudibus aut sanguine sed precibus et ture solo placare deos."
[5] The statues of Serapis were painted black (Clem. Alex. 1, p. 43, ed. Potter).

XXI.]   SECT. I.—THEOLOGY.   433

him to his exact representative in the old Egyptian pantheon. The statues and coins of Serapis, which are chiefly of Asiatic cities, and all of the Greek or Roman times, usually exhibit him with the lineaments of Pluto, and accompanied by Cerberus, but distinguished from that god by having a *modius* on his head[1], to indicate his being the author of abundance, a character well-suited to the primary meaning of Dis and Πλούτων. He also carries a cubit, supposed to have a reference to the rise of the Nile[2], or else to his function as judge in the infernal regions. None, however, of the representations of the ancient Egyptian gods at all correspond with this description, nor do we know with what attributes the Serapis of Memphis or Rhacotis had been figured, before the influence of Greek art, and the mixture of Greek mythology. That he was considered to be Æsculapius was owing to the multitude of cures which were performed in his temple, rather than to any peculiar correspondence in their attributes. The Greeks and Latins concluded probably from the sound, that the name was connected with Apis, Osirapis or Soroapis, " the coffin of Apis ;" we find a representation of Osiris in the character of Apis, that is, with a bovine head[3], but with none of those insignia which the Greek and Latin authors attribute to Serapis. This god was known to the Macedonians before the death of Alexander; after his illness at Babylon, Python, Seleucus and several of his attendants slept in the temple of

---

[1] Millin, Galerie Mythologique, Pl. lxxxvii. No. 346. Visconti, Mus. Pio-Clem. 2, 1.

[2] Suidas, Σάραπις. The graduated pedestal of Ptah is supposed to refer to the rise of the Nile (Birch, Gallery of Antiquities, pl. 6).

[3] Wilkinson, pl. 31, Part 2.

Serapis, for the purpose of ascertaining[1] whether it would be better to remove him to the temple for the chance of his recovery; and the god replied that it was better he should remain where he was. There was at Seleucia[2] in Syria a temple consecrated to a divinity of this name. If Ptolemy, partaking in this reverence for Serapis[3], wished to introduce his worship into Egypt, it was natural that, to avoid offending the religious feelings of his new subjects, he should identify him with some former object of their worship, and Manetho appears to have lent his aid for this purpose. If this god were Osiris, it will be easily understood how Serapis should be considered as corresponding with Pluto, with the Sun and the Nile, all these attributes being combined in Osiris[4].

There are some gods mentioned by the ancients, to whom we find it difficult to assign representatives among the figures on the monuments. Herodotus says[5] that Mars was worshiped at Papremis, and describes the bloody affray which occurred when one body of his priests endeavoured to force their way with his statue into the temple, and another resisted his entrance. A figure of the same deformed proportions as Ptah-Socari, armed with a sword and shield, has received the name of Mars, but with little probability[6]. An armed male figure,

---

[1] Suet. Vesp. 7. The blind man, and the cripple whom Vespasian healed, had been encouraged in a dream by Serapis to apply for his aid.
[2] Tac. 4, 84.
[3] Comp. Arrian, Exped. Alex. 7, 26. Plut. Alexand. § 73.
[4] SOLI SARAPI, ΗΛΙΩ ΣΑΡΑ-ΠΙΔΙ, are common in Latin and Greek inscriptions. Jablonsky, P. 1. p. 225. Serapis, sol inferus. Id. P. 2, p. 234. Orelli, Inscr. c. 4, § 32.
[5] 2, 63, 64.
[6] Birch, Gall. p. 48. This figure is evidently not of the Pharaonic times. Comp. Wilkinson, Pantheon, pl. 24, A. 4.

having the name of *Ranpo*, seems more exactly to answer to the character of Mars[1]. The river-horse was held sacred in the Papremite nome[2], and therefore from analogy we should conclude was sacred to the god of Papremis; but it was an emblem of Typhon[3], and perhaps the god whom Herodotus calls Mars may have been a form of the Evil principle. Hercules again is repeatedly mentioned as an Egyptian god; but Chons, with whom he has been identified (see p. 384), has nothing resembling his Greek attributes. It is uncertain what goddess answered to the malignant Tithrambo[4], whom Epiphanius calls Hecate, or to Thermuthis[5], who appears to have been a divinity of the same unfriendly character. On the other hand, there are several figures which appear from their attributes to be divine, whose functions it is difficult to assign, and who have no correspondence with any divinity mentioned by the Greek and Roman authors.

Upon the whole, we have abundant evidence that the Egyptian theology had its origin in the personification of the powers of nature, under male and female attributes, and that this conception took a sensible form, such as the mental state of the people required, by the identification of these powers with the elements and the heavenly bodies, fire, earth, water, the sun and moon, and the Nile. Such appears everywhere to be the origin of the objective form

---

[1] Wilkinson, pl. 69, 70.
[2] Her. 1, 71.
[3] Prichard, Analysis, p. 122. Comp. Her. (2, 63), "ἐθέλοντα τῇ μητρὶ συμμίξαι," with Horap. 1, 56, "Πρὸς τὴν ἑαυτοῦ μητέρα ἐπὶ γάμον ἥκει," of the hippopotamus.
[4] Jablonsky, P. I, p. 103-121.
[5] Ibid. P. I, p. 116.

of polytheism; and it is especially evident among the nations most closely allied to the Egyptians by position and general character—the Phœnicians, the Babylonians; and in remoter connexion, the Indians on the one side and the Greeks on the other. The conception of a god, however, is formed within man himself; it is from his own consciousness that he derives the idea of power, which he transfers to the outward world, along with the ideas of volition and intelligence, which in himself are inseparable from power. He is hence subjected, in the formation and expression of his religious conceptions, to two counteracting influences, which variously predominate, according to individual and national character; one leading him to multiply the objects of his worship, as his knowledge of the powers of nature extends; the other suggesting the idea of one spiritual essence, informing the material world, in analogy with that by which the human body is animated and controlled. Of the extent to which the latter prevails, it is impossible that we should have satisfactory evidence in regard to an extinct people who have left us no written record of their sentiments. The material symbol of the most refined religious conception, when it comes to stand alone and without commentary, necessarily appears anthropomorphic or even idolatrous. If we had no other means of judging of Christian doctrine but by Christian art, we should suppose that its Deity was represented under a human form, or that it admitted more than one object of worship. It will not therefore follow, that the Egyptian Kneph did not represent the spiritual essence which pervades all nature, or even the Intellect which presides over all, because he is figured as a man, with the head of a ram.

If in the absence of positive information we might venture to draw a distinction, we should say that the older gods, to whom Kneph belongs, appear to represent rather the principles and powers to which the world owes its existence; while Osiris and Isis more distinctly and palpably personify the parts and elements of the material world, and perhaps from this circumstance, among others, became the gods of the whole nation, and representatives to foreigners of the whole Egyptian theology. It might have been expected that the discovery of the hieroglyphic character would have produced more certainty in regard to the original conceptions of the Egyptians respecting their gods, but they have added little to our knowledge. Even if correctly interpreted, they do not exhibit a more spiritual system of belief than we had previously cause to attribute to them.

We can find no sufficient evidence for the opinion that the various gods of Egypt are but symbols and personifications of the attributes and powers of one Being, whom the priests, if not the people, recognised as the only true god. This opinion seems to have been adopted not so much from any direct evidence, as from its appearing the necessary consequence of another assumption, that the doctrine of the Unity of God, being the primæval belief of mankind, must have been held by the original population of Egypt. The only approach to the idea of Unity which we find is that the functions of a supreme god appear to be assigned to subordinate deities, as if all were really but the manifestation of one power. Of the ancients, some represent the Egyptians as believing in no other gods than the elements of nature and the heavenly bodies; others as being the source whence Orpheus and Pythagoras derived their doctrine, that God dwells in the world as the soul in the human body. Each opinion may have been held in Egypt when the Greeks became acquainted with it, and the partisans of each have claimed it to be the genuine sense of their religion. The recognition of God, however, as the intellectual principle, wholly distinct from matter, which presided over creation (the clear doctrine of the Hebrew Scriptures), appears to have been, as regards the Pagan world, the original and independent merit of the school of Anaxagoras[1]. This is the only kind of monotheism which has any definite character or moral value; the rest are a pantheism, which is easily changed into polytheism on the one side, or atheism on the other.

SECT. II.—SACRIFICIAL RITES.—THE SACERDOTAL ORDER.

Sacrifice, the universal expression of the religious sentiments in the ancient world, has a natural origin in the transference of his own feelings from the worshiper to the object of his worship. He takes for granted that his god is pleased with a costly gift, and demands, as a proof of his gratitude for an abundant harvest, a fruitful season, or the increase of his flocks and herds, the offering of the best and choicest of what he has bestowed. If

---

[1] Ar. Met. lib. 1, c. 3. Others say Thales, Cic. N. D. 1, 10.

his gift be of an imperishable nature, he suspends it in his temple; if capable of being consumed, it is either laid upon the fire of the altar, or poured out in a libation, or given to the priest as the visible representative of the divinity. These are *eucharistic* sacrifices, expressing gratitude for benefits received, in a mode analogous to that in which it would be manifested towards an earthly benefactor. Such sacrifices are also naturally supposed to be *propitiatory*, and to produce towards the worshiper a kindly feeling on the part of his god, disposing him to bestow further benefits. The darker passions of humanity, however, are transferred to the heavens, as well as those of benevolence and pity; occasions arise, when the consciousness of guilt or the experience of calamity produces the belief, that the god is angry, and has inflicted or is preparing to inflict evil on the object of his displeasure. Human resentment in similar circumstances is not discriminating. It is not always to be mollified by submission and repentance, but its vengeance may be diverted to some other than the person by whom the offence has been committed. If the penalty of divine displeasure is not wholly to be avoided, it may be commuted; an *expiatory* sacrifice less costly than the life of the offender may be accepted; the shedding of the blood of animal victims may procure for him a remission of the sentence against himself; or if human blood must absolutely flow, some life over which he has power, that of a slave, a captive, or a child, may be offered for his own; if one sacrifice be not sufficient, numbers may prevail, and divine vengeance be averted by a hecatomb.

Human sacrifices were so common in the ancient world, even among nations by no means barbarous[1], that it is in itself not at all incredible that they should have been practised by the Egyptians, notwithstanding the humanity which generally characterized their institutions. We have besides the positive testimony of Manetho[2], that "men called Typhonian were burnt alive in the town of Idithya (conjectured to be Eilithya) and their ashes scattered to the winds." Diodorus informs us what was meant by Typhonian, namely men of a red colour, which was believed to be that of Typhon. This colour, he remarks, was rare among the Egyptians, though very common among foreigners, and these Typhonian men were sacrificed by the ancient kings at the tomb of Osiris[3]. The Greeks believed that a king of Egypt of the name of Busiris had rendered himself memorable and odious by this sacrifice of strangers who had ventured into Egypt, or been driven by storms on the coast. As no such king is found in the lists, it was conjectured that Busiris means " tomb of Osiris[4];" and whether the etymology is sound or not, it is very probable that the tale originated in the custom of offering red-haired strangers, that is, natives of northern regions, to Osiris. Manetho adds, that a king named Amosis abolished the custom, and substituted a waxen

---

[1] Of this practice among the Phœnicians and Carthaginians, no evidence needs to be offered. Of the Arabs see Porphyr. de Abstin. 2, p. 225. Of the Greeks, Wachsmuth, Hellenische Alterthumskunde, ii. 2, 225. Its prevalence among the inhabitants of Palestine, and its abolition by Amosis, who expelled the Hyksos, may lead to the supposition that it was introduced by the Phœnician Shepherds.

[2] Plut. Is. et Osir. p. 380 D. Athen. 4, p. 172.

[3] Diod. 1, 88.

[4] Diod. 1, 88.

image for the human victim[1]. There is no conceivable reason why a high-priest of Egypt should invent a story so little creditable to his nation; while it is quite credible that an inhuman custom, time-honoured and sanctioned by religion, should have existed along with civilized manners, and institutions in their general character humane. No doubt the Egyptian considered a Typhonian man as acceptable a sacrifice to his god, as a Jew or a heretic was deemed by a Spanish Inquisitor; nor does the circumstance that in the latter case it was called a penalty, and not a sacrifice, make any difference in the quality of the act. Herodotus indeed denies the existence of the practice at any time in Egypt; but the reason which he gives for his disbelief is not convincing. "How is it likely," he says, "that the Egyptians, to whom it is not lawful to sacrifice even animals, with the exception of sheep, and pure oxen and male calves and geese, should sacrifice men[2]?" He has himself, however, related that swine, so impure commonly in the eyes of the Egyptians, that a touch of one rendered purification in the river necessary, were nevertheless on one day in the year offered in sacrifice to the Moon and Dionusos[3]. It is not safe to apply reasoning to a thing so capricious as superstition, or to conclude that a custom has never prevailed, because it is incongruous to the manners of a people as we see them. The Mexicans were a highly civilized

---

[1] Porphyr. de Abstin. 2, p. 223. Euseb. Præp. Ev. 4, c. 16. Comp. Ovid, Fasti 5, 621, of the custom of throwing images of bulrushes into the Tiber, as a substitute for an ancient custom of drowning men.
[2] 2, 45.
[3] 2, 47.

people, and their works of art not unworthy to be compared with those of Egypt; yet we know that their *teocallis* were profusely stained with the blood of human victims, even of their own countrymen. The Egyptian priests had contrived to retort the odium of human sacrifices upon the Greeks; they related that Menelaus, when driven into Egypt, seized two youths of the country, and sacrificed them to obtain a favourable wind for his departure —a story evidently framed when they had heard from the Greeks of the sacrifice of Iphigenia[1]. The monuments give us no positive evidence on this subject; for the representation of kings grasping a score of captives by their hair, and preparing to strike off their heads, if not altogether symbolical, has reference to military slaughter, not to sacrifice. It is found on monuments of the Ptolemies, and therefore certainly represents no real fact[2]. It is remarkable, however, that the seal which the *sphragistes* placed upon the victim, in order to mark it as lawful for sacrifice, bore according to Castor[3] "the figure of a man kneeling, with his hands bound behind him, and a sword pointed at his throat." A stamp has been found on which three bound and kneeling human figures appear, beneath the jackal of Anubis, the emblem of the infernal world[4]. Wilkinson says that he has seen in the sculptures a group still more exactly corresponding with the description of Castor[5].

---

[1] Herod. 2, 119.
[2] Rosellini, Mon. Reali, clxv. 3.
[3] Plut. Is. et Osir. p. 363 B.
[4] Leemans' Horapoll. Hierog. pl. 47 a.
[5] Manners and Customs, 5, 352. This author disbelieves the accounts of human sacrifices in Egypt.

The period of the abolition of human sacrifices, or the substitution of some symbolical rite for an actual shedding of the blood of life, is usually placed by tradition in those remote ages, in which the mythical and the historical element are with difficulty discriminated. Thus in Greece, while the narratives of the heroic age are full of human sacrifices, in the historical times they were of rare occurrence, being confined to a few localities[1] and exceptional occasions[2]. When they had ceased in ordinary circumstances in Greece, the Athenians yearly put to death two malefactors at the festival of the Thargelia, with the ceremonies of a sacrifice[3]; and the sacrifice of foreigners in Egypt, who were forbidden by law to enter the country, exhibits the same mixed character of a judicial execution and a sacred rite. Those who, as an expiation (ἀποτροπῆς χάριν), were precipitated from the Leucadian promontory, were in later times at least malefactors[4].

There appear to have been few sacrifices exclusively expiatory among the Egyptians, but whenever a victim was offered, a prayer was repeated over its head, "that if any calamity were about to

[1] If the eldest born of the family of Athamas entered the temple of the Laphystian Jupiter at Alos in Achaia, he was sacrificed, crowned with garlands like an animal victim (Her. 7, 197).

[2] Themistocles sacrificed three Persians to Διόνυσος 'Ωμήστης, before the battle at Salamis (Plut.

Them. 13). The omission of any mention of this by Herodotus cannot weigh against the precise account by Plutarch.

[3] Wachsmuth, ii. 2, 227. Ovid relates how the intended command of a human sacrifice was eluded by the ingenuity of Numa (Fasti, 3, 338):

Cæde *caput*, dixit. Cui Rex, parebimus, inquit;
Cædenda est hortis eruta *cepa* meis.
Addidit hic *hominis*. Summos ait ille *capillos*.
Postulat hic *animam*. Cui Numa *piscis* ait.

[4] Strabo. 10, p. 452.

befall either the sacrificers themselves, or the land of Egypt generally, it might be averted on this head." The head, after being cut off, was not eaten by the Egyptians[1], but thrown into the Nile, or sold to the Greeks in towns where they trafficked. This mode of averting evil was very analogous to the practice of the Jews in regard to the scape-goat. Aaron was commanded, once in the year, to take a live goat, chosen by lot for the purpose, and laying his hands upon his head, to confess over him all the iniquities and transgressions of the children of Israel and put them on the head of the goat, and send him away into the wilderness[2]. By this ceremony the people's apprehension of punishment for their sins was removed, and they could resume their worship without fear of its being unacceptable.

This ceremony was practised with all victims, but the evisceration and burning differed. In a sacrifice to Isis, which was one of the most solemn of all, the animal having been flayed, and the intestines, but not the other viscera, and the internal fat taken out, the neck and limbs were cut off, and the cavity of the body filled with bread, honey, raisins, figs and frankincense, with other odoriferous gums. The whole was then burnt, being plentifully basted with oil. The rites of Isis were partly of a lugu-

---

[1] Wilkinson observes (M. and C. 2, 377), that the head sometimes appears to be used for food by the Egyptians. There may have been exceptions even in the time of Herodotus (2, 39), and the sculptures in general belong to an age much earlier than his.

[2] Levit. xvi. 21. Deut. xxi. 1-9. If the author of a murder could not be found, a heifer was to be brought to the brink of a torrent, and its head struck off. So, according to Lev. iv. 1-12, the high-priests and elders were to lay their hands on the head of the victim, and thus transfer to it the sin of ignorance.

brious character, representing the death as well as the recovery of Osiris. A fast, therefore, preceded, and during the burning the worshipers beat themselves. When it was over, the portions of the victim which had been reserved were eaten, probably by the priests in conjunction with the offerers. Strabo[1] observes respecting the worship of Osiris at Abydos, that no music was used in the rites preliminary to the sacrifice, which was elsewhere the usual accompaniment, as among the Greeks and Romans. We find in the monuments no confirmation of the opinion that the Egyptians originally made only unbloody offerings to their gods[2]. It was probably a fiction, illustrative of the innocence of the primitive times, when the shedding of blood even in sacrifice was avoided[3]. They exhibit, however, a great variety of unbloody offerings. Almost all the characteristic productions of the country appear as gifts on the altars of the gods, especially the papyrus and the lotus, with the vegetables most esteemed for food, the water-melon, the radish and the onion, the grape and the fig, cakes, milk; wine and ointment. Birds, especially the goose or duck of the Nile, were offered in sacrifice by the Egyptians, as by the Jews; a practice less common among the Greeks and Romans. Gifts of objects not to be consumed were also made to the gods, among which the sitting figure of Truth is one of

[1] Ἐν τῇ Ἀβύδῳ τιμῶσι τὸν Ὄσιριν· ἐν δὲ τῷ ἱερῷ τοῦ Ὀσίριδος οὐκ ἔξεστιν οὔτε ᾠδὸν οὔτε αὐλητὴν οὔτε ψάλτην ἀπάρχεσθαι τῷ θεῷ καθάπερ τοῖς ἄλλοις θεοῖς ἔθος. 17, p. 814.

[2] Macrob. Saturn. 1, 7, p. 150. See p. 432 of this volume, note [4].

[3] Vetus illa aetas cui fecimus Aurea nomen
Fœtibus arhoreis et quas humus educat herbis
Fortunata fuit, nec polluit ora cruore.—Ov. Met. 15, 97.

the most common, emblematic of the sincerity of the worshiper. An image of Thoth, the god of knowledge, is frequently presented, or the *sistrum* with the head of Athor, a sceptre, a feather fan, a necklace[1]. The spoils taken in war were also offered to the gods in great variety[2], and *ex votos* suspended in their temples in commemoration of benefits conferred, especially in the cure of diseases[3]. The statues of the gods were anointed with perfumed ointment, which was also placed in vases as a gift before their shrine. The Egyptians were celebrated for the composition of ointments, among which were the Cyprine, perfumed by the Al-henneh plant, and the *sagdas*, of which the composition is unknown[4]. Wine, besides being poured in sacrifice over the head of the victim, was also used in libations. Incense of various kinds was burnt before the images of the gods. In the temple of the Sun, resin was burnt in the morning, myrrh at noon, and *kuphi* at sunset[5]. The composition of this last was complex and elaborate; sixteen fragrant substances entered into it, and those who were employed in compounding it read a formulary from the sacred books[6].

A priesthood numerous, richly endowed, and freed from the care of providing for themselves, like that of Egypt, naturally employs itself in making

---

[1] Rosell. M. R. tav. cxlvi. cxx. cxv. Wilk. M. and C. 5, 372.
[2] Rosell. M. R. lii. lix. lxxi.
[3] Wilk. M. and C. 3, 395.
[4] Athen. 15. p. 689. The *sagdas* was also called *psagdas*, *p* being the Coptic article.
[5] Plut. Is. et Osir. p. 383.
[6] In the composition of the sacred ointment of the Jews, myrrh, cinnamon, sweet reed, cassia and olive oil were employed (Exod. xxx. 22). Stacte, onycha, galbanum and frankincense were to be mixed together, for the perfume which was to be kept in the Tabernacle (ver. 34).

its ritual more minute and elaborate, in multiplying ceremonies and processions[1], and widening the separation between itself and the laity. Frequent and careful ablution is enjoined in Egypt by a regard to health and propriety; the priests bathed themselves in cold water, twice every day and twice every night. They shaved their bodies every other day, to prevent the possibility that vermin should harbour upon them, and wore garments of linen and sandals of papyrus only, that neither wool nor leather, being of animal origin, should be in contact with their persons. Their diet was chiefly flesh of oxen and geese[2]; fish they were forbidden to taste, and beans; both probably from dietetic motives originally[3], though the sanitary rule grew into a religious prohibition[4], and mystical reasons were devised for it, so that to the priest even the sight of a bean was a pollution. In regard to this the practice of different temples varied. The priests of the Casian Jupiter near Pelusium never touched onions, nor those of the Aphrodite (Athor) of Libya garlic; in other temples they abstained from mint, sweet marjoram, or parsley[5]. These refinements,

---

[1] Their ritual was comprised in ten books, "concerning sacrifices, first fruits, hymns, prayers, processions, festivals and such like." Clem. Al. Strom. 6, 758.

[2] Οὐ μόνον συῶν, ἀλλὰ προσέτι αἰγῶν, καὶ οἰῶν καὶ βοῶν (cows) καὶ ἰχθύων ἀπέχονται οἱ Αἰγυπτίων ἱερεῖς. Orig. c. Cels. 5, p. 264. With the exception of swine, cows and fish, it may be doubted if the prohibition extended beyond the nomes in which these animals were sacred.

[3] Herod. 2, 37. Cic. Div. 1, 30; 2, 58. Fish, though not absolutely an unhealthy, is an impoverishing food, and the fish of the Nile are watery and insipid. Rosellini, Mon. Civ. 1, 222.

[4] Plutarch, Is. et Os. p. 383 B. Ταῖς ἱερουργίαις καὶ ταῖς ἁγνείαις καὶ διαίταις οὐχ ἧττόν ἐστι τοῦ ὁσίου τὸ ὑγιεινόν.

[5] Sext. Emp. p. 173, Bekker.

which are recorded by late authorities, indicate a state in which the leisure of the priesthood was employed in systematizing superstition.

The practice of circumcision appears in its origin to have been national and not sacerdotal, and to have had no religious character[1]. According to Herodotus it was first introduced in Egypt, and imitated by other nations. He had found it among the Colchians[2], attesting the presence of the army of Sesostris in his Asiatic expedition; and from them it had been learnt in recent times by the Cappadocians and some other neighbouring tribes. He was uncertain whether the Ethiopians had learnt it from the Egyptians or the Egyptians from the Ethiopians, but inclined to the latter opinion. The Syrians in Palestine, among whom he says it also prevailed, are evidently the Jews. Among the Mesopotamian Syrians it appears to have been unknown. The Phœnicians, who practised it generally, had abandoned it where they had much intercourse with the Greeks. It appears from Diodorus (3, 31) that it was in use among the Troglodytes, who lived chiefly on the shores of the Red Sea, and were probably of Arabian origin. Besides the Jews, the Idumæans, the Ammonites, the Moabites and the Ishmaelites[3] had the same practice. The inhabitants of the cities of the Philistines[4], however, certainly had it not, nor those of the land of Canaan generally[5]. The Jews, however, appear to

---

[1] Her. 2, 37. Περιτάμνονται καθαριότητος εἵνεκε· προτιμῶντες καθαροὶ εἶναι ἢ εὐπρεπέστεροι.
[2] Her. 2, 104.
[3] Hieron. ad Jerem. 9, 25.
[4] 1 Sam. xviii. 27.
[5] Gen. xxxiv. 14. In the time of Josephus (c. Ap. 1, 42) the Jews alone practised it of all the nations of Palestine.

have been the only people in ancient times among whom it was strictly a national religious rite, and who therefore did not wait like the Egyptians till the age of fourteen, when reasons of health or purity might prompt to it, but submitted infants of eight days old[1] to circumcision. The words of Herodotus imply that it was general among the Egyptians, but not that it was strictly universal or commanded by law[2]. From the language of the book of Joshua (v. 9), in which uncircumcision is called "the reproach of Egypt," it should seem as if then it was held disreputable among the Egyptians not to have undergone this rite; in later times it appears to have been confined to the priests[3], and to those who devoted themselves to science and letters. Upon them it was probably imposed by the priesthood, as a troublesome initiation which would assist in excluding those who had no other motive than an idle curiosity[4]. It is even said by Origen, who could not be ignorant of the customs of Egypt at least in his own time, since he was a native of Alexandria,

[1] The narrative of the circumcision of her son by Zipporah (Exod. iv. 24) appears to indicate that it had begun to be neglected by the Jews in Egypt, and that Moses had omitted to perform it on his own sons. It must, however, have been known to Zipporah, since upon the sudden and dangerous illness of her husband, she conceives this to be the cause of the displeasure of Jehovah, and immediately performs the rite with such an instrument as she had at hand.

[2] Just before, speaking of the custom of washing their brazen vessels, he says very emphatically, οὐκ ὁ μὲν ὁ δ᾽ οὔ· ἀλλὰ πάντες· but this is not said of circumcision.

[3] Τοὺς ἱερέας ἐνθάδε μὲν ὁλοκλήρους νόμος
Εἶναι· παρ᾽ ὑμῖν δ᾽, ὡς ἔοικεν ἀπηργμένους.
Anaxandrides Athen. 7, 55. Ἀπάρχεσθαι was the action of the sacrificer, who cut off a small portion of the victim, and offered it to the god. Her. 4, 61. Hom. Od. γ´. 446, ξ´. 422. Joseph. c. Apion. 1, 22; 2, 13.

[4] Pythagoras is said to have been compelled to submit to circumcision, before the priests would admit him to the knowledge of their doctrines. Jablonsk. Panth. Proleg. § vii.

that without submitting to this rite, no one was allowed to study the hieroglyphical character[1]. From the examination of the mummies it appears that the practice was very limited, not extending to one in fifty[2]; but it must be remembered, that a large proportion of these are not of very high antiquity.

According to Diodorus[3], the priests married only one wife, while polygamy was allowed to the rest of the population. The sons were brought up by their fathers and instructed by them in the two kinds of writing, the sacred and the demotic[4]. It appears to be implied by Diodorus[5], though he does not expressly assert it, that the study of geometry and astronomy was also confined to the priests. There was a gradation of ranks among them. Besides the high-priest there was an order of *prophetæ*, who were the presidents of the temple, and whose duty it was to commit to memory the ten sacerdotal books, which contained everything relating to the laws and the gods and the education of the priests. To them also belonged the administration of the temple revenues. The *pastophori* had the

---

[1] Apud Ægyptios nullus aut geometrica studebat, aut astronomiæ secreta rimabatur, nisi circumcisione suscepta. Sacerdos apud eos, aruspex aut quorumlibet sacrorum minister, vel ut illi appellant prophetæ, omnis circumcisus est. Literas quoque sacerdotales veterum Ægyptiorum quas hieroglyphicas appellant nemo discebat nisi circumcisus. Origen, Comm. Ep. Rom. 2, 13.

[2] Madden, as quoted by Pettigrew on Mummies, p. 168. The French Commission, Mem. 3, 83, attest its existence. Wilkinson says—"The antiquity of circumcision in Egypt is fully established by the monuments of the Upper and the Lower Country, at a period long antecedent to the Exodus and the arrival of Joseph," but without specifying the evidence on which he relies. M. and C. 5, 318.

[3] 1, 80.

[4] 1, 81. See p. 326 of this vol.

[5] Οἱ μὲν ἱερεῖς, at the beginning of the section, appears to have its correlative in τὸ δὲ ἄλλο πλῆθος τῶν Αἰγυπτίων, a few lines from the end.

charge of the books relating to medicine; the *stolistes*, from his name, must have had the superintendence of the sacred vestments, and also kept the vessel for libations and the cubit of justice, the standard of long measure. He was also specially charged with the books which contained the rules for the sealing of the victims. The sacred scribes, or *hierogrammateis*, possessed the knowledge and had the regulation of everything relating to the sacred utensils, to measures of capacity, the furniture of the temples and the places specially consecrated to them; the course of the Nile and the topography of Egypt, the order of the sun, moon, and planets, geography, cosmography and hieroglyphics. The *horoscopus* was required to be familiar with the four books of Hermes which treated of astronomy (astrologia), and the *odos* or singer with those which contained the hymns to the gods, and the regulations for the life of the king[1]. It appears that the same degree of strictness was not required from all the orders of priests. According to Chæremon, quoted by Porphyry (de Abstin. 4, 8), "true philosophy" was found in the *prophetæ*, the *hierostolistæ*, the *hierogrammateis* and the *horologi*; the rest, including the *pastophori* (who carried shrines) and the *neocori* (who had the charge of the edifice and its cleanliness), and the rest of the subordinate ministers, were bound to personal

---

[1] The priests of Memphis are enumerated on the Rosetta Stone as οἱ ἀρχιερεῖς καὶ οἱ προφῆται καὶ οἱ εἰς τὸ ἄδυτον εἰσπορευόμενοι πρὸς τὸν στολισμὸν τῶν θεῶν καὶ πτερο- φόροι καὶ ἱερογραμματεῖς. Others are mentioned by the general name of priests, who appear to have come by delegation from the other temples of Egypt.

purity, but not the same strict abstinence as the others.

Herodotus says that in Egypt no woman was invested with a sacerdotal office[1]. It is evident, however, that women were not excluded from all functions about the temples, since he explains the origin of oracles at Dodona and Ammonium by the carrying off of sacred attendants from Thebes[2]. The monuments confirm his statement, when explained with this limitation, for nowhere does a female appear discharging a properly sacerdotal office; nor does the hieroglyphic for priest occur with the feminine termination. Women, however, are found making offerings to the gods; under the Ptolemies, in imitation of the Greeks, they were invested with the office of priestesses[3].

When Herodotus (2, 83) declares that the art of divination in Egypt belonged not to men, but to some of the gods, we learn from his words that the Egyptian priesthood retained in their own hands that powerful instrument for governing the minds of men, the power of predicting the future, or giving commands in the name of the Divinity. In other countries this power was hereditary in certain families, or was supposed to be possessed by individuals, who by superior sanctity had been admitted to the knowledge of the divine mind, or by mystic rites and invocations had obtained it from superhuman sources. In Homer, for example, we

---

[1] 2, 35.
[2] 2, 54. Ἔφασαν οἱ ἱρέες τοῦ Θηβαίου Διὸς, δύο γυναῖκας ἱρηΐας ἐκ Θηβέων ἐξαχθῆναι ὑπὸ Φοινίκων. One of these he describes afterwards as ἀμφιπολεύουσαν ἱρόν Διός.
[3] Rosetta, Inscr. Hierog. of Egyptian Soc. pl. 17, l. 3.

find that Calchas among the Greeks, and Helenus among the Trojans are possessed of a gift of divination, which proceeds from the gods, but is so far inherent in themselves, that they have no need to consult them in special cases. So Tiresias, though he appear specially as the soothsayer of the Ismenian Apollo, predicts, commands and threatens by virtue of the divine knowledge inherent in him, without consulting Apollo. The *gens* of the Iamidæ, the Clytiadæ, and the Telliadæ at Elis, appear for successive generations to have exercised the office of diviners. Others wandered through Greece, offering their skill to individuals or communities. These practices seem to have been unknown in Egypt, where the monopoly of the priesthood would have been encroached upon, by the intervention of those who did not belong to it. It is said indeed by the prophet Isaiah (xix. 3), describing the terror and confusion of the Egyptians, that they should seek to the idols, *and to the charmers, and to them that have familiar spirits.* But he is describing a time of general panic, when " the spirit of Egypt should fail in the midst thereof, and the counsel thereof be destroyed;" a state in which men are tempted to try new and forbidden means of delivering themselves from their perplexities; as Saul, deprived of the oracle of God, sought the witch of Endor.

The most celebrated oracles in Egypt were those of Hercules, Apollo, Minerva, Diana, Mars, Jupiter, and above all that of Latona in the city Buto[1]. The oracle of Hercules was probably at Canopus, where the god had a temple, and its fame seems

[1] Herod. 2, 111, 133.

afterwards to have been transferred to that of Serapis. The chief oracle of Apollo was at Apollinopolis Magna; of Minerva at Sais; of Diana at Bubastis; of Mars at Papremis; of Jupiter at Thebes and Ammonium. The modes of divination in these, Herodotus says, were different, without informing us what they were. One probably practised in all was divination by sacrifices. As the Greeks are said to have learnt their system from the Egyptians, we may presume that in the country in which it was indigenous, as in that into which it was imported, it implied the examination of the entrails of the victims, as well as the manner in which they burnt away upon the altar, with a clear and steady blaze, or a dull, sputtering and divided flame. We read in later times of an oracle at Abydos, in which a god named Besa was consulted by means of written tablets[1] containing inquiries or petitions. The god of Baalbek, whose worship is said to have been introduced from Heliopolis in Egypt[2], was consulted in the same way, and returned his answers in writing; so did some of the Grecian oracles. Ordinarily, however, it is probable that the votary propounded his question, and the *prophetes* (who derived his name from presiding over the oracle[3], not from *foreseeing* or *foretelling*) gave the answer.

It does not appear that augury, or divination from the flight of birds, was in use in Egypt; and we may conjecture the cause to have been,

---

[1] Ammian. Marcell. 19, 12.
[2] Macrob. Sat. 1, 23.
[3] At Delphi and Dodona Πρόμαντις was the equivalent title.

Herod. 2, 55. 6, 66. Comp. 8, 135, where the names are used as synonymous.

that superstition always attaches itself to something imperfectly known, and that in a country like Egypt, without woods or other hiding-places for birds, their habits would be too familiar to influence the imagination. Its uniform climate, in which rain and thunder are unknown, prevented divination from celestial phænomena, which in the electrical atmosphere of Etruria became a most important branch of the art. A thunder-storm would be reckoned among the prodigies, which Herodotus[1] says they most carefully recorded in writing with all their circumstances and consequences, inferring that whenever the prodigy recurred it would bring with it similar results. From these records the priests would expound to the people those events, which excite the curiosity of the popular mind, such as monstrous births, the speech of animals, unusual appearances of the Nile. The vulgar had besides, no doubt, their own modes of judging of the future. Good or evil was anticipated from the actions of Apis, and from his accepting or rejecting the food which visitors offered him; and probably a similar superstition attached to the other sacred animals. From the anecdote which Herodotus relates of Amasis[2], it appears that the oracles did not disdain to answer such questions as with us are proposed to " cunning men and women[3]." Before he came to the throne he had supplied himself by theft with the means of a voluptuous life, and had been often

---

[1] 2, 82. Τέρατά σφι πλέα ἀνεύρηται ἢ τοῖσι ἄλλοισι ἅπασι ἀνθρώποισι.
[2] 2, 174.
[3] Comp. 1 Sam. ix. 6, where Saul is represented as resorting to Samuel, to obtain information respecting his father's asses.

brought by those who suspected him before different oracles, some of which had acquitted and others had condemned him. Having the best possible evidence that the latter were correct, after his accession he paid all honour to their gods, as speakers of the truth, neglecting the former as liars, and giving nothing for the repair of their temples. From the books of Genesis and Exodus, we learn how great was the authority of dreams in Egypt, and that the interpretation of them belonged to the wise men and magicians[1], the *hierogrammateis* and *horoscopi* of the priestly body. Herodotus relates circumstances which show the same influence of dreams[2].

According to Champollion[3], the tomb of Rameses V. at Thebes contains tables of the constellations and of their influences for every hour of every month of the year. Thus in the latter half of the month *Tobi*, "Orion rules and influences at the first hour the left arm; Sirius, at the second, influences the heart; the Twins, at the third, the heart;" and so on[4]. A papyrus in the British Museum, of the age of Rameses III., contains a division of the days of the year into lucky and unlucky[5]. On the sarcophagus of Rameses IV., the twenty-four hours are represented, showing the antiquity of this division. Each has a star placed above it and a figure; twelve male, representing the day, have their face

---

[1] In Hebrew חרטמים, a name probably denoting *writers*. Gen. xli. 8.
[2] 2, 139.
[3] Lettres, p. 239.
[4] Lepsius (Einleitung, 1, 110) denies that the constellations are represented as having an influence upon the parts of the body, which he supposes to refer to some distribution of the heavens, represented under the symbol of the human figure.
[5] Dublin U. Mag. v. 28. p. 187.

turned towards the god Horus, the representative of the Sun; twelve female, towards a crocodile, the symbol of darkness[1]. In a great astronomical picture from the tombs at Bab-el-Melook, a variety of circumstances, connected with the rising and setting of the stars, are evidently indicated[2], but in the present state of our knowledge it is impossible to give the meaning of the Egyptian characters.

Herodotus[3] enumerates, besides sacrifices and divination, three religious ceremonies which the Egyptians had devised, and which the Greeks had borrowed from them. The *introductions*[4] are frequently represented in the monuments. Sometimes a god, sometimes a priest appears conducting a king by the hand to the presence of the tutelary god of the temple[5]. At other times the priest follows, offering a prayer or presenting a gift to the god[6]. The *processions*, πομπαί, were very numerous; spacious temples, lofty colonnades, and avenues of trees or mystic figures afforded an opportunity of making them most impressive to the spectators. The variety of garments by which the priests were distinguished, still more their symbolical head-dresses and the insignia which they carried in their hands, furnished additional means of gratifying the

---

[1] See the posthumous publication of Champollion's Drawings of Egyptian Antiquities, vol. 3, 272, 274.

[2] Ibid. vol. 3, p. 277.

[3] 2, 58. Πανηγύρις δὲ ἄρα καὶ πομπὰς καὶ προσαγωγὰς πρῶτοι ἀνθρώπων Αἰγύπτιοί εἰσι οἱ ποιησάμενοι· καὶ παρὰ τούτων Ἕλληνες μεμαθήκασι.

[4] Comp. Eph. ii. 18. Δι' οὗ ἔχομεν τὴν προσαγωγὴν πρὸς τὸν πατέρα.

[5] Rosellini, M. del Culto, vi. 2, viii. 1. M. Reali, clxiv. 3. In all these cases Horus is the conducting god, if it be not rather a priest wearing the insignia of Horus.

[6] Rosellini, M. R. cxlix. 1, 3. The priest who is represented as following, may be understood according to Egyptian art, as standing *beside* the king.

eye, while the religious character of the spectacle was maintained. Clemens Alexandrinus[1] has described the order in which the five different classes of priests appeared on these occasions, the Singer opening the procession, followed by the Horoscopus, the Hierogrammat and the Stolistes, the Prophetes as highest in dignity closing it. The monuments exhibit these different orders, but not in exact correspondence with this description. The most splendid processions were those in which the images of the gods were carried about and displayed to their worshipers, from whose view they were ordinarily hidden in the recesses of the temples, or if not the images themselves, more portable copies of them. Such processions were called *Comasiæ* by the Greeks, and the priests who carried the images *Comastæ*[2]. It has been supposed that an early reference to this custom is found in the Iliad (α', 424), where Jupiter and the gods are said to have gone to feast for twelve days " with the blameless Ethiopians." According to Diodorus[3], this originated in the custom of carrying the image of Jupiter across the river into Libya and bringing it back some days after. It is very probable, considering how many of the religious edifices of Thebes were on the Libyan side of the river, that such a custom existed; we have indeed positive proof of it in the Ptolemaic times[4], but it could never give rise to a

---

[1] Strom. 6, p. 757, ed. Potter. Compare p. 450 of this volume.

[2] Strom. 5, p. 671, Potter. Ἐν ταῖς καλουμέναις παρ' αὐτοῖς κωμασίαις. Diod. Sic. 3, 4, with Wesseling's note.

[3] 1, 97.

[4] Peyron, Papyr. Græc. 1, p. 3, l. 2. πρὸς τὴν διάβασιν τοῦ μεγίστου θεοῦ Ἀμμῶνος (p. 8, l. 20).

story of his going *up* the river into Ethiopia. These Ethiopians, whom Homer places on the verge of the ocean, that is, the remotest point of the world towards the South, were invested, like the Hyperboreans who lived in the extreme North, with qualities which fitted them to be the associates of the gods; and hence the story of the annual visit of Jupiter and the Olympian deities to them for twelve days. The account of Diodorus betrays itself to be one of those accommodations of Egyptian history and customs to Greek mythology which had begun in the time of Herodotus, but greatly increased before Diodorus wrote. That processions with the images of the gods, however, were made by water, is probable not only from the circumstance that the Nile was the nation's highway, and that the temples generally stood near it, but also from the manner of their transport, even when not taken beyond the limits of the temples. The image of the god, or the sacred animal which was his symbol, is seen placed in a boat (*bari*), sometimes exposed to view, at other times concealed in a shrine; and we find an officer of the court of Thothmes V. described in his tomb as "having charge of the *bari* of Ammon[1]." No other reason for the adoption of this form is so obvious, as that boats were actually employed in early times, and retained as symbols, even in processions wholly made by land.

In form these processional boats, shallow and highly curved at each end, resemble those in which the embalmed bodies are represented as conveyed across the Nile at Thebes to their place of inter-

[1] Rosellini, Mon. Storici, iii. 1, 212.

ment in the Libyan hills[1]. They are adorned at the stern and prow with the characteristic symbol of the gods, as the ram's head of Kneph, the sacred lotus, the hawk's head of Horus. The god himself is either seated in the centre of the *bari*, or this place is occupied by a shrine richly adorned with sacred emblems, in which he is at times concealed, at others disclosed. On the model of such a shrine as this the Ark of the Covenant of the Hebrews appears to have been constructed, which contained the Tables of the Law, the Pot of Manna and the Rod of Aaron. The mixed figure of the Cherubim which were placed at either end and overshadowed it with their wings, has a parallel in some of those Egyptian representations in which kneeling figures spread their wings over the shrine[2]. Sometimes the shrine was not placed on a boat, but the image of the god stood upright upon a platform, supported by poles which the priests carried[3]. In this also we see a resemblance to the Ark of the Covenant, which was furnished with rings through which poles were passed for transporting it from place to place. The shrine was thus borne around the sacred precincts, and rested in some conspicuous place, where incense was burnt and sacrifices and offerings made before it. If the temple was dedicated to more than one god, their images were borne together. Clemens Alexandrinus mentions the re-

[1] See Wilkinson, M. & C. plates 83, 84.
[2] Wilkinson, M. & C. 5, 276. The word כְּרוּבִים, which has no etymology in the Semitic languages, is probably allied to the γρύψ of the Greeks.
[3] Jer. x. 5: "They (the idols) are upright as the palm tree, but speak not; they must needs be borne because they cannot go." Also Is. xlvi. 7.

presentations of two dogs (denoting the upper and lower hemisphere), a hawk and an ibis, as carried by the Egyptians in their sacred processions. The figure of Anubis, with the head of a jackal, which the Greeks took for a dog, the hawk of Horus, and the ibis of Thoth, are often seen among the sacred emblems thus carried; but it does not appear on what occasion these four alone were used.

On the walls of the great temple at Esneh and the palace of Medinet Aboo[1] we find portions of the sacred calendar of these places, in which the order and ceremonies of sacrifice and procession throughout the year have been recorded. These, however, are mere local rubrics for the worship of each place. Unless we should be fortunate enough to discover, among the remains of Egyptian writing, some work analogous to the *Fasti* of the Romans, we must remain ignorant of the yearly cycle of the festivals and sacrifices which the whole nation celebrated. Some of them from their nature were appropriate only to certain seasons of the year. Plutarch says that the ceremony called the disappearance of Osiris was celebrated on the seventeenth of the month Athyr (October), and that it represented the decrease of the waters of the Nile, the cessation of the Etesian winds, the increase of darkness and diminution of light, and the nakedness of the land through the fall of the leaf. The rites of mourning, which Plutarch describes as performed by the priests, for four successive days from the seventeenth of Athyr[2], when they clothed the image of the cow

---

[1] Champollion, Lettr. d'Egypte, p. 203, 360.

[2] Is. et Os. § 39. p. 366.

which symbolized Isis with a black veil, belong necessarily to the decline of the year[1]. The subsequent ceremony at the supposed finding of Osiris, when the priests went to the seashore on the 19th of the month, and mixing a portion of earth with fresh water formed an image of the clay, in the shape of a lunar crescent, crying out that Osiris was found[2], marks the season of the year when the water of the Nile might be expected to return. The festival kept in honour of the return of Isis from Phœnicia, when cakes were offered to her marked with a hippopotamus, the symbol of Typhon, expresses the triumph of light over darkness, at the winter solstice. The feast called the " Entrance of Osiris into the Moon," was celebrated at the new moon of the month Phamenoth or March, the beginning of spring, and was evidently designed to symbolize the renewed fertility of the earth[3]. This was the occasion, probably, on which alone, according to Herodotus[4], it was lawful in Egypt to sacrifice swine, Dionusos and the Moon in his account answering to Osiris and Isis. On the vigil of the festival every man sacrificed a swine before his own door to Dionusos, and then gave it to be carried away by the swineherd of whom he had

[1] See p. 332 of this volume, note [4].

[2] Plut. *u. s.* does not say on the 19th of what month this ceremony was performed; but it cannot have been of Athyr, for the mourning lasted from the 17th to the 20th inclusive. Jablonsky conjectured *Tybi* (January), in which month the lengthening of the days begins to be visible; Wyttenbach *Pharmuthi* (April); Wilkinson, M. & C. 5, 301, *Pachons* (May). None of these alterations has any critical authority, and it appears that Plutarch had omitted the mention of the month.

[3] Plut. Is. et Os. § 43, p. 368.

[4] Plut. *u. s.* Herodotus, 2, 47, says on the *full* moon, but probably the same festival is meant. Lepsius thinks a festival was kept at the beginning and in the middle of each lunation. Einleitung, 1, p. 157.

purchased it. But on the day of the festival itself, the swine that had been sacrificed was eaten, the internal fat, with the extremity of the tail, having been burnt[1]. Another festival fixed by its nature to a particular time of the year was the *Niloa*, which Heliodorus[2] describes as being celebrated about the summer solstice and at the first rise of the waters of the Nile; which was popularly conceived as the mixture of earth and water, the source of all life, but mystically as the union of Isis and Osiris. At this festival the priests were accustomed to drop a piece of money and the præfects gifts of gold into the Nile near Philæ[3].

The *panegyries* differed from the other festivals, as they brought together, not the worshipers at a single temple, or the inhabitants of a single nome, but of all Egypt. The panegyries which in the Rosetta inscription the priests of Memphis decree in honour of Ptolemy Epiphanes, were to begin on the first of the month Thoth, in all the temples of Egypt, and sacrifices and libations were to be performed. But the panegyries of which Herodotus speaks[4], resembled the Olympian and Pythian games, which collected the people from all parts of Greece at one spot. They were all held at temples in Lower Egypt, where the population was most abundant, and the means of transport by the branches of the river and the canals were most ready. The greatest resort of

---

[1] The universality of this festival may account for the circumstance, that notwithstanding their impurity, large herds of swine were kept in Egypt. The tomb of Ranni, a military man, but of the sacerdotal order, at Eilithyia, exhibits a *cen-sus* of his stock of animals of different kinds, and among them are 1500 swine. Rosellini, M. Civ. 1, 266.

[2] Heliod. Æth. 9, 9.

[3] Sen. N. Q. 4, 2, 7.

[4] 2, 58.

all was to the temple of Artemis at Bubastis, which was near the Pelusiac branch of the Nile. A crowd of both sexes embarked on one of the large boats called *bari*, which were used for navigating the Nile. As they were carried down the stream some of the men played on the pipe and the women on the cymbals, whose noisy music was especially adapted to excite the passions, while the rest sang and beat time with their hands; and when they reached any town on the bank, they ran their boat along shore. The celebration of the festival of a female divinity seems in Egypt, as in the festival of Ceres at Eleusis, to have given unusual licence to the female sex, and as they danced and shouted, they jeered the women of the place with indecent gestures[1]. When they arrived at Bubastis they offered numerous sacrifices, and more wine was consumed in this festival (the historian means probably in libations) than in all the rest of the year. The numbers who assembled were estimated by the natives at 700,000 persons, besides children. There is a propensity to exaggeration in all such estimates, which besides can never be accurately made; but from the example of the Jewish Passover, the pilgrimage to Mecca and those of the Hindus, we see how congenial is this resort of crowds to a consecrated spot, to the temper of oriental nations. In regard to the number which flocked to it, the festival of Isis at Busiris came next to that of Artemis. The sacrifice to this goddess has been already

---

[1] The account given by Clemens Alex. Coh. vol. 1, p. 17, Potter, of the gestures of Baubo, in endeavouring to divert the melancholy of Ceres, exhibits a literal correspondence with the words of Herodotus. Even in Sparta the festivals of Diana were not free from licentious words and gestures. See Lobeck, Aglaoph. p. 1086.

described; as the festival had a reference to the death of Osiris, the votaries, men and women, beat their breasts while those portions of the victim were consumed which were placed upon the altar. Herodotus remarks that the Carians who settled in Egypt went beyond the Egyptians themselves in the expression of their grief, and wounded their foreheads with knives, according to the barbarous customs of the Asiatic nations[1]. The festival of Mars at Papremis, however, was celebrated in a manner more characteristic of the fanatical character of these foreigners than of the Egyptians. Sacrifices were performed, as elsewhere; but when the sun was setting, some of the priests endeavoured to wheel back into the temple the image and gilded shrine of the god, which had been taken the preceding day into a sacred edifice near at hand. Their entrance was opposed by the rest, who stationed themselves, armed with clubs, at the gate; and the party who sought admission being aided by the votaries, who had also furnished themselves with clubs, a battle ensued, in which many wounds were inflicted; and, as Herodotus believed, lives lost. The legend of the priests explained the custom as commemorating the forcible entrance which Mars made into the temple, when he wished to visit[2] his mother after a long absence, in which the priests had forgotten his person. More probably it had a reference to the warlike attributes of the god, and may have been a

---

[1] Comp. Deut. xiv. 1. Wounding the forehead at a private funeral is probably there intended; but this was no doubt the origin of the same practice in the funereal mysteries.

[2] There is a doubt respecting the meaning of the passage in Her. 2, 64. Compare note ([3]), p. 435.

substitute for a combat with more deadly weapons. The feast of Isis-Neith at Sais was accompanied with a general illumination on one of the nights. It was performed, according to the custom of the southern nations, not within, but around the houses, by means of shallow saucers filled with oil and salt, and those who were prevented from attending the festival illuminated their respective cities. Neither Herodotus nor any other author has mentioned at what season of the year this festival took place, or what was its import[1]. We may conjecture, that as the inscription in the temple of Neith declared her to be the mother of the Sun[2], this kindling of lamps may have been intended to celebrate her as author of light. In a country whose religion was less symbolical than that of Egypt, we might have been contented to explain it only as a proof of that association of festivity with artificial light, which shows itself in the customs of all nations. The festival in honour of Latona at Buto, and of the Sun at Heliopolis, consisted only of sacrifices. The sacrifice of a swine to Dionusos has been already mentioned. In other respects the festivals in his honour appear to have been conducted, as among the Greeks, with indecent emblems, and processions led by the pipe, while the women followed singing the praises of the god. The choral dances, which from the first formed a part of the festival among the Greeks, and ultimately gave birth to the drama, were unknown to the Egyptians[3], and the festival seems always to have been confined in Egypt to

---

[1] There was a ἱερὸς λόγος, but he does not mention it (2, 62).
[2] See note (¹), p. 3?9.
[3] Τὴν ἄλλην ἀνάγουσι ὁρτὴν τῷ Διονύσῳ οἱ Αἰγύπτιοι, πλὴν χορῶν, κατὰ ταὐτὰ Ἕλλησι. Her. 2, 48.

the villages, as it was in its rudest state in Greece[1]. Herodotus believed that Melampus taught the Greeks the custom of phallic processions in honour of Dionusos, having himself learnt it from the Phœnicians who had settled in Bœotia with Cadmus. The festival which Plutarch[2] calls Paamylia, and supposes to have derived its name from Paamyles, who announced the birth of Osiris to the world, was evidently a phallic ceremony of the kind described by Herodotus.

There were other rites connected with this god in Egypt, of a very different character from the processions and village-festivals which have been just described. "There is at Sais," says Herodotus[3], "in the temple of Minerva, a burial-place of Him, whom in such a connexion I deem it not lawful to mention," that is, of Osiris; "and adjoining to the temple a lake. In this lake imitative representations of his sufferings are performed by night, which the Egyptians call *mysteries*. 1 know more particulars about these things; but let them remain buried in silence." These sufferings were no doubt the adventures of Osiris, when he was enclosed in the chest by Typhon, and afterwards cut to pieces. As the body was floated down the Nile, and carried to Byblos, and as Isis embarked on the Nile to collect the portions of his body, we see why a piece of water was chosen for the performance of these mysteries. The mysteries of

---

[1] Her. 2, 48. σφί ἐστι ἐξευρημένα ὅσον τε πηχυαῖα ἀγάλματα νευρόσπαστα, τὰ περιφορέουσι κατὰ κώμας γυναῖκες. Arist. Poet. 5. Κωμῳδοὺς οὐκ ἀπὸ τοῦ κωμάζειν λεχθέντας, ἀλλὰ τῇ κατὰ κώμας πλάνῃ ἀτιμαζομένους ἐκ τοῦ ἄστεως.
[2] Is. et Osir. § 12, p. 355.
[3] 2, 171.

Ceres, called Thesmophoria by the Greeks, concerning the nature of which Herodotus in the same passage declines to speak, had also been brought from Egypt. The daughters of Danaus had taught this rite to the Pelasgian females of the Peloponnesus. When the Peloponnesus was conquered by the Dorians, and the old inhabitants expelled, Arcadia alone retained its original population and the rites of Ceres. The reason for his silence was in both cases the same; it was inauspicious to mention death and Hades[1] in connexion with a god; Osiris had been killed by Typhon, and Proserpine carried to the unseen world by Pluto. The mysteries related to the deaths and sufferings of the gods[2]. It does not appear that in Egypt they were otherwise separated from the popular religion, than by the circumstance of the nocturnal gloom in which from their nature they were celebrated. Even the Eleusinian mysteries were open to every one who spoke the Greek language and was not stained with crime. Men were excluded by their sex from the Thesmophoria. In the Bacchanalian mysteries, where licence undoubtedly prevailed, means were taken to prevent the entrance of all who did not belong to the association; but these appear to be later corruptions[3].

When we read of foreigners being obliged to submit to painful and tedious ceremonies of initiation, it was not that they might learn the secret meaning of the rites of Osiris or Isis, but that they might

[1] Comp. Her. 2, 132.
[2] Considera sacra ipsa et mysteria; invenies exitus tristes, fata, funera miserorum deorum (Min. Felix, 21, 195). This will explain Cic. Tusc. 1, 12, 13, without supposing with Warburton (D. L. 1, 152) that Euhemerism was taught in the mysteries.
[3] Comp. Liv. lib. 39.

partake of the knowledge of astronomy, physic, geometry and theology, of which the priests were supposed to have exclusive possession. It was only when transferred to Greece, where a public religion was already established with which they were not congenial, that the Egyptian rites connected with the history of Osiris became a secret religion. In their origin they had no immoral character[1]; but large crowds of both sexes cannot be assembled and drawn to a distance from their homes without danger to morals. Secret nocturnal assemblages afford the opportunity of licence, and in the corruption of manners which overspread the Roman empire, the Eleusinian mysteries may have degenerated so far, as to deserve the character given of them by the Christian Fathers. We must not pronounce that the spectacle which would grossly offend our eyes argues a depraved heart in those to whom it bore a sacred character; nor make religion responsible for the mischief which results from *holy fairs*. The Christian Church was compelled to put an end to nocturnal festivals[2] from their flagitious consequences. But it is impossible that either in Egypt or in the days of Athenian independence, licentiousness can have been sanctioned as a part of their religious rites. It was different with the Isiac rites, which make their appearance towards the end of the Roman republic; initiation into them was a source of gain to vagabond priests of both sexes, and they seem often to have been

---

[1] The Bacchanalian religion itself appears in its origin to have been ascetic rather than licentious (Eur. Hipp. 959).

[2] See Warburton, D. L. 1, 169.

abused. Yet even they numbered many among their votaries who were superstitious, but sincere and ascetic in their practice[1], at least for the time.

It is probable that the different orders of Egyptian priests would possess in very different degrees the knowledge of their theological system : while the majority were trained in the ceremonial duties of the temple and the altar, few only were acquainted with their import and history, and the metaphysical doctrines which had either given birth to their religion or been devised for its explanation. Such gradations must exist in every body, even through the difference of natural capacity; in Egypt they seem to have been connected with a graduated scale of instruction, each order being taught to read the books, in which their own duties and the doctrines belonging to them were contained[2]. But it does not appear that the ascent from one step of knowledge to another was accomplished by undergoing a series of trials, increasing in severity according to the sublimity of the truth to be communicated. These have been minutely described by some writers without any warrant either from the monuments of Egypt or from historical sources. They have taken for granted that there must have existed a very close correspondence between the Eleusinian mysteries of Ceres and the ceremonies by which aspirants were admitted to the knowledge of the esoteric doctrines of Egypt. There is no

---

[1] Propert. Eleg. 2, 33.

[2] Αἰγύπτιοι οὐ τοῖς ἐπιτυχοῦσι τὰ παρὰ σφίσιν ἀνετίθεντο μυστήρια οὐδὲ μὴν βεβήλοις τὴν τῶν θείων εἴδησιν ἐξέφερον, ἀλλ' ἢ μόνοις γε τοῖς μέλλουσιν ἐπὶ τὴν βασιλείαν προϊέναι· καὶ τῶν ἱερέων τοῖς κριθεῖσιν εἶναι δοκιμωτάτοις ἀπὸ τῆς τροφῆς καὶ τῆς παιδείας καὶ τοῦ γένους. Clem. Alex. Strom. 5, p. 670, ed. Potter.

evidence, however, that any esoteric doctrines were taught in the Eleusinian mysteries. They were accompanied with various rites, expressive of the purity and self-denial of the worshiper, and were therefore considered to be an expiation of past sins, and to place the initiated under the especial protection of the awful and potent goddesses who presided over them. The mythic history of Ceres, Proserpine and Bacchus, was repeated in symbolical actions; and in these, and in the hymns which were sung, there must have been much that had reference to the unseen world; the very act of initiation into their mysteries was supposed to prepare for the votary a more favourable reception from them, when he reached the realm over which they presided[1]. In this sense the doctrine of a future life may be said to have been taught in them; but it was a part of the popular belief, no esoteric doctrine of the mysteries, nor was it inculcated in any purer and more spiritual form, but in the same mythological garb in which it had been long familiar. In Egypt the belief in a future life was mixed with the doctrine of the metempsychosis, but it is very doubtful whether this entered into the Eleusinian mysteries[2]. There is no trace whatever of the communication of any doctrine at Eleusis respecting the gods at variance with the popular creed, or of a system of cosmogony and metaphysics; and therefore as far as an argument from analogy can avail,

[1] Schol. Aristid. p. 101, quoted by Lobeck, Eleusinia, p. 73. Ἔλεγον οἱ Ἕλληνες ὡς οἱ τὰ μυστήρια μυηθέντες εὐμενοῦς καὶ ἴλεω τῆς Περσεφόνης ἐτύγχανον. Cicero (Leg. 2, 14) expresses himself less mythologically: "Neque solum (a mysteriis) cum lætitia vivendi rationem accepimus, sed etiam cum spe meliore moriendi."
[2] See Lobeck, u. s.

we are authorized to conclude, that what Herodotus calls the mysteries of Egypt conveyed no such information on these points.

Besides annual festivals, the Egyptians, like the Greeks and Romans, must have had others of less frequent occurrence. Such was the finding of Apis, which must have recurred every quarter of a century, if not oftener, as if he survived that term he was put to death. Ptolemy Epiphanes, on the Rosetta Stone, is called " Lord of the Triaconterides," or Panegyry of Thirty Years; and though the corresponding hieroglyphic is wanting, from the fracture of the stone, it has been ascertained from other monuments, and is found as early as the sixth dynasty[1], and is afterwards a regular title of the Egyptian kings. Probably it had reference to some astronomical period, but no satisfactory explanation has been given either of this or of the name *Set*, which is found connected with the hieroglyphic of the Panegyries.

SECT. III.—DOCTRINE OF A FUTURE LIFE.

It appears almost impossible for man not to conceive of himself as composed of two elements, a corporeal and a spiritual principle, to which a different destiny is assigned, when their temporary union is dissolved by death. The larger and grosser part is visibly restored to the earth; but it is only

---

[1] Lepsius, Einleitung in die Chronologie, 1, p. 161, 165, quotes Dion Cassius, 62, p. 1023, as the only passage of an ancient author in which mention is made of a *tria-conteris*. Thrasea, ἐν Παταβίῳ τῇ πατρίδι τραγῳδίαν κατά τι πάτριον ἐν ἑορτῇ τινι τριακονταετηρίδι ὑποκρινάμενος.

by the analogical reasonings of philosophy that men have ever been brought to believe that the soul is involved in the same destruction. The instinct of nature prompts to a belief in its continued existence, which is the more easily cherished, because it has no sensible properties distinct from matter. But wide differences appear among nations, in regard to the degrees of activity and enjoyment attributed to the soul in its separate state. The Jews, before they had become acquainted in the Captivity with the Zoroastrian doctrine of a resurrection, conceived of the grave as a place in which the souls of the dead repose in a state of inactivity and unconsciousness[1], though not of extinction. The question of Samuel to Saul, "Why hast thou *disquieted* me to bring me up?[2]" indicates that the dead were supposed to be simply at rest in the grave, yet in such a state that they might by necromantic arts be temporarily recalled to consciousness. The sublime description of Isaiah[3], in which the dead are roused up to meet the king of Babylon, is framed on the supposition that they are ordinarily in a state of unconsciousness, which might, however, be broken by the strong excitement of curiosity to welcome a new visitant, and of revenge to triumph over a fallen enemy. The condition of the dead as described by Homer is not very different from this. The soul is not annihilated by death, but it is removed to a land of mist and shadows, beyond the remotest habitations of men, where it dwells in such

---

[1] Even the good Hezekiah speaks of death as a state in which there could be no praise of God, and therefore no conscious existence for the pious. Isaiah xxxviii. 18.

[2] 1 Sam. xxviii. 15.
[3] xiv. 9.

a state of feebleness[1] that it cannot exercise its powers till it has been revived by a libation of blood, and thus in some measure reunited to the former cause of its life[2]. The greatest of the Grecian heroes declares that he would gladly assume the place of a hireling, if he might return to the upper world[3]. Neither among the Jews nor the Greeks was this state believed to be one of retribution for mankind generally. Only a few personages of mythic celebrity are represented as undergoing a special punishment for their crimes, which is itself a prolongation or symbolical representation of their history on earth, not the result of any judgement passed upon them before their entrance into the world of spirits. Minos indeed appears exercising the office of a judge *among* the dead, who plead their causes before him; but this is only a continuation of his earthly office, as Orion chases the shadows of the wild beasts whom he had slain, or the heroes in Virgil's Elysium delight themselves in the care of horses, arms and chariots[4]. It was a later conception to make Minos (with Æacus and Rhadamanthys) the judges who decided on the characters of the dead, and allotted them their place with the blessed or the damned[5]. Hesiod in his Works and

[1] Πῶς ἔτλης ἀϊδόσδε κατελθέμεν, ἔνθα τε νεκροί
'Αφραδέες ναίουσι, βροτῶν εἴδωλα καμόντων;
Od. λ', 474. I¹. ψ', 72.

[2] Od. λ', 141, 151. Teiresias is an exception, and by the special favour of Proserpine retains his faculties (κ', 490).

Od. λ', 488.
Æn. 6, 653.

[5] Compare Homer, Od. λ', 567, with Virg. Æn. 6, 429.

Ἔνθ' ἤτοι Μίνωα ἴδον, Διὸς ἀγλαὸν υἱὸν
Χρύσεον σκῆπτρον ἔχοντα, θεμιστεύοντα νεκύεσσιν
Ἥμενον· οἱ δέ μιν ἀμφὶ δίκας εἴροντο ἄνακτα.

Nec vero hæ sine sorte datæ, sine judice sedes.
Quæsitor Minos urnam movet; ille silentum
Concihumque vocat, vitasque et crimina discit.

Days (166) assigns to his heroes a dwelling-place in the Islands of the Happy; but no judgement or probation precedes. The entire race was half-divine, juster and better than its predecessor. Menelaus, according to the prediction of Proteus[1], was to be transferred without dying to the Elysian plains in the extremity of the world, where Rhadamanthys dwells, where Earth yields an easy sustenance to men, and Zephyrs from the Ocean maintain a genial temperature, without snow or thick rain. In this description also there is no mention of a previous judgement.

The state of belief in regard to a future life and retribution among the Jews, for many centuries after their departure from Egypt, whose rites and worship they were so prone to adopt, leads to the suspicion that it was not an object of *popular* faith among the Egyptians themselves in the earliest ages. If it be true that the original reason of embalmment was that the soul was believed not to quit the body till the body decayed, and might be detained in a state of consciousness while that change could be averted[2], we can understand the extraordinary pains which they bestowed in ornamenting their tombs and covering their walls with paintings exhibiting the scenes of daily life; not merely those in which the deceased had been personally engaged; for the variety found in a single tomb precludes this idea; but all that could recall to him the remembrance of his actual experience. They could minister nothing

---

[1] Od. δ', 560.
[2] Serv. ad Æn. 3, 68. Ægyptii periti sapientiæ condita diutius servant cadavera, scilicet ut anima multo tempore perduret et sit corpori obnoxia, ne cito ad alia transeat.

to the gratification of the living, since they would be seen only when a new tenant was added to the occupants of the sepulchre. The reason which they assigned for bestowing so much more pains on their tombs than on their dwellings was, that the tomb was man's everlasting habitation, the house only his temporary lodging[1]. But had it been a popular belief that the soul was either entirely detached from the body or performing its rounds through those of inferior animals, such a conception of the tomb could scarcely have originated. If on the contrary it remained connected with the body as long as it could be preserved from putrefaction, that is, by the embalmer's art, for an indefinite period, we see a sufficient motive for surrounding it with the implements which it had used in life and representations of the scenes amidst which it had been passed. The same motive will explain the custom of painting on the mummy-cases, before tombs were so elaborately adorned, the various articles of dress and armour which the deceased had worn, and of the food on which he had lived. The Egyptian notion then would differ from the Jewish, inasmuch as according to the latter the usual condition of the departed spirit was complete unconsciousness; and from the Greek, inasmuch as the Greek was a state of imperfect consciousness without activity or enjoyment;

---

[1] Diod. Sic. 1, 51. Τὰς μὲν τῶν ζώντων οἰκήσεις καταλύσεις ὀνομάζουσιν, ὡς ὀλίγον χρόνον ἐν ταύταις οἰκούντων ἡμῶν, τοὺς δὲ τῶν τετελευκότων τάφους ἀϊδίους οἴκους προσαγορευούσιν, ὡς ἐν ᾅδου διατελούντων τὸν ἄπειρον αἰῶνα. Here *Hades* is evidently used for a *state* rather than a place, otherwise the sepulchre could not be called the everlasting dwelling. In Ecclesiastes xii. 5, בית עולם, which our Translators have rendered " his long home," is in the Septuagint " his everlasting home," οἶκον αἰῶνος.

whereas, according to the Egyptians, the progress of death could be arrested and the soul kept in a state by which its living condition was closely imitated.

It is generally supposed, however, that the form under which the Egyptians believed in a state after death, was that of the Transmigration of Souls. Herodotus, having mentioned the descent of Rhampsinitus alive into Hades, and the supremacy of Demeter and Dionusos, that is Isis and Osiris, over that region, proceeds[1]: "The Egyptians are the first who declared this doctrine also, that the soul of man is immortal, and that when the body decays the soul enters into another animal successively at its birth; and when it has gone round all the terrestrial and marine animals, and all the flying creatures, it enters again into the body of a man at its birth; and this circuit of the soul is performed in 3000 years. Some of the Greeks have made use of this doctrine, both in former and in later times, as if it were their own, whose names I write not, though I know them." These no doubt are Orpheus and Pythagoras[2], or his preceptor Pherecydes.

There is an ambiguity in the construction of this sentence which leaves it doubtful, whether Herodotus meant to say that the Egyptians were the first who taught the doctrine of the immortality of the soul, or only the first who taught the doctrine of immortality combined with that of transmigration. Evidently the latter part of the sentence must refer to the same doctrine as the former; and as it was

---

[1] 2, 123.   εἰς πᾶν ζῶον τῆς ψυχῆς μεταβολὴν
[2] Diod. 1, 98. Πυθαγόραντ ἦν μαθεῖν παρ' Αἰγυπτίων.

not the doctrine of the soul's immortality only, but also of its transmigration, which Orpheus and Pythagoras taught, it may seem that our author meant to assert the same of the Egyptians. Cicero, however, referring to the same school of philosophy, says that Pythagoras or Pherecydes was the first who taught that human souls were eternal, "animos hominum esse sempiternos[1]." This may seem inconsistent with the facts already stated respecting the belief of the Greeks in the Homeric age. Yet the existence attributed to the *manes* was of that inert and unconscious kind, which partakes more of the quality of death than life; and therefore Herodotus in speaking of the Egyptian and Cicero of the Pythagorean doctrine, may have meant to imply, that they first attributed a real immortality, an indestructible active existence to the soul.

Another question raised respecting this passage of Herodotus is, whether he meant to say that the soul did not quit the body till it was completely resolved and decayed, so that he may have alluded to the practice of embalmment, as intended to delay this change and the commencement of transmigration indefinitely; or whether by "when the body decays[2]," he meant merely to describe death by its usual accompaniment. It appears that the latter was his meaning, or he would have used a tense which would have denoted that the act of decay must be completed.

Herodotus does not speak of this transmigration as connected either with reward or punishment. The soul does not, according to him, pass into the body

---

[1] Tusc. 1, 16.   [2] Καταφθίνοντος τοῦ σώματος.

of a clean or unclean animal, one of a higher or lower rank in creation, according to the guilt or merit of its actions in the body. It accomplishes of necessity the whole round of the kingdoms of animated nature, and at the end of 3000 years again enters a human body. So far the Indian doctrine of metempsychosis agrees with the Egyptian; the soul must pass through the bodies of animals; but when it is added, in order that by the trials which it endures in this process it may be prepared for re-union with the divine soul, of which it is an emanation, this has nothing correspondent in the Egyptian doctrine as stated by Herodotus, who seems to have supposed that the circuit would be perpetual. In the later Pythagoreans we meet with this doctrine of the ultimate reception of the soul into the divine nature; whether it were a part of the primitive philosophy of Pythagoras is doubtful. Ovid represents him as teaching a perpetual transition from the human to the animal body, and *vice versâ*:

> Omnia mutantur; nihil interit; errat et illinc
> Huc venit, hinc illuc et quoslibet occupat artus
> Spiritus, eque feris humana in corpora transit,
> Inque feras noster, nec tempore deperit ullo.—Met. 15, 165.

Whether the Egyptian doctrine comprehended an ultimate return to the Divine Essence, or only a perpetual transmigration, it appears to have been a refinement of sacerdotal philosophy[1], rather than an article of popular belief. The funeral cere-

---

[1] Τὴν τῶν Αἰγυπτίων φιλοσοφίαν εἶναι τοιαύτην—τὴν ψυχὴν καὶ ἐπιδιαμένειν καὶ μετεμβαίνειν (Diog. Laert. Prooem. ii.). Τί οὖν χρὴ ποιεῖν (to obtain assurance of a future life) ἢ τοῦτο; εἰς Αἴγυπτον πορεύσομαι καὶ τοῖς τῶν ἀδύτων ἱεροφάνταις καὶ προφήταις φιλιωθήσομαι (Clem. Rom. Homil. 1, 3, 5, quoted by Creuzer, Comm. Herod. p. 316). Plants are mentioned among the objects into which the soul migrates (Diog. Laert. Pythag. 4), but this seems an addition to the genuine Pythagorean doctrine. Zoega de Or. et

monies and prayers have reference to the hope that the deceased may dwell in peace and happiness, under the protection of Osiris in the invisible world[1]. It is very rare to find among the funereal monuments of Egypt anything which alludes to the metempsychosis. In the tomb of Rameses the Sixth, in Bab-el-Melook[2], the usual judgement-scene is represented, with the addition of a *bari* preceded by a Cynocephalus, on which is the figure of a sow. Behind the sow is another Cynocephalus, an emblem of Thoth or Mercury Psychopompus, who appears to be driving her on. This has been generally admitted to be a representation of the return of a wicked soul to the upper world, condemned by Osiris for its sin to migrate into the body of a swine. Champollion, following out this idea, read the characters which stand above the sow " gluttony," which he supposed to be the vice for which the soul had been condemned to this penance[3]. Rosellini does not confirm this interpretation of the writing, though he agrees in the opinion that the soul's transmigration is here represented. It must seem very strange, however, that the sepulchre of a king should exhibit his soul as condemned to such a degradation, and we may therefore doubt whether the relation of this to the judgement-scene has been rightly apprehended.

If the Egyptian doctrine of transmigration included only the idea of a perpetual round of change,

---

Us. Obelisc. p. 302, not. 15. It was taught by Empedocles, Æl. Hist. An. 12, 7.

[1] Diod. 1, 92. Παρακαλοῦσι τοὺς κάτω θεοὺς σύνοικον δέξασθαι τοῖς εὐσεβέσι. Τὸ δὲ πλῆθος ἐπευφημεῖ καὶ συναποσεμνύνει τὴν δόξαν τοῦ τετελευτηκότος, ὡς τὸν αἰῶνα διατρίβειν μέλλοντος καθ᾽ ᾅδου μετὰ τῶν εὐσεβῶν.

[2] Rosellini, M. d. C. lxvi. p. 378. Wilkinson, M. and C. pl. 87.

[3] Lettres d'Egypte, p. 230. The explanation is repeated in Champollion Figeac's l'Univers, Egypte, p. 131.

it could hardly exist among the Greeks without being combined with punishment and reward. This combination we find already in Pindar[1], but in a very modified form of metempsychosis, a return to the human body, without passing through those of brutes. "Let the possessor of wealth," says he, "know, that the proud souls of those who die, forthwith endure retributive pains. The offences committed in this domain of Jupiter some one judges below, pronouncing sentence by a stern necessity. But the good lead a life free from toil, having the sun equally by night and by day; not harassing the earth by the strength of their hands, nor the water of the deep, for an unsubstantial fare; but lead a life free from sorrow, beside the honoured gods who delight in the sanctity of oaths[2]; while the others undergo pain not to be looked upon. But those who, remaining in either world to the third time, have resolutely kept themselves from all iniquity, travel the road of Jupiter to the citadel of Saturn, where ocean-gales breathe around the Island of the Blessed; and golden flowers glow, some from the ground, some from the bright trees; and others water nourishes, with chains and garlands of which they wreathe their hands, by the just decisions of

---

[1] Ol. 2, 109.

[2] In a fragment of a θρῆνος (Heyne Fr. 1, p. 21), Pindar describes the employment of the good in the invisible world, in language which Virgil has evidently had in view in his description of the Elysian Fields, Æn. 6, 640:

Τοῖσι λάμπει μένος ἀελίου
Τὰν ἐνθάδε νύκτα κάτω·
Φοινικορόδιαι τε λειμῶνες
Εἰσὶ προάστειον αὐτῶν·
Καὶ τοὶ μὲν ἱππείοις γυμνασίοις
Τοὶ δὲ πεσσοῖς, τοὶ δὲ φορμίγγεσσι τέρπονται·
Παρὰ δέ σφισιν εὐανθὴς
Ἅπας τέθηλεν ὄλβος.—Plut. p. 120 C.

Rhadamanthys, whom father Saturn has ever at hand as an assessor. Peleus and Cadmus are reckoned among them, and his mother brought hither Achilles, when she had moved the heart of Jupiter by her prayers[1]."

It is evident that we have here an attempt to connect the old *mythic* notion of a place of happiness for heroes, with the more *ethical* conception of retribution and reward for mankind generally; and this again with the doctrine of transmigration. It is not, however, an Egyptian or Indian transmigration through the bodies of brute animals. The wicked at death are condemned to punishment—of what kind or duration we are not told; the good lead a life of abundance and ease, yet after a time return again to the upper world; and are only admitted to the Island of the Blessed, if they have thrice gone through the trial of a mortal life, and kept themselves from all iniquity. Another fragment of Pindar, quoted by Plato[2], represents human souls, after having paid to Proserpine the penalty of their ancient transgressions, as returning to the light of the sun in the ninth year; and becoming kings and wise men and heroes. But it would be treating a poet too much as a philosopher

---

[1] Here the Scolion of Callistratus placed Harmodius the avenger of Athenian liberty (Brunck, Anal. 1, 155).

[2] Meno, ii. p. 81 B. Pind. Heyn. Fr. Thren. iv.—

Οἷσι γὰρ ἂν Φερσεφόνα ποινὰν
Παλαιοῦ πένθεος δέξηται,
Εἰς τὸν ὕπερθεν ἅλιον κείνων
Ἐνάτῳ ἔτει ἀναδιδοῖ ψύχαν πάλιν.
Ἐκ τᾶν βασιλῆες ἀγανοὶ καὶ σθένει κραιπνοὶ
Σοφίᾳ τε μέγιστοι ἄνδρες αὔξονται·
Ἐς δὲ τὸν λοιπὸν χρόνον ἥρωες
Ἁγνοὶ πρὸς ἀνθρώπων καλεῦνται.

were we to attempt to combine this passage with the quotation from the Second Olympian, and suppose that an interval of nine years was to elapse between each of the three visits of the soul to earth, before it was prepared for admission to the Island of the Blessed. In such purely imaginary delineations we can expect no consistency, even in the writings of the same author. Among the Greek philosophers the doctrine of the Metempsychosis underwent a great variety of modifications. Plato[1], combining the Egyptian period of 3000 years with Pindar's threefold probation, declares that the souls of those who have cultivated philosophy with sincerity, or lived without sensual impurity, if they have thrice chosen this life, recover the wings which the soul had lost when united with the body, and fly away to their native home, at the end of the third period of 1000 years. All others at the close of their first human existence undergo a trial. Some of them are condemned to punishment in the world below, others enjoy happiness in heaven. At the end of the first period of 1000 years, both classes choose their second life; and thus the human soul passes into the life of a brute, and he who was once a man, from a brute again into a man. Ten thousand years must elapse before the souls of ordinary men can regain their wings and fly back to their original abode[2]. The philosopher, however, is not more consistent than the poet; sometimes he uses the common language respecting

---

[1] Phædr. § 61, iii. 249.
[2] Εἰς τὸ αὐτὸ ὅθεν ἥκει ἡ ψυχὴ ἑκάστη οὐκ ἀφικνεῖται ἐτῶν μυρίων· οὐ γὰρ πτεροῦται πρὸ τοσούτου χρόνου (Phædr. u. s.).

Hades and Elysium; sometimes he assumes a transmigration of souls, and again blends both with his own poetical imaginations and philosophical theories[1].

A writer, under the name of Hermes, preserved by Stobæus[2], probably of very late times, thus states the doctrine of transmigration: "All souls proceed from the soul of the universe, and their changes are many, some to the better, some to the worse. Those of reptiles change into aquatic, the aquatic into terrestrial, the terrestrial into aërial, the aërial into man. And human souls as the beginning of immortality are changed into dæmons, and so into the choir of gods; now there are two choirs of gods, one of the wandering, the other of the fixed (stars?). And this is the most perfect glory of the soul. But when it enters into man, if it continue wicked it will never obtain immortality, but will take the backward course to the reptiles." He cannot, however, be received as evidence of the original Egyptian doctrine.

Neither the Egyptian nor the Pythagorean doctrine of transmigration appears to have included that of punishment. But the more popular conception of the state of the dead, as subjected to the judgement of Osiris and existing in the invisible world, which the Egyptians called Amenthe, must have acknowledged a retribution for the conduct during life[3]. Of the state of the just after death we have a curious picture in the papyrus rolls which

---

[1] Phædo, i. 113.
[2] Ed. Heeren, p. 1000.
[3] Ait Mercurius Ægyptius animam digressam a corpore non refundi in animam universi, sed manere determinatam, *ut rationem patri reddat eorum quæ in corpore gesserit.* Tertullian. de Anima, 33.

were frequently enclosed in the sarcophagi along with the mummies. They appear, according to Lepsius, who has published one of them under the title of the Book of the Dead, to have been a sort of passport to the soul through the numerous gates of the heavenly dwelling. Champollion had given them the appellation of the Ritual; but they contain no precepts for honours to be paid to the dead, nor hymns or prayers to be offered to him. The deceased is the person represented, and the papyrus describes his adventures after the soul has left the body. So far it may be called a ritual, that it contains the prayers which he offers to the gods. The French 'Description de l'Egypte' contains an engraving of one of these Papyri[1]; but by far the most complete copy exists in the Royal Museum of Turin, whence the facsimile of Lepsius has been taken. The smaller funeral papyri contain extracts or abridgements of this, some sections being omitted in one, some in another. They appear to have been prepared by the priests; some are in the hieroglyphic, but most of them in the hieratic character. If perfect, they contain a representation of the judgement-scene which we have already described, and which is denominated "Book of the redemption in the hall of the twofold Justice." The deceased addresses each of the forty-two judges by name; it was the business of each of them to punish some particular sin, and of this sin the deceased declares himself innocent. The first step in the progress of the soul through the unseen world is,

[1] Antiquités, vol. 5, pl. 44-46. The funeral papyrus, published in 1805 by Cadet and Hammer, is nearly 28 feet long, and contains 537 columns.

that it issues from the grave, and under the form of different gods addresses invocations to Osiris as Lord of the lower world. In succeeding chapters Thoth is addressed as the champion of Osiris against his enemies, and the deceased appears armed with a lance, and pursuing the Typhonian animals, the crocodile, the serpent, the tortoise and the ass. In a subsequent part he is seen offering to the inhabitants of the celestial regions, embarking on the heavenly waters, ploughing, sowing, reaping and threshing[1]. These Elysian fields are surrounded and permeated by waters; but it is not necessary to suppose that this circumstance gave rise to the Greek fiction of the Islands of the Blessed, which may be purely poetical, or if it have any foundation in fact, may have owed it to the Phœnician settlements in Western Spain and their discovery of the Canaries or Azores[2]. The deity (Seb), whom the Greeks interpreted as Saturn, has no connexion in Egyptian mythology with the unseen world; and Rhadamanthys, though it has been etymologized from the Coptic[3], appears to be a purely Greek word[4]. These are the most important contents of the funeral papyri[5]; there are also varied prayers to the gods, who are all designated as forms of Osiris, and hymns,

---

[1] It is supposed to be in allusion to this future occupation of the deceased, that small representations of a hoe are among the objects offered to the dead. The figures of mummies placed in the tombs have usually a hoe imprinted or painted on the shoulder, along with a bag, supposed to be a seed-bag. Rosellini, M. Civ. 1, 291.

[2] Strabo, 3, p. 150. Gesner de Navig. Phœnic. extra Col. Herc. p. 644 of Hermann's Orphica.

[3] Zoega de Obel. p. 296. He supposes the last part to represent Amenthe.

[4] Ῥαδαμεῖν (see Hesych.) is βλαστάνειν, which joined with ἄνθος expresses very well the flowery luxuriance by which these islands were characterized. See p. 481.

[5] Lepsius, Das Todten Buch, Leipzig, 1842.

which from their division by points, appear to be metrical. The most perfect rolls belong to the flourishing times of the Pharaohs, from the fifteenth to the thirteenth century before Christ. In later times they are brief and fragmentary, and of the Ptolemaic times no single copy has been found.

We are not to expect in the papyri any explanation of the fate of those who were found wanting in the trial of the balance by Osiris. Every one who was embalmed and deposited in the tomb was presumed to have been approved by him; the mummy bore the form of Osiris, and the deceased was called *Osirian*[1] and identified with the god, just as among ourselves, every one who receives Christian burial is assumed to die in peace with the Church and in the hope of a happy immortality. Rosellini and Champollion suppose, that in the tombs of the kings, where according to them the mystical doctrines respecting the soul are set forth, the spirits of wicked men are represented as rejected by the Sun, the ruler of those celestial regions through which they have to take their course. The former gives these as the words which accompany the representation—" They (the reprobate) do not see this great god; their eye does not imbibe the rays from his disk; their souls are not manifested or made illustrious in the world; they do not hear the voice of this great god, who towers above their sphere." Of the good, on the other hand, it is said, " This great god speaks to them and they speak to him; his glory illuminates them in the splendour

---

[1] Thus in the Parisian papyrus " the Osirian Petamon." Rosellini, Mon. Civ. 3, 492.

of his disk while he is in their sphere[1]." Rosellini speaks also of representations in the royal tombs of wicked souls exposed to torments by fire and steel. The connexion of the Sun with the departed spirits is illustrated by a custom which Porphyry records[2]. In the process of embalmment, the viscera were taken out and placed in a chest by themselves, which the embalmer then held up to the Sun, with this prayer:—
"O Sun, and all ye Gods who give life to men, receive me, and give me to dwell along with the immortal gods. For I have ever reverenced the Gods whom my parents taught me, and have honoured the authors of my body; of other men I have neither killed any one, nor deprived him of a deposit, nor have done any other grievous wrong. And if throughout my life I have committed any sin, in eating or drinking, I have not done it on my own account, but on account of these, pointing to the chest containing the viscera, which was then thrown into the river, and the body, as pure, submitted to embalmment."

It would be vain to endeavour to combine these different statements and indications of opinion, into a system which should represent the defined and universal belief of the Egyptian people. We can distinguish with some certainty the philosophical dogma of transmigration, the religious doctrine of retribution, and the popular belief of the continued existence of the soul, still dwelling in the uudecayed body. But other differences must have existed. Our first impulse is to think of the dead as

---

[1] Rosellini, Mon. Civ. 3, p. 323, 328.   [2] De Abstinentia, lib. 4, § 10.

extinct, and their condition as one of mere negation, rest and silence; and this view ever returns and obtrudes itself, even amidst conceptions and modes of speech derived from the belief in their continued existence. The popular and the philosophical doctrine could not remain side by side for centuries, without attempts being made to reconcile them, which became a fresh source of variety. Not only is a future state of retribution the universal belief of Christendom, but this belief is founded upon express revelation; yet how variously has it been conceived! A millennium on earth, purgatory or the sleep of the soul between death and the general resurrection, the eternal suffering, final extinction or final restitution of the wicked—these are only some of the diversities of opinion to which this doctrine has given rise. It must be ever so in regard to what lies wholly beyond the sphere of sense and personal experience. We need not wonder therefore if we cannot frame a conception of the Egyptian belief on this subject, which shall explain everything, from writings which have been only partially preserved, and monuments as yet very imperfectly understood.

CHAPTER XXII.

EMBALMMENT, SEPULTURE, AND FUNERAL RITES.

ACCORDING to Herodotus, on occasion of the death of any person of consequence in Egypt, all the women of the family and female relatives daubed their heads and faces with mud, and leaving the corpse in the house, wandered through the city with their garments girt over the waist, just below the bosom, so as to leave it bare[1], and beating themselves with lamentation. The men, formed also into companies, disposed their garments in a similar way and beat themselves with lamentation. In the paintings which represent the funeral processions, we see men and women thus dressed, in separate bands, flinging dust or mud upon their heads and beating their bosoms. On occasion of a royal funeral, the mourning was universal throughout Egypt. For seventy-two days, that is, while the process of embalmment was going on[2], they rent their garments, and divided into companies of two or three hundred, went about twice a day singing in measured verse the praise of the deceased monarch's virtues[3]. During this time the temples were closed, all sacrifices and festivals suspended, and the people abstained not only from pleasures and luxuries of

---

[1] 'Επεζωσμέναι, Her. 2, 85. Περιεζωσμέναι σινδόνας ὑποκάτω τῶν μαστῶν. Diod. 1, 72.
[2] Genesis l. 3.
[3] Rosellini thinks he has discovered a metrical nænia, in praise of Roei, a priest and basilogrammat of Thebes (M. Civ. 3, 400).

every kind, but even from the use of animal food and wheaten bread[1]. In the case of private persons, the mourning appears to have been suspended during the embalmment[2], which was the next stage. This art was practised by a body of men called *Taricheutæ*, who in the Greek times formed a caste[3], and who appear to have had ranges of buildings allotted to them in which it might be carried on. As it was connected with the manipulation of dead bodies, these buildings were removed from the neighbourhood of the temples. At Thebes they were confined to the Memnonium on the western bank of the river, and as we find a similar restriction placed upon the tanners[4], probably this region, like the Transtiberine at Rome, was allotted to disgusting or unwholesome operations[5]. The office itself, however, was not deemed degrading; the *Taricheutæ* were not rendered impure by it, but were allowed to enter the temples and associate with the priests. It appears as if each *Taricheutes* had a district assigned to him, on the inhabitants of which he alone was allowed to exercise his art; since we find one of them bringing an action against another for encroaching on his *walk* .

The embalmers kept models of three different modes of embalmment, of which one was chosen,

---

[1] Diod. 1, 72.
[2] Her. 2, 85. Diodorus 1, 91, represents them as mourning and fasting till the interment.
[3] They are called τὸ ἔθνος in a Turin papyrus (Peyron, Pap. Græc. 1826, 1, p. 2, l. 24).
[4] Peyron, Pap. Græc. 1, p. 2, l. 21.
[5] Ib. 2, p. 41. "Quare colligere licet ad Memnonia detrusas fuisse artes immundas et quidquid politioribus hominibus facile stomachum movisset."—

............Nec te fastidia mercis
Ullius subeant ablegandæ Tiberim ultra.—Juv. s. 14, 202.

[6] Peyron, 2, p. 48. One had the Memnonium, the other Diospolis or Eastern Thebes.

according to the expense which the relations were willing to incur. The most honourable and most costly was that in which the body was made to resemble Osiris. In preparing it according to this method, the brains were first partially extracted by a crooked iron instrument through the nostrils, or dissolved by some injected fluid and so brought away. Many of the mummies attest the correctness of this account given by Herodotus; the cribriform plate having been broken through in the process of extracting the brain[1]. In other cases the brain has been left; or the hollow filled up with bituminous matter and a fragrant resin. The chief of the embalmers, called the *scribe*, probably as being the one who was in possession of the written formula by which everything was regulated in Egypt, marked on the left side of the body, between the breast-bone and the ribs, the size of the incision, which the *paraschistes* with a sharp flint[2] then made. His service was odious, and having performed it he immediately took to flight, being pursued with stones and curses by the by-standers. The whole of the intestines were then taken out, the kidneys and the heart alone being left, and were carefully washed with palm wine and pounded spices. They are sometimes found within the body[3]; sometimes enclosed in linen and asphaltum and placed beside it; but more commonly they seem to have been deposited in the four vases, called improperly *Canopi*, which have been already de-

---

[1] Pettigrew on Mummies, p. 56.
[2] Sharp flints with a cutting-edge have been found in Egyptian tombs; Wilkinson, 3, 262. (Comp. Exod. iv. 25.)
[3] See p. 405 of this volume. Archæol. 27, 270. Pettigrew, p. 74.

scribed[1]. The cavity was then filled up, according to Herodotus, with myrrh and cassia and all other fragrant resins except frankincense, and the body steeped for seventy days in a solution of natron. This salt, which is found in great abundance in the Natron Lakes, appears to contain, along with a large proportion of muriate of soda, or common salt, a carbonate of soda. The common salt exercises its usual antiseptic power, and the other ingredient, combining with the adipose particles, leaves the fibrous part of the flesh untouched. Herodotus has probably placed the steeping of the body erroneously after, instead of before the filling up of the cavity with aromatic substances. Diodorus does not mention the immersion in natron, but says that during thirty days the body is treated with *cedria* and other preparations, and *afterwards* with myrrh and cinnamon and other substances, which not only preserve it for a long time, but give it a fragrant odour. This cedria was a kind of liquid pitch, obtained from the Syrian *cedrelate* by burning it, and possessed of strongly antiseptic virtues[2]. The body thus prepared was next enveloped in bandages of linen[3], which had been steeped in some resinous substance, probably the gum of the Sont (*Mimosa Nilotica*), which is abundant in Egypt. The art with which they have been applied and combined, so as to envelope smoothly all the limbs, has excited the admiration of professional men. Accord-

---

[1] See p. 406 of this volume. Rosellini, M. Civ. cxxix. 2.

[2] Phny, 16, 21. Cedrium—cui tanta vis est, ut in Ægypto corpora hominum defunctorum eo perfusa serventur.

[3] That they are linen and not cotton, has been decided at last, after very contradictory judgements, by the microscopic examination of the fibre. See Phil. Mag. Nov. 1834. Wilkinson, 3, 115.

ing to Dr. Granville, there is not a single form of bandage known to modern surgery, of which examples are not seen in the swathings of the Egyptian mummies. The strips of linen have been found extending to 1000 yards in length. Rosellini gives a similar testimony to the wonderful variety and skill with which the bandages have been applied and interlaced.

Herodotus, in speaking of the dress of the priests, observes, that they wore white woollen garments thrown over their linen tunics, but that nothing of woollen was ever carried into the temples, nor buried with them. It had been generally supposed that this was an universal law of Egyptian interment; but at Gebel-el-Mokattam, bodies of the workmen have been found wrapt in woollen (p. 131, 140), and what is still more remarkable, the mummy of Mycerinus found in the third pyramid had been similarly enveloped. In the most elaborately executed mummies, as those of kings and priests, not only the arms and legs, but the fingers and toes are separately bandaged[1]. Compresses are placed in various parts, so as to secure an exact application of the bandage to the body, wherever there might otherwise have been a vacant space, into which the air might have gained admission. Within the folds of the inner and outer bandages various objects have been found. The most important of these are the papyri, the nature of which has been already described, in speaking of the opinions of the Egyptians respecting the state of the dead; they are not found,

---

[1] Pettigrew, pp. 95, 99. The Greek mummies had the arms bound separately, the Egyptian not (Wilkinson, M. and C. 5, 474, 5).

however, in all the mummies, but only in those which were expensively prepared ; they have been placed usually on the breast, between the thighs and legs, or the body and the arms. Small figures of Osiris in blue porcelain with hieroglyphical inscriptions are also frequently found either between the bandages or beside the mummies. A scarabæus with a similar inscription was often placed on the breast and in immediate contact with the flesh, or within the cavity of the body, on which the name of the deceased is read ; sometimes, instead of the scarabæus, a small tablet of stone or baked clay, in the form of a funeral stele, inscribed with hieroglyphics, lies on the breast. Besides these, amulets of various kinds, necklaces composed of glass beads or agate and jasper pebbles, ear-rings and finger-rings, bracelets, hair-pins, and other female ornaments, are of frequent occurrence. The body having been swathed, a case was accurately fitted to it, composed of layers of cloth cemented together and forming a substance nearly resembling pasteboard ; it appears to have been moulded upon the body while moist, so as accurately to take its shape, and the contents were secured by its being sewed up at the back[1]. This case was then ornamented with paintings of the most vivid colours, which even at the present day, when first brought into the light and air, have lost little of their original freshness. The head is covered with a mask extending down the shoulders, on which the face is represented ; the conventional colour of yellowish-green being adopted for women and reddish-brown

[1] Pettigrew, 116.

for men. The face has sometimes been gilded; at other times the surface of the body, the head, feet and hands. In a mummy found at Saccara, thin plates of gold were wrapped round each limb and each finger, inscribed with hieroglyphics[1]. Artificial eyes of glass are inserted to aid the appearance of life, and a network of beads and bugles is sometimes spread over the whole front of the body. The whole case is covered with columns of hieroglyphics or emblematic figures, among which the scarabæus, the winged serpent, the ibis, the cynocephalus, or the genii of Amenthe and the goddesses Isis, Netpe and (Tpe) the heavens, are the most common[2]. The hieroglyphics contain usually the name and quality of the deceased, but little besides, except formulary invocations and prayers. Exterior to this is a case usually of sycamore wood, sometimes excavated from the solid tree, at others composed of several pieces, and secured by wooden pegs, which fasten the receptacle and the cover firmly together. This is sometimes again enclosed in a second, and that in a third wooden case, the outermost being also adorned with hieroglyphics and with rich colours and elaborate gilding. The outermost case is of various forms, but most commonly adapted to that of the mummy.

The various processes employed in preparing a mummy are represented in one of the tombs of Thebes, described by Rosellini[3]. Two men are using the drill and bow, as practised by carpenters at the

---

[1] Trans. Roy. Soc. Lit. 2nd series, vol. i. p. 109.

[2] See the mummy represented in the Atlas to Minutoli, tab. xxxvii.

[3] Rosellini, Mon. Civ. 3, 362, pl. cxxvi.

present day; another is piercing a hole with the same instrument in the eye of the mask for the head and shoulders which has been already described, for the insertion of a piece of black enamel in the centre, representing the pupil. In another compartment a man is preparing the cloth for the bandages by steeping it in a vase containing some resinous solution; a second is polishing the surface of the mask with his hand, and a third levigating the plaster with which that and the covering of the mummy are to be overspread, preparatory to the painting. This operation is represented in a third chamber, where the body is laid upon two stools; the saucers for the colours are on the ground, and a boy is preparing them by rubbing on a stone, while an artist, with a pallet in one hand and a pencil in the other, is painting the countenance. In the three upper compartments the completion of the process of bandaging is delineated, and a man distinguished by his dress from the rest, probably the *scribe*, holds in his hand a roll of papyrus, no doubt the Book of the Dead, which is about to be placed among the last folds of bandage over the breast.

Such was the mode in which the body was embalmed, swathed and encased, according to what Herodotus calls the most elaborate method. In the second and less expensive, they made no incision nor extracted the viscera, but injected cedria from below, which remained in the body during the time of the steeping, and, as he had been told, brought away with it the dissolved bowels. But as this substance has no such solvent power, it is probable that in this case also the contents of the body were extracted, and that the cheap oil of cedar was used instead of costly aromatics, to preserve what remained from putrefaction. In the third method, which the poorest of the Egyptians practised, a still cheaper injection of salt and water was used[1], the steeping in natron for seventy days remaining the same. In the two last methods no swathing was employed, but the body given back to the relations as it came from the natron lye. These were not all the methods used; they are only specimens of the most costly, of the cheapest, and of an intermediate process; but each of these admitted of very numerous varieties. Of those which have the lateral incision, some are filled with aromatic matter, others only with asphaltum, to which they trusted chiefly for the preservation of the body, which aromatics alone could not effect[2]. Some of those which are without the incision have evidently been dipped in asphaltum in a liquid state, which has thus coated the whole body; and others simply salted and dried. There were even cheaper modes of making mummies than that described by Herodotus as the cheapest; the corpse being merely filled with salt, or ashes, or chips of bitter wood. The practice of embalmment is at least as old as the Pyramids, and it continued in use till Christianity extinguished the old religion. In this long series of centuries changes took place, on which a chronology of the

[1] Συρμαίη, Her. 2, 88, explained by Hesychius, πόμα δι' ὕδατος καὶ ἁλῶν.
[2] Diod. 19, 99, speaking of the transport of asphaltum from the Dead Sea to Egypt. *Mum* is said to be a Persian word signifying naphtha or liquid asphaltum (Jablonsk. Opusc. 1,472). The Egyptian name for a mummy is, according to Rosellini, *Kols* (M. C. iii. 2, 370).

art has been founded[1]. From the mummy of Menkera it appears that if linen were known in that age, it was not used in swathing the body.

According to Herodotus, when the process of embalmment was completed, the case in which the body was enclosed was deposited in a sepulchral chamber, erect against the wall[2]. This however appears to have been only done in exceptional cases, where the family possessed no *hypogæum*, and had to erect a building for the reception of their dead; or when interment was forbidden or delayed. In the hypogæa the mummies are always found, if undisturbed, in an horizontal position. Herodotus has not described the ceremonies of the funeral, which are detailed by Diodorus[3] and in most points illustrated by the monuments. A formal judgement preceded the interment. A day was fixed by the relatives of the deceased, on which his body should be conveyed across the lake of the nome, and forty-two judges being assembled took their seats in a semicircular bench beside the lake. The *baris* or bark being drawn alongside, before the coffin was allowed to be placed in it for conveyance to the other bank, any one who chose was permitted to accuse the deceased. If these accusations were sustained by the judges, the rites of sepulture were withheld. A false accusation was severely punished. If none were made, or if the accuser appeared to be a calumniator, the relations of the deceased, laying aside their mourning, extolled his virtues; not after the manner of the Greeks, dwelling upon his noble birth,

---

[1] See Birch, in Gliddon's Eg. Arch. p. 88, and p. 131 of this vol.
[2] Οἰκήματι θηκαίῳ, 2, 86. Compare the use of οἴκημα, 2, 100.
[3] 1, 92.

since all Egyptians are deemed equally noble, but on his good education, his justice and piety, his temperance and continence. The surrounding multitude joined in the eulogy with acclamation, and prayed the gods below to receive him to dwell among the pious dead. The bodies of those who had been prohibited from interment remained in their private dwellings, and it sometimes happened that after they had remained above ground for years their children obtained the means of proving the falsehood of the accusations against them, and they were finally committed to the tomb. The only trace which the monuments exhibit of a judgement before interment is that in the funeral processions, when the mummy is taken from the bark and is about to be placed in the tomb, one of the attendants touches it with the instrument which symbolically expresses *approbation*[1]. Other causes, such as an undischarged debt, might delay the interment.

Later writers[2] speak of it as a custom of the Egyptians to keep the embalmed bodies of their friends in their houses, and on festive days to place them on seats and couches and make them partakers in their feast. This is not confirmed by the monuments, but it does appear as if they were sometimes kept in wooden closets and occasionally taken out, not to be placed at a *lectisternium*, but to receive libations and offerings of cakes, flowers and geese[3].

---

[1] Rosellini, Mon. Civ. iii. 2, 437. The meaning of this instrument is ascertained by the Rosetta inscription, where it answers to the Greek ὃν ὁ Ἥφαιστος ἐδοκίμασεν.

[2] Lucian, de Luctu, c. 21. ὁ Αἰγύπτιος, ξηράνας τὸν νεκρὸν σύνδειπνον καὶ συμπότην ἐποιήσατο. (See Wessel. ad Diod. 1, 91.)

[3] Wilkinson, M. & C. p. 384.

The sepulchre was a place of family interment. The inscriptions on the walls, and the mummies, where these remain, often give evidence of the burial of the husband and wife, the sons and daughters; and what is said respecting the pledge of dead bodies and the prohibition of further interment till the debt was discharged, shows that as long as the family remained extant they continued to use the same sepulchre. The ample size and numerous lateral or perpendicular excavations would afford room for the deposit of many generations. It was after dwelling in Egypt that Abraham declined the offer of the Hethites to bury his wife in the choicest of their sepulchres, and purchased for himself and his descendants the cave of Machpelah[1]. A special place of sepulture, however, could not be obtained by the poorest classes. Their bodies, prepared by one of the cheap modes of embalmment, and without coffins to enclose them, were placed in layers, in the deep pits which are found in the grottoes, or along the sides of the passages which branch off from them.

As the cemeteries of Memphis and Thebes were both on the opposite side of the Nile from that on which the principal part of the habitations stood, the bodies must have been conveyed across the Nile for interment, and the ceremony of the judgement may have preceded its embarkation. But the *baris* on which the coffin is placed in the representation of funeral processions is evidently in many cases only a symbol, and not adapted to actual navigation; nor can there have been in every nome a lake, such as the account of Diodorus supposes. If a passage

---

[1] Gen. xxiii. xxv. 9. xlix. 29.

over water were really an essential part of the funeral ceremony, we must suppose that by a lake he meant some one of those canals or branches of the Nile which abounded everywhere; or the lake of the principal temple of the nome, which was generally furnished with an appendage of this kind. It appears, however, from the monuments, that in many cases there was a real transporting of the body, across the river, to the Libyan hills; and all the royal sepulchres, whether pyramids or hypogæa, are on the western side. In the tomb of Nevopth at Benihassan, which is on the eastern side, a small *bari* without sails or oars, but furnished with two rudders, on which a mummy reclines under a canopy, is towed upon the Nile by a larger vessel, with a square sail set[1]; a man stands on the prow with a pole for pushing off, and makes signals with his hand, while several sailors are engaged in handling the ropes. In other instances, rowers, standing or sitting, are pulling the boat[2].

The representation of the funeral procession usually forms the first part of the papyrus rolls when these are entire and on the largest scale, as that of Turin, accompanied by a long description of the funeral prayers and rites. It is also of common occurrence in the tombs with some variation in the details, but a close resemblance in all the

---

[1] Rosellini, M.C. cxxxiii. 1. iii. 2, p. 427.
[2] Ibid. pl. cxxx. Sir G. Wilkinson in his map of Thebes lays down a supposed Lake of the Dead. Rosellini thinks the excavation in question cannot have been intended to contain water. (M. C. iii. 2, 431. Wilk. Mod. Eg. and Thebes, 2. 186.) It must have been 7000 feet long and 3000 broad, a very improbable magnitude if its use was merely symbolical. Memphis had a λίμνη, but it was dug for its defence on the side on which it was not protected by the Nile. (Her. 2, 99.)

principal parts. The body, enclosed in its painted sarcophagus, is first seen, erect or reclined within a tabernacle of wood, richly adorned with emblematic paintings; if reclined, it is usually on a couch, the head and feet of which imitate those of a lion. This tabernacle is itself placed upon a *bari* which rests on a sledge, or a dray with low wheels, and is drawn towards the place of embarkation or interment by hand, or by oxen. A priest in a leopard's skin, the costume of the chief functionary at funerals, walks at the head, and turning towards the sarcophagus holds out a censer with burning incense, or pours a libation on the ground. Besides the tabernacle which encloses the body, another is sometimes seen in the procession, borne on the shoulders of men, in which the vases are contained which hold the embalmed viscera. The groups of mourners are variously disposed. Sometimes the females are hidden from view within a cabin on the deck; or again are mounted on the roof of this cabin, and with dishevelled hair and naked bosoms beat themselves or throw dust upon their heads. When the procession is advancing by land towards the place of sepulture, male and female mourners in separate companies precede or attend upon it, the females naked to the waist, and both with gestures of lamentation[1]. Arrived at the place of interment, which is designated by a portion of a mountain and the portico of a hypogæum, with the eye of Osiris, the mummy is taken from the tabernacle and placed upright by a figure, wearing the jackal mask of the

[1] Tomb of *Roei*, a priest and keeper of a temple in Thebes, and also *basilicogrammat*. (Rosellini, iii. 2, 400.)

god Anubis. On the head of the mummy is a conical figure and a lotus, a frequent offering to the dead. The widow, kneeling on the ground, and casting dust with one hand upon her head, with the other embraces the feet of her deceased husband. In another part of the same procession, a female, kneeling in an attitude of grief near the tabernacle which contains the vases, is designated as sister of the deceased. Three priests stand before it; one with the leopard's skin offers a libation, another incense, and a third holds out the instrument of approbation. Near the entrance of the sepulchre is seen one of those funeral tablets or *stelæ* which are to be found in most collections of Egyptian monuments, exhibiting a *proscynema* of the deceased to Osiris and certain formulary phrases, declaring that offerings are made to the god to obtain his favour and a quiet abode in Amenthe.

There are examples of still more pompous processions. In that of a royal scribe at Thebes, a long train of servants precedes the *bari* in which the mummy is enclosed, with objects of various kinds—small chests for the images of the gods or the ancestors of the deceased, chairs and tables, a chariot with horses, vases, images, fans, costly collars and the insignia of office[1]. Many of these were deposited in the tombs, that the deceased might be surrounded by the objects which had been familiar to him during life, or with which his honours had been associated. Nor was this confined to the insignia of high office; the tools of artificers have been found in their tombs; and it is said to have

---

[1] Wilkinson, Plates, 83, 84.

been a superstition with the natives of Abessinia, which may have been shared by the Egyptians, that it was ominous to use the tools of a deceased person[1]. To this desire of surrounding the dead with objects prized by them during life we must attribute the custom of placing fictile vases in the tombs, where a great variety of them has been found. These vases have been sometimes filled with grain, fruits, eggs, and others have evidently contained perfumes; all designed to carry on an uninterrupted continuity between the present and the future life.

The honours paid to the dead did not even cease with their interment. From the Greek papyri we learn the existence of a custom, which no doubt had been handed down from the Pharaonic times. There was a class of persons, called *Choachutæ* or *Libation-pourers*, whose duty seems to have been to watch over the tombs and see that they suffered no violation[2] (an outrage not unlikely to be committed as they contained valuable property), and from time to time to make offerings of wine, cakes, fruit, flowers and herbs, to the deceased, accompanied no doubt by prayers and propitiatory ceremonies. Duties which begin in feeling and are performed at first in person, degenerate by degrees into forms which are entrusted to hired functionaries who make a living by them. Such appears to have been the case with the Choachutæ[3], whom we find

---

[1] Rosellini, M. Civ. 2, 315.
[2] Peyron, Pap. 1, p. 86.
[3] From the similarity of the letters A and Λ in the writing of the papyri, Dr. Young read this word Χολχυται, and derived it from a Coptic word signifying *to dress*. The error, long ago pointed out by Dr. Ed. Hincks, in the Dublin University Magazine, has been propagated through the works of Peyron, Champollion and Rosellini, who speak of the Colchytæ as an order of priests, specially employed in swathing the mummies.

deriving a revenue from the performance of their duties to a certain number of tombs, and selling it as a profitable right to others of the same profession[1]. These Choachutæ appear also at Thebes to have taken a part in the annual ceremony of carrying the ark of Amun across the river to the Memnonium, and to have had the duty of strewing sand on this occasion along the *dromoi* and courts of the temples, to prevent their being defiled by the mud which would otherwise have been brought into them. Possibly this visit of Amun to the region of the necropolis may have had some reference to the doctrine of a future life, since in the manifold blending of the characters of the Egyptian gods, Amun may have been identified with Ptah and Osiris, the gods of the invisible world[2].

According to the accounts which Diodorus copies, the Egyptian priests represented not only the doctrine of the transmigration of souls, but the whole mythology of the infernal regions and Elysian fields, as borrowed by Orpheus from the Egyptians, thus going, as in other instances, far beyond the statements of Herodotus. Having mentioned the introduction of the mysteries by Orpheus and the identity of Osiris with Dionusos, and Isis with Demeter, Diodorus proceeds[3]: " They say also that he introduced the punishments of the impious in Hades, and the meadows of the pious and the fictitious imagery

---

[1] In a papyrus at Berlin, Horus sells to Osoroeris his liturgical rights over fifteen mummies at Thebes. In another papyrus, a sixth part of the λογεία, or right to make a collection for offerings to the dead, among the relatives of the deceased, is the subject of a contract (Peyron, 1, pp. 88, 89). The names of the parties are all Egyptian, which shows that the custom was not of Greek introduction.

[2] See Birch, Gall. of B. M. p. 5.

[3] 1, 96.

which is current among the many, having imitated the proceedings at funerals in Egypt. For that Hermes, the conductor of souls, according to the ancient custom of the Egyptians, having conveyed the body of Apis to a certain point, gives it over to him who is invested with the mask of Cerberus. Orpheus having showed these things to the Greeks, Homer adapted his poetry to harmonize with this:

> Cyllenian Hermes now call'd forth the souls
> Of all the suitors; with his golden wand
> He led them gibbering down into the shades.
> Od. 24, *ad init.*

" And a little further on he says—

> The streams of Ocean, the Leucadian rock,
> The Sun's pale postern and the land of Dreams,
> Passing, they came at once into the meads
> Of Asphodel by shadowy forms possess'd
> Of mortal men deceased.

" They say that he calls the river Ocean, because the Egyptians call the Nile Ocean in their own language; and that the gates of the Sun are the city of the Heliopolitans; and that the meadow, the mythological abode of the departed, is the place along the shore of the so-called Acherusian Lake, near Memphis, round which are beautiful meadows and marshes, and lotus and reed. And he has consistently said that the dead dwell in these places, because there are the most numerous and the greatest funerals of the Egyptians, the dead bodies being conveyed across the river and the Acherusian lake, and deposited in the sepulchres which lie there." In this account there is so much that is evidently devised to give plausibility to the claim of Egypt to be the source of everything Grecian, that the whole is suspicious. No one who reads Homer with any feeling for poetry can believe, that he meant the Nile by the Ocean, were it even certain that the word had this sense; or Heliopolis by the gates of the Sun. And if any other origin than poetic conception is to be sought, for the picture of the Elysian fields and the meadow of Asphodel, it may be more naturally found in the imagery of the Book of the Dead[1], than the local scenery of Memphis and the broad daylight of a great capital. Diodorus continues—" The other mythological stories of the Greeks respecting Hades accord with the actual practices of Egypt. The vessel which conveys the bodies is called *baris*, and the coin called an obolus is given as passage-money to the ferryman, who is called in the native language Charon. And they say there are near these places a temple of Hecate the Dark, and Gates of Cocytus and Lethe, closed with brazen bolts; and that there are other gates of Truth, and that near them stands a headless figure of Justice." Here again we have evident traces of a forced accommodation of Egyptian usages to Greek mythology. The word *baris*, which means in Egyptian any kind of river-boat[2], instead of being used by the Greeks from Orpheus and Homer downwards for the ferry-boat of Charon, is never so applied till after the Macedonian age. No such custom as that of placing a piece of coin in the mouth of the corpse existed in the Pharaonic

---

[1] See p. 486 of this volume.

[2] It appears to have found its way through the Ionians, the first who became acquainted with Egypt, into use among the Athenians, for a foreign vessel. Comp. Æsch. Pers. 545 (559 Bl.); Suppl. 843; Eur. Iph. Aul. 297.

times, when indeed the Egyptians had no coin[1]. The name of Charon appears to be purely Greek, like χαροπός, denoting fierce-eyed[2], and answering to the description of Virgil—

> Terribili squalore Charon; cui plurima mento
> Canities inculta jacet; *stant lumina flamma.*—Æn. vi.

Acheron, Cocytus and Lethe again are Greek words, and a lake of Grief, a stream of Wailing and a fountain of Oblivion are conceptions so obviously connected with the unseen world, that we need not suppose the poetical Greeks indebted for them to the unpoetical Egyptians[3]. A figure of Justice or Truth, without a head, or rather with a mask, covering not only the eyes but the whole head, is found in the Book of the Dead[4]; but neither this representation, nor the Gates of Truth, afford any ground for inferring that the Greeks borrowed this part of their mythology from the Egyptians, nothing parallel to them being found in old Greek poetry or art.

---

[1] A small plate of gold is said to have been found in the mouth of a mummy (Pettigrew, p. 63); but similar plates are sometimes disposed in other parts of the body, and instead of a general fact, it is one of very rare occurrence that it should be found in the mouth. It had no reference to the payment of the ferryman, but was of the nature of an amulet, or symbol.

[2] Lycophr. 260, 650, an epithet of the eagle and the lion.

[3] Vectorem Charontem, etsi post Homerum, facile commenta est antiquitas; neque adeo ex Ægyptia religione et lacu Mœride illum adumbratum esse necesse est; quin potius Græculi seriores Ægyptiam priscam religionem in hanc partem interpretati esse videntur (Heyne, Exc. ix. ad Æn. vi.).

[4] See Sir G. Wilkinson's Plates, 48.

END OF VOL. I.

ENTR.

KING'S CHAMBER

QUEEN'S CHAMBER

SUBTERRANEOUS CHAMBER

SECTIONS FROM NORTH TO SOUTH

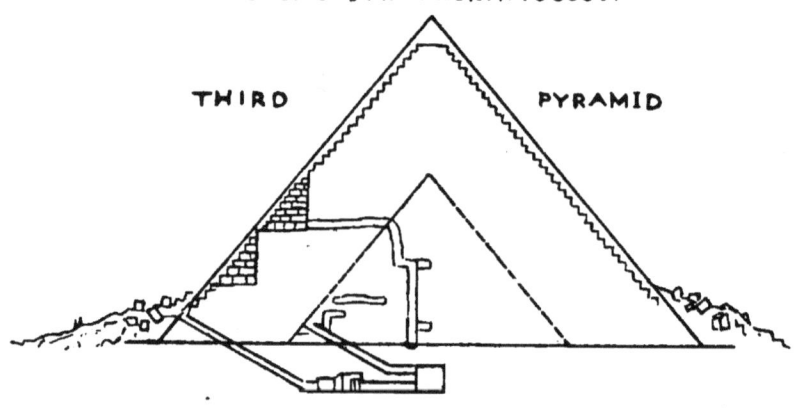

THIRD PYRAMID

VEGETATION — SEASONS OF HARVEST — INUNDATION

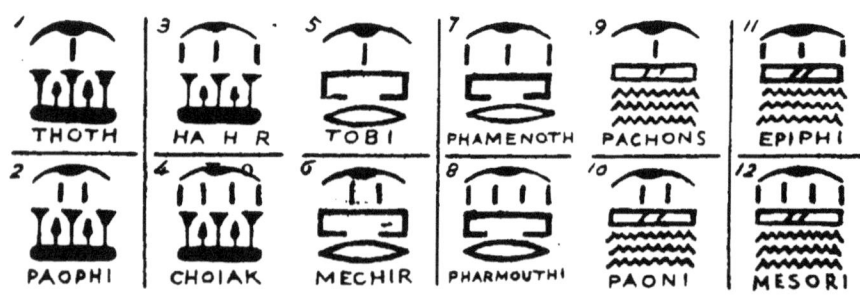

| 1 THOTH | 3 HA H R | 5 TOBI | 7 PHAMENOTH | 9 PACHONS | 11 EPIPHI |
| 2 PAOPHI | 4 CHOIAK | 6 MECHIR | 8 PHARMOUTHI | 10 PAONI | 12 MESORI |

www.ingramcontent.com/pod-product-compliance
Lightning Source LLC
Chambersburg PA
CBHW040408010526
44108CB00045B/2722